Allergy & Candida Cooking Made Easy

God Bless you!
Matthew 19:26
2 Corinthians 1:3-7
Sondra

Sondra K. Lewis

with Lonnett Dietrich Blakley
illustrations by Christine Hicks

Published by
Canary Connect Publications
A Division of SOBOLE, Inc.
Coralville, Iowa

DISCLAIMER

Information contained in this book is intended to be useful and educational. It is not intended to replace medical diagnosis or treatment, but rather to provide recipes and information that may be of assistance in implementing a food allergy, *Candida* control, and/or rotational diet prescribed by your health-care provider. Please consult your nutritionally oriented health-care provider for medical advice before changing your diet.

The publisher and authors declare that to the best of their knowledge all material in this book is accurate. We shall have neither liability nor responsibility to any person with respect to any loss or damage caused, or alleged to be caused, directly or indirectly by the information contained in this book.

There are no warranties with the education of this book. We shall have neither liability nor responsibility to any person with respect to any loss or damage alleged to be caused, directly or indirectly, by the information contained in this book.

First Printing, November 1996

Cover art and printing by Heuss Printing, Inc., 903 North Second, Ames, IA 50010.

ISBN: 0-9643462-1-4
Library of Congress Catalog Number 96–071277

Printed in the United States of America

Printed with soybean ink.

How to Order:
Single copies may be ordered from Canary Connect Publications, A Division of SOBOLE, Inc., PO Box 5317, Coralville, IA 52241-0317; telephone (319) 351-2317. (See order form on page 271.) Quantity discounts are also available. On your letterhead, include information concerning the intended use of the books and the number of books you wish to purchase.

Commonly Asked Questions & Answers

Q: What is *Candida* and what causes *Candida* Related Complex?

Chapter 1 (page 3) covers what *Candida* is as well as the causes, diagnosis, and symptoms of *Candida* Related Complex (CRC).

Q: How can I tell if *Candida* is a problem for me?

The *Candida* Questionnaire and Score Sheet (pages 247–249) developed by William G. Crook, M.D., is a self evaluation which may help you and your health-care professional evaluate if *Candida* may be affecting your health. In addition, certain blood and stool diagnostic analysis tests may be helpful in diagnosing *Candida* Related Complex (page 6).

Q: How is *Candida* Related Complex treated?

Treatment for CRC starts with a simple, effective goal—get the yeast and toxins out of the body tissues and build up the body's ability to keep them out. In addition to diet, treatment can include several facets with the ultimate goal of building up the weakened immune system. See Chapter 2 (pages 7–16) for the dietary and other treatments.

Q: I heard the term "*Candida* die-off" from a friend. What does it mean?

This is also referred to as "yeast die-off." See pages 7, 10, and 16.

Q: How do I begin on a *Candida*-control diet?

The *Candida*-control diet is a yeast-, sugar-, and mold-free food plan which is the cornerstone of CRC treatment (see pages 9–12). While it may seem difficult when first starting, the diet is an accomplishable challenge. Many guidelines, tips, helpful hints, and planning aids are provided in this book to help you incorporate the *Candida*-control diet into your lifestyle (see pages 12–13, 61–64, 65, and 68).

Q: Since I need to omit yeast on the *Candida*-control diet, what are my options for having a sandwich?

You actually have more choices now than when you were using regular wheat bread. The Sandwich Ideas chart on page 180 refers you to purchased bread products (see Resources, page 250) as well as the various bread recipes in this cookbook—all of them delicious alternatives.

Q: Is there a way I can check for food allergies without using expensive tests?

If you suspect food allergies, be sure to read Chapter 3 (page 17). It includes basic information on food allergies such as causes, typical food reactions, and an explanation of how to do a food challenge (pages 10 and 18). In addition, using a rotational diet can aid in identifying foods that could be causing problems (page 21).

Q: How are food allergies treated?

Several short-term and long-term treatments are discussed on page 20—the most important treatment being the use of a rotational diet (see Chapter 4 starting on page 21).

Q: How do I get started on a rotational diet?

Chapter 4 (beginning on page 21) describes the rotational diet including the basic rules. Chapter 8—Meal Planning tells you where to begin and provides meal planning ideas for each Day of the rotation (pages 64–69 and 79–88).

In addition, if your personal food allergies and other dietary restrictions require you to make adjustments in the rotation listed on pages 66–67, the information on pages 26, 60, 64, and 259 will help you create your own personalized rotational diet.

Q: I just learned I am allergic to all the foods I usually eat—wheat, corn, soy, egg, etc. If I cannot eat them now, what can I eat?

You have such a wonderful variety of options available to you that you will wonder why you never heard about or used them before. In Chapter 5—Specialty Foods (starting on page 27), you will learn about grains, nongrains,

continued . . .

continued from previous page
starches, sweeteners, and other foods that will add delicious variety to your meals. Very few of the 350+ recipes in this cookbook contain common food allergens. Wheat is totally omitted unless you count the wheat alternatives, spelt and Kamut.

Learn how to substitute these specialty foods for the ones you are allergic to in your favorite recipes by seeing pages 56–58.

Q: I am allergic to milk. What do I use on cereal?

Check out the variety of milk substitute options on page 58. This listing also includes options for a beverage, cream-based soups and casseroles, and puddings.

Q: All of my favorite snacks are now "NO-NO"s. Any suggestions?

My favorite snacks include several cracker varieties (pages 110–112). Many more snack ideas are listed on pages 63 and 85.

Q: What do I eat for breakfast?

See ideas on pages 62, 68, and 84.

Q: What do I use for a beverage?

Your best option is purified water (see pages 9 and 255). However, additional options are listed in the Beverages and Miscellaneous section of the recipes (page 224).

Q: I don't cook. What do I do?

If you currently use prepared foods and mixes or fast-food restaurants and "carry out" meals in your meal planning, you may find that starting a rotational and *Candida*-control diet, as well as "cooking from scratch," is a challenge. However, if you are committed to improving your health, planning and preparing foods and meals within your dietary restrictions that complement your lifestyle is accomplishable. Read the sections on commitment (pages 1, 25, 61, and 288), About the Recipes (page 95), and kitchen and meal preparation efficiency (70–74). Use the quick and easy (pages 63, 68, and 81) and easy (page 82) meal ideas. And check the lists of "good" prepared food options (pages 78–79) for ideas you can incorporate in your meal planning. But most important of all, you need to realize that improving your health through changing your diet is ultimately your choice and responsibility. By doing so, you can be an essential part of the process in improving your health and your life.

Q: Will I need to cook separate meals for myself and my family?

Many of the recipes in this book emphasize "traditional" foods with slight changes—for instance, tacos, pizza, crackers, lasagna, "Tuna Helper," chili, basic casseroles, sandwiches, etc. (see page 95). Ideas and helpful hints are given to help you introduce new foods and tastes into your family's diet as well as make minor adjustments in meal preparation to provide dishes for other family members. See the Feeding Family references listed in the Subject Index (page 278).

If your family can use regular purchased bread products such as muffins, crackers, tortillas, bread, etc. this will lessen the preparation time you spend—you will only need to supply your personal needs using the recipes for these products.

Q: I work outside the home. What do I take for lunch?

See pages 69, 70–71, 74–75, and 86.

Q: How did you come up with Canary Connect as the name of your business?

See pages xi and 269.

Q: I want to keep up to date on information and treatments for CRC, food allergies, and other related health challenges. What do you suggest?

Subscribe to and purchase the back issues for Canary Connect News, a quarterly newsletter edited by the authors of this book (see pages 268, 270, and 271 for subscription information).

Q: After reading and applying the information in this book, I still have more questions. What do I do?

See the Guidelines for Submitting a Question for Newsletter or Personal Response section on page 269.

TABLE OF CONTENTS

Table of Contents

> *A happy person is not a person in a certain set of circumstances, but rather a person with a certain set of attitudes.*

> *For anything worth having one must pay the price; and the price is always work, patience, love, and self-sacrifice.*
>
> —*John Burroughs*

Reviews of <u>Allergy and *Candida* Cooking Made Easy</u>

A superb book written by a person who's been there! This book should serve as an invaluable resource for any person with yeast-related health problems. I especially recommend it for those who continue to experience problems even though they take antifungal medication, avoid chemical pollutants, and take nutritional supplements.

　—William G. Crook, M.D., author of <u>The Yeast Connection</u>, <u>The Yeast Connection and the Woman</u>,<u>The Yeast Connection Handbook</u>, <u>Chronic Fatigue Syndrome and the Yeast Connection</u>, & <u>Help for the Hyperactive Child</u>

* * * * *

Congratulations on a job well done! The comprehensive information in <u>Allergy and *Candida* Cooking Made Easy</u> will help many people with food allergies and *Candida* yeast infections, especially those recently diagnosed and just getting into treatment. I especially like the care you have taken in suggesting appropriate treats and snacks for each of the four days. In my experience, people just won't stick with a diet that forbids all forms of fun foods. Yours appears to be a very livable plan for eating one's way to recovery—and it's already rotated. Thank you!

　—Marjorie Hurt Jones, R.N., Editor, <u>MFA Collection</u> and <u>Allergy Self-Help Cookbook</u>

* * * * *

Sondra Lewis' knowledge of *Candidiasis* and the treatments for it is very impressive. In <u>Allergy and *Candida* Cooking Made Easy</u> she gives the medical background for problems related to *Candidiasis* and food allergies as well as providing useful techniques to help individuals affected by them feel better. I highly recommend this book to anyone with *Candidiasis* and/or food allergies who is eager to actually get well by putting some much-needed effort into improving their diet while enjoying what they eat.

　—Nicolette M. Dumke, author of <u>Allergy Cooking with Ease</u> and <u>Easy Bread Making for Special Diets</u>

* * * * *

If you were to gather a few books together for a library covering natural foods preparation, this book by Sondra Lewis would be one of the best to add to your shelf. Many books have been written covering the field, however this book occupies a unique place because of its ease of use, helpfulness and applicability, and good basic coverage over a wide range of topics. It is especially valuable because it was developed through the personal needs and hands-on experience of the author. The thoughts and concepts were gathered and developed from a wide range of references, with the references fully documented. Highly recommended from beginner to expert!

　—Larry Hendershot

* * * * *

Finally, a complete guide for my patients and myself. I refer to it all the time.

　—Barbara Schiltz, Nutritionist, New York

* * * * *

I wish to congratulate you on an excellent book.

　—George F. Kroker, M.D., FACAI, Allergy Associates of La Crosse, Ltd., Wisconsin

continued . . .

* * * * *

It was nice to get a cookbook I didn't need to outgas before reading. The "Helpful Hints" section is full of ideas to make the special diet easier to follow. I will often use the substitution tables for grains, thickeners, and eggs to adapt family recipes. Sondra gives detailed instructions on making tortillas and crackers from many types of grains and grain alternatives. The "Specialty Foods" section has fun stories of where different grains come from and explains how to use them. We will enjoy the wild game recipes. And I look forward to using the Resources section to order organic foods I cannot purchase locally.

My 8-year-old son uses the rotations with ease. He simply turns to the list of foods for Day 1 (or 2, 3, or 4) and finds out what to eat for breakfast. He has even taken the book to school to explain his rotational diet to his teacher. It took the mystery out of it for the class.

Now that I am able to add more things to my diet and actually have company occasionally, I enjoy "company meals." I just like the idea of not having to figure out "What's for dinner?"

—Judy J., Iowa

* * * * *

This is the best cookbook I have seen on the subject of Allergy and *Candida*. Compared to other cookbooks, it is much more detailed and has a larger variety of foods and recipes. I like the idea of the four day meal planning and recipes with a wide variety of foods. It makes meal planning much easier to follow. The spiral binding allows the book to lay flat so that it is easier to read when following the recipes. Thank you for a much needed book on Allergy and *Candida*.

—Ross R., Wisconsin

* * * * *

This is the most fantastic cookbook for EI (Environmental Illness) people I have ever seen. It is most exceptional! Sondra has done a great deal of testing and retesting in the process of developing her recipes as well as incorporating many different grains, nongrains, and alternative sweeteners. I have had the opportunity to be a tasting "guinea pig" for her recipes in addition to preparing them for my husband and myself. This is the type of book I needed when I was diagnosed with food allergies and MCS/EI (Multiple Chemical Sensitivities/Environmental Illness). It would have been a Godsend to be able to bring a book of this caliber home to read and use in learning more about food allergies, rotational diet, food families, and cooking with alternative foods.

—Elva W., Iowa

* * * * *

I found this cookbook to be just what I needed for planning meals for my family to keep our food allergies from increasing. Problems with *Candida* have affected five generations of my family, down to my 7-year-old daughter, and being able to prepare meals that help deal with this condition is important to me.

—Jo Ellyn O., Texas

ACKNOWLEDGMENTS

I wish to thank so many for their direct and/or indirect help in making this book a reality.

◊ Almighty God and His Son Jesus Christ, my Lord and Savior, for without their presence and guidance in my life this book would not have been conceived.

◊ Jedn and Iowa Vocational Rehabilitation for their belief in me and the beginning funds that brought Lonnett and I together in the Fall of 1991.

◊ Lonnett for her writing skills in taking my thoughts and words and turning them into understandable sentences.

◊ My great appreciation to all those who came before me in the study of food allergy, rotational diet, and *Candida* Related Complex for their knowledge, inspiring recipes, guidance, and examples through their writings as well as through many kind words of assistance. Just to mention a few—

William G. Crook, M.D.   Marjorie Hunt Jones, R.N.   Nicolette M. Dumke   Sally Rockwell
Charlene Grimmett   Pat Connolly   Natalie Golos   Frances Golos Golbitz
Gail Burton   Stephanie Hayes   Barbara Maynard

◊ Many thanks to Drs. Crook and Kroker for all their assistance with technical information—especially with Chapter 1.

◊ For the positive comments and constructive suggestions, a special thank you to those who reviewed my book

William G. Crook, M.D.   George F. Kroker, M. D.   Marjorie Hunt Jones, R.N.
Nicolette M. Dumke   Larry Hendershot   Barbara Schiltz
Elva   Judy   Ross   Jo Ellyn

◊ Chris for graphic illustrations that add life and fun to my words.

◊ Betty for her artistic flare with photography.

◊ Lonnett, Bob, Elva, Judy, and others for recipe ideas.

◊ Family and friends for their patience, encouragement, prayers, and being part of my quality control and assurance team as "official tasters."

◊ Special Friends—Betty, Elva, Judy, and Lonnett.

◊ MCS/CRC Support Group Friends—Elva, Judy J., Jackie, Judy V., Claire, Janice, Tami, and Nadine

◊ Members of the Caring Connection Writing Circle—Anne, Barbara, Bev, Heather, Martha, Marcia, Susan—for their encouragement, patience, and prayers.

◊ My health-care team—Dr. Kroker, Sorrel, Dr. Kauffman, Kay, Dr. Dole, Dr. Kammeyer, Dr. Zdrazil, Dr. Carr, Betty, "TJ", James, and Laura.

◊ Thanks for the encouragement from fellow food allergy and *Candida* warriors that I have met by phone and mail through my FOS sales.

◊ Thanks for all the encouragement, information, guidance, and support from all of the "beautiful" people I have met and/or talked with through gathering the information provided in this book.

◊ All the people who purchased <u>Allergy & *Candida* Cooking—Rotational Style</u> and/or subscribers to <u>Canary Connect News</u> newsletter. Their encouragement and wonderful feedback encouraged us to keep going.

◊ All the great people at Immuno Labs and Nadine Company.

◊ Paula at GTC.

◊ Business Systems International, Inc.—David and Koreen for their assistance in automating my office with computer equipment/software and education.

◊ And a special tribute to Patricia for reminding us of what we have.

PREFACE

My goal and purpose in developing the rotational diet, recipes, and supplemental materials in this cookbook and resource guide is to reach those persons searching for a healthier lifestyle and/or seeking help with current health problems. My hope is to reach as many people as possible to encourage them to "wake up and smell the roses." This could involve making changes now to prevent the possibility of developing disabling conditions which could drastically affect their lives. Or it could involve implementing special methods to counter conditions already present. Changes in dietary habits, as well as in home, work, and other environments, can be essential steps in preventing the development of or in dealing with the presence of such conditions as *Candida* Related Complex (CRC), food allergies, and/or Multiple Chemical Sensitivities/Environmental Illness (MCS/EI), Chronic Fatigue and Immune Dysfunction Syndrome (CFIDS), and Fibromyalgia (FM).

As a symbol of my goal and purpose, I chose the name **Canary Connect** to illustrate the focus of my endeavors. Canaries were used in coal mine tunnels to warn miners of dangerous coal gases. Since canaries are more sensitive to coal gases than humans, they would stop singing (or even die) when the dangerous gases were present in the mine shafts. Coal miners would then know to leave immediately.

Those of us affected by Multiple Chemical Sensitivities/Environmental Illness (MCS/EI) have come to regard ourselves as warning "canaries" for today's world. Since we are more sensitive to chemicals and other dangerous substances present in today's world, we "human canaries" are singing out the message of danger to any and all who will hear and respond. We "sing" not only to reach those around us, but to connect with other human "canaries" to share information and techniques that may assist us in our daily lives.

> *Every survival kit should include a sense of humor.*

This cookbook and resource guide was developed from the wealth of available information regarding treatments for, as well as from personal experience in dealing with, *Candida* Related Complex (CRC) and food allergies. It presents an eating program which can assist in the treatment of these conditions. Based on those foods allowed on a *Candida* control diet, it uses a rotational format. Using a rotational eating program can help treat current food allergies, lessen the chance of developing new food allergies, and maintain current food tolerances. The rotational format can also be used as a technique for uncovering and identifying food allergies. It is designed so that it can be used for the rest of your life, as well as for shorter time periods.

Although many cookbooks which address CRC and/or food allergies recommend the rotation of foods, only a few of them actually provide a complete rotational format to use. This cookbook not only provides a complete 4-day rotational diet, but it includes meal planning techniques and over 350 recipes to aid you in incorporating it into your daily life.

I wish I could write a rotational diet complete with recipes that everyone could use without modifications. But because of the circumstances and requirements involved for each individual, the specific rotational diet found in this cookbook will not be a "perfect fit" for everyone. However, it can be adjusted and tailored to provide an individually personalized plan using the rules and techniques contained in this cookbook. The basic information and techniques; specialty food information and resources; helpful hints for meal and recipe planning and preparation; and delicious, "healthy" recipes can be of great assistance when working to control *Candida* Related Complex (CRC) and/or food allergies through dietary means. It is an accomplishable goal and this cookbook and resource guide can be the help, encouragement, hope, and

> *Dare to be wise; begin!*
> *He who postpones the hour of living*
> *rightly is like the rustic who waits for*
> *the river to run out before he crosses.*
> *Horace*

support needed to achieve success. It has been for many who purchased and used the first edition of this book, Allergy & *Candida* Cooking—Rotational Style.

YOU CAN DO IT—AND ENJOY THE PROCESS!

Best wishes to you as you begin the adventure of incorporating a food allergy, *Candida*-control, and/or rotational diet into your life. Remember, you are not alone and there are many resources available to you in this endeavor. It is my hope that this cookbook and the quarterly newsletter, Canary Connect News, will be a useful and important part of your journey.

Read . . . Cook . . . Eat . . . Enjoy

and God Bless!

Sondra

If you have a problem you must know that it simply is not going to go away—you might as well face it, tackle it, do something about it.

HOW TO USE THIS COOKBOOK

To receive the full benefit from this cookbook and resource guide, I strongly recommend that you read it in its entirety as you begin a food allergy, *Candida* control, and/or rotational diet. However, if you have a good knowledge base regarding *Candida* Related Complex, food allergies, and the rotary diversified diet, you can begin by scanning Chapters 5–7. Read through the Commonly Asked Questions & Answers found on pages iii and iv and refer to the indicated pages in the text for any that are especially of interest to you. Then read and study Chapter 8—Meal Planning and About the Recipes (page 95) before beginning the rotational diet set forth in this cookbook. *Meal planning is the* **core** *of beginning and remaining on a food allergy, Candida control, and/or rotational diet.*

The most important tool you need to be able to use the information and recipes in this cookbook is a level of **commitment** which grows with experience. The recipes follow the *Candida* control diet as well as a 4-day rotational food plan. The cookbook's format was developed to be user friendly to help the reader avoid the long trial-and-error process often experienced when beginning a food allergy, *Candida* control, and/or rotational diet. Through the helpful information and delicious recipes in this cookbook, and with commitment on your part, success can be achieved quickly with this diet plan.

The recipes and 4-day rotational diet in this cookbook were developed from my first-hand experience with *Candida* Related Complex and food allergies. I did not have all the information and recipes in this book when I first started. It took about 1 1/2 years before I was eating almost all organic foods. My use of specialty foods gradually grew over a five year time period, as did the number of recipes, and the rotational diet was under constant revision over a three year time period. Through the use of this diet and other techniques incorporated into my health-care plan, I experienced enough healing to give me the energy needed to complete the first book, Allergy & *Candida* Cooking—Rotational Style, as well as this updated, revised, expanded, reformatted version, and to produce a quarterly companion newsletter, Canary Connect News. Now the rotation and recipes are available to you just waiting for the addition of your commitment to use them.

If you begin your journey with the attitude shown by the canary on the previous page—"I may be backed into a corner, but I'm not giving up!"—you can achieve more than you may have imagined. The canary shown just inside the back cover (page 288) has used the tools of commitment and knowledge (in the form of this cookbook and the companion newsletter, Canary Connect News) to fight the battle against *Candida* Related Complex and/or food allergies and is doing well in his/her search for better health. Many persons facing these challenges feel discouraged and as though they are "cornered." But it is important to remember that in some ways this is not a bad position to start from. The walls at your back protect you from that direction and the only way you can go is forward. Gather your resources and begin the fight!

Ready to start on your culinary adventure? Give yourself a hug and be proud of yourself for each accomplishment—minor or major. You will be in my prayers as I ask for success and encouragement for you in this endeavor.

The man who removes a mountain begins by carrying away small stones.
—*Chinese Proverb*

Sondra

Enthusiasm is a mental sunshine that keeps everything in us alive and growing.

Every journey begins with a single step.

If you don't know where you're going, you'll end up somewhere else.

Failures are more commonly caused by having made no decisions than by making wrong ones.

1. *CANDIDA* RELATED COMPLEX (CRC)

Following is a review of the literature available on *Candida* Related Complex (CRC) and should not be substituted for medical advice from a nutritionally oriented, health-care professional.

What is *Candida Albicans*?

Yeasts are members of the Fungi Family, which is part of the vegetable kingdom. These single-cell, opportunistic organisms, like their "cousins" the molds, can be found everywhere—in the air, soil, and water as well as in our food and bodies. As part of the body's normal flora, one family of yeasts, *Candida albicans*, lives in the warm, moist mucous membranes of our bodies, particularly in the digestive and genitourinary regions.

Friendly bacteria is another normal flora found in the body. In a healthy body, there is a correct balance between *Candida albicans* and friendly bacteria. However, in a weakened body a reduction of friendly bacteria allows the normally harmless *Candida albicans* to multiply out of control. The resulting overgrowth of this organism, medically termed *Candidiasis* (pronounced can-di-DIE-ah-sis), is a major cause of chronic illness. A graphic illustration of *Candida albicans* overgrowth versus normal balance of friendly bacteria may be found in books by Dr. William G. Crook (including The Yeast Connection Handbook and The Yeast Connection and the Woman).

So What is the *Candida* Related Complex (CRC)?

This often-misdiagnosed illness can manifest itself as a severe chronic systemic infection which can cause extensive tissue damage throughout the body. Several factors may be involved in this systemic infection.

First, when the *Candida albicans* (yeast) in the body multiplies severely out of balance it throws off chemical compounds called toxins. These toxins are picked up and absorbed into the bloodstream and body tissues causing an allergic reaction to them.

Second, an allergic reaction to the *Candida albicans* organism can cause a release of chemicals such as histamines. These chemicals react with different parts of the body resulting in various symptoms.

Third, an overgrowth of *Candida albicans* in the gut (as well as other possible factors) can cause the intestinal mucosa (the gut lining) to become inflamed which weakens the gut wall and allows it to become more permeable. Undigested food particles are then able to leak into the blood stream. The food particles are identified as foreign "invaders" and are attacked by the immune system resulting in allergic reactions (food allergies). This condition is referred to as "leaky gut" syndrome.[1, 2, 3]

Many different names have been used to label the condition suffered by individuals with *Candida*-related health problems including Chronic *Candidiasis*, "The Yeast Connection," the Yeast Syndrome, and "*Candida*." However, George F. Kroker, M.D., of LaCrosse, Wisconsin, has suggested a new name, *Candida* Related Complex or CRC.[4] For simplicity, in this cookbook the term *Candida* Related Complex (CRC) is used to describe any or all health problems attributed to the overgrowth of *Candida albicans*.

What Causes *Candida* Related Complex (CRC)?

There are several factors that allow the normally harmless *Candida albicans* (yeast) to grow out of control. Our twentieth-century American diet, rich in sugar and yeast, encourages yeast growth. The extensive use of antibiotics, while effective in alleviating bacterial infections, can cause complications resulting in yeast overgrowth. For women, hormonal changes relating to the menstrual cycle, pregnancy, or the use of birth control pills encourage yeast growth.

"Leaky gut" syndrome, a condition which results from a breakdown of the gut mucosa[5] (the gut lining), may

---

What Causes CRC
- Diet rich in sugar and yeast
- Antibiotic use
- Steroids (cortisone, prednisone)
- Pregnancy hormonal changes
- Menstrual cycle hormonal changes
- Birth control pills
- Chemical, physical, and emotional stress
- "Leaky gut" syndrome

also contribute to an overgrowth of _Candida albicans_ since it can result in a weakened immune system and an imbalance in the intestinal flora.

When _Candida_ yeast overmultiplies, it releases toxins that weaken the body's immune system. The immune system can also be weakened by physical, chemical, and emotional stress as well as by allergies. In addition, steroids (cortisone, prednisone) suppress the immune system's ability to fight the overgrowth of _Candida albicans_.

A weakened immune system allows germs that cause nose, throat, sinus, ear, bronchial, bladder, and other infections to invade our bodies. Often antibiotics are used to counteract these infections. Extended antibiotic cycles of tetracycline are often used to treat severe acne problems. Unfortunately, antibiotics, including tetracyclines, destroy both friendly and disease-causing bacteria. This leaves the _Candida_ yeast an opportunistic environment for overgrowth because there are not enough friendly bacteria in the body to keep it under control.

Since the yeast is not harmed by antibiotics, it begins to multiply and throw off toxins. It adheres to the cell membranes by sending out projections that penetrate the cell lining.[6] Even after the antibiotics are stopped the friendly bacteria population remains reduced and the yeast continues to overmultiply at a higher rate releasing more toxins into the body.

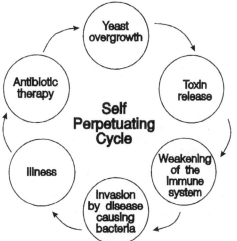

This pattern of yeast overgrowth, toxin release, weakened immune system, invasion by disease-causing bacteria, illness, antibiotic therapy, and resulting additional yeast overgrowth is a self-perpetuating cycle. The yeast overgrowth causes more and more health problems as the cycle repeats again and again. As an additional contributing factor, ill persons often lose their taste for healthy foods and instead desire "junk" foods (particularly sugar-laden desserts) which add to the problem.

The continued use or overuse of antibiotics, birth control pills, and/or steroids is often a major contributing factor in the development of CRC. Too few health-care professionals realize the dangers involved in the extensive use of these substances and the resulting physical changes they initiate.

An analogy used by Dr. George F. Kroker of LaCrosse, Wisconsin, to help patients understand what is happening to them involves the comparison of a heart attack to _Candida_ Related Complex and the underlying causes for both.

When a person has a heart attack, the entire cardiovascular system as well as the heart is involved. Heart attacks do not just "occur." They often are the result of many years of wear and tear on the cardiovascular system from factors such as high blood pressure, elevated cholesterol levels, smoking history, etc. Therefore, a good cardiovascular physician not only focuses on the heart attack, but also on the underlying causes. Treatment includes eliminating or lessening as many of these factors as possible to help prevent a future heart attack.

Dr. Kroker views CRC as a "heart attack of the immune system" with the immune system weakness and the underlying causes for it as the key factors. In 85% of CRC patients, this immune system weakness is caused by allergic illness preceding the yeast-related problems. A very common scenario is one where the CRC patient had recurrent infections as a result of untreated allergies earlier in life. The use of antibiotics in treating these infections set the patient up to have more yeast-related problems. Simply treating CRC directly with a sugar-free diet and antifungal medication may be inadequate if underlying issues such as mold allergy, chemical sensitivity, malnutrition, and immune system weakness are not directly addressed.

To better understand what happens in your body when there is an overgrowth of _Candida albicans_, try this experiment using active dry yeast (bread yeast). Bread yeast and _Candida albicans_ yeast are different, but they desire the same environment and have similar growth patterns. In a clear, two-cup measure, add one package of active dry yeast to one-half cup of lukewarm water (approximately 100—110° F.). Do not stir. Watch what happens over a three-minute period. Add one tablespoon of granulated sugar (again, do not stir) and watch. What you have just seen was yeast in its inactive state and its reaction when given a warm, moist place to live and start to slowly grow. When fed sugar, it grew faster. In fact, within three minutes a population explosion occurred. After ten minutes a thick layer of rapidly growing yeast colony is found on top of the water. If the yeast is allowed to grow with further nourishment but the water becomes cold, the yeast stop reproducing. However, your digestive tract is always a dark, moist, warm place. So to control the yeast's growth in a weakened system where the friendly bacteria are reduced, omit foods on which *Candida* feeds (sweets and other simple carbohydrates) and include supplements which will enhance the friendly bacteria population. (See sections on friendly bacteria enhancing supplements on pages 14–15 and 36–37.)

Who Discovered *Candida* Related Complex (CRC)?

C. Orian Truss, M.D., an allergist and internist, first pioneered the awareness of *Candida* Related Complex, which he called Chronic *Candidiasis*. He has studied the connection between human illness and the yeast, *Candida albicans*, for over twenty years. Many who have benefited from his studies say he deserves recognition from organized medicine for his work, but this will probably not happen in his lifetime.

Only a few in the medical professions have accepted the concept that yeast can cause so many health problems. This is partly due to the fact that the toxic substances produced by the overgrowth of *Candida albicans* have not been specifically isolated or characterized. Nonacceptance or nonrecognition of this condition and the resulting lack of treatment or mistreatment greatly contributes to the continuance and worsening of its symptoms.

Often the health-care professional who recognizes CRC and is working to aid those with the condition has firsthand experience. Whether because of personal health problems or those of a family member, he/she has learned of the underlying causes of the condition and the available treatments to alleviate its effects.

The discovery of CRC is a major medical breakthrough that brings hope to thousands of desperate, distraught people. This is particularly important to persons with CRC who have been mislabeled as "crazy" by many in the medical field. Since Dr. Truss's discovery, many health-care professionals have added additional research and information to the study of CRC and have greatly improved the understanding and treatment of the condition.

Who Treats *Candida* Related Complex (CRC)?

Finding a caring, nutritionally oriented, health-care professional who treats CRC is sometimes difficult. First, ask around your community, including employees at an organic grocery or health-food store, for possible referrals for a physician, chiropractor, and/or certified nutritionist.

If needed, contact one or more of the resources listed on page 260 for more information on physicians who treat CRC in your geographical area. These organizations may require a small monetary donation. Also, for faster service, include a #10, self-addressed, stamped envelope with your request.

Because of the nature of CRC and the many facets involved in its treatment, it is essential for your health-care professionals to be very nutritionally and naturally, as well as medically, oriented in their treatment program; have a thorough understanding of all immune factors that can weaken the system and promote CRC; and have a very caring attitude. Therefore, please keep in mind the importance of these factors in your treatment program when a health-care professional reference is made in this book.

Diagnosis of *Candida* Related Complex (CRC)

Patient history and an evaluation of symptoms are keys to making a correct diagnosis of CRC. The health-care professional pays careful attention to the patient's history of medications (i.e., antibiotics, steroids, birth control pills) that destroy the delicate balance between *Candida albicans* and the friendly bacteria in the body. Symptoms looked for include any from the list on the next page, especially chronic vaginitis or urinary tract infection and yeast and mold allergies. The patient's positive response to the CRC treatment will help confirm a correct diagnosis.

The self-evaluation *Candida* Questionnaire and Score Sheet developed by William G. Crook, M.D. (see Appendix B) may help you and your health-care professional evaluate if *Candida* may be affecting your health.

In addition, some health-care professionals have found certain blood and stool diagnostic analysis tests helpful in diagnosing CRC as well as food sensitivities (discussed in Chapter 3). The tests may include stool analysis for *Candida* and other organisms, digestive capacity, and/or intestinal function and blood studies to measure *Candida* antibodies, antigens, and immune complexes. A list of some laboratories which perform these tests may be found in Appendix C (page 261).

What Are the Symptoms of *Candida* Related Complex (CRC)?

The symptoms of CRC are numerous and complex. This may be the most prevalent reason why physicians either ignore CRC as a real condition or misdiagnose it as an emotional disorder.

Often people say that they are "sick and tired of being sick and tired." People with CRC may be labeled as hypochondriacs if they talk about all their aches and pains. The symptoms may come and go as the body and mind adapt to feeling ill. Or the immune system may wax and wane as it struggles to deal with the demands placed upon it causing symptoms to appear and disappear. Often so many factors are involved that the symptoms are masked like some food allergy reactions (see discussion of masked food allergies, page 17–18).

Following are the most common symptoms of CRC. However, not all symptoms may be exhibited.

ALLERGIC REACTIONS:

- acne
- asthma
- bronchitis
- dizziness
- earaches and itchy ears
- food allergies and/or food cravings
- hay fever
- headaches
- hives
- itchy and/or burning eyes
- mold allergies, symptoms flare up on damp days or in moldy places
- severe chemical sensitivities
- sore throat

EMOTIONAL AND MENTAL PROBLEMS:

- confusion, fretfulness
- extreme irritability and anxiety
- insomnia
- lethargy, fatigue, a "drained" feeling
- loss of libido (loss of sexual drive)
- severe depression
- memory lapses, poor memory, inability to concentrate

INTESTINAL AND URINARY TRACT SYMPTOMS:

- bowel problems, diarrhea, and/or constipation
- gas, abdominal pain, bloating, indigestion
- inflammations of the stomach lining and/or colon
- menstrual complaints, especially PMS
- nausea
- prostate problems
- urinary tract infections
- yeast vaginitis

OTHER PHYSICAL MANIFESTATIONS:

- appetite changes*
- athlete's foot, jock itch, nail fungus
- blurred vision
- myalgias, muscular flu-like symptoms
- numbness, tingling, muscle weakness
- white coated tongue
- tightness in chest
- weight gain or loss

---

*Many CRC patients lose their taste for vegetables and animal protein, foods on which *Candida* does not thrive. Instead they crave and often overeat foods on which *Candida* thrives. Women often experience these cravings a week prior to their menstrual period. For the health-conscious person, food cravings may include honey, granola bars, whole-grain bread, cheese, dried fruit, nut mixes, or peanut butter. Persons who follow an all-American "junk" food diet may crave chocolate chip cookies, pizza, alcoholic beverages, or other refined carbohydrates such as white sugar or bleached flour.

REFERENCES

1. Marjorie Hurt Jones. "Candida—A Different Approach," <u>Mastering Food Allergies</u> (Vol. IV, No. 7, Issue No. 37, July-August 1989), 3.
2. Marjorie Hurt Jones. "Leaky Gut: A Common Problem with Food Allergies," <u>Mastering Food Allergies</u> (Vol. VIII, No. 5, Issue No. 75, September-October, 1993), 1.
3. Marjorie Hurt Jones. "Leaky Gut—What Is It?," <u>Mastering Food Allergies</u> (Vol. X, No. 4, Issue No. 86, July-August 1995), 1.
4. William G. Crook, M.D., and Marjorie Hurt Jones, R.N. <u>The Yeast Connection Cookbook</u> (Jackson, TN: Professional Books, 1989), 25.
5. Marjorie Hurt Jones. "Leaky Gut: A Common Problem with Food Allergies," <u>Mastering Food Allergies</u> (Vol. VIII, No. 5, Issue No. 75, September-October, 1993), 1.
6. Gail Burton. <u>The Candida Control Cookbook</u>, 1.

2. TREATMENTS FOR
CANDIDA RELATED COMPLEX (CRC)

Because of the multifaceted nature of CRC symptoms and causes and the very individualized factors involved, health-care professionals may not use identical treatment programs for all their patients. A treatment program works best if specifically tailored to the patient's needs. Because of these factors, the dietary and additional treatment methods which follow should not be substituted for medical advice from a nutritionally oriented, health-care professional.

Dietary Treatment for CRC

A special sugar-free, yeast-free, mold-free, and diversified diet is the single most important yet most difficult part of CRC treatment. When sweets are omitted from the diet, the yeast "yells" for more sweets, causing you to crave, dream of, and salivate for sweets.

As you succeed in killing off or starving out the overpopulation of *Candida* by using the diet and other treatments discussed later, you may experience a worsening of symptoms. This reaction, called "die off," is the result of your body reacting to the toxins and products given off by the dead *Candida* yeast cells. The greater the amount of yeast killed, the worse these symptoms may be and it may take a few days (or longer) to get rid of the resulting dead yeast products. However, the more yeast you get rid of, the sooner you'll get better.

"You crave, dream of, and salivate for sweets."

Remember, it is the *Candida* yeast that is controlling you and the feelings that you are experiencing. You need to adopt the attitude **"I can beat this!"** Then **you** will be in control.

You may experience a favorable response to the diet in as few as ten days to two weeks. However, it is important to remember that although your major symptoms may disappear, the *Candida* overgrowth was probably well established before it was identified. You must be persistent in the treatment and adhere to the diet for an extended period, for months to perhaps years, to regain and maintain good health.

Even though it seems difficult, especially when first starting, the diet is manageable and can be incorporated into your lifestyle easily with support and guidance. (See more information about support on page 25.)

Your health-care professional may also suggest a low-carbohydrate diet, ranging from 60–100 grams per day. These carbohydrates should be consumed evenly throughout the day and can be gradually increased in amount as you improve. However, a prolonged high-protein/low-carbohydrate diet may cause problems for individuals with CRC in the form of persistent fatigue, weakness, excessive weight loss, and/or malnourishment.

Regular exercise may be recommended to aid in toxin elimination during the treatment. However, if carbohydrate intake is limited, the patient's energy level for exercise will also be limited. Instead eating complex carbohydrates freely (unless you are allergic to them) and limiting simple carbohydrates such as fruits is recommended.

You will probably need to eliminate simple carbohydrates (fruits and sweeteners) for at least the first two weeks and often up to four weeks or longer. Then gradually individual fruits are added to discover which ones can be tolerated and in what amount. After doing this fruit challenge described in "Foods Partially Restricted" (page 10), you may be able to gradually add sweeteners such as brown rice syrup, honey, and pure maple syrup to your diet.

The gluten in gluten grains such as wheat, rye, barley, oat, spelt, and Kamut converts readily to glucose in the body which feeds the *Candida* yeast.[7] In addition, some of these grains are common food allergens so you may desire to test them carefully and watch for immediate and delayed reactions (see page 18).

Remember, everyone is different and only you can listen to your body and make the best decision for you. Since *Candida* Related Complex (CRC) often clouds your ability to concentrate and make decisions, keep a notebook to record all the food you are eating. Record date, time, food eaten, amount eaten, and any noticeable reactions experienced as well as any possible other causes such as environmental factors.

Day/Date	Time	Food & Form Eaten	Amount Eaten	Reaction & Possible Cause
8/25/96	6 pm	Ground Beef Patty Corn on Cob with margarine Sliced Tomatoes	1 medium 2 large ears 1 large	developed a headache approximately 30 minutes after meal that lasted for 2 days—suspect corn

FOOD
AND
REACTIONS
DIARY

Take this notebook and discuss it with your health-care professional for advice on customizing your diet. Also, sometimes a friend experienced in dealing with CRC and its treatment in his/her own life may be able to help you understand what is happening to you and help you adjust your diet. In addition, you may need to adjust your diet with the seasons. For example, because of the way my body reacts it is important for me to eat fewer fruits and other simple carbohydrates when it is rainy, damp, and moldy outside for long periods of time. During these times I crave sweets, but I am much better off if I control these cravings.

Another word on complex carbohydrates—they are good for everyone. The Food Guide Pyramid places complex carbohydrates consisting of whole grains at the base recommending 6–11 servings per day,[8] around 55% of your total daily caloric intake.[9] Complex carbohydrates aid in the prevention and treatment of high blood pressure and heart disease, osteoporosis, and digestive disorders. As quoted in The Yeast Connection Cookbook, in a lecture given in January 1987, Sidney M. Baker, M.D., said that "eating a diet rich in complex carbohydrates is the best way to promote normal bowel flora in the person who has some immune dysfunction."[10]

Food cravings are part of the reason why the diet is the most difficult aspect of the CRC treatment. These cravings add to feelings of denial and lead to low self-esteem when you eat foods that are not on your diet plan. (More information on dealing with these feelings may be found in issues 5 and 6 of Canary Connect News [CCN] where a two part article addresses "Chasing the Blues Away! Working Toward Emotional and Spiritual Healing." See Appendix G, page 271, for subscription information.) In addition, CRC patients may temporarily lose their taste for vegetables and animal protein and their taste buds may be "clouded" by the *Candida*.

Retraining your taste buds to enjoy the foods you can have, including new foods you may not be familiar with, may be difficult, but it is possible. When introducing new foods and flavors into your diet—such as amaranth, buckwheat, quinoa, teff, etc.—do not make a negative judgment after a single trial. Give yourself a chance to learn to like a new food by trying it again and/or using it in a different manner, recipe, and/or food combination. The whole-grain and nongrain entree, tortilla, cracker, bread, biscuit, and muffin recipes in this cookbook will satisfy your desire for yeast breads. And soon you will be able to satisfy your sweet tooth by enjoying some of the dessert recipes. **Don't be a prisoner of your taste buds!**

> **Remember that it takes time to change your taste buds and food cravings. As you kill off the *Candida* yeast, your food cravings will decrease. Be patient with yourself.**

Yeast foods do not actually promote *Candida* growth, but they are removed from the diet because many persons with CRC are allergic to yeast products. After your symptoms have cleared, you can do a challenge by trying a yeast food such as Brewer's yeast or vinegar. (Using a yeasted bread product for this challenge adds too many additional factors.) Watch closely for immediate and delayed reactions.

In addition, as stated by Gail Burton, "All yeast have estrogen receptors and give off female hormones. As both female and male *Candida* patients have hormonal imbalances, it is wise to eliminate all yeast from the diet. Also, due to yeast sufferers' hypersensitivities to fungi in general, baker's yeast can cause problems."[11]

Another factor to consider is that "recent research indicates that antibiotic-resistant strains of microorganisms can be spread by eating meats raised on steroids and antibiotics."[12] Choose meats and poultry raised without the use of antibiotics and growth hormones. Many times these meats have another advantage because the animals are often fed organically raised grains. In addition, organically raised foods are recommended since the chemicals (herbicides and pesticides) in nonorganic foods can possibly weaken your immune system. (For more information on organic foods read Chapter 6—Organics—The Only Way to Go.)

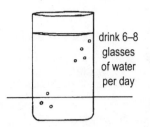
drink 6–8
glasses
of water
per day

It is important to drink 6–8 glasses (approximately 2 quarts) of water throughout each day and to consider using some type of "purified" water: reverse osmosis, distilled, or bottled in glass. All bottled waters are not the same and some may contain pesticides or other contaminants such as may be found in regular tap water. City tap water should be avoided since it contains chlorine and possibly fluoride which generally depress thyroid function and the overall immune system.[13] In addition, consider using a natural toothpaste without fluoride. (See Appendix C, page 255, for information on purchasing "purified" water and/or a home water-purification unit.)

Candida Control Diet

The dietary treatment for *Candida* Related Complex (CRC) is unique to the individual. Since individuals differ, what works for one person may not work for another. The following diet guidelines may need to be modified to fit an individual's personal requirements.

Foods You Can Eat Freely (unless you are allergic to them)

Vegetables and Legumes

Artichoke	Chard	Leek	Radish
Asparagus	Cucumber	Lettuce, all kinds	Rutabaga
Beans, all kinds	Eggplant	Okra	Soybean
Beet	Garlic	Onion	Spinach
Broccoli	Green Bean	Parsley	Sprouts, all kinds
Brussels Sprout	Greens: Beet	Parsnip	Squash, all kinds
Cabbage	Collard	Peas, all kinds	Tofu
Carrot	Kale	Peppers, all kinds	Tomato
Cauliflower	Mustard	Potatoes, white & sweet	Turnip
Celery	Kohlrabi	Pumpkin	Yam

Nuts
Almond
Brazil Nut
Filbert
Macadamia Nut
Pecan
Pine Nut
Walnut

Seeds
Pumpkin
Sesame
Sunflower

Butters
Almond and other nut
　butters (except peanut)
Sesame
Sunflower

Fats
Butter
Oils, unrefined, all
　kinds except peanut

Whole Grains
Barley
Corn
Job's Tears
Kamut®
Millet
Oat
Rice, Brown
Rye
Spelt
Teff
Wheat
Wild Rice

Nongrains
Amaranth
Buckwheat
Quinoa

Starches
Arrowroot
Kudzu/Kuzu
Tapioca

Fish/Shellfish
Cod
Crab
Halibut
Orange Roughy
Salmon
Shrimp
Trout
Tuna
Other fish/shellfish

Poultry
Chicken
Cornish Hen
Duck
Eggs
Goose
Pheasant
Turkey
Other poultry

Dairy
Yogurt, plain and
　unsweetened only

Red Meats
Antelope
Beef
Buffalo
Lamb
Pork, uncured &
　unsmoked only
Rabbit
Squirrel
Veal
Venison
Other red meat

Beverages
Water, "purified" is
　preferred
Sparkling Water
Lemon or Lime in
　Water
Pau D'Arco Tea (see
　pages 16 & 224)

Foods Partially Restricted

For most CRC patients, the following fruits and sweeteners may need to be omitted for the first two weeks and often up to four weeks or longer. Depending upon your response to a food challenge of these individual fruits and sweeteners, you may not be able to add them to your diet or in the quantity or frequency indicated.

Fresh Fruits	Sweeteners
2–3 servings of the following may be eaten per day	**Limit the following to 1–2 teaspoons per day**

Fresh Fruits		Sweeteners
1 medium apple	1 cup grapes (often not tolerated)	Brown Rice Syrup
1/2 avocado	1 medium lemon	Honey
1/2 banana	1 medium orange	Pure Maple Syrup
1 cup blackberries	1 cup papaya cubes	
1 cup blueberries	1 medium peach	
1/2 cantaloupe	1 medium pear	
1 wedge Casaba melon	1 wedge Persian melon	
1 cup cherries	1 cup fresh diced pineapple	
1 cup fresh shredded coconut	1 medium plum	
1/2 large grapefruit		

After major symptoms have cleared, do a food challenge by gradually adding individual foods, in this case fruits, to discover which ones may be tolerated and in what amount. First, select a food you have not eaten in at least two or more weeks. As an example, we will select apple. To eliminate one more factor, the apple will be peeled and only a very small apple or one-half of a medium-size apple will be eaten. For the next 48 hours do not try any other fruits or foods that you are wanting to "challenge." This allows you to check for immediate and delayed reactions because you could have either or both of them for this one particular food.

Keep a notebook to record the food being tried. Record date, time, food eaten, amount eaten, and any noticeable reactions experienced as well as any other possible causes such as environmental factors. If you are very sensitive, it is always better to try a food challenge in a very controlled environment (such as home) where you can avoid being chemically challenged.

FOOD
AND
REACTIONS
DIARY

Day/Date	Time	Food & Form Eaten	Amount Eaten	Reaction & Possible Cause
8/25/96	10 am	peeled apple	small size	no reaction for up to 2 days

After this approximate 48 hour period, if no reactions have been noticed, you can add apple (or your selected food) to your list of allowed foods. In addition, the next time you try apple you may want to expand the challenge by eating the peeling and again waiting 48 hours to check for immediate and/or delayed reactions.

Once a food challenge is completed and no further reactions are noticed, you may select another food or fruit that you would like to try to add to your diet. This time you may wish to select a cherry, blueberry, or some other fruit with skin that you would not peel to add that additional factor to your challenge.

Later you can try the sweeteners listed above. When experimenting with fruits and other sweeteners, I **cannot emphasize enough** trying only a small amount of one at a time and being sure to wait for both immediate and delayed reactions (48 hours) before trying an additional amount or another food.

> **It is essential to make the dietary changes that are most important IMMEDIATELY. These changes include:**
>
> ♦ **Avoid sugar, yeast, etc. in your diet. See listing of "Foods You Must Avoid."**
> ♦ **Omit foods to which you are allergic.**

Foods You Must Avoid

Sugars and Sugar-containing Foods: Brown, granulated, and powdered sugar as well as other sugars such as dextrose, fructose, galactose, glucose, glycogen, lactose (milk sugar), maltose, mannitol, monosaccharides, polysaccharides, sorbitol, and sucrose. Also avoid Sucanat (organic raw sugar), molasses, maple sugar, date sugar, and turbinado sugar. Read all labels of packaged foods to make sure there are no hidden sugars.

Artificial Sweeteners: NutraSweet and Equal (aspartame) often cause allergic reactions. Some can tolerate them in moderation, but be aware that they contain milk sugar or corn sugar which are also common allergens. While saccharin is not generally allowed on the *Candida* control diet, Dr. Crook does allow a limited use of the liquid form (Sweeta or Fasweet).[14]

Common Table Salt: Most table salts contain dextrose and other chemicals. Instead use sea salt or "Real Salt" that may be free of these substances. Be sure to read the ingredients. (Sea salt is processed from ocean water. "Real Salt" is a mined sea salt which was originally deposited on the floor of an ancient ocean long before the advent of modern day chemicals such as herbicides or pesticides.)

Milk and Milk-containing Products: Milk contains lactose, a simple carbohydrate which feeds the yeast, and should be avoided at least until you improve. Also, many persons are allergic to milk. Some can tolerate plain yogurt which is free of fruit, sugar or other sweeteners, preservatives, and additives.

Black Pepper: Black pepper is hard to digest so it is not recommended. In contrast, however, cayenne (red) pepper seems to promote digestion.

Caffeine and Caffeine-containing Products: Avoid coffee, tea, and other beverages that contain caffeine and chocolate. Instead drink water or sparkling mineral water and substitute naturally sweet-tasting carob for chocolate.

Yeast and Moldy Foods:

* Alcoholic beverages, beer, and wine are fermented and/or brewed with yeast.
* Breads, pastries, and other yeast-leavened bakery products.
* Cheeses: Aged, processed, cheese-containing foods are made from mold-fermentation methods and some also contain additives. Avoid foods containing whey, a by-product of the cheese-making process.
* Coffee and tea: Includes all varieties, caffeinated or decaffeinated, except Pau D'Arco tea. Mold collects on beans and leaves during the drying process for coffee and tea. Even though herbal teas do contain molds, some tolerate them. To start, try no more than one cup of herbal tea per day. As an exception, Pau D'Arco tea is beneficial in combating yeast and comes from the bark of trees resistant to fungi.
* Condiments, sauces, and other vinegar-containing foods contain fermented products. This includes mustard, catsup, barbecue, chili, shrimp, soy, steak, and tamari sauces. It also includes vinegar-containing foods such as green olives, horseradish, mayonnaise, pickles, pickled vegetables, relishes, salad dressings, and sauerkraut.
* Cream of tartar is made from the fermented residue in wine barrels and may aggravate CRC symptoms.
* Dried herbs: Mold collects on the leaves during the drying process. When possible, use fresh herbs. One teaspoon of dry herbs equals one tablespoon of fresh herbs. Note: Garlic is really not an herb and, in any form, is beneficial in combating yeast. Cloves also kill yeast.
* Edible fungi: Includes citric acid, morels, mushrooms, and truffles.
* Fermented beverages such as cider and root beer.
* Fruit juices of all kinds except freshly prepared juices and unsweetened cranberry juice. Packaged juice may be made from seconds, fruit that drops off the tree and bruises. Bruised fruit develops more mold growth that is often not cut away before processing. When preparing fresh juices, wash the fruit thoroughly and avoid using fruits of second quality.
* Fruits that are moldy and dried fruits: This may include strawberries and other berries and melons. Dried fruits collect mold during the drying process. Avoid canned fruit.
* Leftovers should be eaten within 24 hours or frozen immediately after the meal for later use.
* Malted products such as barley malt found in many cereals, candies, and malted milk drinks.
* Peanuts and pistachios harbor fungus. Avoid peanut oil and peanut butter.

continued . . .

* Processed and smoked meats such as pickled and smoked meat and fish: This includes beef jerky, corned beef, hot dogs, luncheon meats, pastrami, pickled meat, and sausages.
* Skins of fruits and vegetables accumulate mold during growth. Grapes and tomatoes especially have a fungus which grows on them. Scrub the skins of all vegetables and fruits before peeling or cutting to avoid spreading the mold.
* Tempeh and Miso: Tempeh is a cake of cooked split soybeans held together by a dense, white cultured mold closely related to mushrooms. Miso is a fermented soybean product.

General Tips to Follow in the *Candida* Control Diet

1. Avoid eating any foods you are craving, even if they are listed as acceptable foods. Chances are that you are allergic to the food or that it promotes yeast growth (e.g., fruit, honey) and the yeast is "yelling" for it.

2. Buy fresh or frozen vegetables, fruits, fish, poultry, and meats. Purchase only whole grains, whole-grain flours, raw nuts, and cold-pressed, unrefined oils. Organic and/or natural foods are the best options.

3. Rinse fresh vegetables and fruits thoroughly before using. Dispose of any fruit or vegetable with evidence of mold.

4. Sometimes persons with CRC will react to flours but have no problem eating the whole grain. There are two reasons for this reaction.
   —The oil in flour stored at room temperature starts to deteriorate and mold multiplies.
   —The surface dirt, mold, and pollens that are removed when washing the grain before cooking were not removed before the grain was ground into flour.
   Before you give up on flours and baked goods, try purchasing freshly ground flour and freezing it immediately. If this does not help, try grinding your own flour. Before grinding, sort through the grain to remove any debris and immature grains which otherwise would float to the top when washing it. Also, do what you can to remove dirt from the grain surface by shaking it in a mesh strainer or wiping it with a dry cloth.

5. Read all labels when buying foods to check for ingredients that need to be eliminated from your diet. For instance, many canned tomato products contain citric acid.

6. Mold begins to grow on food within 24 hours, which can be harmful to your health. To prevent this, freeze leftovers soon after preparation. You may store dinner leftovers in the refrigerator for lunch on the following day, but the freezer is better for a longer time period.

7. You may need to omit nuts and seeds in the beginning stages of the diet if you have a sensitive digestive system. However, ground nuts and seeds are easier to digest. In addition, CRC sufferers are mold sensitive and may not be able to tolerate supermarket nuts and seeds. I recommend organic nuts and seeds purchased directly from the grower, such as Jaffe Brothers (see Appendix C). After picking and shelling, the organic growers immediately freeze or refrigerate their nuts and seeds. By purchasing direct from organic growers, various handling steps and time when the product is stored at room temperature are omitted. These are stages when the original low mold count on the nuts and seeds begins to multiply.

8. Choose alcohol-free flavorings and extracts but read the labels for other ingredients that may not be allowed.

9. Read and reread a variety of different materials on *Candida* Related Complex (CRC) so you can fully understand, visualize, and conquer it. (See Appendix D: Recommended Reading.)

10. Some tips for eating at a restaurant or banquet:
    * Plan ahead. Call ahead for the menu, particularly if you are attending a banquet.
    * Skip the appetizer or order a shrimp cocktail without the sauce. Eat the shrimp with just a squeeze of lemon or take your own Picante Sauce (page 227).
    * Order unflavored mineral water instead of wine or a mixed drink.
    * Use oil and a squeeze of lemon for salad dressing. Ask what comes on the salad before ordering to avoid bacon bits, croutons, etc.
    * Order animal protein without sauce—broiled dry is the best choice. Grilled steak or shrimp is a good option. Check that no marinades are used. Take your own Clarified Butter (page 226) and have the restaurant use it instead of their vegetable shortening in preparing your dinner. Also, ask them to scrape the grill to remove most of any remaining shortening and/or food products.

* Order steamed vegetables instead of bread. Skip the bread, crackers, and dessert and take your own muffin, bread, or dessert.
* Order your baked potato dry and take your own Clarified Butter or flaxseed oil. If you usually enjoy your baked potato with sour cream, try substituting Sunflower Mayo or Creamy Italian Dressing (page 188). Also, do not eat the potato skin.
* If you can tolerate herbal tea, sip a cup while others are eating dessert. Or eat slowly, more slowly than the others at your table, so you are still enjoying your meal while they are having dessert.

11. One of the most important tips is to enjoy your meals and make them attractive on the plate. Relax before, during, and after your meals to aid digestion. Eating slowly and chewing every bite also aids digestion. In order to relax before a meal, try to plan and prepare some things in advance. I often wash and prepare my fresh vegetables ahead of time to avoid being rushed when it is time to prepare a meal.

Other Treatments for *Candida* Related Complex (CRC)

Treatment for CRC starts with a simple, effective goal—get the yeast and toxins out of the body tissues and build up the body's ability to keep them out. In addition to diet, treatment can include several facets with the ultimate goal of building up the weakened immune system and moving toward a healthy lifestyle.

Because birth control pills encourage *Candida* growth, you may need to consider a natural alternative method of birth control. Another important step is to avoid the use of all antibiotics and steroids unless absolutely necessary.

Other Treatments for CRC
• Natural birth control methods
• Avoid antibiotics and steroids
• Yogurt intravaginal treatment
• Allergy testing and desensitization treatments
• Stress reduction
• Regular exercise
• Attitude adjustment
• Regular chiropractic care
• Therapeutic massage
• Avoid antacids
• Plant enzymes
• *Acidophilus* supplements
• Natural probiotic enhancer (FOS)
• Vitamin and mineral supplements
• EFAs (essential fatty acids)
• Antifungal medications or supplements

To help remedy chronic vaginal yeast infections, use a yogurt intravaginal treatment at night. Use plain, unsweetened yogurt with live active cultures. Over-the-counter vaginal antifungal creams can help eliminate the symptoms of yeast infection, but they do not attack the cause of chronic infections. The yogurt treatment reintroduces good bacteria into the vaginal system to provide a natural check on the overgrowth of *Candida albicans*. Generally speaking, this has a better and longer-lasting effect on the yeast infection than the over-the-counter antifungal creams.

Since allergies weaken the immune system, seek testing and treatment for them, especially to yeast and mold. Allergies are a serious factor since they fight against the body's immune system and ability to resist infection so they should not be treated lightly. Allergies to mold are a major problem for

persons with CRC because a symptom (such as itchy or burning eyes) can result from an allergic reaction to airborne mold OR from an overgrowth of *Candida* making it difficult to determine the symptom's cause. If you are seeing a physician who is an allergist or a clinical ecologist, you may be tested for an allergy to *Candida*. Sublingual drops or shots may be prescribed to build your body's natural defense system and to lower your allergic reactions to *Candida albicans*.

If you have food allergies, it is best to entirely avoid eating the foods to which you are allergic. Your second choice is to eat them only occasionally on a rotational basis. Eating the foods to which you are allergic on a rotational basis involves eating the food at least four days apart and usually **more** than four days apart. This time spread needs to be long enough that you do not notice any allergic reactions after consuming the food. Using this technique will lighten the load on your immune system. (See Chapter 4—Rotational Diet.)

Stress puts your body into an "alarm mode" that does not allow your immune system to heal. Even though exercise relieves stress, you need to regularly practice other stress handling methods. I suggest prayer, personal Bible study, laughter, deep breathing coupled with progressive relaxation, talks with an understanding friend, and balancing your time indoors and outdoors, especially getting plenty of sunlight and enough restful sleep each night.

Regular exercise is important because it increases circulation, improves digestion, relieves stress, and helps release toxins that have become lodged in the muscles. Sweat created through exercise is a good avenue for toxin removal. Remember to breathe deeply during exercise. Those adversely affected by many odors may have developed a habit of shallow breathing. We need to remember to breathe normally and take deep breaths when our air is of good quality.

A positive mental attitude regarding your health is very important to recovery. A healthy mind and a religious attitude are effective in determining how you handle your situation, work mentally to heal your body, and adopt a healthy life style. Strive for warm fuzzies in your life and reject the cold pricklies that could bring you down. A warm fuzzy is a warm, cozy, comforting hug (mental or physical) that lifts your outlook and attitude. A cold prickly is like that person who said to you, "It's all in your head. There's nothing wrong with you." Cherish warm fuzzies and seek them out at every opportunity.

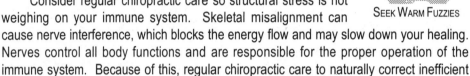

SEEK WARM FUZZIES

REJECT COLD PRICKLIES

Consider regular chiropractic care so structural stress is not weighing on your immune system. Skeletal misalignment can cause nerve interference, which blocks the energy flow and may slow down your healing. Nerves control all body functions and are responsible for the proper operation of the immune system. Because of this, regular chiropractic care to naturally correct inefficient nerve and energy patterns is an important aid to the healing process. It allows the immune system to fight back and attack the overgrowth of *Candida albicans* which is at the root of your health problems.

Likewise, therapeutic massage (Shiatsu and Swedish) enhances energy flow and the release of toxins by keeping the muscles relaxed and loosened. This encourages increased, more complete blood circulation throughout the entire body. Since the circulatory system delivers nutrients to all parts of the body and removes toxins and waste, the increased efficiency resulting from therapeutic massage can greatly aid the body's healing process.

A hug is a great gift... One size fits all, and its easy to exchange.
Lily Biles

Avoid antacids since they promote an acid-free environment in your digestive system which encourages yeast growth. Instead, your health-care professional may suggest charcoal capsules or tablets for stomach distress. However, stomach distress may be caused by the opposite condition—too alkaline an environment. An alkaline stomach does not provide the proper environment for food digestion and therefore may allow undigested food particles to appear in your stool. Repeated occurrences of this situation can lead to constipation, diarrhea, and nutrient deficiency. Hydrochloric acid capsules or tablets may be recommended to aid in digestion as well as to combat yeast growth by returning your stomach to a proper acidic nature.[15]

Undigested food particles in the system due to ineffective digestion (from whatever cause) can add to *Candida* problems as well as contribute to food sensitivities and "leaky gut" syndrome. In <u>Food Enzymes: The Missing Link to Radiant Health</u>, Humbart Santillo states: "Undigested proteins, to which yeast and other allergens attach themselves in the circulation, often enter by way of the digestive tract. One way to prevent this is to take plant enzymes with meals to aid in the digestion of these substances."[16] Plant enzymes are supremely adapted to aiding in digestion because they: 1) function throughout the entire digestive tract, 2) work best in a temperature range of 92–104°F. (body temperature), 3) function in a very broad pH range (3.0 to 9.0—the human gastrointestinal tract pH range is approximately 1.5 to 8.0), and 4) require moisture to perform their digestive function. (See Appendix G, page 273.)

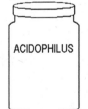

ACIDOPHILUS

To help reestablish a normal flora balance in your digestive tract, take a good quality friendly bacteria supplement, commonly referred to as *acidophilus*. This supplement may contain *Lactobacillus acidophilus* (*L. acidophilus* or *L. dophilus*), *Bifidobacterium bifidum* (*B. bididum* or *L. bifidus*), *Streptococcus faecium*, and/or *Lactobacillus bulgaricus* (*L. bulgaricus*). To evaluate the quality of different brands, read the product label for a listing of ingredients. Also look for substances specifically avoided in their production, such as common allergens—dairy, yeast, grains, soy, etc. Depending upon the bacterial culture medium used, you may need to rotate your friendly bacteria supplement. (See more information about rotation of foods in Chapter 4.) Also, compare different products for concentrations of *Lactobacillus* per gram. Recently a new strain of *Lactobacillus acidophilus*, called NCFM Superstrain, has become available which may be more effective for persons with an overacidic stomach environment which often occurs as a result of CRC. More specific information and research about *Lactobacillus* supplements may be obtained from several companies who market the product. Each company's research supports their product and often differs widely from what another manufacturer's research supports. Individual experimentation may be the best solution when choosing this **VERY IMPORTANT SUPPLEMENT** for your own use. Check with your health-care professional to see if he/she has a specific product to recommend. The *acidophilus* supplement right for one person may not be right for another.

Two factors are especially important when using an *acidophilus* supplement. First, be sure to choose a good quality product that displays an expiration date. Since good quality products contain live active cultures, they have a limited "shelf life" after which they lose much of their effectiveness. Inexpensive *acidophilus* products can be found in the supplement sections of grocery or discount stores. However, they may not contain the effective active cultures and would therefore not be effective in replacing the beneficial intestinal flora. Good quality supplements can be purchased from some health-care professionals, at health-food stores, through food-buying cooperatives, and from mail-order sources such as N.E.E.D.S. (see Appendix C: Resources).

Second, many of the individual *acidophilus* floras (especially *Bifidobacteria*) are acid sensitive and may have trouble surviving through the upper gastrointestinal tract. Because of this, it is important to support the existing beneficial flora in the gut by "feeding" it with a probiotic enhancer such as FOS to help it multiply naturally.

NATURAL PROBIOTIC ENHANCER

100% NUTRAFLORA™

FRUCTOOLIGOSACCHARIDES
CONCENTRATE

FOS (fructo-oligo-saccharides) is a natural probiotic enhancer that "feeds" the beneficial bacteria in the gut, but which cannot be used by *Candida* and other yeast or by certain other harmful bacteria. Since the FOS molecule is too large to be recognized and digested by the body, it reaches the intestines intact where it can be broken down and used by the beneficial bacteria. FOS is a relatively fine white powder with a clean taste. It is about half as sweet as sugar with no aftertaste or bitterness and is very simple to use. (For more information, see page 36–37.)

Your health-care professional will probably prescribe multivitamin and mineral supplements that do not have yeast as a base. Some companies which carry yeast-free supplements are Freeda Vitamins, Nutricology/Allergy Research Group, Twin Labs, Standard Process (except vitamin B supplements), and Metagenics. Again, just as when choosing an *acidophilus* supplement, read the label to make sure the vitamin/mineral supplement is not made from any common allergens or from any food which causes you allergic reactions. If the supplement does not say yeast-free, there is an almost 100% chance that the B vitamins are grown on yeast. In any case, your wisest choice is to purchase a quality brand rather than the inexpensive supplements often found in discount stores or supermarkets.

In addition to multivitamin and mineral supplements, your health-care professional may suggest an antioxidant supplement such as chlorophyll, pycnogenol, silymarin (milk thistle extract), or Nutricology/Allergy Research Group's AntiOx to help eliminate toxins from the blood and gastrointestinal tract. An antioxidant is a "substance that scours the body for unstable oxygen molecules call free radicals, which can cause cell damage."[17] Antioxidant supplements may include beta carotene, dimethylglycine (also called DMG or vitamin B_{15}), selenium, vitamin A, vitamin C, and/or vitamin E. Keeping your colon moving (elimination of solid body waste) every day is also important in the removal of toxins from your body.

Another recommended supplement may be essential fatty acids, commonly referred to as EFAs. Essential fatty acids help in balancing the body systems, including the immune system. EFAs include Omega-3 (EPA) and Omega-6 or gamma linolenic acid (GLA) and are available in vegetable forms (flaxseed oil, evening primrose oil, or borage oil) or an animal form (fish oil supplements). Instead of taking flaxseed oil by the spoonful, its tasty, buttery flavor is good poured on pancakes, muffins, potatoes, vegetables, etc. However, when using flaxseed oil for its nutritional properties, do not add it to foods before cooking them because the oil looses its beneficial factor when heated.

Your treatment for *Candida* Related Complex (CRC) may need to include one or more antifungal medications or supplements. Antifungal medications that must be prescribed by a physician are Nystatin (a powder taken by mouth or a cream for vaginal use), Nizoral, Diflucan, and Sporanox. Nystatin is poorly absorbed by the body so while it is effective in reducing *Candida albicans* in the large bowel it causes no side effects except for a little nausea. The newer antifungal medications, such as Diflucan and Sporanox, are easily absorbed by the body, which enhances their effectiveness in reducing *Candida albicans* in all body tissues.

Paramicocidin is an antifungal supplement derived from extracts of grapefruit seeds and does not need a prescription, but it is usually not readily available over-the-counter. It is often available from health-care professionals such as chiropractors or certified nutritionists who treat CRC or in health-food stores.

As mentioned earlier, garlic and cloves are beneficial in combating yeast. Taking yeast-free odorless Kyolic garlic tablets or capsules is an easy way to benefit from garlic's antifungal properties.

Large amounts of biotin, a B vitamin available in capsules or tablets, is beneficial because a deficiency of biotin allows yeast to overgrow. Biotin is produced by your normal bowel flora. When this delicate balance is disturbed, so is the biotin production that would help keep *Candida albicans* in check naturally.

Pau D'Arco tea is very helpful in discouraging yeast growth. It is a nutritional tea derived from the inner bark of the Pau D'Arco tree. These trees are found in the rain forests of Argentina and are naturally resistant to fungi. I recommend the bulk tea rather than the tea bags because the bag may be made from allergenic materials. Drink 3–6 cups of unsweetened tea evenly and slowly throughout each day, either warm or cold on an empty stomach. (See recipe on page 224.)

Caprylic acid, a short-chain fatty acid, has been found to be antifungal. This is available in capsules, liquid, or tablets and is derived from coconut.

Acu-trol is a four element system which uses Caprol, Bentonite, Psyllium, and beneficial bacteria. Caprol, a mixture of olive oil (including oleic acid) and liquid caprylic acid, has strong antifungal properties. Bentonite aids in intestinal detoxification through its absorptive action on toxic material. Psyllium provides an expansive, adhesive bulk which gently scrapes and cleanses the colon. A good *acidophilus* supplement is used to repopulate the good bacteria. Acu-trol works to cleanse and repopulate the system while limiting the severity of any potential die-off reaction due to the cleansing action of the bentonite and psyllium. (See Appendix C: Resources, page 255.)

Other nonprescription antifungal include oil of oregano (see Appendix C: Resources, page 255), Nature's Herb Myrrh liquid, or Tea Tree Oil from Australia.

Treatment using antifungal medications and supplements most often causes a worsening of symptoms at first, usually during the first two weeks. This temporary increase in symptoms is called "yeast die-off." Also, as with food, you can develop an allergy (sensitivity) to anything you ingest each day. Consider rotating some or all of your vitamin, mineral, antifungal, and *acidophilus* supplements matching the food source from which they are derived with your food rotation.

In Conclusion

Since I am not a physician, chiropractor, or certified nutritionist, I make no medical claims or recommendations for the diet, treatments, or supplements discussed in this book. The information is based on literature, lectures, and my personal experience. Each individual is unique and any treatment initiated needs to be determined by you and your health-care professional. However, it is important for you to read and reread materials about *Candida* Related Complex (CRC) to become as knowledgeable as possible. You need to understand which treatments can be beneficial or detrimental to your recovery. Also, you may by chance read some material and, by taking it to your physician, open his/her eyes to your recovery. No one has all the answers to the complex problem of CRC. Whichever treatment(s) you choose, I cannot emphasize enough that you need an understanding health-care professional to supervise your recovery.

REFERENCES
7. Gail Burton. The *Candida* Control Cookbook (New York, NY: New American Library Books, Div. of Penguin Books USA, Inc., 1989), 4.
8. Department of Agriculture. Food Guide Pyramid: A Guide to Daily Food Choices (Washington, DC: Government Printing Office, 1992).
9. Marjorie Hurt Jones, R.N. Mastering Food Allergies (Vol. V, No. 9, Issue No. 49, October 1990).
10. William G. Crook, M.D., and Marjorie Hurt Jones, R.N. The Yeast Connection Cookbook (Jackson, TN: Professional Books, 1989), 24.
11. Gail Burton. The *Candida* Control Cookbook, 4.
12. Ibid., 5.
13. James Balch, M.D., "Prescription for Nutritional Healing." Seminar presentation, Paul Barry Health Seminars, University of St. Thomas, St. Paul, MN, May 11, 1996.
14. William G. Crook, M.D. The Yeast Connection Handbook (Jackson, TN: Professional Books, Inc., 1996),182–183.
15. Gardiner Harris. "Low Stomach Acidity," Medical Nutrition (Spring 1989).
16. Humbart Santillo. Food Enzymes: The Missing Link to Radiant Health (Prescott, AZ: Hohm Press, 1993), 77-78.
17. Beth Ann Meehan. "Linus Pauling's Rehabilitation," Discover Magazine (Vol. 14, No. 1, January, 1993), 54.

3. FOOD ALLERGIES

Due to the nature of *Candida* Related Complex (CRC) as well as the presence of other contributing factors, many persons with CRC are sensitive to individual foods, additives, and preservatives. It is important to understand the causes and treatments for food allergies and to deal with them to improve your health.

What Is a Food Allergy?

An allergy is an individual's adverse response to a substance such as dust, pollen, food, or a chemical that normally does not cause a problem. For a person with a weakened immune system, repeated exposure to a substance can eventually cause the immune system to reach a state where it cannot deal with the exposure any longer and an allergic reaction develops. Allergic reactions can be as varied in form as there are individuals. Because they are often inherited, you may have a predisposition for allergies. They sometimes appear relatively late in life, but you may be able to think back and remember the subtle effects of allergies throughout your life.

The most common food allergens are foods eaten frequently. The diet of most Americans includes one or more servings of wheat, milk or other dairy products, egg, corn, and/or soy each day. You may not be aware of these substances in your diet. However, if you check the labels of prepared foods, you will find these ingredients in common foods such as salad dressing, catsup, pancake syrup, breakfast cereal, breads, snack cakes, chips, granola bars, etc.

> **Common Food Allergens**
> - wheat
> - milk/dairy products
> - eggs
> - corn
> - soy

When you eat foods to which you are allergic, they cause the lymphocytes (white blood cells) to release proteins called immunoglobulins. These immunoglobulins then react with other cells in your body (tissues of your nose, lungs, skin, digestive tract, etc.) to release chemicals such as histamine. The symptoms (allergic reactions) that you perceive are caused by the histamine reacting with parts of your body.

Food allergies are either fixed or cyclical reactions. Fixed food allergies are the type that you have every time you eat or even breathe the fumes of a small amount of a particular food. A fixed reaction usually appears earlier in life, the first time you consumed the food. The reactions are very strong, often potentially dangerous, and appear soon after contact with the food. They have a lifelong pattern, are very unlikely to disappear, and the food causing the reaction always needs to be eliminated from the diet. Fish and nuts are two common fixed food allergens. Often, people who react to fish and/or nuts need to avoid all fish and/or nuts but have no other allergies.

Fixed food allergies are the result of factors different from those which cause the cyclical form. This book deals with the description, causes, and treatment of cyclical food allergies.

Cyclical Food Allergy Reactions

Cyclical reactions are much different in that you may or may not notice a reaction or may not notice the reaction every time you eat the food. The level of reaction may range from quite weak to severe, is seldom dangerous, and may depend on how much of a particular food you eat or how often you eat it. For example, eating one cup of popcorn once a week may not cause you any noticeable reaction. But if you eat an increased amount (let's say four cups of popcorn once a week) or if you increase the frequency (one cup of popcorn each day), an immediate or a delayed reaction may occur. Constant consumption of a food allergen may cause acute symptoms to temporarily disappear or become chronic as your body tries to adapt to the exposure. Corn and soy are good examples because they are hidden ingredients in several foods consumed daily.

Cyclical food allergies usually depend upon exposure so any food can be an allergen. In the typical Western diet, common food allergens are beef, chocolate, citrus, corn, egg, milk, peanut, shellfish, soy, tomato, wheat, and yeast.

A cyclical food reaction can be either masked or unmasked. An unmasked reaction is when you have a reaction soon after eating a food and/or you know which food causes the reaction. However, the most common reaction is a masked cyclical reaction, which occurs many hours after eating the food. Many times you do not make any connection between your health problems and the foods you eat. Repeated consumption of a food to which you are allergic causes symptoms that become chronic and do not necessarily occur or worsen at the time you eat the food. Instead, symptoms may include feeling slightly stimulated (which may be a good feeling), craving the allergic food, and/or feeling worse if you avoid eating it for a couple of days. A craving leads to over-consumption of the reactive food. Often you feel the food is needed by your body to maintain good health. This pattern is called a "food addiction."

To unmask a food allergy begin by completely avoiding the suspected food(s) for two weeks or longer. Also, read all labels on the foods you eat to be sure you are omitting all sources of the suspected food(s). Your list of suspected foods should include the common food allergens as well as foods you normally eat more than two times a week.

After your chronic symptoms have cleared, eat a small amount of one of the suspected foods. Use a notebook to record date, time, food eaten, amount eaten, and any noticeable reactions experienced as well as any other possible causes such as environmental factors.

Day/Date	Time	Food & Form Eaten	Amount Eaten	Reaction & Possible Cause
8/25/96	8 pm	egg, scrambled with butter	2 large size	Mild headache 2 hours following breakfast lasting until midafternoon Itchy rectum around noon on 8/26 Suspect the butter as well as the egg. Next time try using Clarified Butter or unrefined oil.

Your body's response may appear as a noticeable and/or unexpected reaction. Watch for immediate and/or delayed reactions. A delayed reaction can occur relatively soon (as little as 30 minutes) after eating the food or as long as up to 48 hours later.[18] A delayed reaction is caused by the fact that it takes time for the allergens to travel through the blood stream and encounter the sensitized cells in your body. If you have an immediate or delayed reaction, you should avoid eating the food for three to six months before trying it again.

After this approximate 48 hour period, if no reactions have been noticed, you may want to expand the challenge by eating a larger amount or eating the food two or three times in one day. Again wait 48 hours to check for immediate and/or delayed reactions. Use your notebook to record your responses.

An example of how a food allergy becomes masked is described in <u>Coping with Your Allergies</u>.[19] If a person allergic to peanuts has avoided them for at least ten days or longer, they will probably have a definite recognizable reaction—immediate or delayed—if they eat peanuts or a peanut product. However, if they continue to eat peanuts every day, the reaction occurs but at a lesser level of severity. Eventually the reaction is no longer noticed or associated with the peanuts and has therefore become masked or hidden. The masked reactions become chronic ailments and if you have many masked food allergies, you end up having a lot of chronic ailments. When this acute stage is reached you often feel better when you eat the foods you are allergic to or begin to crave them.

What Causes Food Allergies?

Food sensitivities are the result of the body's immune defense system reacting to the presence of incompletely digested food particles outside the gastrointestinal tract. The gastrointestinal tract is a hollow tube which stretches from the mouth to the rectum and includes the esophagus, stomach, small and large intestines, and the rectum and is designed to breakdown food into usable particles and separate them from materials to be eliminated from the body. The usable particles are allowed to enter the rest of the body where they provide the nutrients needed for proper body function. In a healthy system, the permeability of the gut allows only the beneficial substances to get through.[20]

Unfortunately, many factors can cause the gut lining to become inflamed and to break down or erode. The resulting increased permeability allows substances such as incompletely digested food particles and toxins to freely circulate ("leak") to areas of the body where they normally would not. The body recognizes these substances as "foreigners" and signals the immune system to attack and make antibodies against them. If the attacked substance is a food particle, the body then recognizes the food as a foreign substance and a food sensitivity has developed. This condition is known as "leaky gut" syndrome which triggers a state of continuous and prolonged stress in and on the immune system.[21]

Some causes of gut inflammation which can result in "leaky gut" include:

- *Candida* Related Complex
- Use of antibiotics
- Use of non-steroidal anti-inflammatory drugs (including aspirin, Motrin, Ibuprofen, Advil, Aleve, Naprosine, and Teleprin) (Tylenol is not included in this category.)
- Eating foods to which you are already allergic
- Stress, hurried meals, anxiety, fatigue, etc.
- Alcohol consumption
- Chemotherapy/radiation

Since a "leaky gut" can lead to food allergies and food allergies can contribute to continued or increased gut inflammation, this becomes a self-perpetuating cycle unless steps are taken to correct the gut condition and deal with the food allergies.

What Are Typical Allergic Reactions to Food?[22, 23]

Allergic reactions to foods are numerous and complex. The following are typical reactions. However, not all symptoms may be exhibited and they may vary depending upon the food.

RESPIRATORY:		
• dry mouth	• ringing in ears	• sensitivity to odors
• ear infections	• rubbing nose all the time	

GASTROINTESTINAL:		
• gain in weight	• constipation	• diarrhea
• craving for food, alcohol, or tobacco	• colic	

GENITOURINARY:			
• chronic bladder irritation	• bedwetting	• premenstrual tension	• menstrual cramps

SKIN:			
• sweating	• flushing	• outer ears hurt	• bright red ear lobes

SYSTEMIC:		
• fluid retention in any part of body	• backache	• dark circles under eyes
• unexplained fluctuation of weight	• fatigue	• leg aches
• muscle and joint swelling, redness, and pain	• hyperactive	• muscle aches

CARDIOVASCULAR:		
• abnormal heart rhythms	• severe chest pain	• heart palpitations

CEREBRAL:		
• migraine headaches or chronic headaches	• depression	• convulsive seizures
	• constant anger	• blackouts
• changes of mood: lack of ability to concentrate; feelings of sadness, weariness, frustration, animation, euphoria, aggressiveness, anger, panic, violence, silliness, and/or "spaciness"	• impairment of speaking and reading ability	• psychosis such as manic depression or schizophrenia
	• lack of coordination	• night terrors: scream in the middle of night, eyes open staring
	• loss of balance	
	• excessive hunger or thirst	• "Jeckyll and Hyde" reaction
	• sleepiness or insomnia	• make clucking noise
• inappropriate laughter	• phobias, delusions, hallucinations	• see a difference in handwriting just after eating a food or meal
• crying spells	• amnesia	

Diagnosis of Food Allergies

A clinical ecologist, internist, or allergist who treats food allergies can perform tests to aid in determining food allergies. These can include skin prick (least accurate), sublingual, and/or blood tests (most accurate). Two blood tests are used to measure allergic food responses. The IgE test measures immediate or rapid reactions and the IgG test measures "hidden" or delayed-onset reactions. (See Appendix C, page 261.)

In addition, some health-care professionals closely supervise a special fasting, elimination, and rare food diet to aid in determining food allergies (see <u>The E.I. Syndrome</u> by Sherry Rogers, M.D. for more information).

An important step in the diagnosis of food allergies may be to determine if the symptoms are the result of a food allergy or a food intolerance. While a food allergy is an over-reaction of the body's immune system, a food intolerance does not involve the immune system. A food intolerance is usually caused by an enzyme deficiency that hinders digestion. (For more information on enzymes, see page 14 and Appendix G, page 273.) However, food intolerance symptoms, such as intestinal discomfort, often resemble those of a food allergy. Consult with a health-care professional for help in determining which reaction you are experiencing.[24]

Treatments for Food Allergies

While continuous, long-term treatments are essential in dealing with food allergies, there are some short-term measures which can help if you are experiencing a reaction to a food exposure. —Take 1/4 teaspoon of **baking soda** in 1/2 cup purified water—you may need to repeat the dose. —Use buffered, corn-free, citrus-free **vitamin C powder** dissolved in purified water. You may want to research the source to ensure you can tolerate it. Good resources for this substance are Twin Labs and Allergy Research/Nutricology—both brands may be available in your local health-food store. —**Alka Seltzer Gold** (in the gold box) may also help with food reactions. It is aspirin free and contains: Active Ingredients: heat treated sodium bicarbonate 958 mg., citric acid 832 mg., potassium bicarbonate 312 mg. Inactive Ingredient: a tableting aid. (Citric acid may be a problem for CRC sufferers.) Alka Seltzer Gold often must be special ordered through a pharmacy. —**Alka-Aid** is an antacid which contains: Active Ingredients: sodium bicarbonate 360 mg., potassium bicarbonate 180 mg. Inactive Ingredients: cellulose, glyceryl monostearate, methycellulose, magnesium stearate. It contains no yeast, wheat, corn, soya, dairy/animal products, preservatives, sugar, artificial color or flavoring agents. (See Appendix C, page 255, for mail order source.)

Long-term treatments are the first line of defense in dealing with food allergies and are used to eliminate or control the effects of the reactive foods on the system.

Some allergists or clinical ecologists use desensitization shots or drops in the treatment of food allergies to build the body's natural defense system and lower allergic reactions. In addition, a treatment called EPD (enzyme potentiated desensitization) is now available. (See Appendix C, page 260, for physician referrals.)

FOS (fructo-oligo-saccharides), _acidophilus_ supplements, and three nutritional-support supplements—UltraClear®, UltraClear® Sustain, and UltraClear® Plus (see Appendix C, page 255, for resources)—may be used in combination to treat "leaky gut" syndrome.

To reduce food sensitivity symptoms, the offending food or class of food needs to be identified and eliminated or consumed less often by the sensitive person. Avoiding these foods allows the immune system to rest. If you are extremely allergic to specific foods this is probably the best step to take.

By far the most important treatment for food allergies is the use of a rotational diet. It provides an effective means of controlling food exposures and allowing the body to recover from the effects of a food before it is eaten again. Rotational diet is discussed fully in the next chapter.

> _The real art of living is beginning where you are._   _Martin Vanbee_

> _It is astonishing how short a time it takes for very wonderful things to happen._
>   _Frances Burnett_

REFERENCES

18. Alan Scott Levin, M.D., and Merla Zellerbach. <u>The Type 1/Type 2 Allergy Relief Program</u> (CA: Jeremy P. Tarcher, Inc., 1983), 96.
19. Natalie Golos and Frances Golos Golbitz. <u>Coping with Your Allergies</u>, 85.
20. Marjorie Hurt Jones. "Leaky Gut—What Is It?," <u>Mastering Food Allergies</u> (Vol. X, No. 4, issue #86, July-August 1995), 1.
21. Marjorie Hurt Jones. "Leaky Gut. A Common Problem with Food Allergies," <u>Mastering Food Allergies</u> (Vol. VIII, No. 5, issue #75, September-October 1993), 1.
22. Alan Scott Levin, M.D., and Merla Zellerbach. <u>The Type 1/Type 2 Allergy Relief Program</u>, 18–19.
23. Jerry Springer. <u>Allergies—Making Kids Crazy</u>. Interview with Doris Rapp, M.D. Air Date: December 17, 1992. 45 min., Multimedia Entertainment, Inc., 1944, videocassette.
24. "Sidestepping Food Sensitivities." Informational brochure distributed by Good Earth Restaurants, Corporate Office, 3001 Hennepin Avenue South, Suite 301-A, Minneapolis, MN 55408-2647 [(612) 822-0016].

4. ROTATIONAL DIET

Due to the cause and effect interrelationship involved in *Candida* Related Complex (CRC), it often goes hand-in-hand with food allergies and "leaky gut" syndrome[25] and many persons with CRC will also be sensitive to individual foods, additives, and preservatives. Because of this it is very important to rotate and/or diversity the foods used in the *Candida* Control Diet. This is especially advantageous during the early weeks and months of the CRC treatment program when the body is weakest and there is a greater chance of developing food allergies. In addition, if food allergies are present but unidentified, a rotational diet can help in identifying them and therefore aid recovery.

Rotary Diversified Diet—What and Why

The rotary diversified diet was first developed in 1934 by Dr. Herbert J. Rinkel. It is used by people who (1) have food sensitivities, (2) are diagnosed chemically susceptible, (3) are healthy members of a family prone to food allergies, or (4) are health-conscious individuals.[26]

A rotational diet is more enjoyable and less limiting than other diets with which you may be familiar. It is a controlled, rational way to eat which incorporates flexibility and accomplishes three main goals.

1. Helps in the treatment of current food allergies by allowing the body to recover from the effects of a food before it is eaten again.
2. Greatly lessens the chances of developing allergies to additional foods.
3. Aids in identifying foods that could be causing problems.

Using a rotational format when starting the CRC treatment diet is especially important because feelings of deprivation may surface when foods are removed from the diet. To compensate, the frequent response is to overeat a substitute for the removed food(s). Overeating an individual food increases the chances of developing a sensitivity to it. For example, when I eliminated wheat (my first known food allergen), I substituted rye crackers and popcorn and ate them often. Within two months I had developed allergies to rye and corn. So I substituted rice cakes, ate them often, and as a result developed an allergy to rice. Since a rotational format regulates exposure to an individual food, it can help prevent this cycle by aiding in the treatment of current allergies and lessening the chance of developing new ones.

Eating on Rotation

By following a rotational diet, you gain control over your exposure to foods that cause you cyclical food reactions. A 4-, 5-, 6-, 7-, or 8-day rotational diet maybe used. Whichever cycle length is used, each food eaten on a particular day is not eaten until that day repeats again in the rotation. For example, in the sample 4-day rotation (see Table A) the broccoli and rice on Day 1 will not be eaten again until the following Day 1 with three days in between. The same holds true for a longer rotation. In the sample 5-day rotation (see Table A) broccoli and rice are eaten on Day 2 and are not eaten again until the next Day 2 with four days in between their consumption. The same holds true for other foods in the two sample diets below.

TABLE A

Four-Day Rotation

Day 1	Day 2	Day 3	Day 4	Day 1	Day 2	Day 3
broccoli	shrimp	carrot	orange	broccoli	shrimp	carrot
rice	potato	turkey	beans	rice	potato	turkey

Five-Day Rotation

Day 1	Day 2	Day 3	Day 4	Day 5	Day 1	Day 2
quinoa	rice	amaranth	buckwheat	beans	quinoa	rice
carrot	broccoli	tomato	spinach	asparagus	carrot	broccoli

Four days is generally a long enough rotation to assure maximum bowel transit time (the amount of time your body takes to move food through the complete digestive tract and eliminate the waste part of the food from your body). Persons with chronic constipation may need a cycle longer than 4-days—either a 5-, 6-, or 8-day rotation. A 7-day rotation is not recommended because it becomes too monotonous eating the same foods every Monday, Tuesday, etc. If using a cycle longer than four days, it might be easiest to choose an 8-day rotation. First, this allows maximum bowel transit time. Second, after becoming healthier, switching to the most used 4-day rotation is easy.

When first starting, you may find, as I did, that the 4-day rotation will be long enough for some foods but not for others. In this instance, use the basic 4-day rotation but rotate some foods every eight days. In Table B, notice that rice, spelt, cod, shrimp, potato, amaranth, beans, and asparagus are only eaten on one day in eight, whereas broccoli, turkey, carrot, and orange are eaten every four days.

TABLE B

Day 1	Day 2	Day 3	Day 4	Day 1	Day 2	Day 3	Day 4
broccoli	cod	carrot	orange	broccoli	shrimp	carrot	orange
rice	potato	turkey	beans	spelt	amaranth	turkey	asparagus

What Is a "Day"?

While an expected definition of a day would be the meals you eat between sunrise and sunset (breakfast, lunch, dinner), for the purposes of a rotational diet this 24-hour period can be adjusted to fit individual needs.

For example, persons who cannot handle preparing breakfast may prefer to use *plan*overs (planned leftovers) from dinner the previous evening and would define their rotational day as lunch, dinner, and breakfast the following morning.

If you work outside your home and carry your lunch, you may wish to define your day as dinner, breakfast, and lunch. This will allow you to prepare extra servings for your lunch on the following day while preparing your evening meal.

Basically, then, a "day" consists of any 24-hour period and the meals consumed during that time frame. This can be from midnight to midnight, 3 p.m. to 3 p.m., or any other cycle that works for your particular needs. With careful planning, you can easily and successfully maintain your rotation and enjoy nutritious, delicious meals. (See Chapter 8—Menu Planning.)

Basic Rules to Follow on a 4-Day Rotational Diet

RULE 1. **Simple is better.** Eat whole foods, not highly processed foods that have lost much of their nutritional value and may contain hidden ingredients such as corn, soy, or egg. Eat a wide variety of foods. Diversify your diet by using many different types of fish and other protein sources, vegetables, whole grains, and grain substitutes.

RULE 2. **Do not eat the same food item more often than every fourth day.** For example, eat rice on Day 1, then avoid eating rice until the next Day 1, with three days in between. This means that rice will not be consumed on a schedule of every Sunday or Thursday, but that it will be eaten on whichever day of the week Day 1 of the rotational cycle falls. See Table C.

RULE 3. **Within a rotation, food families are also rotated.** Foods are grouped into botanical food families based on their biological origin. Each food family is assigned a name and a number for identification. Food families are rotated because foods in the same family tend to share common allergens and could react similarly. Eating rice on Day 1, spelt on Day 2, oat on Day 3, and millet on Day 4 is not really rotating foods since you are eating a member of the Grass Family every day. Table D illustrates how all foods from an individual family are eaten on an assigned day.

For a complete listing of food families, see Appendix A. This listing also includes nonedible plants. Persons may need to avoid foods when they are allergic to a weed or plant included in the food family group. For example: if allergic to pigweed, be cautious of amaranth; if allergic to poison ivy, be cautious of cashews, pistachios, and mangoes; and if allergic to lamb's-quarters, be cautious of quinoa, spinach, chard, and beets.

TABLE C

Sunday Day 1	Monday Day 2	Tuesday Day 3	Wednesday Day 4	Thursday Day 1	Friday Day 2	Saturday Day 3
rice	potato	millet	beans	rice	potato	millet

Sunday Day 4	Monday Day 1	Tuesday Day 2	Wednesday Day 3	Thursday Day 4	Friday Day 1	Saturday Day 2
beans	rice	potato	millet	beans	rice	potato

TABLE D

Day 1 Grass Family	Day 2 Lily Family	Day 3 Mustard Family	Day 4 Legume Family
rice	garlic	cauliflower	peas
spelt	onion	Brussels sprouts	pinto bean
oat	leeks	broccoli	garbanzo bean
millet	asparagus	cabbage	lima bean
etc.	etc.	etc.	etc.

RULE 4. **Different foods within a food family may be rotated every other day.** As explained in Rule 3, within a 4-day rotation a particular food is eaten at least four days apart. However, Rule 4 allows foods in a food family to be eaten two days apart. Notice in Table E that each food is eaten every four days yet separate foods in a family are eaten two days apart. Ex.: include rice and spelt on Day 1 and oat and millet on Day 3 (Grass Family); garlic and onion on Day 2 and leeks and asparagus on Day 4 (Lily Family); etc. This allows for more flexibility and variety in planning meals.

TABLE E

Day 1	Day 2	Day 3	Day 4
Grass Family	**Lily Family**	**Grass Family**	**Lily Family**
rice	garlic	oat	leeks
spelt	onion	millet	asparagus

Mustard Family	Legume Family	Mustard Family	Legume Family
broccoli	garbanzo bean	cauliflower	peas
cabbage	lima bean	Brussels sprouts	pinto bean

One exception to Rule 4 to be aware of involves the Grass Family (# 6). Wheat, spelt, and Kamut® are very closely related and should always be assigned to the same day—not divided and eaten two days apart. In addition, if you have an allergy to wheat, be very careful when adding spelt or Kamut® to your diet. Be sure to do a food challenge (see pages 10 and 18) to check for reactions to these grains.

Persons with severe food allergies may need to use additional restrictions to the 4-day rotation, such as:

1. Do not repeat foods or food families twice within one day unless at the same meal.
2. Do not incorporate Rule 4 in your rotation.

The rotation outlined on pages 66–67 does not use Rule 4 for all food families. As an example, the Nightshade Family (# 74) is assigned only to Day 2 and eaten only four days apart rather than members of the family being split every other day.

RULE 5. **Foods may be moved to another day providing that the complete food family is also moved.**

Example 1. Moving foods on a permanent basis. To move cabbage (member of the Mustard Family, #36) from Day 1 to Day 2 you must move other assigned Day 1 members of the Mustard Family to Day 2 (see page 66). Also, this requires moving Day 3 members of the Mustard Family to Day 4 (see page 67).

MOVING VAN

Example 2. Use "Floating Foods" to allow for creativity and flexibility within the regular 4-day rotation. A "floating food" is any food that may sometimes be eaten on a day which is two days later than its assigned day. It works best if the "floating food" is consumed less often because when you properly "float" a particular food it is eaten six days apart (five days in between). See Table F for an example using wild rice.

TABLE **F**

Day 1	Day 2	Day 3	Day 4
Wild & Brown Rice with Herbs & Pecans			

Day 1	Day 2	Day 3	Day 4
		Wild Rice Pasta Salad	

When I planned the rotation diet outlined on pages 66–67 and began developing the recipes, I gradually added foods that I desired to "float" between Days 1 and 3 and between Days 2 and 4. Looking at these food lists for each day you will find an asterisk (*) by parsley and cinnamon indicating that these foods float between Days 1 and 3. Also, you will find garlic, oregano, and chili powder indicated as foods that float between Days 2 and 4. These are the few foods defined as "floating foods." Each of the recipes in which these foods occur does not have a warning asterisk to remind you to omit them for four days before eating them again.

There are other foods in this rotational diet that I occasionally "float" from Day 1 to 3 or from Day 2 to 4 or vice versa. For example, wild rice is in recipes on Day 1 as well as on Day 3. Remember, when using a "floating food" it is important to avoid eating it for four days before eating it again as Table F illustrates. To assist you with meal planning, every attempt has been made to asterisk (*) any foods in the recipes that are temporarily moved ("floated"). However you can float any foods by following Rules 2, 3, and 4.

Example 3. Allow "Fun Foods" to brighten your day. There are some foods that I call "Fun Foods" because they are members of a food family with no other or only a few other foods in their family. These foods can be moved with ease, just remember to allow three days between the times you consume them. Below is my list of "Fun Foods" along with their food family number and the day on which they are normally assigned. Some of the "Fun Foods" are unassigned. As an example let's consider Brazil and macadamia nuts. Since these nuts are each a member of a different food family and there are no other foods in their family, they can be eaten on any day of the rotation as long as they were not consumed within the last four days. I usually use macadamia nuts in Day 4 recipes and Brazil nuts in Day 2 recipes. However, there are also a few recipes on Days 1 and 3 that include these nuts. Again, to assist you with meal planning, every attempt has been made to asterisk (*) any unassigned "Fun Foods" in the recipes. Also, since macadamia nuts are sometimes difficult to find as well as more expensive, I personally use Brazil nuts in recipes on any day when I have not consumed them in the past four days and do not plan to consume them in the next four days.

Example 4. Moving foods on a temporary basis. Occasionally I like to eat asparagus with scrambled eggs on Day 1. This can be accomplished if I plan ahead and make modifications within my rotational diet. Usually I eat the Lily Family on Days 2 and 4 as illustrated in Table E. To temporarily move asparagus from Day 4 to Day 1, omit eating the Lily Family on Day 4 before and Day 2 after you eat asparagus on Day 1. In addition, you must avoid eating asparagus on the Day 4 after you eat this food combination on Day 1. See Table G for a visual example. On the next repeat of the rotational cycle return to eating foods from the Lily Family as Table E on page 23 illustrates.

List of Fun Foods

Food Family Number	Food	Day Assigned in Rotation
1	agar-agar and kombu	Day 4
10	pineapple	unassigned
16	banana and plantain	Day 2
17	ginger	unassigned
20	vanilla	unassigned
23	filberts (hazelnut)	Day 3
26	macadamia nut	unassigned
33	nutmeg	unassigned
35	poppy seed	unassigned
44	flaxseed and flaxseed oil	unassigned
50	maple granules	unassigned
54	okra	Day 2
59	papaya	unassigned
62	Brazil nut	unassigned

Day 1	Day 2	Day 3	Day 4	Day 1	Day 2	Day 3	Day 4
	Lily Family		Lily Family	Lily Family	Lily Family		Lily Family
	garlic onion		Omit All	asparagus	Omit All		eat leeks omit asparagus

Example 5. Choose to substitute other foods rather than move foods. Sometimes moving foods is more difficult than creatively substituting. Carefully evaluate any move to be sure it does not cause too many problems and seriously consider adapting the recipe to use foods assigned on a particular day before attempting a move. As an example, when developing a stuffed green pepper recipe, I needed to move rice from Day 1 to Day 2. This meant I would have to move or omit eating all other foods from the Grass Family such as Kamut, rice, spelt, teff, etc. on Day 1. In addition, I would have to omit eating all food items from the Grass Family such as barley, oat, millet, rye, wild rice, etc. on the following Day 3. I decided that this particular move was too restrictive and instead chose to use garbanzo beans in my Stuffed Green Peppers.

RULE 6. **Be your own best friend and helper.** Relax, be understanding, and be kind to yourself. You may be feeling overwhelmed by your health situation and the many changes you know you will be making to help your system heal. But you can better deal with dietary and lifestyle changes if you develop a **positive sense of helping yourself.** Rest your mind; be flexible, optimistic, and calm; and give yourself time to retrain your taste buds and to learn to use the many new foods and cooking techniques offered in this cookbook. Do not dwell on what you cannot eat. Instead, concentrate on how the foods you can eat are leading you to a well-nourished, healthy lifestyle. This will help you develop a positive attitude on how you are guiding yourself toward improved health. After eating on rotation for a while, you will realize it is an achievable and extremely healthy way to eat.

> If you feel "stuck" on your limited diet, begin to change your attitude by focusing on what you <u>can</u> eat and enjoy. This will help you stay on your food allergy, *Candida* control, and/or rotational diet.

To accomplish rotating foods successfully, start with defining your commitment level. Start gradually and work up to a higher level of commitment. One way to accomplish this is to start with rotating grains, then add meats to the rotation followed by vegetables and then fruits. Finally, add spices and oils to the rotation.

If you get off rotation, for whatever reason, don't become discouraged and drop all of it because you cannot handle it all or as quickly as you might wish. You may have added rotation steps too soon for your situation. Don't worry about the past. Look forward and start fresh. Go back to an earlier rotation step such as just rotating your grains, then add the other foods gradually. Do not try to be a "one hundred percenter." Allow yourself some freedom, especially when traveling or on special occasions.

This is a personal commitment you are making and your individual time and energy levels need to be a factor in the decision. Make it realistic for you and your situation. But remember, you are changing your lifestyle **to benefit yourself**. Only you can truly define and set your personal commitment level and ultimately responsible for following through on this commitment. Work with what you can handle and soon, with support, you can accomplish more than you ever dreamed.

RULE 7. **Seek support.** Seek nonprofessional help from understanding friends or family, a local CIIN or HEAL support group (see Appendix C, page 261) or a food cooperative (see Appendix E). Also, an overeaters support group may help. If necessary, seek professional help from a counselor. (For more information on choosing a counselor see issues #5 and 6 of CCN, page 271.) Other than the support of friends, I have found the best solution for myself is education. Read and reread information about *Candida* Related Complex (CRC), food allergies, rotational diet, etc. until you fully understand, visualize, and conquer it.

Success with a *Candida* control and/or rotational diet does not come overnight. Build your personal support system as you are able. It may take time to find the people and services that will benefit you, but the end result will be well worth it.

Personalizing a Rotational Diet

Depending upon your personal food allergies and other dietary restrictions, as well as availability and personal food likes/dislikes, you may need to adjust the rotational diet outlined in this book (pages 66–67) or develop a complete personalized rotational diet. There are businesses who will assist you in developing a personalized diet (see Appendix C, page 259) or follow the steps below.

Adjust the rotational diet in this cookbook by using the following steps.
1. Photocopy diet on pages 66–67 and two copies of form on page 60.
2. With a pencil, cross out all foods that you can not eat due to food allergies or other dietary restrictions. Also, indicate the time frame by foods that are only available during a specific time of year.
3. Look at the foods remaining and evaluate whether there are enough foods on each day to form a balanced diet. Look for a cross section of animal and/or other protein sources, carbohydrates, starches, and vegetables as well as fruits and sweeteners (once you can add them to your diet).
4. If you decide that you do not have enough foods on certain days, follow the basic rules outlined in this chapter and begin moving foods from one day to another. Be sure to move the complete family as explained in Rule 5, Example 1 on page 23. OR choose allowed foods to assign to desired days of the rotation. To accomplish this, proceed through the food categories in the following order:

  - Start with Grains, Flours, & Baking Foods and Higher Carbohydrate Vegetables such as: root vegetables— potatoes, parsnips, turnips, rutabaga, sweet potato; squashes—pumpkin, acorn, butternut, and other winter squashes; and legumes—peas, lentils, and dry beans.
  - Then proceed with Animal Protein and/or other protein sources such as beans, nuts, seeds, amaranth, quinoa.
  - Next consider the Lower Carbohydrate Vegetables.
  - Finally add nuts, seeds, herbs, spices, fruits and sweeteners. As you consider nuts, seeds, and vegetables, also decide on an oil for each day.

Use the custom diet for a few rotations before proceeding to the next category. Also, at each step do not concern yourself with rotation of other foods in the lower categories until you reach that level. This will allow you to become accustomed to your diet and successfully adjust to your new lifestyle before proceeding. However, it is best to attempt to eat a wide variety of foods (that you are not allergic to) in the lower categories and, if possible, adapt to eating a particular food no more often than every other day.

About This Cookbook

This cookbook offers you a food allergy, *Candida* control, and 4-day rotational diet that will enhance your health and well being with the use of a wide variety of foods. In addition, it introduces you to several "new" foods and provides information on preparing and purchasing them. Each day of the rotation has a list of assigned foods with a wide variety of recipes and meal planning ideas to support the rotation. The recipes may use unfamiliar ingredients but they have only slight changes in flavor and texture. Before you know it your taste buds will not crave or need the original. Learn to enjoy the flavors of new foods combined with old favorites.

As you work with the rotational diet offered in this cookbook and the food family charts in Appendix A, you will learn to recognize food families and be able to vary your diet according to your individual food allergies and/or to suit your taste. After using a rotational diet, you soon may be able to safely tolerate foods that previously caused you moderate to severe reactions. This is possible because you have allowed your body's immune system to have an appropriate rest period and recover to the point where you have regained a tolerance to many previously offending foods. You may regain tolerance to some foods in as little as 3–4 weeks where for other foods it may take 2–6 months or longer. However, some food allergies may be permanent or fixed. You soon will realize good, tasty, nutritious meals are available and will not miss the foods you cannot eat.

REFERENCES

25. Marjorie Hurt Jones. "Leaky Gut: A Common Problem with Food Allergies," Mastering Food Allergies (Vol. VIII, No. 5, Issue No. 75, September-October, 1993), 1.
26. Natalie Golos and Frances Golos Golbitz. Coping with Your Allergies (New York, NY: A Fireside Book, Published by Simon and Schuster, Inc., 1986), 85.

5. SPECIALTY FOODS

This chapter is devoted to specialty foods in various forms that you can use to add diversity to your diet, especially if you are eating on rotation and/or are allergic to foods such as wheat and corn. It includes an introduction to grains and nongrains as well as individual description sections on grains, nongrains, starches, sugar substitutes, and miscellaneous foods. Each individual listing is divided into sections on Properties, History, and Uses. In some cases a "Sondra's Thoughts" section is included which gives my personal thoughts and suggestions on the specific food item.

The specialty foods listed are generally available in health-food stores, through food-buying cooperatives, and/or from mail-order sources. Check you local grocery store as well since more places are now carrying some of these specialty foods. Appendices C, E, and F provide information on Resources, Cooperative Food Warehouses in the United States, and Organizations Providing Information on Organic Food Production and Availability for your use in locating the foods you wish to purchase.

Introduction to Grains and Nongrains

Whole grains and whole-grain products have been staple foods for thousands of years in almost all cultures. Today they are used as a common source of carbohydrates and an inexpensive source of protein.

Amaranth, buckwheat, and quinoa are differentiated as nongrains because, although they are prepared and act a lot like a grain in both whole-grain and flour form, they are not a part of the Grass Family (#6). Each is in a distinctly different food families: amaranth—Pigweed Family (#30); quinoa—Goosefoot Family (#28); and buckwheat—Buckwheat Family (#27). (See Appendix A: Food Families.)

Whole grains are seeds that contain three natural components:
- **bran layer:** a tough outer coating which protects the grain and is rich in fiber and minerals
- **germ:** contains vitamin E, essential fatty acids, and proteins which provide food for the plant seed to sprout and develop a root system
- **endosperm:** the starchy bulk layer of the grain, rich in complex carbohydrates and proteins, which nourish the seedling during the early growth period before the leaves begin to photosynthesize

Refined grains have been degermed or polished, which removes the germ and bran layers and lowers the nutritional value. For example, "pearled" barley is a refined product that has undergone six scourings between Carborundam wheels which removes the bran and germ. As a result the barley loses between 74–97% of its protein, fat, fiber, and minerals.[27] Another example of refined grain is the white (wheat) flour common in American diets. Wheat loses up to 80% of its nutrients in the refining process. Persons who use refined white flour commonly respond by saying it is "enriched." But why use a product that has had more than twenty nutrients removed and only four added back—thiamin, niacin, riboflavin, and iron?[28] In addition, the B vitamins used to "enrich" refined flour often have a yeast growth source which CRC patients should avoid. Refined flours are also subjected to a bleaching process, which destroys the essential amino acid or protein part of the flour.

Another property of some flours is gluten, a type of protein that controls bread's ability to raise. When flour containing gluten is mixed with water, kneaded, and beaten, it forms an elastic framework that stretches as either yeast or another leavening agent causes it to grow. When you bake the dough this gluten framework sets up to form the structure of the baked good.

The gluten-containing grains are wheat and other wheat relatives (spelt and Kamut), rye, oats, and barley, in descending order of more-to-less gluten. The essentially gluten-free grains and nongrains are amaranth, buckwheat, corn, millet, quinoa, rice, sorghum, and teff.

According to the Rodale Research Center in eastern Pennsylvania, all grains and grain-like foods do contain some traces of gluten. However, the essentially gluten-free grains and nongrains should be all right for celiacs who cannot digest gluten. This is because the gluten in these foods is chemically bound and unavailable to enter into any reactions in the body.[29]

Special Note: Celiacs are unable to digest gluten. According to Marjorie Hurt Jones,[30] celiacs who continue to eat gluten-containing foods develop abdominal symptoms such as gas pain, bloating, cramping, etc., because the gluten is not digested and erodes their intestinal villi. The intestinal villi are very important for the absorption of soluble nutrients in our body. Celiacs who continue to ingest gluten-containing foods show signs of malnourishment no matter what they eat.

Washing and Cooking Whole Grains and Nongrains

Grains and nongrains should be rinsed to remove dirt and hulls before cooking. Guidelines for washing and cooking grains and nongrains, along with a chart listing amounts and cooking times, is found in the Grain and Nongrain recipe section (page 96).

Purchasing and Storing Whole Grains and Whole-grain Flours

The key to purchasing fresh whole grains is to check for unbroken grains as they can last for a long time if properly stored. Store grains in a cool, dry, dark place in glass jars with tight-fitting lids. For often-used grains that are not stored for long periods use glass jars and store in a cupboard or pantry. For grains to be kept for a longer period of time, store in glass jars in the freezer. For freezer-stored grains, remove the amount to be prepared and return container to freezer. Allowing the grain to warm up and then refreeze can create a mold problem.

A pleasant aroma is the best clue to freshness in whole-grain flours. Any "off odors" could indicate mold or rancidity in the flour. This rancid odor comes from the flour being stored too long at an improper temperature. The germ part of the whole grain and its oil become rancid if exposed to air and heat for any length of time. Rancid flour has a distinct bitter taste. Store whole-grain flours in glass jars with tight-fitting lids in the freezer.

Grains

Kamut

PROPERTIES Kamut (pronounced Kah-moot) is a trade name associated with a variety of an ancient Egyptian gluten-containing grain related to durum wheat. Each golden-colored kernel is two to three times the size of a wheat kernel and has a distinctive hump in the middle. A member of the Grass Family (#6), Kamut has a wonderful, rich, and almost-buttery taste. It is commonly found in the form of whole grain (berries), flakes, puffed, cold breakfast cereal, flour, and pastas.

Though it is related to durum wheat, studies have indicated that many wheat-sensitive persons can tolerate Kamut, especially on a rotational basis. However, since Kamut and wheat are closely related, persons who react allergically to wheat should do a food challenge to assess the advisability of consuming it since Kamut could cause a similar allergic response. (For a description of a food challenge, see pages 10 and 18.)

With 30% more protein than common wheat varieties as well as more of eight out of nine minerals (especially magnesium and zinc), Kamut is higher in nutritional value than any other strain of wheat. Kamut contains higher levels of 16 of the 18 amino acids found in wheat and has significantly higher levels of all of the major fatty acids.

HISTORY It's believed that Kamut originated in the Tigris and Euphrates area of the Middle East, possibly in Egypt. It first came to the United States in 1949 when a U.S. airman stationed in Portugal was given 36 kernels of Kamut. He was told that the kernels were gathered from a stone box found in an excavated tomb from an Egyptian pyramid. (This account is questionable since there is no documentation that ancient and mummified seeds found in the pyramids are able to grow.) Intrigued, the airman mailed the seeds to his father, a Montana wheat farmer. When planted, 32 of the 36 seeds germinated and within 6 years 1,500 bushels of Egyptian wheat filled a Montana granary. It received some local attention at the county fair as "King Tut's Wheat," but eventually the novelty diminished, the large wheat went for cattle feed, and the grain was all but forgotten.

In 1977, a Montana agricultural scientist and wheat farmer (Bob Quinn, Ph.D.) and his father (Mack) launched a search to find some of the ancient grain they remembered as "King Tut's Wheat." The Quinns saw a future for the ancient strain of wheat and, by scouring the barns and cellars in the Montana wheat belt, they located a one-pint jar of seeds. For the next ten years they worked to increase the grain, carefully selecting and propagating it on their ranch near Big Sandy, Montana. Quinn named the grain Kamut, an ancient Egyptian word for wheat.

Unlike modern-day wheat, Kamut has not been hybridized and "scientifically improved." Since it is self-pollinating, it can grow in a field right next to common wheat and not interbreed or "cross" with it. The Kamut plants grown today are replications of the ancient ones.

USES Kamut flour resembles finely ground cornmeal, and can be used for almost any purpose where you would use whole-grain wheat flour. Most baked goods made with Kamut flour turn a pretty golden brown. As a good rule of thumb, when replacing whole-wheat flour with Kamut flour, use one tablespoon less Kamut per cup of flour. Since Kamut is a whole grain, it is more like whole-wheat flour and would probably not be an accurate replacement in recipes using white flour.

Kamut pasta has a delicious firm texture and does not get waterlogged like normal wheat pasta. Kamut flakes are similar in appearance to oatmeal and can be cooked for a hot cereal or used to make delicious granola bars and "stove-top" stuffing. See Day 1 recipes for more uses for this versatile grain.

*   *   *   *   *   *   *

Millet

PROPERTIES Millet is a tiny, bright yellow, gluten-free seed that is covered with a hull. The hulls, which have a dull shine, are removed before the grain is used in cooking. Even though it is from the Grass Family (#6), many who do not tolerate other grains can eat millet without experiencing grain-like allergic reactions. This might be because they have never eaten this grain or have not eaten it as much as other grains.

The gentle, lightly sweet flavor of millet is enhanced by herbs and spices, vegetable and meat stocks, and fruits. Since it is rich in iron, potassium, calcium, B vitamins, and protein, millet has many nutritional benefits.

HISTORY Millet is a hardy plant that survives most any growing conditions from drought-dry to water-logged soil and it appears in as many as 6,000 variations around the world. Millet was considered a "holy plant" in China around 2800 B.C. and was a popular ancient staple of India, Egypt, and North Africa. In Java, millet was grown as a border around rice fields to activate growth and encourage abundance in the rice crop. Today, millet is still a major food source in Asia and North Africa. However, in Great Britain and the United States it is most recognized as bird seed and cattle feed.

The key element in millet, silica, is a crystalline compound also found in quartz crystals. The silica is responsible for opening the millet plant to light and warmth. This factor may have contributed to the legend that millet has the ability to transmit spiritual energy.

USES Millet is available in several forms such as hulled grain, flour, flakes, and puffed millet. Cooked hulled millet has a soft, dry texture, but it can also be cooked to a creamy texture such as in Creamy Millet Cereal and Salmon Millet Dinner. Dry roasting millet before cooking enhances its flavor and helps to blend in the flavors of other combined foods such as in Basic Millet with caraway. Some of my favorite Day 3 combinations are to flavor millet with apples and cinnamon in Millet Pudding or to add it to turkey and vegetables in Millet Turkey Vegetable Stew. Puffed millet is a dry cereal similar to puffed rice. Millet flour can be used in baking, but I have found that it must be used with egg as a binding agent for the end product to hold together.

Since millet turns rancid quickly after hulling, it should be stored in glass jars in the refrigerator or freezer.

*   *   *   *   *   *   *

Rice

PROPERTIES Rice, a gluten-free grain in the Grass Family (#6), is the second most produced food in the world. There are many varieties available in a range of colors from off-white to black. Generally rice has a rather plain flavor that provides an excellent canvas waiting to be colored with other foods and spices. The only limiting factor is the imagination of the cook. Natural rice is a great source of B vitamins.

HISTORY Rice originated in India, Southeast Asia, and China around 4000 B.C. Today it is grown in many parts of the world, including Asia, China, Africa, Australia, India, Italy, Spain, South America, and the United States. It likes warm, moist growing conditions and has the highest water content of all grains.

Some of the various rice varieties you may encounter are short-, medium-, and long-grain brown rice; sweet brown rice; Basmati; Texmati; Calmati; and specialty rice varieties such as mahogany, black japonica, field run japonica, royal, and wehani.

USES Brown rice is available in many forms including whole grain, flour, puffed, rice cakes, flakes, pastas, and creamy hot cereal. Brown rice flour generally has a drier consistency than wheat flour and it is very popular with people who cannot tolerate wheat.

SONDRA'S THOUGHTS You should avoid using polished rice, Minute Rice, and other highly processed rice products. They are usually not organically grown and most of the natural vitamins and fiber are removed during processing. In addition, there is no way of knowing if the nutrients added to these processed products include yeast-based vitamins.

*　　*　　*　　*　　*　　*　　*

Spelt

PROPERTIES A member of the Grass Family (#6), spelt is a gluten-containing grain related to wheat. The nutrients in spelt dissolve rapidly in liquid and become more readily available to the body with only a minimum of digestive work.

Possibly due to its high level of solubility, this delicious, easily digestible grain may be tolerated by many wheat-sensitive persons. However, recent research has indicated that wheat-sensitive persons should be very cautious when attempting to add spelt products to their diet.[31, 32] Since spelt and wheat are closely related, spelt products can cause similar responses for persons with a wheat allergy. A food challenge should be used to assess the advisability of adding spelt to a personalized rotational diet. (For a description of a food challenge, see pages 10 and 18.)

Spelt grain is a light golden brown in color and closely resembles wheat grain in appearance and size. It may be found in several forms such as whole grain, flour, flakes, and pastas. Spelt has a nutty flavor similar to whole wheat, and the flour is an excellent substitute, with minor adjustments, for whole wheat flour in recipes.

One of spelt's most outstanding features is its high nutritional value. It contains all of the basic materials for a healthy body, including protein (up to 40% more than commercial wheat), fats, carbohydrates, vitamins, trace elements, and minerals. Spelt is particularly rich in B vitamins and in polyunsaturated fats (essential fatty acids) and has a higher content than wheat in several amino acids (up to 65% more).

HISTORY Spelt is not a hybrid like commercial wheat. It is among the first original, natural grains known to man. Spelt originated in central Asia (the Tigris-Euphrates River valley) and was later brought to Europe where it gained great popularity. It can be grown without fertilizer and pesticides, requires a minimum of care, and grows in varying terrains and any climate, even those with difficult winters. Due to its resistance, spelt is not sensitive to typical grain diseases. The spelt kernel is tightly surrounded by a strong husk or hull, which must be removed before the grain can be used for cooking. This protective covering guards the spelt grain against all types of pollutants in the air, even radioactive fallout. It also protects the grain during storage, ensuring the freshest possible product after dehulling and milling.

Modern research has proven that spelt was grown in Europe more than 9,000 years ago. It is also mentioned by name in some translations of the Bible (Exodus 9:31–32 and Ezekiel 4:9).

According to lore, in the Middle Ages St. Hildegard of Bingen, a Benedictine nun, received a vision that she should feed spelt to the patients under her care. Soon "terminal" patients were recovering and, as word spread of her work, people began to flock to her clinic. Writings on her life state that many were helped by her special nutritional regimen, which is a testimony to the valuable nutritional characteristics of spelt.

Today, spelt is very popular in European countries, specifically Germany, Italy, France, Switzerland, and Austria, where it is considered a "gourmet" food. It was introduced into the United States food market by Purity Foods of Okemos, Michigan in 1990 and is steadily gaining popularity as people learn of its incredible benefits. Before it gained more recognition, spelt was used mostly in cattle feed in the United States.

USES To substitute spelt flour for whole-wheat flour in a recipe, a good rule of thumb is to either increase the amount of flour used by 20–25% or start with only 3/4 of the liquid called for in the recipe. (You can add small additional amounts of liquid if needed.)

> *When things start going your way, it's usually because you stopped going the wrong way down a one-way street.*
>
> *Los Angeles Times Syndicate*

Teff

PROPERTIES   Teff is an ancient, gluten-free grain. Even though teff is from the Grass Family (#6), it is in a
subgroup by itself separate from other members of this family. For this reason many who do not
tolerate other grains can eat teff without experiencing grain-like allergic reactions.

There are many varieties of teff, but only brown, ivory, and red are grown in the United States. The word teff
means "lost" and is appropriate since the seeds are very tiny. The smallest of the grains, it takes 150 teff grains
to equal one wheat kernel. Because the grains are easily lost in the fields, harvesting is very labor intensive. The
crop can also be lost if water falls prematurely on the seed panicles, causing the water-soluble bran to decompose.

Teff's mild, pleasing, slightly molasses-like flavor is so delicate that it allows the flavor of other ingredients to
come through such as in many teff recipes that use sesame and/or pear. Brown teff flour has both brown and
white particles and the finished food products have a very dark, rich, brown color like. Cooked teff grain has a
gelatinous texture. Ivory teff has an even milder flavor but turns a faint green color when cooked.

In addition to its versatile flavor and basically nonallergic properties, teff is very nutritional. Rich in iron,
calcium, and potassium, teff has as much as five times the amount of these elements as may be found in other
grains. Teff is high in copper and zinc as well as protein and soluble and insoluble fiber.

HISTORY   Teff comes from Ethiopia and has been used and loved there for thousands of years. Ethiopia and
teff survived invasions by the Egyptians, Romans, Arabs, and Europeans. Even though the teff fields
were burnt, the Ethiopians could easily carry the tiny seed into hiding because only about two pounds of seed were
needed to plant the next year's crop.

When Wayne Carlson was a Public Health worker in Ethiopia, he learned about and enjoyed eating teff.
When he returned to the United States, he missed having teff in his diet and decided to try to grow it in the United
States. In southwestern Idaho, near the Oregon border, Mr. Carlson found a valley with a terrain and climate
similar to Ethiopia and began raising teff there. For the first five years he raised teff for a limited market. Now,
since 1988, he grows enough to sell to the health-food markets. Brown and ivory teff are marketed by direct mail
from Mr. Carlson's company. In addition, Arrowhead Mills distributes his brown teff. (See Appendix C: Resources.)

USES   Teff grain is dried for cooking into cereal or for grinding into flour. The flour can be used in crackers,
tortillas, muffins, pancakes, and desserts. Most teff recipes I have seen contain ingredients such as
gluten-containing grain, eggs, starch, sweetener, and/or milk. However, I have successfully developed recipes
without many added ingredients. This is especially helpful when rotating and/or eliminating foods due to allergies.
Teff may act as a mild laxative, so as with any other new food add it to your diet slowly.

SONDRA'S THOUGHTS   When I first tried teff, I did not enjoy the flavor of either the brown or ivory varieties. But
I continued to eat teff cereal and before I finished my first pound I was in love with it.
My initial reaction to teff's flavor may have been influenced by the high *Candida* level I was experiencing at the
time. My favorite teff recipes include crackers, pancakes, and as breading on Oven Fried Chicken or Catfish.

*   *   *   *   *   *   *

Wild Rice

PROPERTIES   While wild rice is a member of the Grass Family (#6), it is in a different subgroup from rice and is
technically an aquatic grass seed. Brown-black in color, it is a very thin grain that can be as long
as one inch in length. It has a very strong flavor so a little goes a long way when it is included in recipes. Wild rice
has a greater concentration of B vitamins, magnesium, and zinc than rice, is low in fat, and has one of the highest
protein contents among grains. It is also rich in carbohydrates, which are easily converted to energy in the body.

HISTORY   Wild rice is indigenous to the lakes and rivers of Minnesota and Canada where it is still harvested
today. It has been a staple food of the Chippewa Indians and an important part of their heritage for
centuries. Because wild rice is harvested by hand, its price reflects its scarcity and labor-intensive processing.
Considered a gourmet food by many, wild rice aficionados maintain that it is well worth the cost.

USES   Wild rice is available in the whole grain and in 100% wild-rice pasta. As it cooks, the grain opens to show
a soft white-gray inside against a curling brown-black cover. Some of my favorite wild-rice recipes are
Salmon or Turkey Vegetable Salad with 100% Wild-Rice Pasta and Wild & Brown Rice with Herbs. Also, I enjoy
Northwest Natural brand Halibut Medallions, which contain wild rice, served on a "hamburger" bun.

Nongrains

Amaranth

| PROPERTIES | Amaranth is a gluten-free nongrain from the Pigweed Family (#30), which is tolerated by many who are allergic to grains. However, if you are allergic to the pigweed pollen, you may have a sensitivity to amaranth. Amaranth can be purchased in four forms—whole grain (referred to as seeds so it does not get confused with true grains from the Grass Family), flour, roasted bran flour, and puffed (popped).

Amaranth grows best at low altitudes with Kansas and Nebraska offering the best growing conditions in North America. While amaranth has many advantageous growth characteristics, its nearly wild nature offers many challenges for farmers. The seeds need a lot of moisture for approximately three weeks to germinate and to support early growth. But the mature plants require very little moisture and thrive on neglect and drought. It is planted in rows and wild pigweed is commonly found among the plants. The seeds will mold on the stalk with too much moisture in late summer and early fall or will fly away in the wind if the air is too dry. The six-foot seed stalks survive best when picked by hand. As an added advantage, amaranth roots are shallow (just below the surface) and they crowd out most of the weeds making chemical herbicides unnecessary.

The small amaranth seeds range in color from tan to black. The cooked whole seeds have a gelatinous texture and are coated with a thick, shiny film that makes them shimmer like caviar.

Amaranth has a wonderful, nutty, slightly sweet flavor that is intensified if the seed is dry-roasted before cooking. Black seeds can add a bitter taste, so try to purchase amaranth with as little black seed in it as possible.

Amaranth contributes to good nutrition because of its high level of vegetable protein with a good balance of amino acids. It is especially high in lysine which is low in most grass grains. Amaranth is lower in carbohydrates than grains from the Grass Family. It is rich in vitamins and minerals, including vitamin B complex, iron, calcium, and phosphorus. Puffed amaranth is very high in dietary fiber, much higher than grains from the Grass Family.

| HISTORY | Amaranth originated with the Aztecs in Mexico and in South America centuries ago. In 1521, Cortez banned amaranth and it nearly vanished, but four and a half centuries later in 1972 a botanical team found it growing wild in Mexico. They collected some of the seeds and were successful in growing it in the United States. Amaranth was also known in ancient China, and today China is its major producer, followed by Mexico and Central America. Amaranth means "immortality," an appropriate name considering its history.

| USES | Amaranth seeds are harvested and dried to be cooked as cereal or used as a thickening agent. The seeds can be ground into flour for baked goods or sprouted and used as you would alfalfa sprouts. Those not allergic to grains and not following the rotational diet in this cookbook can take advantage of the nutritional value, sweetness, and moisture of amaranth by substituting this flour for a portion of the flour called for in your favorite recipes. Replace the amount of flour called for with 1 part amaranth flour to 3–4 parts wheat flour. (For example: 1 cup wheat flour = 1/4 cup amaranth flour + 3/4 cup wheat flour.)

However, when using only amaranth in a recipe, this gluten-free flour requires the addition of a starch or a natural gum to compensate for the lack of gluten properties. As a general rule of thumb, use 75% amaranth flour and 25% potato starch, arrowroot starch, tapioca starch, soy flour, pea flour, or ground nuts. Amaranth flour feels very fine and delicate. The soft, smooth texture and high moisture content of the amaranth doughs require a lot of tender loving care. Amaranth tortillas seem to be the hardest to make. Amaranth works best in thin and/or crispy products such as tortillas and crackers. However, I have succeeded in making "hamburger" buns, pizza crust, and cookies. Puffed amaranth can be used as breading, a snack, or a texturizer in recipes such as cookies or granola.

For the home gardener it is not beneficial to grow amaranth for the seeds because it is too labor intensive to harvest and dry. However, amaranth leaves can be harvested to eat as a green. When leaves are harvested they grow back and the plant produces fewer seeds. Pick the leaves from the heavy center stalk and steam or stir fry for 10–15 minutes. Or toss the leaves whole or in pieces into soup or stew approximately 10–15 minutes before serving. You may freeze the leaves to use year round; simply blanch as you would spinach.

| SONDRA'S THOUGHTS | I succeeded in growing amaranth in my garden and would encourage you to add this interesting crop to your garden. I have included several Day 2 recipes that use amaranth greens—Vegetarian Lasagna, Vegetarian Pizza, Low Carbohydrate Lasagna, and Steamed Amaranth Greens. You can obtain seeds from Nu-World Amaranth, Inc. and Seeds of Change. (See Appendix C: Resources)

Some mail-order sources will freshly grind amaranth flour to order. However, the freshly ground flour I have purchased does not seem as fine as the organic flour distributed by Arrowhead Mills. The more coarsely ground flour seems to be okay for preparing crackers, but I do not like it as well for other food products, especially tortillas. Do not purchase amaranth flour in too large an amount because if it stands for many weeks the oils can go rancid, become bitter, and develop a strong odor. Store the flour in glass jars in the refrigerator or freezer. Also, ask when new shipments are expected. For the freshest source, you may choose to order all four forms plus the garden seeds directly from the grower, Nu-World Amaranth, Inc. (see Appendix C: Resources).

*   *   *   *   *   *   *

Buckwheat

PROPERTIES Despite its name, buckwheat is not related to wheat but is instead a gluten-free nongrain from the Polygonaceae Family, sometimes known as the Buckwheat Family (#27). Other members of this family are rhubarb, garden sorrel, and dock (a weed).

Grown in northern climates, buckwheat does well in adverse conditions and thrives in locations where other crops fail. The bush-like plant grows quickly, adapts well to poor soils and moist cool climates, and can even be planted in July and harvested in 70 days.

Buckwheat has a shallow root system and smothers out the weeds around it. In addition, no known insects harm the fruit of the plant (seeds). Because of these two factors, little or no chemical application is needed when growing buckwheat.

The plants have many glorious white and pink blooms. Each flower produces one triangular-shaped seed (fruit of the plant) covered with a protective hard outer black hull. This fruit, called groats, is white with hints of green, gray, and tan. If you roast buckwheat groats, then called kasha, they become deep brown in color with a strong aroma. A field of fragrant buckwheat blossoms attracts many bees to produce buckwheat honey, which is darker and more flavorful than clover honey.

Buckwheat has a strong earthy flavor. Some say that you either love it or hate it, but I feel you can learn to love the flavor if you do not enjoy it at first. When you are first getting used to the flavor of buckwheat, be sure and try the raw groats because roasting intensifies the flavor as well as the color and aroma.

Buckwheat groats are rich in B vitamins, especially thiamin and riboflavin. They also have large amounts of vitamin E, are rich in phosphorus and potassium, and are high in iron and calcium. Buckwheat is the best food source of rutin, a bioflavonoid which functions in the body to strengthen the walls of the blood vessels and help prevent arteriosclerosis. A good source of protein, buckwheat has seven usable amino acids, is especially high in lysine, and is best complemented by combining it with peas, beans, or dairy products.

There are three grades of buckwheat flour: whole grain, dark, and light. Whole-grain flour is made by grinding groats still covered with the protective outer black hull. Dark buckwheat flour is also made by using hull-covered groats. However, additional hulls are added before grinding into flour. Commercial light buckwheat flour is made from groats with most of the hulls removed.

For more general or nutritional information on buckwheat and the various buckwheat products available, contact: Buckwheat Institute, PO Box 440, Penn Yan, NY 14527.

HISTORY Originally buckwheat came from the plains of China and Siberia. The Chinese cultivated this ancient nongrain for hundreds of years before traders took it from Asia to Europe. Then early-American settlers transported it to the United States. By the 1800s it was an important crop in the United States, but then wheat and corn became more widely used and buckwheat faded in popularity. Buckwheat is the basis of many delicious whole-food dishes in Asia and Europe (piroshki, kasha varnishkas, kasha knishes) and in Japanese cuisine, mostly in the form of a pasta called soba.

USES Buckwheat groats are very porous and cook quickly (about 15 minutes). Because of this porous nature, when you rinse the groats before cooking them you should do so quickly. Raw or roasted whole groats may be cooked by simmering or baking and served as a potato substitute or used in other Day 4 recipes such as stir fry. You may coarsely grind the groats into grits to cook for breakfast as Creamy Buckwheat Cereal. Or finely grind them into White Buckwheat Flour (page 105) for use in recipes. Raw buckwheat groats may be stored in an air-tight container in a cool, dry place for eight months or longer.

SONDRA'S THOUGHTS I have been told by some wheat-sensitive people that they are also sensitive to buckwheat. If you are reacting to whole-grain or dark buckwheat flour, it may be because the hard outer hull has not been removed and it is adding too much fiber to your diet. At one time I felt that I was sensitive to buckwheat when I was only eating foods prepared with whole-grain buckwheat flour. When I switched to using mostly buckwheat groats with the outer hull removed and/or grinding the groats into White Buckwheat Flour using my blender, I noticed that my problems with buckwheat disappeared. An added advantage was that I had much better success in cooking with the White Buckwheat Flour than with the whole-grain buckwheat flour.

Another reason why you may feel you are allergic to buckwheat is that you may be eating buckwheat pancakes made from a prepared mix. Be sure to read the label because many buckwheat pancake mixes include other ingredients such as wheat flour instead of using buckwheat flour only. Be aware also that allergic reactions to buckwheat may be due to a sensitivity to the weed "dock."

SOURCES If you do not desire to prepare your own White Buckwheat Flour (page 105), check with mail-order sources to locate one which freshly grinds flours to order or purchase directly from Birkett Mills (see Appendix C: Resources).

*   *   *   *   *   *   *

Quinoa

PROPERTIES Quinoa (pronounced keen-wah) is a gluten-free nongrain from the Chenopodium or Goosefoot Family (#28) and is tolerated by many who are allergic to grains. There are 2,000 known varieties of quinoa. Other members of this family are spinach, beets, chard, and a weed called lamb's-quarters.

The highest quality quinoa only grows at high altitudes—6,000–15,000 feet. It can thrive in thin, dry air and poor, sandy soil. In addition, it is able to withstand the strain of intense radiation from the sun and the below-freezing temperatures found at high altitudes.

All of the 2,000 varieties have very elliptical seeds, approximately the size of millet. The color ranges from off-white to black. Imported quinoa is an off-white plump kernel whereas domestic quinoa is gray and slightly smaller. Black quinoa is truly black with a hint of purple, very small, not readily available, and considered a delicacy like wild rice.

Quinoa has a slightly bland character that can easily be enhanced with vegetables, apples, meats, etc. to create a delicious, light, fluffy dish. The subtle, nutty taste makes it a great side dish with almost any meal, or add it to soups, salads, and casseroles (see Recipe Index, Quinoa recipes).

Quinoa is a complete protein source, containing all eight essential amino acids. In fact, this protein source is so good that The National Academy of Sciences has called it "one of the best sources of vegetable protein in the vegetable kingdom." Also, this essential amino acid balance is close to the ideal set by the United Nations Food and Agriculture Organization. Quinoa protein is equal in quality to that of dried milk and close to that of mother's milk. Quinoa is also high in vitamin E, B vitamins, calcium, phosphorous, and iron.

HISTORY Quinoa has been cultivated in the Andes Mountains of South America since 3000 B.C. The Inca Indians named it quinoa, meaning "the mother grain," for its life-giving properties. Quinoa was as important to the Incas as the buffalo was to the American Indian. The Incas used the whole plant in their daily life. Young plants supplied deep, green, leafy vegetables. The seeds were their staple nourishment. The stalks were used for fuel in high altitude areas where wood was unavailable. Finally, the ash from a quinoa fire was used with coca leaves in a manner similar to chewing tobacco, producing a mild narcotic effect.

The Incas realized quinoa's life-giving properties to such an extent that they encouraged pregnant and lactating mothers to eat quinoa every day for healthy babies and an adequate milk supply. Also, if needed, mothers made a thin gruel for their babies from cooked quinoa flour to supplement their milk.

Quinoa was so important to the Incas that it was considered sacred, and as part of their ceremonial rights the Inca ruler planted the first row each year with a gold planting stick. Also, the grain was mixed with blood to form dolls for religious rituals.

In 1982, Steve Gorad, founding president of the Quinoa Corporation, traded an Andean farmer the shirt off his back for quinoa seeds. This launched the Colorado quinoa growing program under the supervision of Colorado State University. Some quinoa is grown in the Rocky Mountains, but most of our supply comes from the plant's original home—Peru and Bolivia. These low-income South American farmers do not use chemicals because they either do not have access to them or cannot afford them.

Quinoa seeds have a bitter coating called saponin which functions as a natural repellent to insects and birds and protects the seeds from the high intensity of the altiplano sun. Before cooking the seeds you need to wash them two or three times to remove this saponin coating. The tiny wet seeds will not slip through a mesh strainer because the seeds rest on top of each other when you pour slowly. The saponin coating is not harmful, just very bitter. Interestingly, the Incas saved the foam from washing quinoa to use as shampoo.

To remove the bitter saponin coating so the seed can be ground into flour, the Quinoa Corporation prewashes their quinoa in South America prior to importation. In addition, they have developed a system of belts along which they jostle the whole seeds. This method, called pearling, uses friction rather than chemicals to buff off the saponin (outer-most edge of the kernel).

| USES | Quinoa can be considered a fast food within whole-grain cookery since the seeds cook very quickly. Cooked whole seeds are delicious served several different ways. As the whole quinoa cooks, the germ (outside of the grain) unfolds, disclosing a glistening translucent partial spiral which resembles caviar. Also, pancakes and muffins made from quinoa flour with the addition of a starch are delicious.

Starches

Arrowroot

| PROPERTIES | Arrowroot is an edible starch made from the rootstocks of the *Maranta arundinacea* (West Indies or "true" arrowroot) plant. It is a fine, silky white powder with a faint licorice aroma. Its fine texture allows it to thicken quickly when cooked at lower temperatures and for a shorter time period than other starches. When boiled in water, it yields a transparent, odorless, pleasant-tasting jelly. Being almost pure starch, arrowroot supplies no vitamins and contains only 0.2% protein. It is easily digested and an excellent thickening and binding agent for use by persons requiring a bland, low-salt, and/or low-protein diet. *Maranta arundinacea* is the only food in the Arrowroot Family (#19) and has been assigned to Day 2 in this rotational diet.

| HISTORY | "True" arrowroot is probably a native of Guyana and western Brazil and is cultivated throughout the West Indies, Southeast Asia, Australia, and South Africa. The plants reach a height of 5–6 feet and have large, arrow-shaped leaves and a few short-stalked white flowers. The plants are harvested when the root tubers are gorged with starch just before the plant's dormant season. The peeled roots are grated in water, the resulting mixture is dried to a powder, and the powder is then purified by several washings.

| USES | Arrowroot can be used as a thickening and binding agent in foods where you may have previously used cornstarch or tapioca starch. In this rotational diet, it is used as a thickener in Day 2 stews and casseroles and as a binding agent in amaranth baked goods. Arrowroot thickens to produce a clear, nongummy texture. An appropriate ratio would be to use 1 tablespoon of arrowroot to thicken 1 cup of liquid. Use 2 tablespoons to achieve a firmer texture for your final product. To reduce crumbliness in nongluten baking, substitute 3/4 cup of arrowroot for 1 cup flour as a binder.

| SONDRA'S THOUGHTS | Arrowroot is also produced from plants (which can involve seven other families) other than *Maranta arundinacea*. Since it can be difficult to determine the exact source, I have assigned most of the possible arrowroot source families to Day 2. The Cyad Family (#4), Tacca Family (#13), and Canna Family (#18) have arrowroot as their only member and are easily assigned to Day 2. The Ginger Family (#14) includes spice ginger that is an unassigned "Fun Food." I normally use ginger in Day 2 and 4 recipes, making it easy to use a possible arrowroot from this family on the correct day. The two families that have the most-used foods to be aware of as an arrowroot source are the Banana Family (#16) and Spurge Family (#47). Bananas are assigned to Day 2 so an arrowroot source from this family would not be a problem. However, there is a possibility that tapioca starch flour from the Spurge Family (#47) could be marketed as arrowroot. The Spurge Family is assigned to Day 3 and tapioca is a thickener used in that Day's recipes. Tapioca starch flour is very similar in texture and appearance to arrowroot, but does not have as strong an aroma and may have a slightly finer texture.

It is also possible that an arrowroot product could be diluted with potato starch. Since the Potato Family (#74) is also assigned to Day 2, this should not cause a problem with rotation unless you are allergic to potatoes.

The best advice I can give you regarding arrowroot sources would be to watch for any possible reactions when you consume it. If you have a reaction, research the plant source used to make the arrowroot product you purchased. Try changing to a different brand, particularly one that uses a different source. As with most food products, be sure to read labels and make the best possible choice you can given the information you have.

Kudzu (Kuzu)

PROPERTIES — Kudzu (also spelled kuzu) is an oriental culinary thickener popular in macrobiotic cooking. Usually sold in a white chunk form, kudzu is a starch powder extracted from the roots of the wild kudzu vine which may be used for the same thickening purposes as arrowroot or tapioca starch. As a member of the Legume Family (#41), kudzu is assigned to Day 4. In addition, since it is more expensive than other thickening agents, using kudzu on this Day actually is more economical since there are fewer recipes requiring a thickener.

HISTORY — Kudzu is a tenacious, perennial vine which thrives in the rugged, volcanic, mountainous terrain and rural regions of Japan, other areas of eastern Asia, and in southeastern United States.

Japanese folklore attributes this deep-rooted plant's strong thickening characteristic to its ability to grow through hard mountain soil, splitting bedrock in its path. For centuries skilled craftsmen have followed a time-honored process, which takes over 100 days, to extract the kudzu starch. The roots are hand harvested at full maturity during the cold winter months. To extract the starch, the roots are crushed and the resulting mash is washed and filtered several times, using pure mountain water. The resulting kudzu cakes are set in wooden boxes to dry naturally and are then crumbled into a chunky powder.

In addition to its culinary uses, kudzu is also used in traditional folk medicine in Japan. However, in the United States its primary use is for thickening puddings, gravies, clear soups, sauces, and jellied fruit desserts.

USES — Since the chunks are difficult to measure accurately, I have found that grinding them into a powder in my blender greatly simplifies this process. Store the white powder in a glass jar and measure as the package or recipe directions say for the chunks. A good ratio is 1 tablespoon of kudzu powder for 1 cup of liquid. The kudzu must be cooked for its thickening power to work. The powder may be added directly to cold foods before cooking or dissolved in a small amount of cold liquid before being added to hot food and simmered for 10–15 minutes. Kudzu produces a slightly thinner gel, but it is clear, not cloudy like cornstarch.

☆   ☆   ☆   ☆   ☆   ☆   ☆

Tapioca

PROPERTIES — Tapioca starch is prepared from the root of the cassava plant (*Manihot esculenta* [bitter cassava] or *Manihot aipi* [sweet cassava]). As a member of the Spurge Family (#47), it is assigned to Day 3 for use as a thickener or binder. The familiar granular "pearl" form of tapioca is commonly used in puddings. Also, a fine white tapioca starch flour similar in behavior and consistency to cornstarch or arrowroot is available. Tapioca is quite nutritious and digestible.

HISTORY — The cassava plant is native to the West Indies and to South America. After it was introduced into Asia during the 19th century, it became a common food in that part of the world as well.

USES — When cooked, granular tapioca swells, thickens, and becomes translucent. Tapioca granules and starch flour are used as a thickener in soups, sauces, and puddings. The starch flour is also used as a binder in baked goods, especially in my Day 3 recipes using quinoa. A general rule of thumb is to use 1–2 tablespoons of flour or 4 teaspoons of pearls per 1 cup of liquid to be thickened. Tapioca starch flour may be labeled as tapioca starch or tapioca flour and is not as easy to locate as the granules.

Sugar Substitutes

FOS (Fructo-oligo-saccharides)

PROPERTIES — FOS (Fructo-oligo-saccharides) is a relatively fine white powder that has a clean taste about half as sweet as regular sugar with no aftertaste or bitterness. Also known as NutraFlora or neosugar, it consists of natural sugar (sucrose, common table sugar) to which an additional molecule has been attached. With the added molecule, the resulting FOS molecule is too big for humans to digest.[33] Because FOS is not broken down in the digestive process, it is essentially noncaloric and the blood sugar level remains stable (no sugar spike).

FOS reaches the intestines intact where it is broken down and used by beneficial bacteria and is therefore categorized as a probiotic enhancer. At the same time, FOS cannot be used by *Candida* and other yeast, or by salmonella, *E. Coli.*, and certain other harmful bacteria.[34, 35, 36, 37] Due to this characteristic, FOS is often beneficial in the treatment of "leaky gut" syndrome as well as *Candida* Related Complex (CRC).

FOS occurs naturally in small amounts in a variety of fruits, vegetables, and grains.[38] It is produced commercially by using a special enzyme to add an extra molecule to sucrose. It does cost more than other sweeteners, but the benefit of having an easy-to-use sweetener that also supports beneficial intestinal flora far outweighs the price consideration. In this rotational diet, FOS has been assigned as a Day 3 sweetener. However, many people use it more often than every four days for its therapeutic properties.

| HISTORY | FOS has been used in Japan as a low-calorie, "non-nutritive" sweetening, bulking, and health-promoting agent for nearly a decade with no adverse reactions to date.[39] However, as with many supplements, overingestion of FOS (5 teaspoons/day for men, 6 teaspoons/day for women) may result in diarrhea.[40]

| USES | FOS is a pleasure to eat. For maximum health benefit, a good time to take it is on an empty stomach before meals, but it can be added to almost any food. Perhaps the simplest way to enjoy FOS is to place 1/4 teaspoon of the powder form (or more, if desired) directly in your mouth. With the addition of moisture, the FOS will tend to form a small ball and dissolve like a piece of candy. In fact, except for the lower sweetness level, FOS tastes and dissolves a little like cotton candy and is helpful in satisfying a "sweet tooth" craving.

FOS does not dissolve as readily as sugar so it takes a little more stirring when added to cold liquids. You will find it included in Day 3 recipes such as Quinoa Pancakes, Quinoa Cereal, and Basic Quinoa. In addition, you can move it to Day 2 to use as a sweetener in plain yogurt.

| SONDRA'S THOUGHTS | As a probiotic enhancer, FOS is an ideal addition to your health-care regimen, especially when you are taking an *acidophilus* supplement. There are some *acidophilus* supplements on the market that have FOS included in them. I would recommend that you not use these combined products since you have no control over the ratio of FOS to *acidophilus*. Also, FOS has an indefinite shelf life while the *acidophilus* product has a limited one.

To learn more about the health benefits that can be achieved through including FOS as a regular part of your health-care regimen, contact Canary Connect (see Appendix G, page 273). Request the FOS packet that includes information on dealing with CRC and food allergies through using FOS. Appendix G (page 274) also contains a list of available research articles/abstracts on the use and benefits of FOS.

| SOURCES | FOS (in the delicious powder form) is available by mail order from Canary Connect (see Appendix G, page 273) at wholesale and discounted retail prices. An economical 1 pound size of FOS is available if using it as a sweetener or for long-term use

* * * * * * *

Honey

| PROPERTIES | Honey, probably the most commonly used natural sweetener, is 99% naturally predigested and therefore requires little additional processing by the digestive tract. The resulting absorption and energy boost occurs quickly with little or no strain on the digestive system. Honey is a thick, sticky syrup in texture. The darkness or lightness of its golden color indicates how strongly it is flavored and how rich it is in mineral content. In addition, a honey's base source plant affects its individual flavor and color (buckwheat honey is probably the "darkest" honey available). Darker honeys have a much stronger, distinctive flavor and contain higher levels of minerals such as iron, copper, sodium, potassium, magnesium, manganese, calcium, and phosphorous. In addition, honey contains small amounts of C and B vitamins.

Honey generally is the least chemically contaminated sweetener available because bees exposed to pesticides usually don't make it back to the hive. Labeling such as "U.S. Grade A" or "Fancy" refers to the level of filtration used in processing and does not give any indication of quality or freedom from chemical contamination.

Honey can come from many different floral sources. For rotational purposes it is important to know the source of any honey you wish to use and to purchase only honey that is labeled with this information. Be sure to read the label carefully because it is a common practice to mix different source honeys to create a marketed brand.

The source for Berry Honey can be from raspberries, blackberries, or a combination of both. Orange Blossom Honey can be from a variety of citrus fruits such as orange, grapefruit, tangerine, and tangelo. Clover Honey and Alfalfa Honey also may contain pollen from other source plants. Baker's Honey may include titi, oil seed, goldenrod, Brazilian pepper, Chinese tallow, purple loosestrife, salt cedar, horsemint, and buckwheat and is not a good choice for persons on rotation.

Tupelo Honey is light amber in color, has a mild pleasant flavor, and, if it is pure, never granulates. It has a low glucose-to-water ratio and is likely to remain liquid with no special treatment. The tupelo tree is mostly found along the Apalachicola River in northwestern Florida and southern Georgia.

As a general rule for honey, the best processing is the least processing. You should avoid honey that has been subjected to heat or chemicals or that comes from beehives sprayed with antibiotics or other chemicals. Be sure to choose honey that is labeled "undiluted" because some marketed honey is diluted with corn syrup.

| USES | Because honey is 20–50% sweeter than sugar, substitute 2/3 to 3/4 cup of honey for 1 cup of sugar. However, recipes in this cookbook have been developed using much less honey and they are still enjoyed by those who normally eat sweets. To facilitate the measuring process and help the honey slide out without sticking, moisten the measuring cup or spoon with water or oil. In addition, decrease the amount of liquid in the recipe by 1/4 cup for each 3/4 cup of honey used. The addition of a pinch of baking soda to baked goods will help neutralize honey's natural acidity. Honey browns more easily than sugar so the oven temperature should be decreased by 25–30°F, and the pan should be placed on the middle or top oven rack.

Due to its ability to absorb and retain moisture, honey has a "keeping" quality which retards the drying out that occurs in baked goods. The flavor of baked goods made with honey is actually better the day after baking. Because using honey as a sweetener will add an additional flavor factor to your end product, it is better to use a lighter, more mildly flavored honey.

Honey should be stored at room temperature in a dry place. Be sure to keep the lid and rim of the jar clean so that the lid will close tightly. Almost all honey naturally crystallizes over time. It is easy to reliquify honey by placing the container in a pan of warm water (not hot) until the crystals disappear. This process does not affect the taste or purity of the honey.

Honey is assigned as a Day 4 sweetener. To use honey in this rotational diet, you must remember that it contains bee protein and can be used only once in four days regardless of its base source plant. Because of the bee protein, you cannot use a rotation of Berry Honey on Day 1, Sage Honey on Day 2, Avocado Honey on Day 3, and Orange Blossom (citrus) or Buckwheat Honey on Day 4 even though these base source plants come from different families. In addition, you may wish to avoid honeys with a base source plant to which you are allergic.

> **HH:** Store syrups such as brown rice syrup and honey at room temperature in a container with a tight-fitting lid. Wash the rim of the container after each use before replacing the lid.

*   *   *   *   *   *   *

Maple Granules

| PROPERTIES AND USES | Maple granules are a dehydrated form of 100% pure maple syrup. Maple syrup, a concentrate of maple-tree sap, has long been used as a mainstay natural-food sweetener. Pure maple syrup is a member of the Maple Family (#50). Because it is in a family by itself, it is listed as an unassigned "Fun Food" in this rotational diet (see explanation on page 24).

I use maple granules to sweeten Day 3 oat cereals and apple crisps.

*   *   *   *   *   *   *

Brown Rice Syrup

| PROPERTIES | Brown rice syrup is a rather opaque golden liquid with a consistency similar to honey. It has a pleasant, lightly sweet taste and is only about 20% as sweet as sugar. A member of the Grass Family (#6), brown rice syrup is excellent to use when only a touch of sweetness is needed.

Sweet Dreams Organic Brown Rice Syrup from Lundberg Family Farms is made by grinding organic brown rice into a meal, cooking it to a slurry, and mixing it with a small amount of natural cereal enzymes (less than 1%). This process converts the starches to complex natural sugars (maltoses). The liquid is then squeezed from the slurry and cooked until thickened. No artificial additives, stabilizers, or chemicals are used in Lundberg's process.

| USES | Brown rice syrup may be used to top your favorite Day 1 pancakes, rice cakes, or breads. One of my favorite Day 1 desserts is Amazing Sugarless Cookies sweetened with brown rice syrup.

Stevia

PROPERTIES Stevia is a natural herbal sweetener that is approximately 100 times sweeter than sugar. With a faintly licorice-like flavor, the white powder extract most commonly used in cooking and baking is the purest form of stevia available. Stevia is also available in a brown liquid extract and as crumbled *Stevia rebaudiana* leaves. A member of the Composite Family (#80), *Stevia rebaudiana* is a small shrub which grows wild in the province of São Paulo near the southern border of Brazil, on the frontier with Paraguay. While a teaspoon of white stevia extract powder has the same sweetening power of 24 cups of sugar, it contains only 8 calories. Since it is not absorbed by the body and has such a low caloric content, stevia does not trigger a rise in blood sugar levels. It has been researched extensively since 1899 and found to be completely nontoxic, in contrast to many artificial sweeteners available today. Because of these properties, stevia has been used effectively in the treatment of diabetes, high blood pressure, and infections, as well as in weight-loss programs.

HISTORY The *Stevia rebaudiana* plant was first scientifically studied in 1899 by Moises S. Bertoni, a Paraguayan botanist who recognized its highly concentrated sweetening power. Stevia has long been used by the Guarani Indian tribes to sweeten teas and foods. In the city of Birigui, in São Paulo province, Brazil, stevia is so popular that it is used to sweeten milk shakes, juices, and coffee in almost all bars and restaurants. During World War II there was some speculation among scientists that stevia might be useful as a sweetener in the United States because sugar was at a premium. Unfortunately, the plant was not cultivated for industry outside of South America and the idea never materialized. More recently the Japanese have been using stevia to sweeten their diet foods since all artificial sweeteners are banned in Japan.

USES Unlike some artificial sweeteners, stevia is stable at any temperature and is very useful for sweetening beverages and cereals to baked products. Because of its concentrated sweetness, typically no more than 1/4 teaspoon of the powder extract is needed to sweeten a whole recipe. In fact, adding too much stevia to a recipe can make it bitter. For a cup of tea a few grains (less than a "pinch") are usually sufficient. Because of its high potency as a sweetener, it is best to move cautiously when you first begin using stevia. Start with slightly less than is called for until you learn how much to use to satisfy your personal taste. All of the recipes in this cookbook that call for stevia use the white powder extract, referred to as "white powder concentrate."

SOURCES While stevia has not been approved for marketing as a sweetening agent in the United States, it is available as an herbal supplement. Check the herbal product section in stores or mail-order sources.

Miscellaneous Foods

Carob

PROPERTIES A member of the Legume Family (#41), carob is a high-protein, low-fat, low-calorie, caffeine-free tropical bean that is an excellent substitute for chocolate or cocoa. Unlike cocoa, which has a naturally bitter taste, carob's natural sweetness allows you to use much less sweetener while having cocoa's rich brown color and consistency. Carob powder is slightly lighter in color than cocoa, but its aroma and flavor are very similar. An additional advantage of carob use is that it usually costs about one-fifth as much as chocolate.

HISTORY The carob tree is an evergreen which can reach a height of fifty feet. They are found in hot climates with an abundance of rain, primarily near the shores of the Mediterranean Sea. Also, carob trees can be found in the semiarid regions of the United States. The trees require very little pruning, need no spraying because they are remarkably free from fungus diseases and insect pests, and in most soils need no fertilization until the tree begins bearing fruit. The fruit is a fat leathery pod which averages from three to twelve inches in length and contains five to fifteen brown seeds in a sweet pulp. Most trees start bearing fruit five years from budding with an average yield of 250 pounds per acre. At eight years the yield increases to 2,500 pounds per acre, and at twelve years the yield may be as much as 5,000 pounds per acre.

The name carob seems to have no single, accepted origin. The plant is also variously known as the honey locust, the algarroba, the caroubler, and the Egyptian fig. Many believe the "locust" mentioned in the Bible as the food John the Baptist ate were carob pods, which is why carob is still known as St. John's bread and sometimes as locust pod.

Carob powder in raw or toasted form contains the entire seed pod except for the seeds. The pod is processed into pulp, dried, toasted, and pulverized into the final product. Carob powder has been available in the United States since the 1920s as a roasted cocoa replacement.

Carob seeds are extensively used in the manufacture of gum tragacanth, a widely used food additive. In addition, they are used for animal feed, and an oil is extracted, called algarroba oil, which is used for medicinal purposes. Carob seeds, uniform in weight, are thought to have been the original carat weight used by jewelers.

| USES | Carob can be used to make treats such as Carob Cake Brownies (page 241). Carob chunks can be used as a naturally sweet snack. Carob should only be used in the powder or chunk form. Commercial "carob chips" usually include ingredients such as sweeteners, whey, nonfat milk solids, hydrogenated palm oil, cottonseed oil, and lecithin (soy) most of which should be avoided on a *Candida* control diet.

* * * * * * *

Clarified Butter (Ghee)

| PROPERTIES | Clarified butter (also known as ghee) is the pure oil derived from butter when the milk solids are separated and removed and the water is cooked out (butter is over 16% water). Since it does not contain the milk sugar that may affect persons with *Candida* Related Complex or lactose intolerance, clarified butter is a versatile oil beneficial even for persons on a dairy-free regimen.

| HISTORY | In India and the Middle East, ghee has been a staple oil and a practical way to preserve butter for many centuries. Often called "royal oil," ghee was used as a medicinal supplement for healthy skin, mental alertness, good digestion, and improved memory and was renowned for its rejuvenating properties. For a deep restful sleep, a teaspoon of ghee stirred into warm milk was prescribed. Traditional herbal remedies were usually mixed into a small amount of ghee and then eaten, which allowed the herbs to be assimilated into the cells more quickly. Placed into tiny vessels with cotton wicks, ghee was also used for candles in special ceremonies and on festive occasions.

| USES | Since clarified butter is a pure oil it may be used as you would other oils assigned to Day 2. Use it for sautéing and frying since it does not burn or smoke like other oils. (It adds a special touch to Fried Potatoes.) Experiment with it, with or without herbs, as a topping for baked potatoes, spaghetti squash, amaranth pasta, shrimp, crab, or lobster. Take it along when dining out. For a rich buttery flavor in baked dishes, replace the butter listed in the recipe with half the amount of clarified butter.

| SONDRA'S THOUGHTS | Clarified Butter is commercially available under the product name Ghee (see Appendix C: Resources). However, it is relatively simple to make (page 226).

* * * * * * *

Flaxseed and Flaxseed Oil

| PROPERTIES | A member of the Flax Family (#44), flaxseeds are flat, oval, pointed at one end, and range in color from light to dark reddish brown or yellow. Ground flaxseed, made by grinding the seeds in a blender, is brown in color and a good source of dietary fiber. Flaxseed oil has a fairly bright yellow color, relative little odor, and a light buttery taste.

Flaxseed oil is important because of its high levels of essential fatty acids, Omega 3 and 6, which are essential to proper body function and are not produced by the human body. These essential fatty acids (EFAs) are key factors in the regulation of cholesterol metabolism; the maintenance and regulation of the function and integrity of cell membranes; and the production of prostaglandins, which are the very active biological substances that regulate nearly every body function. Prostaglandins have an active role in the inflammatory process, healing and repair process, immune system, neural circuits in the brain, cardiovascular system, digestive and reproductive systems, and body thermostat and calorie-loss mechanism. It is easy to understand why a deficiency in Omega 3 EFAs can contribute to such ailments as water retention; dry, scaly, or oily skin; goose flesh (bumps on back of arms and buttocks); high cholesterol; high blood pressure; arthritis; dry eyes; breast tenderness; premenstrual symptoms; and severe menstrual cramps. To adequately process the Omega 3 EFAs for use in the production of prostaglandins, the body must also have adequate amounts of magnesium, B vitamins (B3, B6, B12), selenium, zinc, iron, and vitamin C.[41, 42]

As stated in the book <u>Chronic Fatigue Syndrome and the Yeast Connection</u> by Dr. William G. Crook, "During the past decade, almost without exception, physicians treating patients with yeast-connected health problems have used EFA (essential fatty acid) supplements as an essential part of their treatment program."[43] The usual recommended amount of flaxseed oil to be taken daily is one or two tablespoons.[44,45] It may be taken by itself, but because most oils are not palatable in their individual forms, it is easier to include the flaxseed oil in or on the food you eat. When used primarily for its nutritive qualities, flaxseed oil should never be cooked because the heating process destroys the essential fatty acids.

HISTORY Flaxseed and flaxseed oil have been used for 5,000 years. However, it is only recently that the extent of its beneficial effects has been uncovered. Flaxseed oil is common in Europe and was common in the United States until the beginning of World War II. Flax is an annual plant grown mostly in the colder regions of the world. Because of the cool, long days common to its northern latitudes, Canada is the world leader in high-quality flax production. The majority of the world's flax production (about 85%) is centered in Canada, the United States, Argentina, India, and the Soviet Union.

The name "linseed oil" used to be interchangeable with "flaxseed oil." But in recent years there has been an international effort to separate the use of "flaxseed" and "linseed." "Flaxseed" refers to products that are produced for human consumption. "Linseed" is used when referring to products that have been denatured, made unfit for human consumption, and used commercially in paints, varnishes, and other like substances.

USES Whole or ground flaxseed can be cooked in water to create a flour binder for use as an egg substitute in baking. Flaxseed oil is excellent for use in uncooked salad dressings; for a topping on pancakes, biscuits, cooked vegetables; or for a buttery taste on any other food. It can be blended half-and-half with butter or clarified butter to form a "soft" spread. Since the heating process destroys the EFAs, add flaxseed oil to any dish after it is cooked when using it for its nutritive qualities.

Heat, light, and air (oxygen) must be eliminated during processing and storage for flaxseed oil to maintain its freshness. Purchased flaxseed oil should have an expiration date on the container indicating its effective shelf life. In addition, both ground flaxseed and flaxseed oil go rancid very quickly so they should be refrigerated or frozen.

SONDRA'S THOUGHTS Since I use flaxseed oil for its nutritive qualities and I have no problems with consuming it on a continued basis, I include it on all four days of my personal rotation. However, if you need to rotate flaxseed oil, it may be placed on any day you choose because it is in a family by itself (#44).

* * * * * * *

Guar Gum

PROPERTIES Guar gum is a fine white powder derived from the seed pod of the guar plant, *Cyamopsis tetragonolobus*. As a member of the Legume Family (#41), guar gum has been assigned to Day 4. Guar gum adds fiber to foods and is used commercially as a binder in low-gluten or no-gluten flour baked goods to help them rise and hold moisture. It is also used in the production of ice cream to promote a smooth, soft texture and to keep ice crystals from forming. Because of its highly absorbent character, guar gum thickens instantly when mixed with cold liquid.

HISTORY The guar plant is native to India and is cultivated in the United States today for use as forage as well as for the production of guar gum.

USES I use guar gum as a binder for buckwheat baked goods and tortillas. Since it thickens so quickly, the following tip will help you use it effectively in your baking. If making a recipe which will require a good amount of mixing, add guar gum to dry ingredients before combining them with liquid ingredients. However, since guar gum will have a tendency to clump when combined with liquids, in recipes where only minimal mixing is required add it to liquid ingredients, quickly whisk it in, and immediately add liquids to dry ingredients. The recommended ratio is 1 teaspoon of guar gum to thicken 1 cup of liquid.

Since guar gum may actually increase permeability in the intestinal tract, persons with "leaky gut" syndrome should avoid using it.[46]

It never hurts to crack a smile.

Nothing in life is to be feared. It is only to be understood.
Marie Curie

Tahini

| PROPERTIES AND USES | Tahini is a light colored butter made by grinding raw whole or skinned sesame seeds. It has its own interesting flavor, different from the flavor of plain sesame, and can range in consistency from very oily to somewhat dry. Tahini is a member of the Pedalium Family (#75), and can be used to replace peanut butter as a spread on rice cakes or breads. It also makes an excellent topping to replace jelly on your favorite Day 1 muffin or pancake recipe. In addition, it can be used as an egg substitute in recipes by using a mixture of 1 tablespoon tahini and 3 tablespoons of water.

*   *   *   *   *   *   *

Vitamin C Crystals

| PROPERTIES AND USES | Unbuffered vitamin C crystals are used for two purposes in recipes. In baking, they act as a leavening agent when used in combination with baking soda (for more explanation, see page 55). In "mayos" or salad dressings, their tart taste makes them a good replacement for vinegar or citrus juice (such as lemon).

The texture of unbuffered vitamin C crystals resembles salt. They can be labeled as crystals or unbuffered. The buffered form of vitamin C is a powder and is used to reduce allergic reactions (see page 20 for more explanation). When purchasing a vitamin C crystal product, be sure to choose a brand that is yeast-, citrus-, and corn-free as well as free of other common food allergens. You may also wish to research the product source to avoid possible allergic reactions.

| SOURCES | Unbuffered vitamin C crystals are available through mail-order sources (see Resources, page 254). A brand found in many health-food stores is KAL C-Crystals.

> *Just remember conditions are never "just right."*

REFERENCES

27. Sheila Phillips. "Natural Foods Primer: Grains." Info sheet from Blooming Prairie Warehouse, 2340 Heinz Road, Iowa City, IA 52240.
28. Ibid
29. Marjorie Hurt Jones, R.N. "New Foods and How to Use Them," The Human Ecologist, no. 52 (Winter 1991), 1. Referenced as a "telephone conversation with Rodale Research Center, Kutztown, Pennsylvania."
30. Marjorie Hurt Jones, R.N. Super Foods (Coeur d'Alene, ID: Mast Enterprises, Inc., 1990), 27.
31. Harold M. Friedman, M.D., Robert E. Tortolani, M.D., John Glick, M.D., and Richard T. Burtis, M.D. "Spelt is Wheat," Allergy Proceedings, Vol. 15, no. 4 (July-August 1994), 217-218.
32. John W. Yunginger, M.D. "Food Ingredient Labeling: How Many Ways Can Wheat Be Spelt?" Allergy (Proceedings, Vol. 15, no. 4 July-August 1994), 219-220.
33. Peter J. Perna, Ph.D. "Fructooligosaccharides (FOS)An All Natural Food Which Promotes *Bifidobacteria* and *Lactobacillus*" (Broomfield, CO: Center for Applied Nutrition, ZeaGen, Inc., 350 Interlocken Blvd.), 1.
34. H. Hidaka, T. Eida, T. Takizawa, T. Tokunaga, and Y. Tahiro. "Effects of Fructooligosaccharides on Intestinal Flora and Human Health," Bifidobacteria Microflora Abstract (Vol. 5, issue 1, 1986), 37-50.
35. R.C. McKellar and H.W. Modler. "Metabolism of Fructooligosaccharides by *Bifidobacterium sp.*," Applied Microbiology Abstract (Vol. 31, 1989), 537-541.
36. 10 T. Mitsuoka, H. Hidaka, and T. Eida. "Effect of Fructooligosaccharides on Intestinal Microflora," Die Nahrung Abstract (Vol. 31, issue 5-6, 1987), 436.
37. H.W. Modler, R.C. McKellar, and M. Yaguchi. "*Bifidobacteria* and *Bifidogenic* Factors," Journal of Canadian Institute of Food Science and Technology (Vol. 21, issue 1, 1990), 29-41.
38. Peter J. Perna, Ph.D. "Fructooligosaccharides (FOS)An All Natural Food Which Promotes *Bifidobacteria* and *Lactobacillus*." 1.
39. J.E. Spiegel, R. Rose, P. Karabell, V.H. Frankos, and D.F. Schmitt. "Safety and Benefits of Fructooligosaccharides as Food Ingredients," Food Technology (January 1994), 85-89.
40. Ibid.
41. Ingeborg M. Johnston, C.N., and James R. Johnston, Ph.D. Flaxseed (Linseed) Oil and the Power of Omega-3: How to Make Nature's Cholesterol Fighters Work for You (New Canaan, CT: A Good Health Guide, Keats Publishing, Inc., 1990), 26.
42. "Fresh Flax Oil" (Monument, CO: A pamphlet published by Allergy Resources, Inc.).
43. William G. Crook, M.D. Chronic Fatigue Syndrome and the Yeast Connection (Jackson, Tennessee: Professional Books, 1992), 256.
44. Ibid.
45. "Fresh Flax Oil."
46. Jones, Marjorie Hurt, R.N. "Leaky Gut—What Is It?," Mastering Food Allergies, X, no. 44, issue #86 (July-August 1995): 7.

6. ORGANICS—THE ONLY WAY TO GO!

One of the most important considerations in incorporating a rotational diet and/or a healthier eating plan into your lifestyle is the quality of foods used. I cannot say enough in support of purchasing organic food products on a consistent and almost exclusive basis. Chemical exposures are reduced by using organic foods. In addition, you help support an environmentally sound, self-sustaining, and renewing method of food production which is a priority to avoid further damage to our environment and world. For these and other reasons, I emphatically believe that organics is "The Only Way to Go."

If you have never purchased organic foods or have done so only on a limited basis, the task of locating a convenient source(s) and changing your buying habits can seem formidable at first. Remember, as with other major changes recommended in this book, you may start gradually and work up to a higher level of organic food use. Do as much as you are able at first. Then gradually increase your commitment as you feel comfortable to do so. The goal is to make your life healthier and easier, not to add more stress. This will provide an opportunity to learn as you go not only in locating the best sources for you, but also in acclimatizing your lifestyle and taste buds to new foods and eating habits.

What Is Meant by "Organically Grown" Food?

Specific methods and standards are involved when you speak of "organically grown" food products. In general, organic growers use production methods which:

- maintain the long-term fertility of soils by fostering the creation of humus, replenishing organic matter, balancing mineral levels, and increasing microbial life.
- avoid materials which cause pollution or are known to be harmful to health, such as synthetic fertilizers, insecticides, fungicides, herbicides, hormones, or antibiotics.
- use local, renewable resources and allow farmers a decent return and healthy satisfaction from their work.

Organic foods are grown in nutrient-rich soil, usually ripened before picking, and some of the tastiest, most nourishing foods you will ever eat. They are produced without the use of pesticides, herbicides, or other chemicals and are not artificially ripened using various chemical processes. Organic meats are obtained from animals raised on certified organic grains and hay and without added drugs such as hormones and antibiotics. In addition, organic food is processed and distributed using methods that retain freshness and nutritional quality without the use of synthetic or artificial fumigants, preservatives, additives, or irradiation.

The basic principle of organic agriculture is that a healthy plant grows from healthy soil and is more resistant to pests and diseases. If a problem does arise during the growth cycle, many times it is controlled by sophisticated biological technologies involving natural predators, biodegradable botanical sprays, resistant plant varieties, mechanical and pheromone traps, and other natural methods.

Many states have enacted organic food standards which are used in the certification process for organic growers, processors, and vendors. Following is a listing of what these standards provide.

1. Control over the use of the word "organic" in advertising and labeling of food products.
2. Standards for methods of growing and processing products to be sold as organic, which restrict the use of synthetic fertilizers, pesticides, herbicides, hormones, and antibiotics for a minimum of three years before a grower may apply for certification.
3. Record-keeping requirements for growers, processors, and vendors, including sworn statements to accompany products sold as organic.
4. Opportunity to obtain private certification for products that meet even higher quality standards than those established.
5. A means of enforcing the standards that will protect both consumers and growers.

The label "certified organic" on a food product involves a significant commitment on the part of organic producers to achieve and maintain organic certification for their products.

Since there are many phrasings used in labeling organic foods, be aware of the following definitions as you choose which product or produce to buy.

Biodynamically Grown Food. This term refers to a special type of organically grown food that meets or exceeds all organic growing standards. The aim of this practice, which is more known in Europe than in the United States, is to produce the highest-quality nutrition for both humans and animals, while developing a self-contained farm ecosystem that regenerates land, plants, animals, and people.

"Certified Organically Grown." These foods are grown by organic methods and certified by an independent organization or association of organic growers who verify that the farm meets particular criteria. The name of the certifying organization should accompany this label, and many have logos that are easy to recognize. This is the best assurance that the food is organically grown.

"Organically Grown" or "Organic." This label by itself is generally meaningless, unless the store has its own definition posted near the produce bin. Sometimes this term is used by stores that have signed statements from the grower which describe the precise growing practices. In these cases, the store must take the grower's word as truth, for there is neither time nor money to send knowledgeable people to inspect the farms, run pesticide tests, or perform all the other necessities to certify the produce.

"Represented" or "Claimed Organic." This label is generally used when the farmer has told the store that the produce is organic, but nobody has checked on it. Usually no signed statement of growing practices has been submitted.

"Transitional Organic." This usually means the farm is growing organically but hasn't been doing it for the required period to meet state or private certification.

"Unsprayed." This simply indicates that the food has not been sprayed with pesticides. It also usually means that the food has not been colored, gassed, or waxed, but it probably is not from a farm with a soil-building program and may not be as carefully harvested or packaged. Artificial fertilizers have probably been used.

"IPM" (Integrated Pest Management) or "Ecologic." This indicates food grown on a farm that is using a lesser amount of pesticides than nonorganic farmers or that may be in the process of converting to organic methods.

Why Is It Important to Purchase Organic Food?

Consider some of the procedures that have become a normal part of nonorganic agriculture over the past years. The consequences of these procedures are alarming, not only for the living beings that consume agricultural products, but also for the earth where they are produced.

There are 1.5 billion pounds of pesticides used in the United States each year on agricultural food products. This amounts to nearly 5 pounds of poisonous sprays for each person. About 45,000 different agricultural chemicals are used and 150 of these regularly appear as residue in food, with about two dozen of them at toxic levels. Several of the chemicals used in these applications are known carcinogens (cancer causing agents) and have been linked to birth defects, miscarriages, mutations, Alzheimer's disease, and various degenerative diseases. Many fruit and vegetable crops are sprayed twenty or more times a year with five or more of these active ingredients.

In addition, the use and overuse of agricultural chemicals is destroying our soils and poisoning our water supplies. These chemicals not only kill the destructive insects and weeds for which they are intended, they also kill beneficial insects, birds, fish, and animals. As a side effect, the destructive insects and weeds can develop resistance to these chemicals, which leaves chemical experts searching for ever stronger and more deadly remedies to use in this vicious cycle.

As a means to "protect" the general public from overexposure to the chemicals approved for use in the United States, the EPA (Environmental Protection Agency) is set up to regulate use levels and monitor the residue levels found in foods. Unfortunately, due to possibly unreliable licensing safety tests for chemicals, untimely and inadequate laboratory processing, and a lack of adequate personnel, it is practically impossible for the EPA to adequately control the general public's exposure to these chemicals.

Regarding the nonorganic fruits and vegetables in your local grocery store, an added consideration is that in January and February over 70% of the fresh produce in the United States comes from Mexico. Most of the rest comes from other foreign countries. Many times these countries do not have bans prohibiting the use of chemicals that have been tested and rejected in the United States. As an example, DDT has become a favorite chemical for foreign coffee growers. You were exposed to residues of this dangerous insecticide this morning if your coffee was not organic.

Why subject yourself and your family to the effects of these chemicals when there is a healthful, highly nutritious alternative in organic foods?

How and Where Do I Get Organic Foods?

Because of the set standards described above, it is relatively easy to identify organically grown and produced foods. Any product that is labeled "certified organic" is done so in compliance with state laws that define and regulate organic products. Through the certification and documentation process, you can be assured of the organic quality of the food products you are purchasing.

You will probably find, as I have, that you will use a number of sources to purchase organic foods. Five of the most-used sources are discussed below, but keep your eyes and ears open for other possible organic food outlets in your area.

One of the best-known sources for organic foods is your local health-food store. It varies from store to store, but generally these businesses will carry a wide range of organic products, from flours, grains, oils, and packaged foods (such as cereals or pastas) to fresh produce and meats. Also, the store may be a cooperative where a purchased membership entitles you to lower prices. Ask people in your neighborhood or check your local telephone directory or yellow pages for headings such as grocers or health-food products.

Appendix E provides a list of cooperative food warehouses located in the United States. By combining with others interested in purchasing organic food products and sharing time and energy, you could join or form a food-buying club that can purchase organic products at a savings from these warehouses. Contact a warehouse in your area to learn more about what a buying club is, the existing buying clubs in your area, and/or how to start one. Since the required buying club purchasing level for individual items is likely to be in case lots, forming or joining a club with participants having needs and interests similar to your own will greatly improve the club's effectiveness in saving money.

If your locality has a seasonal farmer's market that has regularly scheduled sale days, go and check out the vendors. Many organic growers use this outlet to market their products. It may mean some planning ahead, but you could find some excellent produce to can and/or freeze for off-season use.

Ordering organic products through mail-order sources can be beneficial in two special ways. First, chemical exposure is likely to be less from leafing through a mail-order catalog than from traveling to special stores (long or short distance) and cruising aisles. And second, you expend less energy when you let the post office or UPS deliver products to you rather than going to the store. In Appendix C: Resources, you will find a listing of mail-order companies for organic food products. Some companies will use special packaging (such as cellophane rather than plastic) if you react to specific materials. Check with each company regarding their options in this area.

> When incorporating organic fruits, vegetables, meats, grains, etc. into your diet, order these products by mail if they are not available in your area. (See Appendix C, page 250.)

Also, in Appendix F you will find a listing of Organizations Providing Information on Organic Food Production and Availability around the United States that can provide you with information on organically grown products and their availability in your area.

> *There are two ways of meeting difficulties: you alter the difficulties or you alter yourself meeting them.*
> *Phyllis Bottome*

Having Your Own Organic Garden

By far, the best way to obtain economical organically grown produce is to grow it yourself. When this is possible, it can be a rewarding way to help guarantee that you are eating the safest and best quality food available. By planning ahead to can or freeze the garden abundance, you can enjoy these foods year round (see Canning and Freezing—Creating Your Own Organic Storehouse, page 48).

Be aware that organic gardening (just like any form of gardening) requires a time and energy commitment to make it worthwhile. If you do not have the energy or interest level that a garden would require, ask friends or relatives to grow the organic produce for you or consider hiring someone to do the garden work, possibly for a share of the produce.

If gardening is something you enjoy, remember it is not necessary to raise a huge garden to reap benefits. You can start small, maybe with one or two crops such as tomatoes and edible pea pods.

There are several excellent books available on organic gardening techniques. A portion of them are listed in Appendix D: Recommended Reading. They focus on such varied techniques as the use of compost, mulch, natural insect control, companion planting, and organic seed and gardening product sources. These techniques are briefly described below.

Compost

You can turn grass clippings, leaves, vegetable peelings, apple cores, and other organic materials into a nutrient-rich soil supplement for your yard or garden through composting. By composting you can help recycle the yard waste and food scraps that make up about one-fourth of the waste produced in the United States.

A compost pile should be at least four feet long by four feet wide by three feet tall to hold heat. There are many styles of compost bins available for purchase. If you build your own, the sides of the pile can be left unsupported or held by cinder-block or chicken-wire walls built to allow air to pass through.

A compost pile requires a good mixture of ingredients, such as dry leaves or straw (carbon-rich materials) and green grass clippings, certain kitchen wastes, and/or manure (nitrogen-rich material). By adding soil to the compost pile you introduce the microorganisms necessary for decomposition. Moisture is also required in the decomposition process, and the compost pile should be as moist as a wrung sponge. If necessary, sprinkle it periodically with water during dry weather.

Air flow is important as well, so the pile should be prevented from collapsing or compacting under the weight of too much water or debris. By alternating layers of green material, dry material, and soil and turning the mixture every few weeks, you can achieve a faster rate of decomposition. A healthy compost pile will be warm because heat is released when organic material decomposes.

Chop or shred big items before adding them to the compost pile. This will speed the rate of decomposition. Do not add meat, bones, cheese, or grease to the pile as they take a long time to decompose and will attract animals. Also, while horse, cow, or sheep manure is rich in nitrogen and beneficial to the compost pile, do not use dog or cat droppings as they may carry disease.

The compost pile will shrink as the materials decompose. The process may take a period of weeks or months, depending on the care the pile receives, but when the compost is dark and crumbly and has an earthy smell, it is ideal to use. Add a one- to three-inch layer of compost to your garden, spread it around individual plants, or use it as potting soil.

Mulch

Mulch is used to cut down on your garden maintenance by controlling weeds and moisture levels. In fact, correctly applied mulch can totally eliminate weeding. Consisting of any material used to cover the ground, mulch comes in basically two categories—organic and nonorganic materials. Both are used in the organic garden.

Usually applied 2–6 inches deep, organic mulches function exceptionally well to hold moisture in the soil, especially if put down after a rain. The deeper the mulch, the more it cools the ground and retains moisture. Always wait until the soil is completely warm and weed before putting down organic mulch. Stop weeds by placing a layer or two of newspaper first, holding it in place with a little soil, and then mulching 4 inches deep in organic material. (Soybean ink printed newspaper is best, but don't use colored or glossy paper as it contains toxic ink.) Since organic mulches decay and add nutrients to the soil, they can be tilled under in the fall.

If your garden does not drain well, organic mulch should be applied in a thin (2–4") layer or not at all to avoid creating a too-wet situation which can damage plants. In addition, warmth-loving plants such as peppers, eggplant, and tomatoes should not be mulched too deep since this keeps their roots too cool.

Although they may not look as nice, nonorganic mulches stop all weeds until they are taken up in the fall. Black poly (plastic) mulch is beneficial for warmth-loving plants because it warms the soil. It can be put down early in the spring before any weeds get started. If applied later, the poly will smother the weeds. The edges should be weighted down every 2–6 feet (depending on size) with heavy objects such as bricks, rocks, or logs. Mark an "X" on the poly to indicate proper spacing for plants, or cut small slits for seeds. For vining plants, it may be beneficial to put a very thin layer (1/2" to 1") of organic mulch on the poly to keep vines from burning in extremely hot weather. Poly mulch MUST be removed in the fall.

Following is a listing of mulches:

A. Organic Mulches:
   - Grass Clippings—Make sure no pesticides or herbicides have been used on the grass.
   - Leaves—It's best to let them set for 6–12 months. Never use walnut leaves as they contain juglone, a natural fungicide harmful to many garden plants.
   - Hay or Straw—The older the better because of weed seeds.
   - Sawdust—Use sparingly or lime annually. Be sure it is not from treated lumber as this is very toxic.
   - Cocoa Hulls—Wonderful mulch, but expensive.
   - Corn Husks and Cobs—Good for loosening hard ground.
   - Bark and Wood Chips—Nice mulch. Call electric companies as they often have them available.

B. Nonorganic Mulches:
   - Black Poly—Six mil preferred. Available at lumber yards.
   - Carpet—Tends to fall apart rapidly and makes a mess.

Natural Insect Control

There are many steps an organic gardener can take to help prevent or control insect damage. Planting resistant varieties is an important first step. Maintaining a nutriently well-balanced soil in your garden helps produce healthy plants that are better able to withstand insect damage. You can also help reduce insect and disease problems by keeping weed growth to a minimum. Many destructive insects that carry diseases thrive in weed-infested areas.

Rotating crops on a three-year cycle is also an essential part of insect control. Keep crops of the same family (such as broccoli, cabbage, and cauliflower or tomato and potato) away from plots where they were grown the past two seasons. This will help prevent damage from pests that may have wintered over in the soil and are waiting for a new crop to destroy.

By placing natural deterrent plants such as marigold, onion, garlic, shallots, mint, tansy, nasturtium, and radish throughout the garden, you can help keep a fairly wide variety of detrimental insects away.

Taking steps to encourage "beneficials" to inhabit your organic garden is a positive measure in pest control. Beneficial insects such as ladybugs, spiders, ground beetles, assassin bugs, damsel flies, green lacewing, praying mantis, and a wide variety of wasps and flies are avid hunters of plant eating or detrimental insects.

The first and most important step to encourage beneficial insects is to use NO poison chemicals. Incorporating plants such as flowers and herbs that supply nectar, pollen, rest stops, and breeding grounds can encourage beneficial insects to inhabit your organic garden. Important helpful plants include dill, parsley, fennel, angelica, and Queen Anne's lace, yarrow, petunia, cosmos, zinnia, nasturtium, marigold, and sunflower.

Other beneficial creatures such as toads, birds, and bats offer assistance in controlling detrimental insects. Provide a small moist shelter that will attract toads by placing a shallow dish of water inside a flower pot on its side near your garden. Attract insect eating birds such as bluebirds, swallows, martins, wrens, phoebes, warblers, and the titmouse by providing birdhouses and baths. Bats are also important insect consumers.

Organic gardening is dependent upon a healthy balance of these beneficial techniques. By maintaining a naturally balanced system, you can greatly improve your ability to control the amount of insect damage to your crops. If a major insect problem arises, intervene with caution. Remember you are altering the natural process. Never use diatomaceous earth on your garden* as it is an indiscriminate killer of all soft-bodied insects, including beneficial ones. Rotenone is deadly to fish and other aquatic life. If intervention is absolutely necessary, insecticidal soaps, traps, and microorganisms, such as Bt, are probably the safest and have the least negative impact. Keep in mind that such measures are only a shortcut and that the best long-term solution is a healthy balance of beneficial plants, insects, and animals.

Companion Planting

Attract beneficial insects, birds, and animals; prevent insect destruction and disease; and improve plant health and yield by intercropping a mixture of plants that benefit one another.

Use a common location for plants that share similar nutritional needs. In the summer heat, sun-loving plants, such as corn or tomatoes, serve as natural shade for the cool weather plants, such as lettuce or spinach. Plants with deep root systems are good companions to shallow-rooted plants. This enables both plants to thrive since they are not competing for space or moisture.

Consult books on companion planting such as Country Woman: A Handbook for the New Farmer and Carrots Love Tomatoes (see Appendix D: Recommended Reading) to avoid such practices as planting onions with peas or tomatoes with fennel which can actually reduce plant yield and vigor.

Organic Seed and Gardening Product Sources

By raising your own organic produce you have a low-cost and need-specific source for the foods you want to use regularly. For a good resource for organic seeds and garden supplies, check with your local health-food store or warehouse for possible product sources in your area. Gardening centers may also stock or be able to direct you to a resource for the seeds and products you need for your organic garden.

A good mail-order source for organic seeds is Seeds of Change and for organic plants is Natural Gardening (see Appendix C, page 255).

Canning and Freezing—Creating Your Own Organic Storehouse

Having my own organic storehouse helps me stay on my rotational diet throughout the winter, especially with regard to vegetables. Several books on canning and freezing are available at your local library, however do contact the local office of your state's Department of Agriculture Extension Service. They have low-cost booklets containing the most up-to-date standards for canning and freezing. Following is a list of tips I have learned through my years of canning and freezing.

Use Proper Equipment. Purchase helpful tools to do your canning and freezing.
- A large food processor is helpful for slicing vegetables such as beets.
- Purchase a juicer to make tomato sauce, beet juice, apple or pear sauce, etc.
- Purchase a large pressure canner. For canning it does not need to be stainless steel because the food will not touch it directly. I like my 22 pint model that will hold up to 7 quarts or 22 pints.
- Large stainless steel kettles for washing large amounts of food, blanching tomatoes and removing the skins, or cooking beets are essential.
- A spare refrigerator is helpful. Some people have one in their basement or heated garage.

Follow Updated Procedures. Due to the recent development of lower-acidity tomato hybrids, the canning procedures for tomatoes have changed so acquire updated tomato canning information from your Agricultural Extension Office. The basic change involves adding some sort of acetic acid to the tomatoes. Citric acid is recommended, however lemon juice is a better choice for those with *Candida* Related Complex. Squeeze several lemons at a time and freeze the juice to thaw when canning tomatoes. To save time, use Santa Cruz's Organic 100% Lemon Juice. Ask your health-food store or cooperative warehouse to stock this

---

* For chemically sensitive persons, diatomaceous earth is the most appropriate insect control substance to use around your home. But do not use it in your garden.

product in pint jars. Use one tablespoon of lemon juice per one pint of tomatoes or tomato sauce. For thick sauce (more like paste), use an additional amount of lemon juice. If you choose to freeze tomatoes, the lemon juice is not needed.

Start Simple. Concentrate on foods that are relatively quick and easy to process. For example, to freeze green peppers simply remove the seeds and inside membranes; cut into strips or dice; package; and freeze. Also, other vegetables such as zucchini and eggplant are easy to process. Simply peel, slice or dice, package, and freeze.

Include those foods that you cannot purchase locally or by mail order (especially through the winter). My list includes eggplant, parsnips, green pepper, peapods, zucchini, and asparagus.

Individually Freeze. A method I use to freeze several foods such as green peppers, zucchini, eggplant, peapods, asparagus, and parsnips is to freeze them in single layers on baking sheets so that they are individually frozen. After freezing, package in cellophane or plastic bags. This allows me to pour out just the amount I need to use and return the unused portion to the freezer.

Blanching. To blanch you apply high heat and steam to vegetables for a short amount of time. Use a steamer pan (my preference), steamer basket, or microwave. Time varies depending on type and size of vegetable, method used, amount blanched at one time, and to some degree personal preference.

Immediately following steaming time, place vegetables in ice water for twice the amount of time that you applied heat. Drain. Package and freeze.

The blanching process stops the ripening of the vegetables to prevent them from acquiring a strong green grass-like taste. Most freezing charts will recommend blanching all vegetables including green peppers, zucchini, and eggplant—three vegetables that I do not blanch. You may have different tastes and may choose to blanch them.

Divide Process into Several Steps. Whenever possible, split big canning jobs into stages with rest breaks in between. For example: make it a family affair.

1. Stem green beans while relaxing and watching television.
2. Wash, drain, and place beans in a large kettle in spare refrigerator.
3. The next morning, rinse again, fill jars, pour boiling water on them, adjust the lids, and start the pressure canning process.

This way the task is divided into steps and successfully completed without overexertion.

Do Small Amount Each Day. Some preserving, such as freezing pear sauce, is a long messy project so my preference is to prepare and freeze a year's supply in one day. However, with vegetables such as green peppers, zucchini, eggplant, peapods, and asparagus I freeze a small amount each day. These vegetables are easy to freeze and use very little equipment. Often during meal preparations I peel, slice, dice, blanch (if needed), and freeze extra garden or purchased produce. Before long I have a storehouse of vegetables in my freezer ready for easy use during the winter.

HH: Food Freezers

I recommend a chest freezer with a push button manual defrost feature (found on most Sears & Roebuck models). This feature facilitates defrosting by heating the sides of the chest freezer and melting the ice formations very quickly. When defrosting you can be ready to replace the food in about 15–30 minutes. Chest freezers usually only need defrosting once a year. You may need to straighten or rearrange the food a few times in between, but the more energy-consuming defrosting process is kept to a minimum. Also, purchasing a few extra hanging baskets facilitates storing more food in better order. I also use several small plastic baskets that fit on the bottom of the chest freezer. They help keep food products separated and organized as well as facilitate food removal for defrosting.

If you can afford or need more than one food freezer, you may want to consider an upright manual defrost model so you can store grains and flours in glass jars. You can also store leftover soup, casserole, etc., in glass jars in this freezer to give you a "quick and easy meal" supply for the days when you do not have as much time or energy to cook. Extra muffins, biscuits, breads, buns, crackers, etc., can be easily stored on a freezer shelf. Or, better yet, store them in small plastic baskets that line one or two shelves of the upright freezer. (The manual defrost is recommended for the upright freezer to avoid the repetitive thawing/refreezing that can result from an automatic defrosting system.)

Sit Down Whenever Possible. To save energy, process as much as possible while sitting down. For example, I stem green beans and edible pea pods when sitting in a recliner.

Delegate. Hire someone or recruit family members to assist you.

Estimate Needs. Choose the recipes that you desire to prepare during the winter when certain vegetables are not available. Decide how often you would want to prepare them and calculate the quantity of the individual vegetables you will need.

For example, I can fresh garden green beans each summer. My family consumes 2–3 pints every 8 days (2 1/2 pint average). Since fresh green beans are available for 56 days (8 weeks), that leaves 309 days each year when I may need canned beans. To estimate my canned bean requirements, I divide 309 by 8 days then multiply by amount consumed (2 1/2 pints) to reach the amount I need to can—97 pints [309 days ÷ 8 days = approximately 39 x 2.5 pints (per 8 days) = 97 pints].

I estimate preparing Millet or Quinoa Turkey Vegetable Stew four times per year when parsnips are not available. The recipe calls for 1 1/2 cups of parsnips so I will freeze 6 cups of them for use in this casserole.

"Quick Meal" Kits—Freeze Vegetables in Convenience Packages. Prepare and freeze vegetables in amounts needed for a recipe. For example, in one bag I freeze the amounts of tomatoes, onion, eggplant, and zucchini needed to prepare Minestrone Soup. (In addition, when I cook Garbanzo Beans and Broth, page 166, I freeze leftovers in a wide-mouth pint jar and mark them for Minestrone Soup.) Later I can mince and saute garlic (or use dehydrated minced garlic when in a big hurry), add the frozen convenience package and spices, and begin the simmering time all in 5–10 minutes. This makes an Easy Meal without planning ahead to purchase the vegetables and spending time in the kitchen preparing them.

Save Time, Money, and Energy. Canning and freezing takes a little time, especially during late summer or early fall, but later saves you time, money, and energy. Enjoy preparing several meals with ease during the off-season, including pizza and spaghetti sauce, stews, soups, and stir fries.

In Conclusion

As a final thought, organic agriculture is not only important for you and me, it is essential to the well-being of the earth and all the creatures of the air, land, and water. So the next time you consider purchasing one of those "picture perfect" vegetables that has been sprayed with chemicals multiple times to keep away the bugs, just remember

IF THE BUGS WON'T EAT IT, WHY SHOULD YOU?

> *Don't wait for a crisis to discover what is important in your life.*

> *The world is round, and the place which may seem like the end may also be only the beginning.*
> *Ivy Baker Priest*

7. QUINTESSENTIAL ODDS AND ENDS

While helpful hints and important information appears throughout this cookbook, this chapter focuses on specific techniques and information that will help you make the best possible use of the specialty foods and recipes in your journey towards better health.   Subjects covered include: Nutritional Information; Suggested Measuring Equipment Supplies; Accurate Measuring; Leavening Agents; Substitutes for Wheat Flour in Baking and Thickening; Sugar, Egg, Milk, and Herb Substitutes; Oven Temperatures; How to Season Cast Iron/Using Cast Iron Cookware/Care of Cast Iron Cookware; and Blank Food Rotation Chart.

Nutritional Information

Nutritional analyses and food exchanges for individual serving or specified amounts of end product are provided for most of the recipes in this cookbook.   They can be used as a general guideline to help you make beneficial food and recipe choices.   Persons not counting calories or carbohydrates and not on a diabetic diet may use the nutritional information in a more general, comparative way. The information is listed in tables as shown at right and gives figures on calories, protein in grams, carbohydrates in grams, fiber in grams, total fat in grams (plus a breakdown of saturated fat content in grams), cholesterol in milligrams, and sodium in milligrams. Since values may vary from brand to brand in food products, the nutritional information given in this book should be used as a guideline only and not as an exact measurement.

Nutritional Information/Serving
Calories:
Protein (g):
Carbohydrate (g):
Fiber (g):
Total fat (g):
Saturated (g):
Cholesterol (mg):
Sodium (mg):
Food Exchanges/Serving

The nutritional information and food exchange calculations were made using version 6.0 of The Food Processor® Plus from ESHA Research, Salem, OR [1-800-659-ESHA (3742)]. If you are accustomed to dealing with food exchange information, the figures arrived at from using the ESHA program may look "funny." This is because ESHA hand calculates the exchanges based on the actual calories and grams of protein, carbohydrate, and fat. This allows for greater accuracy since the figures are reflections of the nutrient content rather than general exchanges based on nutrient amounts for set serving sizes. The food exchange categories used in the program are based on the Exchange Lists for Meal Planning published by The American Diabetes Association and the American Dietetic Association which was revised in 1995 to include the "new" exchanges of "very lean meat" and "other carbohydrates." The table below shows the amount of nutrients in one serving from each category.

FOOD EXCHANGE ANALYSIS CATEGORIES AND NUTRIENTS PER SERVING

Groups/Lists	Carbohydrate (grams)	Protein (grams)	Fat (grams)	Calories
Carbohydrate Group				
Starch	15	3	1 or less	80
Fruit	15	—	—	60
Milk				
Skim	12	8	0–3	90
Low-fat	12	8	5	120
Whole	12	8	8	150
Other Carbohydrates	15	varies	varies	varies
Vegetables	5	2	—	25
Meat/Meat Substitute Group				
Very lean	—	7	0–1	35
Lean	—	7	3	55
Medium-fat	—	7	5	75
High-fat	—	7	8	100
Fat Group	—	—	5	45

The nutritional information figures for specialty food products used in these recipes were gathered from product labels when available. Manufacturers and distributors such as Arrowhead Mills, Birkett Mills, Bob's Red Mill Natural Foods, Ener-G Foods, Grain Place Foods, Jaffe Brothers, Mio Amore Pasta, Muir Glen, Now Foods, etc. were also contacted to gather this information.

The abbreviations used in the Food Exchange section of the Nutritional Information/Serving tables are given at right.

Food Exchange Abbreviations		
Br	=	bread
VLM	=	very lean meat
LM	=	lean meat
Veg	=	vegetable
Fat	=	fat
Oth Carb	=	other carbohydrate
Fr	=	fruit

The following information should be noted regarding the nutritional information and food exchange figures given in this book.

- The calorie count and food exchange figures may seem higher compared to those found in other cookbooks. This may be due to the fact that a more realistic portion size was used for calculations in an attempt to base information on a "real-world" scenario.

- Whenever two or more options are given for an ingredient (ex. sesame or almond oil), the first option has been used in the nutritional analysis unless otherwise stated.

- For some recipes, such as All-in-One Salad, too many possible combinations exist to allow for the nutritional analysis information to be provided for them all. A chart giving the analysis for some individual foods can be found on pages 196–197 to allow you to determine the nutritional information for the specific combination you use.

- Ingredients used in recipes for bakeware, griddle, etc. preparation, such as oil and flour, were not included in the nutritional analysis for the recipe.

- Some baked goods recipes may seem high in fat content. This is a result of oil often being used for flavor and moisture since fruit is omitted. The easy dropped biscuit and griddle bread recipes are designed to offer the lowest fat and sodium content possible using alternative flours.

- Many baked goods may seem high in sodium due to the fact that baking soda is used for leavening rather than yeast and baking powder. Often lowering the baking soda or salt amount in a recipe destroys the raising properties in gluten-free and alternative grain products.

- If sodium content is a concern for you, in many of the entree, soup, and other recipes the salt may be reduced and other seasonings added or increased to improve flavor.

- In recipes calling for ground beef, extra lean ground beef figures were used for the nutritional analysis.

- Because of the wide variance possible, homemade meat broths are not included in the nutritional analysis figures.

- For optional ingredients listed in recipes, when no specific amount is given or an "as desired" indication is listed, they are not included in the nutritional analysis unless otherwise indicated.

- For those recipes listing a choice option of Brazil nuts or macadamia nuts, Brazil nut figures were used for the nutritional analysis unless otherwise indicated. An example of the different values between these two nuts, may be found on page 176 where separate analyses are provided for the Cream of Broccoli and Cream of Cauliflower Soup recipes.

- Nutritional information figures were not available for maple granules, guar gum, and flaxseed. Because of this these substances were not included in the nutritional analysis for recipes containing them.

We would love to hear from you regarding how helpful/useful it was to have the nutritional analysis available for the recipes. In addition, would you like to have the nutritional analysis provided for recipes that appear in Canary Connect News? You may include your comments regarding the nutritional analysis information in the Other Comments section of the cookbook Evaluation Form (see page 275) or you can write to us at: Canary Connect Publications, a Division of SOBOLE, Inc., PO Box 5317, Coralville, IA 52241-0317. Thank you for your comments and suggestions. We enjoy hearing from you and appreciate your input.

We should be patient with everyone, but above all with ourselves.

Suggested Measuring Equipment Supplies

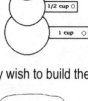

⇒ At least two sets of metal dry-measuring cups (1/4, 1/3, 1/2, and 1 cup).

⇒ One 1/8 cup metal dry-measuring cup is handy. A coffee measure that can be purchased separately usually measures approximately 1/8 cup.

⇒ Clear glass measuring cups of various sizes to measure liquids and foods such as cooked meats and vegetables, especially if measuring over 1/2 cup. Pyrex brand are great since they have handles that allow cups to nest inside of each other for storage. Also, they have easy-to-read red painted increment markings which allow for easier accurate measuring than other brands which only have indentation markings. You may wish to build the following set over time:

- two 1-cup measures
- two 2-cup measures
- one 4-cup measure
- and possibly one 8-cup measure

⇒ At least two sets of metal, long-handled measuring spoons. The long handles (approximately 5 inches in length) work well for getting small amounts of spices, etc. out of narrow-neck bottles. I prefer to take the set apart and store the individual spoons on four separate small hooks conveniently located in mixing area of kitchen.

⇒ At least one 1/8 teaspoon measure. This may be from a set of short-handled plastic measuring spoons. The 1/8 teaspoon measure is the only plastic spoon I use because the static cling makes it difficult to get an accurate measurement. This 1/8 teaspoon is important in measuring very small amounts of stevia (see accurate measuring below).

Accurate Measuring

For some recipes amounts are given as a guide (e.g., casseroles, salads). After preparing these recipes a couple of times, exercise your own creative cooking skills and use the "dump" or "sprinkle" method of measuring.

In contrast, accurate measuring of ingredients is the best guarantee of success in baking, especially when using wheat-free, gluten-free flours and thickeners.

A. To measure dry ingredients such as flour, starch, etc., use a set of dry measuring cups (1 cup, 1/2 cup, 1/3 cup, 1/4 cup).
   1. Choose measuring cup appropriate to amount to be measured.
   2. Fill cup a little over full with ingredient, especially on back side (side nearest handle).
   3. Using a table knife held vertically, move back side (straight edge) across top of measuring cup to level off ingredient. Have some type of container underneath to catch excess.

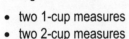

B. To measure small amounts of dry ingredients such as starch, leavening agents (e.g., vitamin C crystals, baking soda, baking powder), salt, seasonings, etc., use a set of measuring spoons (1 tablespoon, 1 teaspoon, 1/2 teaspoon, 1/4 teaspoon).
   1. Choose measuring spoon appropriate to amount to be measured.
   2. Dip measuring spoon into ingredient until a little over full, especially on back side (side nearest handle).
   3. Using a table knife held vertically, move back side (straight edge) across top of spoon to level off ingredient. Have some type of container underneath to catch excess.
   4. Special Note: Usually salt and seasonings do not need to be measured as accurately. Simply shake spoon gently to level ingredient.

C. To measure very small amounts (1/8, 1/16, 1/32 teaspoon) of dry ingredient such as white powder stevia:
   1. Fill 1/8 teaspoon measure with stevia and level it off as described above.
   2. Using tip of a very thin-bladed knife, divide stevia in half. The stevia will hold its form well enough to then take tip of knife and push half of the 1/8 teaspoon (1/16 teaspoon) of stevia out of measuring spoon and into bowl, etc.
   3. To measure 1/32 teaspoon, divide the 1/16 amount in half and then only push off one fourth of amount in the 1/8 teaspoon measure.
   4. Special Note: When first learning to measure in these very small amounts, push measurement into a small separate container before adding ingredient to mixing bowl.

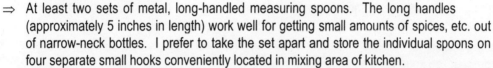
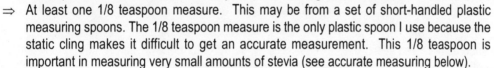

D. To measure very small amounts of dry ingredient such as salt or seasonings, use the pinch method. A pinch is the amount pinched between index finger and thumb. Recipes in this cookbook are based on an approximate equivalent of 10 pinches of sea salt per 1/4 teaspoon.

E. To measure liquid ingredients such as water, juice, syrup, oil, etc., use a clear liquid measuring cup with red painted lines to mark the fractional divisions of the measure.
    1. Place liquid measure on a level table or counter.
    2. Bend down so your eyes are level with red lines on measure.
    3. Liquids are measured at bottom of meniscus (ma-NIS-cus). The meniscus is the saucer-like depression which you see along the top edge of liquid. Add liquid gradually until the meniscus is lined up with desired red mark on liquid measuring cup.

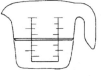

    4. Special Note: The difference in amount of liquid measured at top versus bottom of meniscus is only a small amount and does not make a significant difference in some recipes. However, in many wheat-free baked products the difference in amount of liquid can cause doughy centers and other problems. This simple measuring tip is easy to learn and can make all the difference in your success with these recipes.

F. Use measuring spoons to measure small amounts of liquid ingredients, but be careful that measured liquid does not "round up" on spoon and add additional liquid.

> **HH:** Oils that become thick at refrigerator temperatures, such as olive and sesame oil, are easier to measure if you store them in a wide-mouth jar. This enables you to measure the thicker consistency of these oils by spooning them out rather than warming to reliquify them and then pouring them out.

> **HH:** When measuring syrups (e.g., brown rice syrup and honey), lightly coat the measuring utensil with oil first. This makes the removal of the syrup from the utensil much easier. If the recipe calls for oil, simply measure the oil before the syrup. If the recipe does not call for oil, use water on the measuring utensil. However, water does not work as well as oil.

Measuring Equivalents

Here are some simple fractional equivalents to assist when measuring odd amounts (such as 3/8 teaspoon, 5/8 teaspoon, 7/8 cup, etc.) and/or preparing one-half or double a recipe:

1 gallon	=	4 quarts or 8 pints or 16 cups
1 quart	=	2 pints or 4 cups
1 pint	=	2 cups
1 cup	=	16 tablespoons
7/8 cup	=	14 tablespoons or 1 cup less 2 tablespoons
1/2 cup	=	8 tablespoons
1/3 cup	=	5 1/3 tablespoons or 5 tablespoons + 1 teaspoon
1/4 cup	=	4 tablespoons
1/8 cup	=	2 tablespoons
1 tablespoon	=	3 teaspoons
1/2 tablespoon	=	1 1/2 teaspoons
7/8 teaspoon	=	1/2 teaspoon + 1/4 teaspoon + 1/8 teaspoon
3/4 teaspoon	=	1/2 teaspoon + 1/4 teaspoon
5/8 teaspoon	=	1/2 teaspoon + 1/8 teaspoon
3/8 teaspoon	=	1/4 teaspoon + 1/8 teaspoon
1/8 teaspoon	=	one half of a 1/4 teaspoon
1/16 teaspoon	=	one half of a 1/8 teaspoon or one-fourth of a 1/4 teaspoon
1/32 teaspoon	=	one fourth of a 1/8 teaspoon

<u>Measuring Abbreviations</u>

To assure accurate interpretation of measurements, there are very few abbreviations used in this cookbook. For your reference, the following is a list of common abbreviations.

T. or Tbs. or Tbsp.	=	tablespoon
t. or tsp. or teas.	=	teaspoon
c. or C.	=	cup
pt.	=	pint
qt.	=	quart
gal.	=	gallon

Life is a mixed bag of blessings and disaster. Living is the art of storing up enough joy to tide us over the rough spots.

Attitudes are contagious! Is yours worth catching?

Leavening Agents

A leavening agent has two parts—an acid substance and an alkaline substance. The reaction between these two substances is what causes the food to "raise."

Most people are familiar with baking powder. Often the ingredients of a non-alum baking powder are calcium acid phosphate, baking soda, and cornstarch. Another type of baking powder is Featherweight brand whose ingredients are potato starch, calcium phosphate, and potassium bicarbonate. When using Featherweight brand baking powder, substitute 1 1/2 teaspoons for 1 teaspoon of regular baking powder.

You can also make your own baking powder by using:
      1 teaspoon of baking soda
      2 teaspoons of some type of starch or flour
      2 teaspoons of cream of tartar
Mix the three ingredients together and store in an air-tight container. It can be used like regular baking powder at an approximate ratio of 1 1/2 to 1 3/4 teaspoons of homemade to replace 1 teaspoon of regular baking powder.

Baking powder contains both parts of the leavening agent—the acid and the alkaline. However, for many people with allergies using regular baking powder (especially on a daily basis) is a problem because of an allergy to corn. Featherweight brand baking powder, which has a potato starch base, may cause a problem for persons allergic to the Nightshade Family (# 74). Homemade baking powder may be a problem for persons with CRC because cream of tartar is made from the fermented residue in wine barrels.

Another available leavening option is unbuffered, corn-free vitamin C crystals combined with baking soda. Almost all of the baked product recipes in this cookbook that require a leavening agent use this combination. To convert your personal recipes from baking powder to vitamin C crystals and baking soda, start with the formula:

1/4 teaspoon of vitamin C crystals	plus	1 teaspoon of baking soda	equals	1 1/2 to 2 teaspoons of regular baking powder

Since it adds a salt flavor, when baking soda is used in a recipe the amount of salt may need to be reduced.

Since most of the baked goods recipes call for vitamin C crystals and baking soda, this is one combination of ingredients that is not rotated. If you have reaction problems when using vitamin C crystals, you may need to research the source used to make the brand you are using. Locate different brands of vitamin C crystals that use different sources and rotate them or use other leavening agents instead. At publication date, very little testing has been done toward using other leavening agents in these recipes. If you need to use something other than vitamin C crystals, I highly recommend that you purchase issue #62 (Volume VII, No. 2, February 1992) from the <u>MFA Collection</u> by Marjorie Hurt Jones. In this issue, she discusses leavening agents and the different acid and alkaline substitutes (see bottom of page 263 for address).

Substitutes for Wheat Flour in Baking and Thickening

Various cookbooks have lists of flour and thickener substitutes. The following is a compilation of the options listed in several cookbooks. While this list may help to convert some recipes, it is important to note that often substitutes must be used for other ingredients as well (e.g., sugar, egg, baking powder, yeast, etc.). When many different factors are involved in converting a recipe, it is often necessary to test, adjust, and retest the new version to get a quality product.

Substitute for 1 Cup Wheat Flour in Baking

Amount	Substitute
1 cup	amaranth flour with addition of a starch
1/2 cup	barley flour
3/4 cup	brown rice flour plus 1/4 cup sweet rice flour
1 cup	buckwheat flour
3/4 cup	garbanzo bean (chickpea) or other bean flours
1 cup	millet flour
1 1/3 cups	oat flour
1 cup	quinoa flour with addition of a starch
7/8 cup	rice flour
1 1/4 cups	rye flour

Substitute for 1 Cup of Whole-wheat Flour in Baking

Amount	Substitute
1 cup	Kamut flour
1 cup	Spelt flour—reduce the amount of liquid by 25%

For thickening, replace 2 tablespoons of wheat flour with 1 tablespoon of arrowroot starch, bean flour, cornstarch, kudzu starch, nut flour, potato starch, rice flour, or tapioca starch flour or 1 teaspoon of guar gum. These measurements are the amounts required to thicken 1 cup of liquid for sauces. Double listed amount when using substitutes to thicken puddings.

Use a whisk to dissolve the starch or flour in cool or room temperature liquid (not hot) before adding to hot food. Cook as little as possible to thicken food. Prolonged cooking of starches tends to break them down and the mixture loses the thickening effect and sometimes becomes watery. If this happens, try adding more thickener.

Sugar Substitutes

Below is a list of sugar substitutes gathered from natural cooking sources.

- Substitute 3/4 cup of honey or rice syrup for 1 cup sugar, then reduce the liquid by 1/8 to 1/4 cup. Honey browns more easily than sugar so the oven temperature should be decreased by 25–30°F. and the pan should be placed on the middle or top oven rack. Since honey is 20–50% sweeter than sugar, recipes in this cookbook have been developed using much less honey and they are still enjoyed by those who normally eat sweets.
- Substitute 1 cup fruit juice for 1 cup of sugar and 1 cup of liquid.
- Omit sugar and substitute 1/4 teaspoon of stevia (white powder concentrate) per 1 1/2 cups of flour listed in recipe.
- Omit the listed measurement of sugar and substitute with double the amount of FOS. Liquid may need to be adjusted (lowered) since FOS causes baking doughs to become sticky.
- Use 1 cup DevanSweet™ organic brown rice sweetener to replace 1 cup of sugar. DevanSweet™ is rich in complex carbohydrates and other essential nutrients found in rice. Since it is made from organic brown rice syrup, doughs tend to be a little sticky. You may wish to slightly reduce the amount of liquid in the recipe (start with 2 tablespoons less liquid per 1 cup of sweetener used).
- Use 2/3 cup of Wax Orchards Fruit Sweet for 1 cup sugar. Also, reduce liquids by 1/3 the amount of Fruit Sweet used. (For example, if 1 cup of Fruit Sweet is used, reduce other liquids by 1/3 cup. If 2/3 cup of Fruit Sweet is used, liquids should be reduced by 1/4 cup less 1 teaspoon.) Ingredients of Fruit Sweet are concentrated pear, peach, and pineapple syrup.
- Use 1 1/4 cups of Granular FruitSource sweetener and fat replacer for 1 cup of sugar. Ingredients of FruitSource are rice syrup and grape juice concentrate and may not be a good sweetener substitute for persons with CRC.

continued . . .

Sugar Substitutes (continued)

Since my taste buds are reeducated and my sweet tooth is now much lower, I reduce the amount of sweetener called for in regular recipes. If you have omitted sweeteners from your diet for a period of time, you may be able to do the same.

When working with recipes that call for honey, reduce the amount of honey and sweetness by using the following substitute.

- Replace 1/4 cup honey with a scant 3 tablespoons of water.

Egg Substitutes

Most of the recipes in this cookbook do not call for eggs. They were designed without eggs or list an egg substitute alternative. Eggs are needed in recipes for three main reasons: (1) flavor, (2) binding quality, and (3) raising quality.

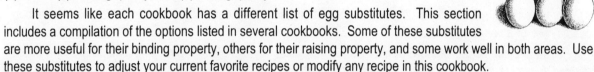

It seems like each cookbook has a different list of egg substitutes. This section includes a compilation of the options listed in several cookbooks. Some of these substitutes are more useful for their binding property, others for their raising property, and some work well in both areas. Use these substitutes to adjust your current favorite recipes or modify any recipe in this cookbook.

To Replace 1 Egg in a Recipe Use:	Good for
1 tablespoon ground flaxseed or flax meal with 3 tablespoons water Mix and add to recipe.	leavening
1 tablespoon whole or ground flaxseed with 1/4 cup water in saucepan While stirring constantly, bring to boil on high. Cook on medium for 1–2 minutes until thickened to consistency of egg white.	binding & leavening
1 tablespoon psyllium seed husk mixed with 3 tablespoons of water Let it stand briefly before adding to recipe.	binding
1 tablespoon tahini with 3 tablespoons of water	
2 tablespoons starch (arrowroot, kudzu, tapioca, potato, cornstarch) or bean flours with 2 tablespoons water Dip food product into solution before coating with breading.	breading
1 tablespoon lecithin granules with 3 tablespoons water	
1/4 cup tofu	binding
1 tablespoon garbanzo bean flour with 1 tablespoon oil	
3 tablespoons thick pureed fruit.	
Ener-G Egg Replacer by Ener-G Foods For best results, mix powder with recommended amount of liquid and let stand 10 minutes before adding to recipe. Ener-G Egg Replacer contains potato starch, tapioca flour, leavening (calcium lactate, calcium carbonate, citric acid), and carbohydrate gum.	leavening
2 teaspoons baking powder* mixed with 2 tablespoons water For a second egg in the recipe add only an additional 1 teaspoon baking powder* and 2 tablespoons water.	
1/2 teaspoon baking powder*, 2 tablespoons flour, and 1 1/2 teaspoons oil	
2 tablespoons apricot mixture (see recipe below) This may not be a good substitute for persons with CRC. However, the idea and recipe are from Sally Rockwell's Coping with Candida Cookbook.	
1 teaspoon plain unflavored gelatin dissolved with 3 tablespoons water Place in freezer. Take out when thickened and beat until frothy.	binding

To replace 1 egg white in a recipe, use 1 tablespoon plain unflavored gelatin dissolved in 1 tablespoon water. Whip. Chill and whip again.

Apricot Mixture for Egg Replacer

Measure 1 cup of dried apricots into a bowl. Cover with boiling water and let stand until fruit is soft. Puree in blender or food processor. Cover and store in refrigerator.

*Remember that regular baking powder contains corn so avoid these substitutes if sensitive to corn or on non corn assigned Days if following a rotation.

Milk Substitutes

Often persons with *Candida* Related Complex (CRC) need to omit dairy milk from their diet. This not only presents a problem in having a beverage, but creates a dilemma when preparing milk-based soups and casseroles and in making some baked products.

For a beverage, use some type of "purified" water, mineral water, carbonated water, Pau D'Arco tea (iced or hot), or Dacopa (iced or hot). Also, see page 224 for more hot or cold beverage ideas.

For a milk substitute in baking use:

◊   an equal amount of water for the required amount of milk or buttermilk. When substituting water in a pancake recipe, start by using a equal substitution amount. Cook one pancake to test for raising properties and then, if needed, make adjustments in remaining batter—add more water to thin batter or add more flour to thicken batter to increase the raising properties.

◊   an equal amount of fruit juice for listed amount of milk, especially good for also adding sweetness.

For hot or cold breakfast cereals, use Mill Milk oat milk, Imagine Foods organic original rice dream beverage, sesame milk, or a variety of nut milks (see page 223 for recipes).

For soups, use Brazil, cashew, or macadamia nut milks. My experience with using almond or filbert milk in creamed soups resulted in a product that was not as tasty.

For creamy-based casseroles such as Chicken or Tuna Rice Casserole or Chicken or Tuna Noodle Casserole, use sesame milk.

For custards and puddings, use almond, cashew, Brazil nut, or macadamia nut milk.

Most of the recipes in this cookbook have the milk substitute proportions incorporated into the ingredients and preparation steps so you do not need to make the nut milk separately ahead of time.

Prepared soy milks in dry powder and liquid form are commercially available, but may not be a good choice for persons with food allergies or CRC. Soy is a common food allergen and may need to be avoided by persons with food allergies. Also, the dry powder form of soy milk is often not organic and the prepared liquid soy milks have other ingredients in them—such as whey and barley malt—which should be avoided by persons with CRC.

For more information on milk substitutes, I highly recommend that you acquire a copy of issue #53 (Volume VI, No. 3, March 1991) of the MFA Collection by Marjorie Hurt Jones which contains an article entitled "Alternatives to Milk." The address is at the bottom of page 263.

Herbs—Substituting Fresh for Dry

Most recipes in this cookbook use dried herbs. If dried herbs are a problem for you, especially during the early stages of treatment, use fresh herbs instead.

1 teaspoon of dried herbs = 1 tablespoon of fresh herbs

To prevent fresh herbs from spoiling before being used, wash, drain, chop, and freeze them. However, using frozen herbs makes accurate measuring more difficult. You may need to use the "dump and taste" method of seasoning your recipe with frozen herbs.

Oven Temperatures

The oven temperatures found in the recipes are given in degrees Fahrenheit (F.). At times you may find a recipe from another source which does not list a specific oven temperature but which instructs you to use a "slow" or other level of oven. The chart at right gives the temperature ranges associated with these descriptions to aid you in adapting recipes.

Temperature	Descriptive Term
250° and 275°F.	very slow
300° and 325°F.	slow
350° and 375°F.	moderate
400° and 425°F.	hot
450° and 475°F.	very hot
500° and 525°F.	extremely hot

How to Season Cast Iron

Items needed: cast-iron cookware to be seasoned (griddle, skillet, etc.); electric burner with heating surface about the same size as cookware; oven; roll of paper towels; stiff brush (fingernail brush will work); and liquid lecithin.

1. If handle is wooden, remove it during seasoning process.

2. Place cookware on cold range burner. Turn range on low and warm cookware just enough to peel off label and glue.

3. Remove cookware from heat. Turn off range. Wash cookware with mild soap and stiff brush. Rinse and dry thoroughly with paper towels.

4. Return cookware to cold range burner. Turn burner on medium-low.

5. Onto warm cookware, pour a thin stream of liquid lecithin in a circular motion (similar to pouring syrup on pancakes). Pour most liquid around outer edge.

6. Spread lecithin evenly over top surface with paper towel, leaving only a thin layer on cookware. Be sure to include corners and crevices. Surface may be rough and damage paper towel. If so, use another towel to finish spreading lecithin. Remove any pieces of paper towel from cookware. Spread lecithin on entire handle if it is cast iron.

7. Place coated cookware in **cold** oven. Turn oven on and set at 300°F. Heat cookware for 30 minutes.

8. Remove and, while warm, wipe off excess lecithin with paper towels. Do not turn off oven.

9. Repeat steps 5 through 8 ten times making sure your cookware remains warm enough to spread lecithin. If cookware remains warm, you can return it to the warm oven rather than taking time to cool oven for each repeat. If cookware becomes cold, start the repeat process beginning with step 4—cold cookware and oven.

Special Notes: Only need to season handle a couple times. Often directions with cookware instruct you to season the outside edge and bottom. I do not recommend this because of the oily mess it makes on range and in oven. To eliminate oven spills, place a large baking sheet on lower rack and cookware to be seasoned on upper oven rack. Clean oven immediately after completing seasoning process to remove burnt odor and any spills.

Using Cast-Iron Cookware

When you first begin using seasoned cast-iron cookware, you may need to use slightly more oil than called for in the recipes. As you continue to use the cookware, it becomes more seasoned and will require less oil. Making a large quantity of tortillas, which uses very little oil, removes some of the seasoned finish from a griddle. But after preparing other foods which use oil, the seasoned finish will be restored.

A cast-iron griddle is great for pancakes, tortillas, and griddle breads. All recipes in this cookbook that call for a griddle were developed using a seasoned cast-iron griddle with electric range control set on low to medium. Other griddles and ranges may vary.

A cast-iron skillet is great for roasting grains and nongrains, simple fried meats that do not require the addition of liquid for steaming, and stir-fry vegetables. Cast iron is especially good for stir-fry vegetables because you need less oil which allows the natural flavor of vegetables to emerge. Avoid cooking acidic foods such as tomatoes in cast iron because acid can remove the seasoned finish.

Care of Cast-Iron Cookware

To protect cast-iron cookware it is important to heat it slowly beginning with a cold burner or oven. Never place cold cookware on a preheated burner or in a preheated oven.

Most people will tell you not to wash cast-iron cookware after each use. However, I prefer to wash cooled cookware quickly (do not leave it to soak) with mild soapy water and a sponge similar to the type recommended for nonstick-coated cookware. Rinse and dry immediately with paper towel. To save on paper towel usage, use a small old cloth that is only used for this purpose. Do not wash cast-iron cookware in an automatic dishwasher.

Always store cast-iron cookware in a warm dry place with the lid off to prevent moisture collection. The under-oven drawer of an electric range is excellent for storage of cast-iron cookware.

Foods for Day ____	**Foods for Day** ____
Grains, Flours, & Baking Foods	Grains, Flours, & Baking Foods
Higher Carbohydrate Vegetables	Higher Carbohydrate Vegetables
Lower Carbohydrate Vegetables	Lower Carbohydrate Vegetables
Animal Protein	Animal Protein
Fruits	Fruits
Sweeteners	Sweeteners
Oils	Oils
Herbs & Spices	Herbs & Spices
Seeds & Nuts	Seeds & Nuts

*Foods that float between Days 1 and 3   **Foods that float between Days 2 and 4

Unassigned "Fun Foods" (See explanation on page 24.)

8. MEAL PLANNING

If you have read How to Use This Book and Chapters 1–7 prior to beginning this chapter, you will have a good knowledge base for understanding the information on Meal Planning. If not, I do suggest that you at least read How to Use This Book and follow its recommendations.

Chapters 1–7 provide the information that will give you a solid knowledge base for incorporating a *Candida* control, food allergy, and/or rotational diet into your life. The wide range of subjects includes: Chapters 1–4, basic information on *Candida* Related Complex, food allergies, and rotational diet; Chapter 5—Specialty Foods; Chapter 6—Organics–The Only Way to Go!; and, for tips, techniques, and options for easier and more effective cooking, Chapter 7—Quintessential Odds and Ends.

The Basics

Meal planning is the core of following a *Candida*-control and/or rotational diet. When planning a meal, be creative and use a wide variety of foods. The phrase "rotational diet" originally comes from the term "rotary diversified diet" so remember to incorporate diversity into meal planning. A positive attitude and planning will make all the difference in successfully using the diet. For instance, do not feel deprived because you are allergic to foods. Instead, feel lucky. In many ways you have more choices and variety in your meals than others. Many people today use prepared foods and mixes or fast-food restaurants and "carry out" meals in their meal planning. If you currently use this form of meal planning, you may find that starting a rotational and *Candida*-control diet, as well as "cooking from scratch," is a challenge. However, if you are committed to improving your health, planning and preparing foods and meals within your dietary restrictions that complement your lifestyle is accomplishable.

Advanced planning can simplify meal preparation. By using advanced planning and other information in this chapter, as well as in the rest of this book, you will have the tools to:
- make staying on a *Candida*-control and/or rotational diet easier.
- develop meals that will properly nourish your body.
- add diversity to your diet.
- make your mealtimes colorful, relaxing, and fun.
- develop a shopping list and system that enables you to:
  —purchase what you need.
  —decrease impulse buying of nonessential or improper foods.

If you feel you are not a person who can organize or plan, make the planning and organizing aspect of this diet a game, challenge, or goal. Use advanced planning to save preparation time in the kitchen and free more time for other things. I think of planning as prayer. Practicing prayer, especially before making decisions, makes life bearable and easier to handle. Following God's answers to prayer smooths your path and often saves you time.

Where to Begin with a Candida Control Diet

Begin by deleting sugar and yeast from your diet. See the "Foods You Must Avoid" list beginning on page 11. Read all labels. Hide or give away all food in your home that you are not allowed to eat.

If other members of the family need the not-allowed foods, at least move them out of sight, such as to a cupboard that you do not need to open. If you have other family members to cook for besides yourself, try fixing only foods that you may have that they will also eat. Have carry-out food for other

> **HH:** It is essential to make the dietary changes that are most important **immediately**. These changes include: Avoid sugar, yeast, etc. in your diet. Also, as soon as possible, omit foods to which you are allergic.

family members if necessary. Do whatever is necessary so you will not be tempted to eat not-allowed foods. After the initial healing, your food cravings and feelings of denial will disappear. Then not-allowed foods that other family members are eating will not affect you.

If you need to eat fruit, limit yourself to a small amount of peeled apple or citrus fruit. Be sure to choose fruit that is free of mold, firm, and of good quality. Wash thoroughly before peeling or cutting.

Plan meals with two words in mind—**THINK VEGETABLES.** Choose a wide variety of fresh vegetables that are of good quality, organic if at all possible, and free of evidence of mold and spoilage. Even though we can not see it, there is mold on the skin of all foods. Thoroughly scrub the skins of all vegetables before peeling or cutting to avoid spreading mold.

Complete your meals with small amounts of meats (free of antibiotics and steroids if possible), beans, and whole grains. If you have leftovers, freeze immediately or refrigerate and eat within 24 hours.

Breakfast and meals away from home will be the more difficult meals to plan. The time and energy you have available for meal preparation are important factors to consider. In addition, food cravings may make choosing appropriate foods more difficult. Many times familiar as well as "new" foods will not taste good because *Candida* is clouding your taste buds and brain.

I understand the struggles and challenges you are experiencing. And I often hear the same questions "How do I change what I eat?" Prepare it all from scratch! "How do I learn to cook and/or learn to prepare foods that I have never heard of?" This cookbook and resource guide and the newsletter Canary Connect News (see page 271 for subscription information) can help you with all of these processes.

First, you need to **BELIEVE IN YOURSELF** and **TAKE CHARGE**. Do not let the *Candida* control you. Allow yourself the time needed to make the changes. Take one step at a time. Give yourself the opportunity to learn to like the new-to-you alternative foods that are available. Retraining your taste buds is possible. Try different combinations or prepare the food a different way. For example, you may not like teff cereal but enjoy teff prepared as crackers or as breading for fish and chicken.

To help you get started, the following meal planning ideas use only foods that you may already have in your kitchen or can get at the supermarket.

Getting Started Breakfast Ideas

◊ hot cereal such as oatmeal, oatbran, grits, or rice bran garnished with one or more of the following:

    —real butter or Clarified Butter (page 226)   —cinnamon
    —unrefined oil (best to avoid corn oil)   —Nut Milks (page 225)
    —small amount of additional salt
    —raw nuts/seeds such as pecans, almonds, sunflower seeds, pumpkin seeds

◊ steamed rice with cinnamon, ginger, curry powder, and/or nuts

◊ rice cakes with butter or Clarified Butter (page 226), nut butter (avoid peanut butter), or tahini

◊ eggs (well cooked)

◊ Denver Eggs (page 162) with rice or potatoes

◊ sweet potato or winter squash such as butternut squash which is naturally more sweet. Garnish with:

    real butter or Clarified Butter (page 226)   —cinnamon
    unrefined oil (best to avoid corn oil)   —leftover pork or fresh pork side

◊ leftover vegetables, fish, meat, lentils, beans, etc. from evening before or frozen from a previous meal

◊ fried potatoes or rice with onions, peppers, and/or leftover meat

◊ tortillas (warmed) with butter, almond or other nut butter (avoid peanut butter)

◊ breakfast burrito: scrambled eggs with onion, pepper, and tomato in tortilla

◊ fresh cooked, steamed, or raw vegetables

◊ raw, fresh vegetable juice

◊ boiled potatoes with salt, cayenne (red) pepper, butter

Getting Started Easy Lunch/Dinner Ideas

◊ Plan meals with the following three components. Notice the vegetable/salad component is listed first. That is where the emphasis needs to be placed during the beginning of the *Candida*-control diet.

1. Choose a variety of vegetables, the more the better. Prepare them stir-fried, steamed, or in combination recipes such as Zucchini with Tomato, Italian Eggplant, Italian Nightshade Casserole, or Kale/Cauliflower. Special Note: If you have difficulty finding tomato products without citric acid, allow yourself to use the citric-acid-containing products occasionally. However, you should add the purchase of citric-acid-free tomato products to your "To Do Soon" List (see below).

AND/OR

Prepare a salad with a variety of greens and raw veggies. Also, there are several combination side salad recipes in this cookbook. Use Lemon/Oil Dressing (page 190) or use 1 teaspoon or more of freshly squeezed lemon or orange juice in place of vitamin C crystals.

2. Choose simple meats—grilled, broiled, skillet-fried, oven-fried, or breaded with spices/herbs and whole wheat or alternative flours used in this cookbook (as a guide, see recipes such as Oven Fried Chicken, Oven Fried Catfish, and Breaded Pork Chop).

3. Choose one of the following in small amounts—brown rice, sweet potato, white potato prepared a variety of ways (except not deep fat fried), winter squash such as butternut or acorn, or beans. See breakfast ideas listed above for a variety of ways to prepare and season your choice from this list. There is also a wealth of easy-to-prepare recipes in this cookbook which include easily found ingredients. My favorite recipe of this type is Spiced Baked Potatoes.

◊ Choose to prepare any of the delicious one-dish-meal/casserole-style recipes in this cookbook, such as "Tuna Helper," Pasta Primavera, Sesame Goulash, Salmon Millet Dinner, Beef Stew, Minestrone Soup, Tuna Broccoli Chowder, Salmon Cauliflower Chowder, Lentil Casserole (three variations), Chili.

NOTE: If you feel you need catsup on your meats, potatoes, eggs, etc., do not despair. See page 226 for a Quick (Easy) Catsup recipe or try the Picante Sauce recipe on page 227. If you have not purchased vitamin C crystals yet, substitute lemon juice as described above for use in salad dressings. (Purchasing vitamin C crystals allows for more variety with recipes in the cookbook—especially for salad dressing, "mayo," and baked goods.)

Getting Started Snack Ideas

◊ Raw vegetables
◊ Celery sticks with almond butter or tahini
◊ Rice cakes with almond butter or tahini
◊ Raw nuts/seeds such as almonds, filberts, sunflower seeds, pumpkin seeds

Getting Started Meals Away from Home Ideas

◊ All-in-One Salad (page 191) or Chef Salad (page 190). Use 1 teaspoon or more of freshly squeezed lemon or orange juice in place of vitamin C crystals.
◊ Soup prepared with leftovers such as—veggies, beans, meat, veggie or meat broth, potato or cooked rice. Use the many soup recipes in this cookbook as a guide.
◊ Tortilla sandwich with leftover meat, greens, or sprouts with raw vegetables
◊ See other Meals Away from Home Ideas (page 86)

"To Do Soon" List

Now that a few days have passed and you have started the *Candida*-control diet, you need to broaden your food base and add more variety as well as possibly avoid additional foods due to allergies. (You may have done this earlier. If so, that's great!) Before you can move further in your meal planning you must acquire some additional foods. To do this, visit your local health-food store (this could possibly involve traveling to a larger city). Or better yet, let your fingers do the walking and order by mail (see Resources starting on page 250). Individual needs may vary, but I recommend you begin acquiring and using an assortment of the following food supplies to enjoy diversity and "new" flavors.

* Sea or Real salt (without dextrose)
* Vitamin C crystals
* FOS, sweetener and probiotic enhancer
* Stevia white powder concentrate, sweetener
* Flaxseed and flaxseed oil
* Almond butter and/or other nut butters (avoid peanut butter) and tahini (sesame butter)
* Alternative grains/nongrains—brown rice, teff, millet, amaranth, quinoa, buckwheat groats
* Variety of dry beans, peas, lentils
* Variety of pastas—rice, amaranth, wild rice, 100% buckwheat Soba (plus Kamut, spelt, and rye which I recommend to add last)
* Alternative flours—amaranth, quinoa, carob, legume (plus Kamut and spelt which I recommend to add last)
* Variety of starches—arrowroot, tapioca, potato, kudzu
* Variety of nuts/seeds—almonds, pecans, Brazil, macadamia, filberts, sesame seeds, sunflower seeds
* Look at the prepared foods list (pages 78–79) and add these items gradually.

Having a supply of alternative grains/nongrains will allow you to add Basic Grains/Nongrains as the starch component of your meal. I especially like to prepare the quick-cooking varieties—millet, quinoa, and buckwheat. Also, if you take 2–3 minutes in the evening you can start your breakfast for the following morning by preparing Slow Cooker Cereals (page 98).

Once you have a supply of alternative grain/nongrain flours, you can add "breads" to your meals. Dropped biscuits are the quickest bread form—they take only 5–6 minutes to prepare and 10 minutes to bake. Preparing quick and easy griddle breads can add sandwiches to your meal choices. Also, the easy cracker recipes are wonderful with soup or as a snack.

Where to Begin on a Rotational Diet

As a first step to meal planning, read through the list of foods assigned to each Day of the rotational diet outlined on pages 66–67. On a piece of paper or in the book margin, note the foods on each Day that you can incorporate in your diet. This will depend on your individual food allergies and other dietary restrictions. Evaluate if there are enough foods on each Day to form a balanced diet. Look for a cross section of proteins, carbohydrate starches, vegetables, and fruits (once you can add fruits to your diet).

After you have looked through the food lists and have decided that you **do have enough foods that you can eat on each Day**:

- Look through the recipes. Pay particular attention to the ingredients and choose recipes that you can eat or modify slightly to fit your requirements.
- Make a list of or indicate in the Recipe Table of Contents (beginning on page 89) the recipes that encourage you and that will allow you to follow your dietary restrictions. This list will help as you begin actual meal planning and preparation.

If you do not have enough foods to eat on each Day, your first task is to modify the list of foods for each Day according to your dietary restrictions. Help in this process is found on page 26. If you need help beyond the scope of this book, refer to Appendix D: Recommended Reading for reference materials on rotation. If you prefer to receive personalized help, refer to Section 3 in Appendix C on page 259.

After making a list of food changes to develop a 4-day rotational diet personalized for your needs—either by yourself or with assistance—you may require assistance with recipes and meal planning. If you need more help beyond the information contained in this book, see page 259 on how to receive the author's assistance.

Ingredient Substitutions within Recipes

A few recipes list substitution options. While many recipes do not specifically give an option, a substitution can often be incorporated into them. Substitute ingredients may be easily understood by looking at the many recipes typed in chart form. For example, in the pizza crust recipe (page 148) it is easily seen that arrowroot or tapioca starch may be substituted and vice versa. Many times the reason an option is not given is that it would break the rotation set up in this cookbook.

Vegetables, grains/nongrains, and/or meats are usually items you can substitute in each of the recipes. Consider length of cooking time and/or color when making substitutions. For example, if you make a vegetable, grain/nongrain, and/or meat substitution, note that the cooking time for the recipe may need to be adjusted depending upon the needed cooking time for the substitute food(s).

Chapter 7—Quintessential Odds and Ends provides help for developing a substitute. Begin by reading the various substitution listings for flours, starches, eggs, milk, sugar, and leavening agents. Following are some additional common substitution situations.

- The cereal recipes on each Day do not have to include the nut milk listed. You may substitute additional water or another milk substitute.
- The "Mayo" recipes found on each Day use a nut or seed base with the addition of a starch for thickening. Each of the base ingredients and/or starches in these recipes could be substituted for those in other recipes. Use this option when you do not have a particular starch on hand or have moved a particular food to another Day.
- To produce a standard product, often a starch or other binder is necessary when baking with gluten-free, nongrain flours. Arrowroot is used on Day 2 with amaranth, tapioca starch on Day 3 with quinoa, and kudzu starch or guar gum on Day 4 with buckwheat. In the substitution lists on page 56 (For Thickening) you will notice that arrowroot, tapioca, potato, kudzu, and cornstarch can easily be exchanged in the recipes, but guar gum is not an equivalent exchange with a starch.

> **HH:** Oils may be stored in freezer in their original containers to extend shelf life. To use the oils, thaw and store in refrigerator.

- Oils can be substituted in any of the recipes. However, check the nut, seed, or vegetable source family with regard to the possible need to move other members of the food family.

"Plain Food" Meals

When I first began using a rotational diet, I was encouraged by books and others to eat "plain food" meals. "Plain food" meals usually have three components—meat, starch, and vegetables—which are cooked separately. When implementing a major dietary change, it can seem simplest to cook the individual allowed foods in this manner—i.e., warm up tuna, cook brown rice, and steam broccoli. While these meals are often easy to plan and prepare, they can become very boring and tasteless when eaten for extended periods. In addition, they add to the clean-up process since each component is prepared in a separate cooking utensil—saucepan, skillet, dish, etc.—which cannot be washed until after the meal.

While "plain food" meals can be useful when doing meal planning, remember that not only is preparation and cooking time a factor, but clean up should be considered as well. It is possible to prepare a "plain food" meal without using a large number of cooking utensils or having a sink full of dishes waiting for you after your meal. By preparing casseroles you not only streamline your clean up process, but you introduce variety and new flavors through food combinations. Using complementary-flavor foods can also help eliminate the need to use condiments and sauces such as catsup which might otherwise be used on plain food dishes. The food's appearance is also often enhanced when the different colors and textures are combined.

continued on page 68

Foods for Day 1

Grains, Flours, & Baking Foods
6   Kamut, rice, spelt, teff, wheat

Higher Carbohydrate Vegetables
36   turnip

Lower Carbohydrate Vegetables
6   bamboo shoots
7   Chinese water chestnut
28   beets, chard
36   broccoli, cabbage, radish, collards, bok choy
65   celery, parsley*

Animal Protein
88   catfish
98   tuna
103 halibut, sole
124 chicken, chicken egg, Cornish hen, pheasant, quail

Fruits
40a pear
40b apricot, peach, nectarine
40c raspberry, strawberry

Sweeteners
6   rice syrup
40a pear

Oils
40b almond oil
75   sesame oil

Herbs & Spices
34   cinnamon*
36   dill, dry mustard
65   cumin

Seeds & Nuts
22   pecan
40a almond
75   sesame seeds

*Foods that float between Days 1 and 3

Foods for Day 2

Grains, Flours, & Baking Foods
19   arrowroot starch
30   amaranth
41   garbanzo bean flour (chickpea)
74   potato starch

Higher Carbohydrate Vegetables
41   garbanzo (chickpea), lima beans
74   potato
79   pumpkin**

Lower Carbohydrate Vegetables
11   onion
54   okra
74   tomato, green pepper, eggplant
79   spaghetti and zucchini squash, cucumber**
80   lettuce

Animal Protein
82   shrimp, crab, prawn, lobster
87   cod (scrod), pollack
129 rabbit
137 beef, buffalo, plain yogurt
n/a red snapper

Fruits
16   banana, plantain
45   grapefruit, lemon
56   kiwi
79   melons

Sweeteners
Currently recipes for Day 2 are developed using stevia or honey floated from Day 4.

Oils
69   olive oil
80   sunflower oil
137 butter, ghee (clarified butter)

Herbs & Spices
11   garlic**
63   allspice, clove
73   basil, marjoram, rosemary, sage, savory, thyme, oregano**
74   cayenne (red) pepper, chili powder**

Seeds & Nuts
79   pumpkin seeds**
80   sunflower seeds

**Foods that float between Days 2 and 4

Unassigned "Fun Foods" (See explanation on page 24.)

| 10 pineapple | 20 vanilla | 33 nutmeg | 50 maple |
| 17 ginger | 26 macadamia nut | 44 flaxseed and flaxseed oil | 62 Brazil nut |

Foods for Day 3

Grains, Flours, & Baking Foods
6 barley, corn, millet, oat, rye, wild rice
28 quinoa
47 tapioca starch
52 cream of tartar

Higher Carbohydrate Vegetables
36 rutabaga
65 parsnips

Lower Carbohydrate Vegetables
28 spinach
36 cauliflower, Brussels sprout, kale
65 carrots, parsley*

Animal Protein
103 flounder, turbot
106 salmon, trout
121 duck, goose
126 turkey, turkey egg

Fruits
34 avocado
40a apple
40b plum, prune, cherry
52 raisin, grape

Sweeteners
28 FOS—NutriFlora™
(see page 273 for ordering information)
40a apple

Oils
22 walnut oil
36 canola oil

Herbs & Spices
34 bay leaf, cinnamon*
65 caraway, fennel, cilantro, coriander

Seeds & Nuts
22 walnut
23 filbert (hazelnut)

*Foods that float between Days 1 and 3

Foods for Day 4

Grains, Flours, & Baking Foods
1 agar agar, kombu
27 buckwheat
41 carob powder, kudzu (kuzu), legume flours
80 Jerusalem artichoke flour

Higher Carbohydrate Vegetables
41 peas, lentils, & all other beans not on Day 2
70 sweet potato
79 pumpkin**, acorn, butternut, & other winter squash

Lower Carbohydrate Vegetables
11 asparagus, leeks
27 sorrel
41 green beans
79 cucumber**
80 artichoke

Animal Protein
87 haddock   130 squirrel
91 sea bass   134 pork
95 mahi mahi   135 venison
100 swordfish   137 lamb, goat
102 ocean perch   n/a orange roughy

Fruits
27 rhubarb
45 orange, tangerine, tangelo
93 blueberry, cranberry

Sweeteners
27 buckwheat honey
41 clover honey
80 stevia

Oils
41 soy oil
80 safflower oil

Herbs & Spices
11 garlic**
73 oregano**
74 chili powder**
80 tarragon

Seeds & Nuts
41 roasted soy beans
48 cashew
79 pumpkin seeds**

**Foods that float between Days 2 and 4

Unassigned "Fun Foods" (See explanation on page 24.)			
10 pineapple	20 vanilla	33 nutmeg	50 maple
17 ginger	26 macadamia nut	44 flaxseed and flaxseed oil	62 Brazil nut

continued from page 65

While casseroles do not always involve fewer cooking utensils, they do have an advantage in that while the casserole is cooking in the oven you are able to wash up the preparation pans and dishes. When your meal is finished the only clean up remaining is the casserole dish, table dishes, and any flatware or drink containers used. This makes after-meal clean up

> **HH:** Clean up kitchen and dishes throughout meal preparation.

quicker, easier, and more relaxing. Also, since most casseroles take up to 1 hour to cook, you can often clean up the kitchen and still have some time to relax before your meal. Some casseroles—such as Chicken or Tuna Noodle or Rice Casseroles—expand this advantage even further because they can be prepared earlier in the day and put in the refrigerator until time to bake them.

The best examples of time-saving "plain food" meals are the following which can be prepared in one cooking utensil resulting in a very tasty meal with a minimum of clean up.

Day 1—Denver Eggs	Day 3—Salmon Millet Dinner
Day 1—Tuna Rice Dinner	Day 3—Turkey Vegetable Stew (two variations)
Day 1—Tuna "Helper"	Day 4—Easy Meal Banquet
Day 1—Sesame Goulash	Day 4—Ham and Bean Stew
Day 2—Beef Stew	Day 4—Pork and Buckwheat Pasta Casserole

All Days—Many of the hearty, complete meal soups

Meal Planning Ideas

Beginning on page 80 several meal planning idea sections are given to help you choose food and recipe combinations for complete meals, preparation time available, and type of meal to be served. Many times an individual recipe is a complete meal and does not need other foods or recipes to complement it. Meal planning ideas are divided into several categories.

- Quick & Easy Meals—These meals can be prepared from start to finish in approximately 30 minutes. The actual time will depend somewhat on the size of recipe being prepared because vegetable preparation usually takes the most time. A few take a slightly longer time with time average indicated.

- Quick & Easy with Advanced Planning—Using some advanced planning, preparation, and/or *plan*overs (planned leftovers) makes these recipes quick and easy additions to your meal plans. Look through the meal planning sections and notice how using advanced planning greatly increases the list of Quick and Easy Meals.

- Easy Meals—These recipes take longer from start to finish, but the actual preparation time spent in the kitchen is very short. The longer completion time is usually due to cooking style and required cooking time (e.g., oven, slow cooker, simmering time to blend flavors, etc.).   **EZ**

- Lower Carbohydrate Meals—These are not just "cave man diet" suggestions, but are meals that have a lower carbohydrate level. [The "cave man diet" is a regimen having a very restricted carbohydrate level (60–80 grams per day) which may be needed by some during the early weeks of a *Candida*-control diet. If knowing the carbohydrate levels of the foods you eat is important for your personal diet, note that most recipes list a nutritional analysis. Often casserole, soup, or salad recipes give you better control over the amount of carbohydrates because individual foods are measured rather than being "guesstimated" as when serving grains as a side dish.

- Breakfast Ideas—For each Day there is a selection of foods such as cereals (prepared in the slow cooker or on top of the stove), pancakes, muffins, biscuits, etc. that make excellent breakfast choices. Try including vegetables or a protein source in your breakfast to add variety and help balance your diet by eating more than just carbohydrates at the start of the day. Everyone's metabolism is different, as is the way each individual body deals with the overgrowth of *Candida*, and you will need to adjust what you prepare for breakfast depending on your own system's needs. I often eat leftover fish, meat, or vegetables from the evening before for breakfast.

- <u>Snack Ideas</u>—Snack ideas for those times between meals when you need a little something to carry you through. I attempt to keep several varieties of crackers in the freezer for my favorite snack.
- <u>Meals Away from Home</u>—These are ideas that work well for when you are away from home during mealtimes. Meals away from home, such as lunch at work, will vary depending upon the work place lunchroom facilities available or what management will allow. If I worked away from home on a regular basis, I would encourage my management to be supportive of my health requirements by:
  - ◊ allowing me (as well as others) to store food in a refrigerator or at least in my cooler in the coolest area of the building.
  - ◊ adding a microwave to the lunchroom for all to use.
  - ◊ allowing me to bring my lunch in a 1-quart size slow cooker ready to plug in and cook or reheat.
- <u>Special Occasion Meals</u>—This section contains recipe and meal ideas for special times such as brunches, potlucks, and when company comes for dinner. Rotation does not have to be tossed out the window for guests. Many of these suggestions take more preparation time. However, carefully planning so many things can be done in advance will allow you to be relaxed when company arrives.

For example, one of my favorite company meals is Shrimp Tofu Lasagna (made with asparagus), Carob Cake Brownies, and Dacopa beverage (a Day 4 Special Meal). To prepare this meal and still allow yourself time to relax and be ready for guests, use the following schedule.

1. Before lunch, prepare brownies and icing. While brownies are baking, clean up kitchen and prepare Soy Lasagna Noodles. Place noodles in refrigerator or freezer as described in recipe.
2. Sometime after lunch, plan some relaxation time as a break from the standing time involved in the brownie and noodle preparation.
3. By 2 or 3 o'clock, prepare lasagna sauce.
4. Approximately 75 minutes (1 hour and 15 minutes) before anticipated serving time, perform lasagna recipe steps 4–6. This allows approximately 15 minutes to layer lasagna in pan and 60 minutes to bake.
5. Have guests arrive approximately 15–30 minutes before anticipated serving time. This will allow 30 minutes or more after placing the lasagna in the oven to set the table and have a few minutes of relaxation before guests arrive as well as time to relax with your guests before serving dinner.

As a special note, this recipe can be prepared with uncooked whole-wheat or spelt lasagna noodles in place of the soy noodles. If you do not have enough time to prepare Soy Lasagna Noodles for everyone, prepare just enough for yourself. Assemble the lasagna in a Corning 10-inch square casserole dish using Soy Lasagna Noodles for one portion and spelt or whole-wheat noodles for the other three portions. Be careful to mark which corner has the soy noodles so you can be sure to place that portion on your plate when serving. My guests have eaten the Soy Lasagna Noodles and not noticed any lack of flavor in comparison with other foods that they would eat. I have had very good compliments on this company meal.

Dacopa beverage is a coffee substitute made from dahlia tubers. It is a nice decaffeinated beverage to offer with dessert for company. It looks like instant coffee and is very easily prepared by dissolving it in boiling water. Each guest can then mix their own beverage in individual mugs or coffee cups to the strength they prefer. Offer honey or FOS in place of sugar and goat, soy, or nut milk in place of cream for those accustomed to cream and sugar with coffee. My guests have enjoyed this drink hot or cold.

This is just one example of a company meal where you can do most of the meal preparation earlier in the day. This gives you a chance to relax throughout the day so you can be well rested when company arrives and enjoy your visit with them.

The Secret to Efficient Meal Planning: Organization

With our busy lifestyles, we are continually searching for something quick and easy to prepare for mealtime. Several recipes in this cookbook are quick and easy and can be prepared from start to finish in as little as 30 minutes. A working person may decide to prepare Quick and Easy meals on Monday through Friday and more difficult or time-consuming meals and recipes on the weekend when more time is available to spend in the kitchen.

Most of the recipe completion time required involves vegetable preparation and cooking time. In some instances, you can cut preparation time by choosing purchased frozen vegetables such as green beans, peas, lima beans, broccoli, mixed vegetables, onions, asparagus, and/or carrots. In addition, you can freeze some vegetables yourself such as eggplant, green peppers, pea pods, and/or zucchini. Learn more about creating your own organic food supply as well as "quick meal" kits beginning on page 48.

In order to supply yourself with easily accessible breads (muffins, hamburger buns, crackers, tortillas) and desserts (once you can tolerate fruits and/or alternative sweeteners), you will need to plan time when you can be in the kitchen for longer periods. By preparing breads and/or desserts and freezing them in individual portions, adding breads and desserts to your meals becomes as easy as using commercially prepared food products.

Also, when you are preparing a meal (perhaps even a quick and easy meal) prepare an additional amount to be used at a later time. This "*plan*over" (planned leftover) food can be put in the freezer to use for the next rotation—four, eight, or more days later. Or use the *plan*overs for your lunch the following day if you are following a dinner/breakfast/lunch "Day" rotation.

> **HH:** Use the freezer to your advantage. Prepare at least double the amount needed and freeze extra portions to use for "instant" meals later. Try to always keep one or two meals for each day in the freezer for those "no time" or lazy-feeling days.

For example, for dinner on Day 1 prepare Oven Fried Chicken, steamed rice, and stir-fry vegetables. The whole chicken may be fried or the bonier pieces may be cooked separately (see Chicken Broth, page 130). The broth may be used in a casserole or soup for the next day's lunch or frozen for later use. Cooked meat from these pieces may be made into a salad, casserole, or soup for the next day's lunch or frozen for later use. Also, when cutting up vegetables for stir-fry, cut up extra amounts to be used in soup or salad or eaten raw for the next day's lunch. If you are going to make a salad, prepare your choice of "Mayo" or salad dressing while dinner is cooking. The next day while fixing breakfast, combine the prepared salad ingredients or cook the soup. Pack the salad in a cooler or the soup in a thermos and you are ready to go. This same principle can be used with several meals on all four days.

The above example would be used by persons following a dinner/breakfast/lunch "Day" plan (see page 22 for explanation). If you are using the breakfast/lunch/dinner plan (as I usually do) or the lunch/dinner/breakfast plan (as I occasionally do), you may find the following tips helpful. To shorten preparation time, decide total quantity of vegetables needed for a particular day. Then use one slot of time to prepare all of them, such as:

* during the cooking time for the evening meal the night before,
* while breakfast is cooking,
* sometime during the morning,
* or while preparing lunch.

Doing all of the vegetable preparation at one time assists in preparing meals faster for that day.

Another technique I use is to prepare the same meal for lunch and dinner. When preparing lunch, I make three servings of the recipe and put two in the refrigerator to be reheated for my husband and myself for dinner.

Your freezer can be an important tool in making meal preparation quicker and easier. Keep some cooked rice, millet, quinoa, buckwheat, and beans frozen ready to pull out and add to a recipe. If you look through the recipes, you will note several that list using these previously cooked ingredients. Also, many of the casseroles and soups use a broth of the Day. When roasting a chicken or turkey or making a beef, buffalo, pork, or venison roast, save the broth and leftover meat to use in future meals.

The list of helpful *plan*overs (planned leftovers) can go on and on. You can help determine the list of foods you want to have handy in the freezer by looking through the recipes you have chosen to prepare. Check to see if the recipes use foods such as cooked meat or cooked grains or nongrains (e.g., cooked chicken, cooked rice). Another good indicator is when the recipe lists another recipe title with a page location. If so, more than likely the referenced recipe is something leftover from a pervious meal or an advanced preparation item. You could make the needed food just before making the recipe which uses it, but it is much easier and faster to have the already-prepared food in the freezer.

> **HH:** An assortment of glass jars with tight-fitting lids is useful for storing and/or freezing leftovers such as meat or vegetable broths, cooked beans, soups, salad dressings, "Mayos," etc. Begin by saving jars that you purchase food in, such as Chuck's Seafood tuna or salmon, or you can purchase wide-mouth canning jars which are easier to use and clean. They come in several sizes such as half-pints and pints (handy for freezing leftovers), quarts, tall half-gallons, and gallons (for storing grains and flours). These jars are available in the canning section of many discount, hardware, and grocery stores. The half-pint, half-gallon, and gallon sizes are in lower demand and may need to be special ordered.

> **HH:** Using a wide-mouth funnel when filling jars makes the process easier and helps prevent spills.

> **HH: Food Storage Wraps**
>
> If you are corn-sensitive, avoid using wax paper. It may be dusted with a corn product. If you are chemically sensitive, avoid using plastic wrap or bags since they are made from petroleum. In addition, a chemically sensitive person should not use aluminum. Use cellophane instead. Cellophane is a plant fiber product and can be purchased on a roll similar to wax paper or in bag form. Use scissors to cut the cellophane roll. The bags come in various sizes as well as in pleated and flat styles. If you can not find cellophane locally, see page 255 for mail-order sources.
>
> Cellophane rips very easily, so handle it with care. The bags also deteriorate over time so do not purchase too large a supply at one time. When using a cellophane bag to freeze foods, place a self-adhesive label on it to mark contents and then place it into another slightly larger cellophane bag or a plastic self-closing bag (such as zip lock).

It's All in the Timing!

Many meal planning ideas outlined on pages 80–81 include only one recipe as a complete meal. Often the directions in these recipes are written to assist you in preparing the meal in the least amount of time possible. For beginning cooks, just learning to cook is a challenge and putting a meal together with several recipes is just too much. Also, during the early stages of *Candida* treatment when we feel like we are trying to think through oatmeal or walking through a maze, we (experienced and beginner cooks alike) need all the help we can get with meal preparation. Following are sample preparation outlines to help you dovetail the preparation of several recipe or food items for one meal.

Several listed meal planning ideas are "Plain Food" Meals (see page 65) which consist of three basic components—meat, starch, and vegetable. The preparation of these meals is easy to organize.

First, consider the length of cooking or baking time as well as actual preparation time you need to spend. As an example, let's choose the following Day 3 Quick & Easy Meal.

Menu Item	Cooking Time	Preparation Time
Ground turkey patty	20 minutes	5 minutes
Basic Quinoa or Millet	20 minutes (allows for 5 minutes to bring to boil)	5 minutes (especially needed for quinoa)
Kale/Cauliflower	25 minutes	5 minutes for kale

To begin meal preparation, choose the food item that takes the longest to prepare and cook. Kale takes a total of 30 minutes, so begin there. Quinoa and turkey pattie take about the same amount of time. I choose to start the quinoa before the turkey since it can be removed from heat and allowed to set for 5 minutes (keep covered). (See step 4 of Basic Grain/nongrain Cooking chart, page 96.) A suggested meal preparation chart would be as follows:

Start At	Preparation Step
6:00	Wash and begin cooking kale.
6:05	Rinse and begin cooking quinoa.
6:10	Make turkey pattie and begin cooking. Turn as needed throughout cooking time. Quinoa—cover, reduce heat, and set timer for 15 minutes.
6:15	Clean and prepare cauliflower.
6:20	Add cauliflower to kale. Add more water if needed. Set table.
6:25	Test quinoa for doneness—if done remove from heat.
6:30	Transfer food to serving dishes or directly to plates. Say table grace, eat, and enjoy.

Add advanced planning to make an easy meal quick. For example, see the Day 4 Easy Meal below. Yes, this meal takes all day to cook, but your actual preparation time is only about 15–20 minutes.

Menu Item	Preparation Step
Roast Pork	Begin in slow cooker on low during breakfast preparation
Basic Buckwheat Groats	Rinse and begin cooking approximately 25 minutes before desired serving time. If you like them cooked with leeks, as I do, plan ahead to have leeks washed, sliced, and frozen (no blanching required)—ready to use.
Frozen Green Beans	Begin cooking just before starting buckwheat.

This meal allows you up to 15 minutes after setting the table to plan or do some advanced preparation for the next day (Day 1) such as cut up chicken fryer for Oven Fried Chicken.

As a second example, any meal with beans uses this simple time schedule. During dinner meal preparation on day before (Day 3) when preparing beans for Day 4, take 5 minutes or less to rinse and begin soaking your choice of dry beans. Also, if you will be in a hurry in the AM, prepare and/or measure out other ingredients in the bean recipe, such as onion, leeks, and seasonings (except salt). In the AM, take another 5 minutes to rerinse and drain beans. Transfer to slow cooker, add water and seasonings, and allow to cook on low all day while at work. Special Note: Remember to add salt before serving.

HH: Read through each recipe before starting. Confirm that you have all necessary ingredients. Place them in mixing area and, after you use each item, set it aside or put it away. Use a table knife or other straight edge to mark your place in the recipe. These tips will help you especially if you are interrupted.

Using a preparation time table for meals involving several dishes can be very helpful, as with the following Day 2 Quick & Easy Meal.

Sloppy Joes with Garbanzo Bean Griddle Bread garnished with sprouts and thinly slice zucchini Lettuce with Day 2 Easy Oil & Spice/C Dressing

(Special Note: This preparation time table assumes that only a single member of the family needs Griddle Bread. Have purchased buns or bread slices for the remainder of the family. If you need to prepare more breads—start them earlier, have more than one griddle, and/or use a large griddle that will hold 2 or 3 breads at one time.)

Start At	Preparation Step
6:00	Preheat griddle.
6:01	Begin cooking ground beef.
6:03	Chop onion, continue step 1 of Sloppy Joes recipe.
6:05	Mix up griddle bread batter (step 2 of recipe).
6:10	Stir meat. Test griddle for hotness and begin cooking first bread.
6:12	Wash lettuce, allow to drain.
6:16	Turn griddle bread. Stir meat, add tomato paste and water—step 2. Mix up Easy Oil & Spicy/C Dressing. Tear lettuce into individual salad bowls.
6:21	Remove first griddle bread and start next one. Stir Sloppy Joes. Slice zucchini. Set table—including salads and garnishes for sandwiches.
6:27	Turn griddle bread. Clean up dishes and kitchen or relax a moment.
6:30	Stir Sloppy Joes, taste, add extra seasonings if needed. Place in serving bowl and set on table.
6:32	Remove second griddle bread. Say table grace, eat, and enjoy.

HH: Organize kitchen to make meal preparation easier and more efficient. Use as many of the following tips as possible.

- Keep measuring and mixing equipment in the same cupboard.
- Set up food staples cupboard as close to measuring and mixing cupboard as possible.
- Organize food in cabinets, shelves, refrigerator, and freezer according to Days. May wish to use different-colored tags or labels to color code foods for each Day.
- Arrange counter-top space for food preparation steps. Have measuring and mixing space near measuring and mixing equipment cupboard. Set up food cleaning and chopping area near sink.
- Store less frequently used items on higher shelves or in harder-to-reach corners. Save more accessible storage areas for items used most often.
- Always return food and equipment items to assigned storage area.
- Store long-handled measuring spoons on hooks under upper cupboards near mixing area. Use a separate hook for each spoon size.
- Keep hot pads or mitts and trivets for hot pans or dishes near stove area.
- Store serving and eating utensils near table.
- Store oils in freezer in original containers to extend shelf life. To use, thaw and store in refrigerator.

Use a long-range preparation schedule for more complicated meals, as the table below for Easy Thanksgiving Feast illustrates. Then break down the tasks to be done the day of the meal into a schedule like the previous ones listed.

Easy Thanksgiving Feast

Menu	Preparation Schedule
Cranberry Spritzer	Day before—Chill ingredients. Combine ingredients just before serving.
Roast Turkey	Day before—Clean bird, tuck or sew wings, and tie legs. Place in oven 4 hours or more (depends upon size) before serving.
Dill "Stove-Top" Stuffing	Day before—Prepare your choice of vegetables, and boil turkey neck for broth. If desired you may remove meat from neck and add. Prepare 20 minutes before serving
steamed broccoli, cauliflower, and/or carrots	Day before—Prepare your choice of fresh vegetables. Cook 10 minutes before serving
Apple Salad	Day before—Prepare " Mayo" and vegetables. In the AM—Dice apples, combine, and chill.
Kamut Dinner Rolls	Day before—Measure ingredients. Begin mixing 1 hour before serving. Bake while turkey is being carved.
canned cranberry sauce	Day before—Chill.
Pumpkin or Squash Pie	Day before—Prepare.
Dacopa beverage	Prepare as needed before serving.

The Right Tool for the Right Job

Having and properly using the correct equipment is by far one of the best ways to save time in the kitchen and therefore to save energy and money. Throughout this cookbook you will find Helpful Hint **(HH)** squares. Many of these are about equipment recommended for accomplishing a particular task. The list of recommended equipment includes the following. If you do not have this equipment, you may desire to gradually add it to your kitchen.

⇒ Digital Timer (page 124)
⇒ Measuring Equipment (page 53)
⇒ Curved-Sided Bowl (page 106)
⇒ Strainer and Colander (page 97)
⇒ Splatter Screen (page 198)
⇒ Knives (page 201)
⇒ Cutting Board (page 198)
⇒ Cast-Iron Griddle and/or Skillet (page 59)
⇒ Blender with Glass Jar (page 189)
⇒ Stand Mixer with Beaters and Dough Hooks (page 102)
⇒ Food Processor (page 206)
⇒ Counter-top Grill (page 157)

⇒ Slow Cooker—one regular-size and one 1-quart size (page 98)
⇒ Toaster Oven (page 75)
⇒ Stainless Steel Cookware and Bakeware, including Steamer Pan (page 200)
⇒ Covered Casserole Dishes, especially four to six Corning Grab-It bowls with glass lids as well as the plastic lids and one Corning 10-inch square casserole with glass lid
⇒ An Assortment of Glass Jars and Wide Mouth Funnel (page 71)
⇒ Food Freezer(s) (page 49)

Reheating

While having *plan*overs (planned leftovers) in the freezer to use for future meals is a great help, it can sometimes be a challenge to thaw and reheat them. Here are some basic tips.

A microwave oven is the easiest and fastest way to thaw and especially reheat several casseroles. But if you do not have or cannot use a microwave oven, reheat foods using the following methods.

- To reheat tortillas, muffins, or other bread products, start with a pan of water. A skillet or very-wide-topped pan works best. A large amount of water is not needed, only enough to be brought to and kept at a steaming state for the thawing and reheating time period. Place a splatter screen (page 198) over the top of the pan. The baked good should be in a closed cellophane bag—fold top over or use tape to close bag. Place bag on the splatter screen over the steaming water. Turn bag often enough so that the baked goods are thawed and heated evenly. Freezing baked goods in individual portions in cellophane bags sealed with tape makes it easy to thaw and reheat.

- Since muffins are larger, they really need to have some thawing time at room temperature before being placed on a splatter screen over steaming water. They are best when thawed first and just warmed to create a fresh-baked taste.

- When reheating casseroles a steamer pan and Corning Grab-It bowl are quite handy. I often freeze casserole *plan*overs in glass jars or Grab-It bowls. If frozen in a glass jar, thaw the casserole enough to remove it from the jar and transfer it to a Grab-It bowl. Purchase a steamer pan large enough for a Grab-It bowl to set down inside the steamer insert. Fill the bottom of the steamer pan with water to about 1/2 inch from the bottom of steamer insert. Heat water to boiling. Put glass lid on Grab-It bowl and set it in steamer insert. Then put the lid on the steamer pan. Open up both lids (steamer pan and Grab-It bowl) to stir casserole often. The pan and Grab-It bowl will be hot so remember to use hot pads when handling them. For casseroles that should not be stirred, such as lasagna, it is best to use a slow oven (300°F.) for thawing and reheating.

- Pizza can also be reheated in a slow oven (300°F.). To facilitate this process, begin with the following tips on freezing *plan*over pizza. Cut pizza into slices, loosen from bottom of pan with spatula, and separate slices. Place pizza pan in freezer to individually freeze slices (around 30–60 minutes). After slices are frozen, transfer the number of pizza slices you will want for a serving to a cellophane bag and close with tape or twist-tie. Mark contents with a self-adhesive label listing the type of pizza and date. Store in freezer where it will not be "knocked around" and damaged. Pizza slices should be thawed in the refrigerator during the day or overnight. Place pieces on a stainless steel baking sheet (does not have to be oiled). Place baking sheet in a slow oven (300°F.—do not preheat). Check pizza occasionally to see if it is ready. If you have a microwave and can use one, you may thaw the pizza and even start it reheating in the microwave. But be aware that using the microwave will cause the dough to become very soggy—especially amaranth dough. The best option is to thaw the pizza in the refrigerator and reheat it in the oven. For reheating individual servings, a toaster oven might be a nice addition to your kitchen. It is more efficient than heating up the whole big oven for just one or two pieces of pizza.

> **HH: Toaster Oven**
> Having a toaster oven allows you to heat only the cooking space you need since you do not need the entire stove oven for one small casserole dish or to reheat a few pieces of pizza. When you shop for a toaster oven, take along the dishes you are likely to use in it to be sure they will fit.

- To thaw items in glass jars (such as soups), set jar(s) into a container of warm water so that the water covers as much of the jar sides as possible without "floating" the jar or reaching the lid. Change the water as it cools. As soup begins to thaw, chip away thawed portion and pour it into the pan you will use to reheat the soup. Continue process until soup is thawed enough to remove entire jar contents. (Special Note: Freezing in wide-mouth jars with straight sides aids in this process.)

The alternative thawing options listed above can be avoided if you plan your meals at least 1–2 days in advance and thaw items in the refrigerator. Do not thaw foods at room temperature except for a brief period of time. Thawing at room temperature can lead to the possibility of food-born illness and it is much safer and easier to develop habits that will make refrigerator thawing your standard method.

Creating a Shopping List

Developing and maintaining a food storehouse (a stored supply of nonperishable food staples) can seem a monumental task at first. However, you will soon have a valuable resource to help in your journey toward better health. The process is not a "snap," but it is an accomplishable challenge. If possible for your situation, you may be able to build your storehouse in stages.

The lists of food staples below, which are divided by the rotational Days, give you a starting point for stocking your storehouse. On pages 78 and 79 you will find lists of prepared foods, divided by rotational Days. When purchasing and using prepared foods, be sure to read the labels carefully. Not all of them are a "perfect fit" in the rotational diet given in this book. You need to be aware of the ingredients which break rotation and plan accordingly.

You can customize these lists to your individual needs by first making photocopies of them. Cross off the food items you need to eliminate because of food allergies and add or move other items that you will use in your rotation. Keep these customized lists in a file folder or 3-ring binder along with pages where you keep notes on resources you have used, dates and amounts ordered, item order numbers, and/or other information that will aid you in stocking your storehouse. By using photocopies of the lists, you can keep the originals to recopy later should you need to modify your customized list if/when your dietary needs change.

Day 1 Staples

Grains
basmati rice, brown and/or white
brown rice, long-, medium-, or short-grain
   (2# brown rice = 6 cups) (2# white rice = 5 cups)
Kamut grain (1# = 2 2/3 cups)
spelt grain (1# = 2 2/3 cups)
teff grain (1# = 1 1/4 cups)
rice, Kamut, spelt flakes (cooked cereal)
   (14oz. = 5 cups)

Flours and Starches
Kamut flour (2# = 6 1/2 cups)
rice flour (2# = 3 cups)
spelt flour (2# =6 1/2 cups)
teff flour (1# = 3 cups)

Oils
almond and/or sesame oil

Sweeteners
DevanSweet™
Lundberg Family Farms Sweet Dreams
   Organic Brown Rice Syrup

Herbs and Spices
cumin, dill weed, dry mustard, parsley

Nuts and Seeds
almonds (1# = 3 cups)
almond butter
pecans (1# = 5 cups)
tahini
sesame seeds (1# = 3 1/4 cups)

Day 2 Staples

Nongrains
whole amaranth (1# = 2 cups)

Flours and Starches
amaranth flour (10oz. = 2 1/4 cups)
arrowroot starch (1# = 4 1/2 cups)
garbanzo bean flour (22oz. = 5 cups)
potato starch (1# = 2 2/3 cups)

Beans
garbanzo beans (chickpeas) (1# = 2 1/2 cups)

Oils
butter or ghee (clarified butter)
olive and/or sunflower oil

Sweeteners

Herbs and Spices
basil, oregano (leaf), summer savory
cayenne (red) pepper–ground or leaf
garlic, dehydrated minced/fresh cloves/powder
marjoram, rosemary, chili powder

Nuts and Seeds
Brazil nuts (1# = 3 1/2 cups)
sunflower seed (1# = 3 1/2 cups)

Start your shopping list with the following food items that you may need on all four days.

- sea or Real salt
- baking soda
- vitamin C crystals
- flaxseed oil
- flaxseed

- EnerG Egg Replacer
- Pau D'Arco tea
- Dacopa beverage
- sparkling mineral water
- spring water

To complete your shopping list, check the recipes you plan to prepare to learn which perishable food items you need—e.g., fresh or frozen vegetables and fruits, meats, eggs, yogurt, or tofu.

Day 3 Staples

Grains and Nongrains
hulled millet (28 oz.= 4 1/4 cups)
whole quinoa (12 oz. = 2 cups)
wild rice (1# = 3 cups)
oatbran (1# = 4 cups)
rolled oats (1# = 6 1/2 cups)

Flours and Starches
barley flour (1 1/2# = 3/4 cups)
cream of tartar
oat flour (24 oz. = 1 1/2 cups)
quinoa flour (24 oz. = 5 cups)
rye flour (2# = 7 1/2 cups)
tapioca starch (1# = 4 1/2 cups)

Oils
canola, filbert, and/or walnut oil

Sweeteners
FOS, available in 1#, sweetener form at discounted
    prices from Canary Connect, see page 273
    (1# = 3 1/3 cups)
100% pure maple granules (4 oz. = 1 1/4 cups)

Herbs and Spices
bay leaf, caraway seed, cilantro, coriander,
cinnamon

Nuts and Seeds
filberts (hazelnuts) (1# = 3 1/2 cups)
walnuts (1# = 4 2/3 cups)

Day 4 Staples

Nongrains
buckwheat groats (1# = 2 1/2 cups)

Flours and Starches
carob powder (1# = 4 3/4 cups)
Jerusalem artichoke flour (6oz. = 1 cup)
kudzu (kuzu) starch
    (3.5 oz. = 3/4 cup ground into powder see pg. 36)
legume flours—lentil, white bean, black bean
    lentil (24oz. = 4 1/4 cups)
    black bean (24oz. = 3 3/4 cups)
soy flour (24oz. = 7 1/2 cups)
white buckwheat flour (or prepare your own, pg. 105)
    (1# = 2 3/4 cups)

Beans
adzuki beans (1# = 2 3/4 cups)
black turtle beans (1# = 2 1/2 cups)
kidney beans (1# = 2 2/3 cups)
lentils (1# = 2 cups)
navy beans (1# = 2 1/4 cups)
pinto beans (1# = 2 1/2 cups)
split peas (1# = 2 1/4 cups)

Oils
pumpkin seed, soy, and/or safflower oil

Sweeteners
honey
stevia (1 oz. = almost 1/4 cup)

Herbs and Spices
tarragon
Watkins Salsa Seasoning Blend or
    other Mexican blend spices

Nuts and Seeds
cashews (1# = 3 1/2 cups)
macadamia nuts (1# = 3 1/2 cups)
pumpkin seeds (1# = 2 cups)

Other
kombu (seaweed)

> *Don't submit to being a prisoner of time. Learn to use your time. Don't let time use you.*

On these two pages are lists of prepared foods, divided by rotational Days, which you may wish to include in your food storehouse. When purchasing and using prepared foods, be sure to read the labels carefully. Not all of them are a "perfect fit" in the rotational diet given in this book. You need to be aware of the ingredients which break rotation and plan accordingly.

When using prepared foods, be sure to watch for reactions. Prepared foods may not be as free of mold as foods you would make at home because there may not be as much care taken in their processing. In addition, prepared foods may not be as good for you to use during the early stages of a Candida-control diet. If you have any doubts about whether or not you are reacting to a prepared food item, do a food challenge (see pages 10 and 18) to help determine if it is causing you problems.

Day 1 Prepared Foods

Animal Protein
Chuck's Seafood tuna (7 1/2 oz. jar)
Northwest Natural Halibut Medallions

Cereals Served Hot (H) or Cold (C)
C–Arrowhead Mills Nature O's (contains wheat)
C–Arrowhead Mills organic Puffed Kamut
    (6oz. = 6 cups)
H–Arrowhead Mills Rice & Shine cereal
C–Erewhon Kamut Flakes
H–Lundberg Family Farms Creamy Rice™
    Cereal
C–New Morning natural Kamutios
C–New Morning Oatios (contains wheat)
C–puffed rice (6oz. = 11 cups)

Crackers
Edward & Sons brown rice snaps
    (flavors—unsalted sesame or onion/garlic)

Frozen Foods
Alvarado St. organic sprouted wheat tortillas
Francis Simun's flat breads and bagels
Kamut bread, sour dough
Nature's Hilights™ brown rice pizza crust
Spelt bread, sour dough

Pasta
Kamut, rice, and/or spelt pastas

Other
Casbah couscous pilaf (contains wheat)
Casbah lentil pilaf (contains rice/lentils)
Imagine Foods org. original rice dream
    beverage
Imagine Foods pudding snacks
Imagine Foods rice dream frozen dessert
pear juice
rice cakes

Day 2 Prepared Foods

Animal Protein
Seafarer's Choice medium peeled & deveined
    shrimp (Schwan's Sales, see page 258 in Resources)

Cereals Served Cold
puffed (popped) amaranth (4oz. = 5 1/3 cups)

Frozen Foods
Cascadian Farm org. Country-Style Potatoes
Francis Simun's flat breads and bagels
Nu-World Amaranth flat bread/pizza crust
SnoPac org. baby lima beans
SnoPac org. Potatoes O'Brien

Pasta
Mio Amore amaranth pasta (8oz. = 3 1/2 cups)
sunflower seed (1# = 3 1/2 cups)

Other
Annie's vinegar-free Green Garlic Vinaigrette
    salad dressing
Casbah hummus mix
Eden org. canned garbanzo beans, no salt
Featherweight baking powder
Garden Valley org. roasted garlic tomato salsa
Millina's Finest org. Tomato/Basil pasta sauce
Mountain Sun Organic Lemonade
Muir Glen organic tomato paste
Muir Glen organic tomato puree
Santa Cruz brand organic 100% lemon juice
Seven Stars original plain org. yogurt

Day 3 Prepared Foods

Animal Protein
Chuck's Seafood salmon (7 1/2 oz. jar)

Cereals served Hot (H) or Cold (C)
C–puffed millet (6oz. = 11 cups)
H–Arrowhead Mills Bits of Barley cereal
H–Ancient Harvest quinoa flakes

Crackers
Ryvta® Toasted Sesame Rye crackers
Wasa original light rye crackers

Frozen Foods
corn tortillas
Francis Simun's flat breads and bagels
rye bread, sour dough

Pasta
Mio Amore Rye Pasta (8oz. = 3 cups)
Mio Amore Wild Rice Pasta (8oz. = 2 1/cups)
Ancient Harvest quinoa pasta (wheat-free)
   (8oz. = 2 2/3 cups)

Other
apple juice
oat milk
Santa Cruz Natural Organic Applesauce

Day 4 Prepared Foods

Cereals to Cook
Cream of Buckwheat Cereal
   (or prepare your own, see page 98)

Frozen Foods
Francis Simun's flat breads and bagels
SnoPac organic cut green beans

Pasta
100% Buckwheat Soba Noodles
Eden Foods kudzu & sweet potato pasta
Eden Foods mung bean pasta

Other
Eden org. canned black & other beans, no salt
R.W. Knudsen 100% Just Cranberry Juice

Getting Started with a Rotational Diet

Before reading this section, take time to read the first part of this chapter as well as About the Recipes (page 95). Look through the recipes and read the many Helpful Hints given to aid you in food processing and meal preparation. This information will be of great help to you as you move forward in the process of beginning a rotational diet. Once you have read this material, many of you may still have one more question—"How do I begin?"

Begin at the Beginning

Take a few minutes to glance at the following items:
- the list of foods assigned to each Day, found on pages 66 and 67,
- Chapter 9: Recipe Table of Contents, and
- the meal planning ideas beginning on page 80. (These are only ideas to help you get started. You will be able to develop more as you become acquainted with the rotation.)

In the Meal Planning section, the first listing is Quick and Easy Meals. These meals can be prepared in 30 minutes or less and are the best place to start as you begin your rotation. Look at these meals and set up a plan for your first four days of rotation. You may want to set up two rotations (8 days) at this point to save time later. Choose a Quick and Easy meal you feel you can accomplish for each meal to be prepared for that set of days. Add your breakfast idea for each day. Remember, some Quick and Easy Meals may be used for both lunch and dinner or for dinner and the next day's lunch, depending on which plan you are following. Using one recipe for two meals would cut down on the number of Quick and Easy Meals that you need at the start.

continued on page 88

QUICK & EASY MEALS

Day 1

◊ Tuna Broccoli Chowder

◊ Stir-Fry Meal for Day 1 with your choice of pasta

◊ Grilled Fish for Day 1
  Cream of Broccoli Soup

◊ Pasta Primavera

◊ Chuck's Seafood tuna
  Your choice of pasta with flaxseed oil, dill, and/or ground cumin
  Stir-fry or steamed vegetables: broccoli, collards, chard, celery, and/or cabbage

◊ Bare Bones Collard Rolls

◊ Denver Eggs

◊ Tuna "Helper"

◊ Vegetarian Day 1 Spaghetti

◊ All-in-One Salad (Tuna)

Day 2

◊ Grilled Shrimp with lemon
  Boiled potatoes with Clarified Butter
  Zucchini with Tomato

◊ Minute Steak and Garbanzo Bean Gravy
  Mashed potatoes
  Lettuce with Day 2 Creamy Veggie Salad Dressing

◊ Vegetable Shrimp Soup

◊ Ground meat patty
  Creamed Potatoes or Spiced Baked Potatoes (45 min.)
  Tomato and zucchini slices

◊ Sloppy Joes with Griddle Bread
  Lettuce with Day 2 Easy Oil & Spice/C Dressing

◊ Tacos with Griddle Bread

◊ Canned garbanzo beans or frozen lima beans cooked with zucchini slices, chopped green pepper, amaranth greens, and/or tomato

◊ Ground meat patty or minute steak
  Amaranth pasta with pasta sauce
  Lettuce with Day 2 Easy Oil & Spice/C Dressing

Day 3

◊ Egg Drop Soup
  Quinoa Biscuit

◊ Salmon Patties
  Basic Millet with Caraway
  Raw carrot slices

◊ Ground turkey patty
  Basic Quinoa or Millet
  Steamed Brussels sprouts or Kale/Cauliflower

◊ Grilled Fish for Day 3
  Steamed Parsnips
  Steamed Spinach or Kale with flaxseed oil

◊ Salmon Millet Dinner

◊ Ground turkey patty
  Wild rice pasta
  Steamed cauliflower

◊ All-in-One Salad (salmon)

Day 4

◊ Pork Cutlet with Gravy
  Peas
  Green beans

◊ Easy Meal Banquet

◊ Pork Chop
  Sweet potato with flaxseed oil
  Green beans

◊ Grilled venison
  Basic Buckwheat Groats
  Asparagus spears

◊ Lentil Sloppy Joes (45 min.) with Griddle Breads garnished with sprouts
  Asparagus spears

◊ All-in-One Salad (using canned beans)

QUICK & EASY MEALS WITH ADVANCED PLANNING

Day 1

◊ Sesame Goulash

◊ Chicken Spaghetti

◊ Chicken Broccoli Chowder
  Teff Crackers

◊ Chicken Broccoli Soup
  Kamut Muffin

◊ Chicken Rice Soup
  with steamed collards or chard

◊ All-in-One Salad for Day 1 (Chicken)
  with your choice of crackers

◊ Chicken or Tuna Salad with chard on your
  choice of tortillas or Teff Griddle Bread
  Celery sticks

◊ Chicken Collard Soup
  with or without crackers, muffin, or biscuit

Day 2

◊ Chef Salad for Day 2
  Amaranth Crackers

◊ Garbanzo Bean & Potato Soup
  Green pepper strips

◊ Vegetable or Nightshade Beef Soup
  (with/without beans)
  Amaranth Crackers

◊ Tacos with Amaranth Tortillas

◊ Vegetable Shrimp Soup (with Beans)
  Soy Bread

◊ Garbanzo Bean Pattie with Griddle Bread
  Lettuce with Day 2 Easy Oil & Spice/C Dressing

Day 3

◊ Millet or Quinoa Turkey Vegetable Stew
  Quinoa Biscuit

◊ All-in-One Salad for Day 3 (Turkey)
  Quinoa Muffin

◊ Turkey Parsnip Soup or Turkey Kale Soup
  Crackers or muffin

◊ Turkey Salad with spinach on Quinoa Tortilla
  Beets (floated from Day 1)

◊ Salmon Salad with spinach on purchase
  sourdough rye bread
  Vegetable/Apple Salad

◊ Quinoa Tortilla with planover Roast Turkey
  Kale/Cauliflower

◊ Creamed Turkey on Rye Toast

◊ Three Color Salad with muffin, crackers or
  biscuit

Day 4

◊ Stir-Fry Buckwheat and Vegetables with or
  without Shrimp or Meat

◊ Lentil Pattie (45 min.) with Griddle Breads
  Steamed peapods

◊ Ham and Bean Stew

◊ Pork and Buckwheat Pasta Casserole

◊ Pork Fajita
  Asparagus spears

◊ Venison and Buckwheat Pasta Casserole

◊ Venison and Bean Stew

◊ Pork and Bean Burritos

◊ Buckwheat Tortilla with planover Roast Pork,
  sorrel, and Day 4 "Mayo"
  Asparagus spears

◊ 7 Layer Salad (if no fresh pork side available, omit
  it and serve salad with grilled pork cutlet)

◊ Black Bean Pattie with Griddle Bread
  Green beans

Easy Meals

Day 1

◊ Oven Fried Chicken
  Basic Brown Rice with/without chard
  Coleslaw
◊ Tuna Rice Dinner
  Celery sticks
◊ Chicken Rice, Spelt, or Kamut Loaf
  Basic Kamut or Spelt
  Stir-Fry Vegetables for Day 1
◊ Easy Chicken Meal or Soup
◊ Tuna Noodle or Rice Casserole
  Radishes
◊ Chicken Noodle or Rice Casserole
  Radishes
◊ Baked Fish for Day 1
  Basic Brown Rice
  Steamed broccoli
◊ Roast Chicken
  Dill "Stove Top" Stuffing
  Steamed collards

Day 2

◊ Spicy Baked Fish
  Garbanzo Beans and Broth
  Lettuce with Creamy Italian Salad Dressing
◊ Spaghetti Squash with Spaghetti Meat Sauce
  Lettuce with Lemon/Oil Dressing
◊ Easy Steak Dinner
  Boiled, diced potatoes or Garbanzo Beans
  Cucumber slices
◊ Chili
  Green pepper strips
◊ Minestrone Soup
  Baked Fish for Day 2
◊ Your choice of pizza
  Lettuce with Creamy Italian Salad Dressing
◊ Your choice of lasagna
  Lettuce with Lemon/Oil Dressing
◊ Beef Stew

Day 3

◊ Turkey Oatmeal Loaf
  pasta salad with Day 3 pasta and Filbert Mayo
  Spinach salad
◊ Turkey Barley Soup
  Biscuit or Crackers
◊ Baked Fish for Day 3
  Stir-Fry Vegetables for Day 3
  Rye pasta with flaxseed oil or Whipped
  Parsnips
◊ Chef Salad for Day 3 (Spinach) with Creamy
  Veggie Salad Dressing for Day 3
  Muffin or crackers
◊ All-in-One Salad for Day 3 (Turkey/Quinoa) or
  Turkey quinoa Pasta Stew
  Apple Quinoa Crisp
◊ Rainbow Trout
  Basic Millet
  Fresh spinach with Creamy Veggie Salad
  Dressing for Day 3

Day 4

◊ Breaded Pork Chop
  Day 4 Stir-Fried Vegetables
  Baked Beans
◊ Squash and Meatballs
  Green beans
◊ Roast Pork or Venison
  Basic Buckwheat Groats
  Green beans or asparagus spears
◊ Tomato-Free Chili
  Green beans
◊ Tofu and Asparagus in Black Bean Sauce
◊ Scalloped Potatoes and Ham
  Green beans
◊ Lentil Casserole
  Cucumber slices
◊ Amazing Spaghetti Sauce with buckwheat
  soba pasta or Eden brand mung bean pasta

LOWER CARBOHYDRATE MEALS

Day 1

◊ Chicken or Tuna Broccoli Chowder

◊ Chicken Broccoli Soup
  with/without crackers

◊ Chicken Loaf (Choice of three varieties)
  Stir-Fry Vegetables for Day 1
    OR a steamed Day 1 vegetable

◊ Easy Chicken Meal or Soup

◊ Grilled Fish for Day 1
  Celery stick with almond butter
  Cream of Broccoli Soup

◊ All-in-One Salad for Day 1 (Tuna or Chicken)
  with or without the pasta or grain

Day 2

◊ Low Carbohydrate Lasagna
  Lettuce with Lemon/Oil Dressing

◊ Easy Steak or Rabbit Dinner
  Cucumber slices

◊ Chef Salad for Day 2

◊ Grilled steak
  Stir-Fry Vegetables for Day 2

◊ All-in-One Salad for Day 2 (Shrimp)

Day 3

◊ Salmon Cauliflower Chowder

◊ All-in-One Salad for Day (Salmon or Turkey)
  with or without pasta

◊ Egg Drop Soup

◊ Chef Salad for Day 3 (Spinach) with Creamy
  Veggie Salad Dressing for Day 3

◊ Grilled or Baked Fish for Day 3
  Steamed Spinach with flaxseed oil

Day 4

◊ Cream of Asparagus Soup
  Orange Roughy

◊ Stir-Fry Meal for Day 4

◊ Baked or Grilled Fish for Day 4
  Asparagus spears

Breakfast Ideas

Day 1

◊ Your choice of Day 1 muffins, pancakes, French toast, biscuits, or cooked cereals

◊ Arrowhead Mills Rice and Shine Cereal

◊ Lundberg Family Farms Purely Organic Hot Rice™ Cereal

◊ Erewhon Kamut flakes or puffed Kamut cold cereal with almond milk or rice milk

◊ Fresh fruit

◊ Rice cake with almond butter or tahini

◊ Any planover Day 1 vegetable, fish, casserole, or soup

◊ Chicken eggs cooked your favorite way

◊ Scrambled Eggs with Bok Choy

Day 2

◊ Amaranth Cereal

◊ Amaranth Griddle Bread with Kiwi Sauce

◊ Fresh fruit

◊ Yogurt Delights I, II, III, or IV

◊ Any planover Day 2 vegetable, fish, casserole, or soup
   —steamed potato
   —Fried Potatoes with onions & green pepper
   —Low Carbohydrate Lasagna

Day 3

◊ Your choice of Day 3 muffins, pancakes, biscuits, or cooked cereals

◊ Puffed Millet cold cereal with oat milk or Filbert Milk

◊ Arrowhead Mills Bits of Barley cereal

◊ Fresh fruit

◊ Any planover Day 1 vegetable, fish, casserole, or soup

◊ Turkey eggs cooked your favorite way or float chicken eggs from Day 1

◊ Millet or Quinoa Pudding

Day 4

◊ Buckwheat Muffins, Pancakes, Bread, or Cereal

◊ Lentils with fresh side (uncured, unsmoked bacon)

◊ Split Pea Soup

◊ Stir-Fry Buckwheat and Vegetables

◊ Fresh fruit

◊ Any planover Day 4 vegetable, fish, casserole, or soup

◊ Sweet potato or butternut squash with flaxseed oil and pumpkin seeds

SNACK IDEAS

Day 1

◊ Broccoli buds
◊ Celery stick with almond butter
◊ Rice cake with tahini
◊ Teff, Kamut, or Spelt Muffins
◊ Teff, Kamut, or Spelt Crackers
◊ Puffed Kamut
◊ Almond-Sesame Granola Bars
◊ Amazing Sugarless Cookies
◊ Almonds or pecans
◊ Fresh fruit
◊ Pear Crisp

Day 2

◊ Green pepper strips
◊ Cucumber slices
◊ Zucchini slices
◊ Sliced tomatoes
◊ Amaranth Crackers
◊ Soy Bread
◊ Sunflower seeds
◊ Amaranth Carob Cookies
◊ Lemon Pudding
◊ Yogurt Delight I, II, III, or IV
◊ Grapefruit Spritzer Beverage
◊ Fresh fruit

Day 3

◊ Carrot sticks
◊ Cauliflower buds
◊ Quinoa Muffins
◊ Quinoa Crackers
◊ Filberts or walnuts
◊ Oatmeal Cookies
◊ Oat or Quinoa Biscuits
◊ Apple Salad
◊ Apple Oat or Quinoa Crisp
◊ Millet or Quinoa Pudding
◊ Fresh fruit

Day 4

◊ Cucumber slices
◊ Buckwheat Muffin
◊ Buckwheat Crackers
◊ Roasted soybeans or cashews
◊ Carob Cake Brownies
◊ Buckwheat Yeast-Free Bread with Rhubarb Jelly
◊ Blueberry Tofu "Cheesecake"
◊ Orange Buckwheat Cake
◊ Carob Pudding
◊ Carob Shake
◊ Spritzer—3 varieties

MEALS AWAY FROM HOME

Day 1

◊ Chicken Turnip Soup with crackers or muffin

◊ Day 1Tortilla (or Teff Griddle Bread) sandwich with Egg, Tuna, or Chicken Salad
Celery sticks

◊ Tortilla sandwich with planover Roast Chicken with fresh collards
Fresh broccoli or Coleslaw

◊ Easy Chicken Meal—take to work in a 1-quart slow cooker ready to plug in and cook for 4 hours

◊ All-in-One Salad for Day 1 (Tuna or Chicken) with crackers or muffin

◊ Any planover casserole if you have a microwave available to reheat it

Day 2

◊ Your choice of the many Day 2 soups with or without crackers

◊ Amaranth Tortilla (or Griddle Bread) with Shrimp Salad and lettuce
Cucumber slices

◊ Amaranth Tortilla with planover Roast Beef and tomato slices
Green pepper strips

◊ Your choice of the many Day 2 salads with or without crackers

◊ Potato Salad with planover roast beef

◊ Any planover spaghetti, lasagna, or stew, if you have a microwave available to reheat it

◊ All-in-One Salad for Day 2
with crackers or biscuit

Day 3

◊ Turkey Parsnip Soup with fresh spinach and crackers

◊ All-in-One Salad for Day 3 (Turkey or Salmon)
Qunioa Muffin

◊ Quinoa Tortilla (or Griddle Bread) sandwich with planover Roast Turkey and fresh spinach
Vegetable/Apple Salad

◊ Salmon Cauliflower Chowder
Carrot sticks

◊ Three Color Salad
Biscuit, muffin, or crackers

◊ Turkey Loaf Sandwich on Quinoa Griddle Bread with raw cauliflower

Day 4

◊ Beans and Beans
Cucumber slices

◊ Quick Bean Soup
Raw Jerusalem artichoke with Macadamia Nut "Mayo"

◊ Cucumber and Pea Salad with or without planover Roast Pork or fresh side (uncured, unsmoked bacon)

◊ Venison or Pork and Buckwheat Pasta Casserole

◊ Your choice of planover "Chili"
Raw Jerusalem artichoke with Macadamia Nut "Mayo"

◊ Lentil or Split Pea Soup with fresh side (uncured, unsmoked bacon) or planover Roast Pork
Zucchini slices (floated from Day 2)

◊ All-in-One Salad for Day 4
with crackers or biscuit

SPECIAL OCCASION MEALS

Day 1

◊ BRUNCH—Breakfast Brunch Squares
Celery stuffed with almond butter
Dacopa

◊ COMPANY—Oven Fried Chicken
Wild & Brown Rice with Herbs
Steamed broccoli and/or Coleslaw
Pear Custard
Dacopa

◊ COMPANY—Tuna or Chicken Cabbage Rolls
Kamut or Spelt Dinner Rolls
Celery sticks
Teff Pear Cake
Iced Pau D'Arco tea

◊ POTLUCK—Cold Oven Fried Chicken
Coleslaw
Sparkling mineral water

Day 2

◊ COMPANY—Grilled steak
Baked potato or Scalloped Potatoes
Lettuce with Creamy Italian Salad Dressing
Blueberry Tofu "Cheesecake" with Amaranth
Crust (moved from Day 4)
Dacopa

◊ COMPANY—Tofu Lasagna
Lettuce with Lemon/Oil Dressing
Carob Amaranth Cookies
Iced Pau D'Arco tea

◊ PICNIC—Grilled hamburgers with Quick
Catsup and Amaranth Bun
Potato Salad or Kidney Bean Salad
Tossed greens, cucumber, and tomato with
Creamy Italian Salad Dressing
Zucchini Amaranth Cookies
Sparkling mineral water

Day 1

◊ BRUNCH—Egg (Cheese-free) Soufflé
Carrot sticks
Biscuits with applesauce or Apple Crisp
Pau D'Arco Tea

◊ EASY THANKSGIVING FEAST—
Cranberry Spritzer (moved from Day 4)
Roasted Turkey
Dill "Stove Top" Stuffing (floated from Day 1)
Steamed broccoli, cauliflower, and/or carrots
(broccoli floated from Day 1)
Apple Salad
Kamut Dinner Rolls (floated from Day 1)
Butternut Squash Pie (squash moved from Day 4)
Dacopa
—I have prepared this menu with the addition
of canned cranberries and Libby's Pumpkin Pie
for family and company and they were all
delighted and "stuffed."

◊ LUNCHEON WITH GRANDPARENT—
Salmon Cauliflower Chowder
Raw carrot slices
Oat Granola Bar
Iced Pau D'Arco tea

Day 2

◊ CHILI FEAST—
Your choice of 1 or more of the following:
—Mexican Medley Beans
—Tomato-Free "Veggie" Chili
—Tomato-Free Chili
—Tomato-Free Vegetarian Chili
Raw vegetable floated or moved from other
Days
Blueberry Tofu "Cheesecake"
Dacopa

◊ COMPANY—Shrimp Tofu Lasagna
Carob Cake Brownies
Dacopa

continued from page 79

Purchase Your Supplies and Take the Plunge

Using your meal plan outline, make a list of the recipe ingredients needed. Decide where you need to purchase them. If you have a local health-food store that can provide all or at least some of the items, shop there. Or use Appendix C: Resources (page 250) to order the needed foods. Once you have all the foods on hand, set your day and say "I'm starting with Day 1 today." Put a smile on your face and be ready to go.

> **HH:** Plan meals, make a shopping list for needed items, and shop only from that list. Diverting from your shopping list without careful consideration (e.g., impulse buying) may cause you to divert from either the *Candida* control or rotational diet.

If you only planned for four days, on Day 3 of your rotation you will need to set up your plan for the next four days. Choose another set of Quick and Easy Meals to prepare for the next four days and purchase the needed foods. Do realize that if ordering foods is necessary, you will need to plan a little further in advance to keep your storehouse stocked. Then you can keep going on your rotation without waiting for food supplies.

Expand Your Horizon

As you plan the second set of four days using the Quick and Easy Meals, start thinking even further ahead to what you can prepare to make the Quick and Easy Meals with Advanced Planning. This may involve such steps as cooking extra Basic Buckwheat Groats to put in the freezer. Then you can prepare another delicious, quick and easy meal such as my favorite, Stir-Fry Buckwheat and Vegetables.

When planning the third set of four days, plan some time when you can prepare some of the Easy Meal ideas—many are quick as far as preparation time, but require some advanced planning on your part. This may involve rinsing and soaking beans or starting your breakfast cereal the night before. Or cut up vegetables the evening before to quickly start Easy Steak Stew in the slow cooker in the morning. As you look at the Easy Meal ideas, you will find many more examples that can add variety to your diet.

Congratulations, You Did It!

Now you are well on your way. You have completed 12 days of the rotational diet. You may have had to change your plans a little along the way, but you have started. Build from there. Repeat some of the same meals that you chose earlier. After all, think about it. How often did you really have that much variety before? What was your previous standard breakfast—cold cereal or hot cereal every morning? Or maybe you had an English muffin. Now you have a much greater variety in your diet. Even if you choose the same thing for each Day 1, 2, 3, or 4 on your rotation, you are having at least four different things for breakfast. For instance, perhaps you prepare Teff Pancakes every Day 1, Amaranth Cereal each Day 2, Creamy Millet Cereal (or better yet, Millet Pudding, which is delicious for breakfast) on Day 3, and lentils or, my favorite, Buckwheat Pancakes on Day 4. If you only chose these four breakfast items and repeated them every four days, you still have more variety in your breakfasts than the "normal" person has or that you once had.

As you continue using the rotational diet, you will become accustomed to the process that works for you in planning your meals and keeping your storehouse stocked. You will learn the techniques that will smooth out the process for you and make your life easier and full of wonderful, nourishing, and varied meals. And best of all, you will know that you are an essential part of the process in improving your health and your life.

Believe in yourself and keep up the good work!
You can do it!

9. RECIPE TABLE OF CONTENTS

SALADS AND DRESSINGS

Day 1

Day 2

Day 3

RECIPES IN BACK ISSUES OF CANARY CONNECT NEWS
(See page 271 for ordering information)

RECIPE	ISSUE #
Birthday Celebration Ideas	3
Cherub (Angel) Food Cake (Day 1 Recipe)	3
Fresh Strawberry Pie	2
Ice Cream	7
Pear Crisp	3
Quinoa Carob Cake	3
Picnic and Potluck Ideas	2
Pumpkin Pie—Several Variations	4
Rice Carob Cake	3
Rhubarb Crisp	2
Spinach/Water Chestnut Salad	4
Strawberry-Rhubarb Crisp	2
Sweetener-Free Butternut Squash Pie	4
Thanksgiving/Christmas/New Years Celebration Ideas	4
Traveling Food Ideas	6

SPACE FOR YOU TO WRITE IN RECIPES FROM FUTURE ISSUES OF CANARY CONNECT NEWS
(See page 271 for subscription information)

RECIPE	ISSUE #
Cheese-Free "Cheesy" Beans	
Dairy-free Whipped Topping	8
"Jello" substitute recipes	
Oven Fried Fish	
Yogurt Dip	

10. RECIPES

The information presented in this chapter includes recipes, an indication of each recipe's assigned Day in the rotation, and helpful hints for food preparation and time management. The recipes are divided into the following sections: Cereals and Basic Grain/Nongrains; Breads, Muffins, Pancakes; Main Dishes (Poultry, Red Meats, Italian, Seafood, Egg Cookery, Basic Bean Cookery, Soups, and Sandwiches); Salads and Dressings; Vegetables; Desserts; and Beverages and Miscellaneous. Vegetarian recipes are found throughout (see Recipe Table of Contents, pages 89–94).

About the Recipes

Many of the recipes emphasize taste and variety while also emphasizing "traditional" foods with slight changes. The recipes may list ingredients you are not accustomed to, but there are only slight changes in flavor and texture. Before you know it your taste buds will not crave or need the original version. In addition, the similarities will help other family members become accustomed to eating the same foods as you do, which will save you meal preparation time.

A low percentage of these recipes contain common food allergens such as wheat, corn, soy, egg, and dairy. Wheat is totally omitted unless you count the wheat alternatives, spelt and Kamut (see Chapter 5—Specialty Foods).

Since accurate measuring is important in recipe preparation, especially for baked goods and gluten-free grains, read the section on Accurate Measuring on pages 53–54 before preparing the recipes in this cookbook (this is essential if you are a beginning cook).

Three Color Salad
(Day 3 Recipe)

3/4 cup	Basic Quinoa (page 96), chilled
1 cup	carrot, shredded
about 1 cup	fresh spinach, torn

Before beginning a recipe, read through it to be sure you have all the ingredients. The ingredient and amount sections of the recipes are formatted with the amount column on the left and the ingredient column on the right with a small space in between. This allows you to move your finger down the list of ingredients very quickly to see if you have all of them before you start. If you do not usually keep a specific food product on hand or know you have a limited amount of an ingredient, a quick glance to the left will let you check the amount needed for the recipe. This format allows you to check the list quickly without constantly moving your eyes back and forth. When preparing a fraction of (1/2, 1/4) or multiplying (doubling, tripling) a recipe, first calculate the measurements of ingredients. Write these amounts in the margin of the cookbook or on a separate piece of paper.

The recipe instructions are written in detail using a numbered, step-by-step outline. At first glance, many of the recipes may appear long and complicated and as though they will take a great deal of time to prepare. Please take the time to read through the directions to discover that in reality they are an easy step-by-step guide to preparation. The numbered outline helps you refer back to each step as you are completing it. Once you complete a step you can then review the next step before beginning it.

Before beginning actual recipe preparation, set up your mixing and/or cooking area. This may involve clearing away extra items on your counter to make space. At first this may seem time consuming, but once you have practiced it a few times it will become "old hat" and you will have learned to appreciate the time that can be saved by using this simple technique. As you read through the recipe, take note of the various preparation items you will need. For example, for muffins you would include the following items in your mixing area: recipe, ingredients, dry cup measures, measuring spoons, 1-cup liquid measure, table knife for leveling ingredients, bowl for mixing, bowl to catch extra flour when measuring, rubber spatula, whisk, muffin tin, 1/4 cup dry measure for dipping batter evenly into tin, and small rubber spatula to remove batter from measure to tin. In the baking area you would include a preheated oven, timer, cooling rack, and sharp knife to assist in removing muffins from tins.

When setting out recipe ingredients in the mixing area, organize them in the order listed in the recipe (the order you will most likely use them). After using each item, set it aside or put it away. Use a table knife or other straight edge to mark your place in the recipe. These techniques will especially help if you are interrupted.

Basic Grain/Nongrain Cooking Chart

Grain/ Nongrain & (Assigned Day)	Amount of Grain/ Nongrain	Amount of Liquid	1/4 Teas. Sea Salt and/or Optional Seasonings	Simmering Time	Yield	Number of 1/2 Cup Servings
Amaranth (Day 2)	1 cup	2 cups		30 minutes	2 1/4 cups	4 1/2
Barley, hulled (Day 3)	1/2 cup	2 cups		45 minutes	2 1/4 cups	4 1/2
Buckwheat Groats, raw, unroasted (Day 4)	1 cup	2 cups	½ cup sliced leeks	15 minutes	3 cups	6
Kamut (Day 1)	1 cup	3 cups		2 1/2 hours	3 cups	6
Millet, hulled (Day 3)	1 cup	2 cups	½ teas. caraway seed	15 minutes	4 cups	8
Quinoa (Day 3)	1 cup	2 cups	1 teaspoon FOS	15 minutes	4 cups	8
Rice—Brown Basmati (Day 1)	1 cup	2 1/4 cups		30 minutes	3 cups	6
Rice—Brown Long-/ Short-Grain (Day 1)	1 cup	2 1/4 cups		30 minutes	3 cups	6
Rice—White Basmati (Day 1)	1 cup	2 cups		15 minutes	2 1/2 cups	5
Spelt (Day 1)	1 cup	3 cups		2 1/2 hours	3 cups	6
Wild Rice (Day 3)	1 cup	2 1/2 cups		40 minutes	3 cups	6

1. Before cooking grains/nongrains, they should be rinsed to remove dirt and hulls.

   * Place measurement of your choice of grain/nongrain in a 2 1/2 quart saucepan
   * Add 2 1/2–3 cups of water and gently stir with your hand or a spoon
   * Skim or gently pour off and discard immature grains, hulls, or other debris that floats to the surface
   * Drain off water. To drain smaller or medium-size grains, pour water and grain into a fine-mesh strainer. For larger grains such as spelt and Kamut, a small-holed colander can be used.
   * Keep in mind the porous or nonporous nature of the grain. Quick-cooking grains such as quinoa, buckwheat groats, and millet are very porous and should be rinsed very quickly to keep them from absorbing the rinsing water. If too much water is absorbed during rinsing, it can change the texture of the cooked product.
   * For quinoa the rinsing process should be repeated 2–3 times to remove the saponin layer (pg. 35).

2. Combine rinsed grain/nongrain and your choice of liquid (vegetable or meat broth or water) with 1/4 teaspoon or more sea salt and/or seasonings in a stainless steel, 2 1/2 quart saucepan.

3. Bring to boil on high. Cover. Reduce heat to between low and medium. Allow to simmer for designated cooking time as indicated above.

4. Remove from heat. Stir to fluff. Serve immediately or cover and allow to set 5 minutes.

Special Note: For best results, do not uncover or stir during cooking time. If it is necessary to check progress during cooking time, do so quickly to minimize steam loss. DO NOT STIR as this will disrupt the even cooking of the grain. If tasting for doneness, use a fork to gently remove a small amount from surface of the grain/nongrain. Different stoves and different pans may require adjustments in time, temperature, and amount of liquid used. The above cooking chart was developed using stainless steel waterless cookware.

Sondra's Thoughts: My family and I dearly love brown Basmati rice. The cooking fragrance is, "Mmmm! Who is cooking popcorn?"

Thorough preparation makes its own luck.
—Joe Poyer

HH: Handy Equipment

A set of various sizes of fine-mesh strainers are very useful for washing small-size to medium-size grains such as quinoa, amaranth, teff, millet, rice, and buckwheat. They can also be used to strain meat broth or sift carob powder.

Roasted Grains/Nongrains

(Roasting intensifies the delicious taste of the grain/nongrain and/or seasoning.)

1. Prepare as Basic Grain/Nongrain (previous page) except insert the following roasting steps after step 1.

2. Transfer rinsed and drained grain/nongrain to a cold, heavy-bottomed pan. I prefer a well-seasoned cast-iron skillet (see How to Season Cast Iron on page 59). For millet, add caraway seed (optional).

3. Place skillet on range. Turn burner to medium-high. Roast, stirring almost constantly, for first roasting time as indicated in chart below or until the grain/nongrain has become rather dry.

4. Lower heat to medium low and continue to roast, stirring constantly for second roasting time as indicted in chart below or until you can smell an intense aroma. Be careful not to burn it.

5. Transfer roasted grain/nongrain to boiling salted water and continue to cook as described on previous page.

Grain/Nongrain	1st Roasting Time	2nd Roasting Time
Amaranth	6 minutes	4 minutes
Millet	4 minutes	4 minutes
Buckwheat	6 minutes	4–9 minutes

Special Note: Roasted buckwheat groats, usually called Kasha, are available in health-food or other stores .

Personal Note: I have only tested this recipe with Amaranth, Millet, and Buckwheat, however any grain/nongrain may be roasted.

Basic Grain	Calories:	Protein (g)	Carbohydrate (g)	Fiber (g)	Total fat (g)	Saturated (g)	Cholesterol (mg)	Sodium (mg)
Amaranth	162	6.3	28.7	6.59	2.83	.72	0	128
Barley, hulled	145	5.1	30.1	7.07	.94	.2	0	123
Buckwheat Groats	112	3.6	22.4	3.15	.49	0	0	100
Kamut	87	4.7	21.3	2.67	.67	0	0	89
Millet, hulled	73	2.4	16.5	1.46	.73	0	0	67
Quinoa	79	2.8	14.6	1.25	1.23	.13	0	71
Rice—Brown Basmati	111	2.6	24.2	1.47	1.09	.25	0	91
Rice—Brown Long-/Short-Grain	115	2.7	23.8	1.86	.93	.19	0	94
Rice—White Basmati	147	3.1	32.6	.27	.5	.17	0	107
Spelt	87	4.7	21.3	5.33	.67	0	0	89
Wild Rice	108	4.2	22.6	1.32	.36	.05	0	92

Nutritional Information per 1/2 Cup Serving

Food Exchanges per 1/2 Cup Serving:

Amaranth: 1.8 Br .4 LM	Millet: .9 Br	Rice—White Basmati: 1.8 Br
Barley: 1.4 Br	Quinoa: .9 Br .2 LM	Spelt: 1 Br
Buckwheat Groats: 1.3 Br .2 Veg	Rice—Brown Basmati: 1.4 Br	Wild Rice: 1.3 Br
Kamut: 1 Br	Rice—Brown: 1.4 Br	

HH: Freeze leftover cooked grains/nongrains in single (or family–size) servings or in amounts needed for use in various recipes such as Three Color Salad, Millet or Quinoa Pudding, soups, and casseroles. Wide–mouth ½ pint or pint canning jars are an excellent size and stack relatively well in the freezer This preplanning makes more meals "Quick & Easy" and encourages you to stay on your rotational diet on those days that you need "A Break Today."

Slow Cooker Cereals

Grain/Nongrain & (Assigned Day)	Amount of Grain/ Nongrain and Flour	Amount of Liquid	Sea Salt	Optional	Yield (Servings)
Teff Cereal I (Day 1)	1/2 cup brown teff grain	2 cups water OR 1 3/4 cups water and 1/4 cup nut milk (see chart on next page)	1/4 teas.		2 cups (2)
Teff Cereal II (Day 1)	1/3 cup brown teff grain and 2 tablespoons teff flour		1/4 teas.		2 cups (2)
Kamut or Spelt Cereal (Day 1)	2/3 cup Kamut or spelt grain		1/4 teas.		2 cups (2)
Amaranth Cereal I (Day 2)	1/2 cup amaranth seed		1/4 teas.		2 cups (2)
Amaranth Cereal II (Day 2)	1/3 cup amaranth seed and 2 tablespoons amaranth flour		1/4 teas.		2 cups (2)
Millet Cereal I (Day 3)	1/3 cup hulled whole millet		1/4 teas.		2 cups (2)
Quinoa Cereal I (Day 3)	1/3 cup whole quinoa AND 2 tablespoons quinoa flour		1/4 teas.	1/4 teas. FOS	2–2 1/4 cups (2)
Quinoa Cereal II (Day 3)	3/8* cup whole quinoa		1/4 teas.	1/4 teas. FOS	2–2 1/4 cups (2)
Buckwheat Cereal I (Day 4)	1/3 cup buckwheat groats OR 1/3 cup purchased Cream of Buckwheat Cereal		1/4 teas.		2 cups (2)

*3/8 cup = 1/4 cup + 2 tablespoons

Special Note: Grind Kamut or spelt grain or unroasted buckwheat groats in a blender just long enough to prepare a coarse meal.

1. Rinse and drain teff, amaranth, millet, and quinoa grains prior to cooking. Quinoa should be rinsed two to three times to remove saponin layer (page 35).

2. Combine your choice of ingredients in a 1-quart size slow cooker. Cook overnight and awake to enjoy this ready-to-eat, mouth-watering cereal.

3. Stir before serving. Enjoy this cereal plain or serve with your choice of toppings listed in chart on next page.

Special Note: These recipes are too small to cook in a standard-sized slow cooker, but they can be easily doubled or tripled if desired. Cook on low if slow cooker has two settings.

Recipe idea from <u>Mastering Food Allergies</u> newsletters.

HH: Slow Cooker
I recommend the Rival brand Crockette slow cooker mainly because the crock insert lifts out of the heating base, which makes it easier to clean. This size is especially useful for slow cooker cereal.

HH: By taking a few minutes to start slow cooker cereal before you go to bed, you can wake up to a very easy, delicious breakfast as well as enjoy the wonderful aroma of cooked cereal when you enter your kitchen in the morning.

Cereal	Nut Milk Option	Serve With
Teff I & II	Sesame or Almond Milk (page 225)	1 tablespoon raspberries or Pear Sauce (page 230)
Kamut or Spelt	Sesame or Almond Milk (page 225)	1 tablespoon raspberries or Pear Sauce (page 230)
Amaranth I, II, & III	Brazil Nut Milk (page 225)	1 tablespoon Kiwi Sauce (page 229)
Millet I & II	Filbert Milk (page 225) or oat milk	2–3 tablespoons peeled, diced apple
Quinoa I, II, & III	Filbert Milk (page 225) or oat milk	2 tablespoons unsweetened applesauce and a dash of cinnamon
Buckwheat I & II	Cashew Milk (page 225) or soy milk	2 tablespoons blueberries and/or a few grains or stevia

Nutritional Information per Serving

Cereal (All analyses done without nut milk)	Calories:	Protein (g):	Carbohydrate (g):	Fiber (g):	Total fat (g):	Saturated (g):	Cholesterol (mg):	Sodium (mg):
Teff Cereal I	175	6.1	35.9	7	.88	0	0	275
Teff Cereal II	156	5.3	31.7	6.12	.83	0	0	274
Kamut Cereal	174	9.4	42.9	5.36	1.34	0	0	266
Spelt Cereal	174	9.4	42.9	10.72	1.34	0	0	266
Amaranth Cereal I & III	182	7.1	32.3	7.41	3.18	.81	0	277
Amaranth Cereal II	148	5.7	26.1	5.39	2.47	.53	0	273
Millet Cereal I	96	3.2	21.8	1.93	.96	0	0	266
Millet Cereal II	146	4.9	33.1	2.92	1.46	0	0	277
Quinoa Cereal I	138	4.7	25.3	2.23	2.13	.17	0	275
Quinoa Cereal II	121	4.2	22.3	1.91	1.88	.19	0	273
Quinoa Cereal III	159	5.6	29.3	2.51	2.47	.25	0	275
Buckwheat Cereal I	106	3.4	20.9	2.9	.46	0	0	276
Buckwheat Cereal II	120	3.9	23.8	3.3	.52	0	0	288

Food Exchanges per Serving:	Teff I: 2.2 Br	Teff II: 1.9 Br	Kamut or Spelt: 2 Br
Amaranth I & III: 2 Br .5 LM	Amaranth II: 1.6 Br .4 LM		Millet I: 1.2 Br
Millet II: 1.8 Br	Quinoa I: 1.6 Br .2 LM		Quinoa II: 1.3 Br .3 LM
Quinoa III: 1.8 Br .3 LM	Buckwheat I: 1.3 Br		Buckwheat: 1.5 Br

Stove Top Prepared Cereals

Grain/Nongrain & (Assigned Day)	Amount of Grain/ Nongrain and Flour	Amount of Liquid	Sea Salt	Simmering Time	Yield (Servings)
Amaranth Cereal III (Day 2)	1/2 cup amaranth seed	3 cups water*	1/4 teas.	35–45 minutes	1 3/4 cups (2)
Millet Cereal II (Day 3)	1/3 cup hulled whole millet	2 cups water*	1/8 teas.	20 minutes	1 cup (1)
Quinoa Cereal III (Day 3)	1/2 cup whole quinoa 1/4 teaspoon FOS (optional)	2 1/2 cups water*	1/4 teas.	20–25 minutes	2 1/2 cups (2)
Buckwheat Cereal II (Day 4)	3 tablespoons buckwheat groats OR 3 tablespoons purchased Cream of Buckwheat Cereal	1 1/2 cups water*	1/8 teas.	10 minutes	1 cup (1)

*May replace 1/4 cup of water with 1/4 cup of nut milk—see chart above.

Special Note: Grind buckwheat groats as described in Slow Cooker cereals.

1. In saucepan, heat water and salt to boiling.

2. Add your choice of grain/nongrain. Stir. Reduce heat. Cover and simmer for time indicated. Stir occasionally. Add more water if needed. Serve as described in chart above.

Oat Bran Cereal
(Day 3 Recipe)

1 cup	water
1/8 teaspoon	sea salt (or slightly less)
1/3 cup	oat bran

In saucepan, heat water and salt to boiling. Add oat bran, stir, reduce heat, and cook for 1–2 minutes. Stir constantly to prevent boiling over or sticking. Cover, remove from heat, and allow to set 3–5 minutes to thicken.

Yield: 1 cup   1 serving

Oatmeal Cereals
(Day 3 Recipe)

Rolled Oats in Microwave

2 2/3 cups	water
1/2 teaspoon	sea salt
1 1/2 cups	old fashioned rolled oats

In large glass saucepan, heat water and salt to boil. Add oats, stir, and cover. Cook in microwave for 4 minutes on cookmatic level 5 or medium power. Allow to set 3–5 minutes to thicken. Yield: 3 cups 3 servings

Rolled Oats Cooked on Stove Top

3 cups	water
1/2 teaspoon	sea salt
1 1/2 cups	old fashioned rolled oats

In large kettle, heat water and salt to boil. Add oats, stir, and reduce heat to medium–high. Cook at a gentle boil for 5 minutes, stirring constantly. Remove from heat, cover, and allow to set 3–5 minutes to thicken. Yield: 3 cups 3 servings

Serving Suggestion: Serve above cereals with oat milk, cinnamon, maple granules, and/or peeled, diced apple.

USED FOR ANALYSIS: Analysis does not include suggested serving ideas.

Oat Granola
(Day 3 Recipe)

1 cup	rolled oats
1 cup	oat bran
1/4 cup	walnuts, chopped
2 tablespoons	maples granules* (omit if use apple juice)
1/4 cup	water or apple juice concentrate
1/2 teaspoon	alcohol-free cinnamon extract (optional)
2 tablespoons	canola or walnut oil

1. In a mixing bowl, combine cereals, nuts, and maple granules. Add extract to liquid. Gradually add to dry ingredients while stirring to evenly coat mixture. Gradually add oil while stirring to evenly coat mixture.

2. Scatter mixture lightly in 9x13-inch baking pan. Bake in oven at 250ºF. for 45–60 min.

(stir every 10–15 minutes) until dry and slightly crunchy. Be careful not to burn. Cool completely. Store in glass jar in freezer.

Serving suggestions:
—Eat plain for crunchy snack or as topping for Vanilla Rice Dream (realize rice is a Day 1 food).
—Enjoy as breakfast cereal served with Filbert Milk (page 225) or oat milk.
—Enjoy as topping on microwave-baked apple. Peel and dice fresh apple. Place in serving bowl, sprinkle with cinnamon, top with granola, and cook in microwave on high for 1–2 minutes or until apple is tender. Serve warm.

Yield: 2 cups 4 servings

*Maple is an unassigned "Fun Food", see explanation on page 24.

USED FOR ANALYSIS: Maple granules not included in analysis.

Nutritional Information/Serving				
	Oat Bran	Oatmeal	Granola/Water	Granola/Apple Juice
Calories:	76	145	239	268
Protein (g):	5.4	6.1	8.2	8.3
Carbohydrate (g):	20.5	25.3	30	36.8
Fiber (g):	4.78	3.98	5.95	6.01
Total fat (g):	2.18	2.34	14.28	14.34
Saturated (g):	.41	.42	1.43	1.44
Cholesterol (mg):	0	0	0	0
Sodium (mg):	278	358	3	7
Food Exchanges	1 Br	1.5 Br .6 Fat	1.6 Br 1.6 Fat	1.6 Br .5 Fr 1.6 Fat

Wild & Brown Rice with Herbs*
(Day 1 Recipe)

1 cup	brown rice—Basmati, long- or short-grain
1/4 cup	wild rice*
2 1/2 cups	water
1/4 teaspoon	sea salt
1/4 teaspoon each	marjoram, rosemary, tarragon*
as desired	chopped pecans or almonds

Prepare same as Basic Grain/Nongrain (page 96). Simmer 40 minutes. Add nuts and stir at step 4.   Yield: 3 3/4 cups   serving size, 1/2 cup

Nutritional Information/Serving	
Calories:	140
Protein (g):	3.3
Carbohydrate (g):	24.3
Fiber (g):	1.99
Total fat (g):	3.51
Saturated (g):	.37
Cholesterol (mg):	0
Sodium (mg):	76
Food Exchanges/Serving	
1.4 Br .5 Fat	

*Wild rice is assigned to Day 3, omit it on Day 3 just before and after eating this recipe on Day 1. Also, realize these spices do break rotation but sometimes you need some spice in your life! To keep with rotation, omit tarragon from recipe and avoid spices in Mint Family (#73—see Herb and Spice listing on Day 2) on Days 2 and 4 before and after eating this recipe on Day 1.

Rice and Chard
(Day 1 Recipe)

Ingredients as in Basic Rice (page 96) or Wild & Brown Rice with Herbs (recipe above)	
1–2 cups	chard, washed, torn into small pieces, packed

Prepare same as Basic Grain/Nongrain (page 96) except lay chard on top of rice in step 2. Continue.

Special Notes: If your entire family does not prefer to eat the chard mixed with the rice, lay folded leaves on top instead of tearing into small pieces. After cooking, carefully remove chard to a separate serving dish before fluffing rice. I have prepared this recipe using only 1 cup of green chard without my husband realizing that the rice was cooked with chard. When cooked with chard, the rice does have a slightly stronger taste and a slight greenish-red color.

Basmati Rice Cereal/Dessert
(Day 1 Recipe)

3/4 cup	cooked Basmati rice (page 96)
1/2 cup	Almond Milk (page 225)
1 teaspoon	brown rice syrup
1 tablespoon	chopped almonds

In small saucepan, combine all ingredients and heat to serving temperature. Stir occasionally to prevent scorching. If desired, add a dash of cinnamon and more rice syrup. Serve for breakfast or dessert.

Yield: 1 serving

Nutritional Information/Serving	
Calories:	325
Protein (g):	8.8
Carbohydrate (g):	44.8
Fiber (g):	4.53
Total fat (g):	14.36
Saturated (g):	1.59
Cholesterol (mg):	0
Sodium (mg):	273
Food Exchanges/Serving	
2.2 Br .2 VLM 2.4 Fat	

Special Note: This recipe can be prepared with other cooked rice, but Basmati rice is my favorite.

Creamy Sweet Rice and Almonds*
(Day 1 Recipe)

1/2 cup	cooked rice
1/4 cup	Organic Original-Lite Rice Dream Beverage*
2 tablespoons	raw almonds, chopped

Combine in small saucepan, heat on low, stirring often. Serve warm for breakfast or dessert. Or combine ingredients and serve cold.

Yield: 1/2 cup   1 serving

Nutritional Information/Serving	
Calories:	246
Protein (g):	6.4
Carbohydrate (g):	48.1
Fiber (g):	3.16
Total fat (g):	10.86
Saturated (g):	1.14
Cholesterol (mg):	0
Sodium (mg):	204
Food Exchanges/Serving	
1.8 Br .5 VLM 1.8 Fat	

*Organic Original-Lite Rice Dream Beverage is made from organic brown rice with addition of safflower oil and sea salt. 1 cup = 130 calories. May not be a good non-dairy beverage to consume in large amounts for people on a *Candida*-control diet, especially in the first 2–4 weeks. Also, safflower oil does cause a break in rotation.

Kamut® or Spelt Yeast-Free Bread, "Hamburger" Buns, & Dinner Rolls
(Day 1 Recipe)

	Kamut	Spelt
water	1 1/2 cups	1 1/4 cups
sesame oil	1/4 cup	
flour	1/2 cup Kamut	5/8 cup Spelt (5/8cup = 1/2 cup +2 tablespoons)
baking soda	1 1/2 teaspoons	
unbuffered, corn-free Vit. C crystals	1/2 teaspoon	
flour	3 cups Kamut	3 cups Spelt
sea salt	3/4 teaspoon	

1. Preheat oven to 350ºF.
2. Oil and flour baking dish(es)—stainless steel does not need to be floured.

For Bread	9x5-inch loaf pan
For "Hamburger" Buns	3 (8-inch square) pans OR 2 (10x14-inch) baking sheets
For Dinner Rolls	8-inch square pan

3. Measure amount of water and oil in separate containers. Set aside.
4. In small bowl, whisk together first listing of flour, baking soda, and vitamin C. Set aside.
5. Set up mixer with dough hooks.* In large mixer bowl, whisk together second listing of flour and salt.
6. Add water. Mix on low (stir) speed to moisten flour. Then beat mixture on medium (mix) speed for 3 minutes. Dough will become cohesive and climb up hooks. Scrape sides with rubber spatula throughout mixing process.

> **HH:** A stand mixer, either KitchenAid or Oster brand, with dough hooks is recommended for these breads. You spend less energy and have more control mixing up the dough than if you were using a hand-held mixer.

7. Add oil and mix on medium to mix oil into dough, scraping sides.
8. Turn mixer to low, add set aside flour mixture and continue to mix (scraping sides) until all flour is moistened. Then beat for 30 seconds on medium.
9. For bread: Lightly oil hands. Shape into smooth-topped loaf. Place in prepared pan.

    For "hamburger" buns: Lightly oil hands. Divide dough as equally as possible into 12 portions. Shape each into flat portion approximately 3½–4 inches in diameter. Place in prepared pans, smooth side up. Reoil hands as needed.

    For dinner rolls: Lightly oil hands. Pinch off a 2-inch portion of dough. Shape into roll. Place in prepared pan, smooth side up. Repeat to prepare 16 rolls. Reoil hands as needed.
10. Bake according to time table below or until toothpick comes out clean when inserted into center:

	Kamut	Spelt
For Bread	55–60 minutes	50–55 minutes
For Hamburger Buns	15–18 minutes	13–15 minutes
For Dinner Rolls	25 minutes	20 minutes

11. For Bread and Buns: Within 5 minutes after baking, turn out bread and buns. Cool on wire rack. Slice bread into approximately ½-inch slices and slice buns in half horizontally when slightly or completely cooled.

    For Dinner Rolls: Cut rolls along divisions. Remove from pan, pull apart, and place in towel-lined basket. Serve warm.

continued . . .

12. May be frozen. Freeze bread with sheets of cellophane or wax paper between slices.

Yield: 1 loaf of bread (12 or 16 slices), 12 "hamburger" buns, or 16 dinner rolls

*If using mixer without dough hooks, reserve ½ cup flour from second listing and knead this reserved flour into dough by hand after step 7.

Recipe idea for Spelt Bread & Buns is from Allergy Cooking With Ease by Nicolette M. Dumke, p.47.

Nutritional Information per Slice, Bun, or Dinner Roll				
	Kamut/slice or bun	Kamut/slice or roll	Spelt/slice or bun	Spelt/slice or roll
Calories:	189	141	194	146
Protein (g):	6.1	4.6	6.3	4.8
Carbohydrate (g):	35.8	26.9	36.2	27.2
Fiber (g):	3.49	2.62	7.25	5.43
Total fat (g):	5.41	4.06	5.45	4.09
Saturated (g):	.64	.48	.64	.48
Cholesterol (mg):	0	0	0	0
Sodium (mg):	291	218	291	218
Food Exchanges per Slice, Bun, or Dinner Roll				
	1.8 Br .9 Fat	1.4 Br .7 Fat	1.9 Br .9 Fat	1.4 Br .7 Fat

Preparation of Muffin Pans, Baking Dishes/Sheets, and Loaf Pans for Baking

Use same oil as used in recipe. Use amount of oil recipe directs for oiling pan. If recipe does not give specific amount, begin with 1/4 teaspoon oil and add more only if needed. Follow recipe instructions for oiling pan. (Some recipes, such as crackers and pizza crust, emphasize spreading oil with fingertips so fingers become lightly coated with oil, which aids in spreading dough.) If recipe does not give specific instructions, follow procedure below.

- Use 1/4 teaspoon oil for 12 muffin cups
- Drop a very small amount of oil into each muffin cup. If you run out of oil before adding it to all 12 cups, do not add more oil until after completing next step.
- With your fingers or using a 2 inch square of cellophane (cut several at a time to have handy to use), spread oil around in each cup making sure to completely coat bottom and sides. Use extra oil remaining on cellophane square to coat any muffin cups that did not have oil in them.
- Add more oil if needed to coat each cup.
- If recipe calls for muffin pan to be floured, immediately sprinkle each cup with a small amount of flour. Again use same flour as used in recipe.
- Immediately shake muffin pan quickly from side to side and front to back to spread flour at least around the bottom. Amount of flour needed varies depending on kind used, but usually is 1 teaspoon for 6 muffin cups.
- Add more flour if needed.
- Remove excess flour, if any, by turning oiled and floured muffin pan upside down over sink and gently tapping on bottom.

Use same procedure with baking dishes except dribble 1/4 teaspoon oil around in pan before spreading.

Buckwheat Yeast-Free Bread and "Hamburger" Buns
(Day 4 Recipe)

1/2 cup	White Buckwheat Flour
2 teaspoons	baking soda
1/2 teaspoon	unbuffered, corn-free vit. C crystals
2 cups	White Buckwheat Flour (page 105)
1 teaspoon	guar gum
1/4 teaspoon	sea salt
1 1/2 cups	water
1/4 cup	safflower oil
1 cup	frozen blueberries, thaw but do not need to drain (optional)

Nutritional Information/Slice or Bun		
	w/o blueberries	w/ blueberries
Calories:	108	113
Protein (g):	2.6	2.6
Carbohydrate (g):	14.4	15
Fiber (g):	2.04	2.21
Total fat (g):	5.18	5.26
Saturated (g):	.55	.55
Cholesterol (mg):	0	0
Sodium (mg):	256	257
Food Exchanges/Slice or Bun		
without blueberries: .9 Br .9 Fat		
with blueberries: .9 Br .1 Fr .9 Fat		

1. Preheat oven to 350°F.
2. Oil and flour needed baking dish(es):

| For Bread | 9x5-inch loaf pan |
| For "Hamburger" Buns | 12 custard cups |

3. In small bowl, whisk together first listing of flour, baking soda, and vitamin C. Set aside.
4. Set up mixer with beaters. In large mixer bowl, whisk together second measurement of flour, guar gum, and salt.
5. Add water and oil. Mix on low (stir) speed to moisten flour. Then beat on medium (mix) speed for 2 minutes. Scrape sides with rubber spatula throughout mixing process.
6. Turn mixer to low, add set aside flour mixture and continue to mix (scraping sides) until all flour is moistened. Then beat for 30 seconds on medium speed.
7. Optional, add blueberries and stir.
8. <u>For bread</u>: Transfer batter to prepared loaf pan. Use a rubber spatula to spread evenly and smooth on top. Bake 55–60 minutes or until toothpick comes out clean when inserted into center of loaf.
   <u>For "hamburger" buns</u>: Portion rounded ¼ cup of batter into each custard cup. Spread evenly in dishes and smooth on top. Bake 40 minutes or until toothpick comes out dry when inserted into center of buns.
9. Within 5 minutes after baking, turn out bread or buns. Cool on wire rack. Slice bread and buns when slightly or completely cooled. May be frozen. Wrap bread individually or place sheets of cellophane or wax paper between slices.

Yield: 1 loaf of bread (12 slices) or 12 "hamburger" buns

Serving Suggestion: Great for breakfast served toasted or untoasted. Variation without blueberries, serve with Rhubarb Jelly (page 229).

HH: There are several ways to test doneness of baked goods.
- Insert toothpick into center of baked good such as bread or muffins. Toothpick will come out clean when baked good is done.
- For recipe such as Soy Bread, bread is done when it sounds hollow when lightly tapped on surface.

White Buckwheat Flour
How to Prepare Using Raw Buckwheat Groats
(Day 4 Recipe)

1. Before processing, sort through buckwheat groats to remove debris and immature grains which otherwise would float to top when washing groats. Also, pour groats by small amounts into fine-mesh strainer over sink and gently shake strainer to remove small debris.

2. Add groats to blender. Blend on highest speed until finely ground. To check progress, stop blender occasionally to feel consistency of flour with fingers. For best results blend 2 cups at a time for 1 1/2–2 minutes.

3. During processing time leave motor running, open lid insert of blender top, and use narrow spatula to loosen partially ground groats from sides of blender jar. Do not touch blade with spatula. (This step is not necessary if using KitchenAid blender.)

Yield: 2 cups of groats will yield almost 2 1/2 cups of flour

Special Note: For best nutritional value, flour should be used immediately or at least stored in glass jar in refrigerator or freezer.

Soy Bread
(Day 2 Recipe)

1 cup	soy flour*
1/2 cup	arrowroot starch
2 1/4 teaspoons	Featherweight brand baking powder**
1/2 teaspoon	sea salt
2 tablespoons	soy oil*
1 cup	water

Nutritional Information/Serving	
Calories:	109
Protein (g):	4.0
Carbohydrate (g):	11.2
Fiber (g):	.48
Total fat (g):	5.71
Saturated (g):	.82
Cholesterol (mg):	0
Sodium (mg):	136
Food Exchanges/Serving	
.6 Br .3 VLM .4 Fat	

1. Preheat oven to 375°F.

2. Oil and flour bottom and sides of an 8-inch square baking pan.

3. In mixing bowl, whisk together dry ingredients. Add water and oil. Mix thoroughly.

4. Transfer batter to prepared pan and spread evenly. Bake for 20 minutes. Bread is done when it sounds hollow when tapped on top surface.

5. Cool 5–10 minutes. Cut into 8 pieces (4x2). Serve for breakfast, with meal (with or without wheat-free gravy), or as snack. May be frozen.

Yield: 8 servings

*Soy is assigned to Day 4, so avoid eating soy on Day 4 just before and after serving this recipe on Day 2.

**At publication date, I have not been successful in preparing this bread using vitamin C crystals and baking soda as the leavening agents. For those allergic to potatoes, do realize that Featherweight brand baking powder contains potato starch.

Recipe idea from Rotational Bon Appetité! by Hayes & Maynard, p. 38.

Destiny is not a matter of chance;
it is a matter of choice.

Amaranth "Hamburger" Buns
(Day 2 Recipe)

1 3/4 cups	amaranth flour
1/2 cup	arrowroot starch
1 1/2 teaspoons	baking soda
3/8 teaspoon	unbuffered, corn-free vitamin C crystals
1/2 teaspoon	sea salt
3/4 cup	water
3 tablespoons	olive or sunflower oil

Nutritional Information/Bun		
	3 count	5 count
Calories:	452	271
Protein (g):	9.4	5.6
Carbohydrate (g):	63.2	37.9
Fiber (g):	5.39	3.24
Total fat (g):	17.02	10.21
Saturated (g):	1.83	1.10
Cholesterol (mg):	0	0
Sodium (mg):	985	591
Food Exchanges/Bun		
3 count: 4 Br .5 LM 2.6 Fat		
5 count: 2.4 Br .3 LM 1.6 Fat		

1. Preheat oven to 350°F.

2. Oil and flour desired baking dishes:
    3 Corning Grab-It bowls for Kaiser-size buns
    5 custard bowls for smaller-size buns (my preference)

3. In large bowl, whisk together dry ingredients. Make a "well" in the center.

4. In smaller bowl, whisk water and oil together for 15 seconds to disperse oil in water. Immediately add to dry ingredients and mix thoroughly with rubber spatula until evenly moistened (do not beat). Dough will be delicate and stiff but manageable.

5. To portion, first press dough evenly and firmly into bottom of mixing bowl. Then use knife to cut into 3 or 5 equal portions.

6. Lightly oil hands. Flatten each portion and place in prepared bowls. Bake 30 minutes or until toothpick comes out clean when inserted into the center of buns.

7. Within 5 minutes after baking, turn out buns. Cool completely on a wire rack. Slice each bun in half horizontally. If centers are slightly doughy, lightly toast halves in toaster or toaster oven. May be frozen. Best to thaw at room temperature. Thawing in microwave causes buns to become doughy.

Yield: 3 or 5 buns

Recipe idea from <u>Allergy Cooking with Ease</u> *by Nicolette M. Dumke, p. 48.*

HH: Several recipes include instructions to make a "well" in the center of combined dry ingredients. To accomplish this, distribute dry ingredients in mixing bowl so there is an indentation (hole) in the center where liquid ingredients will be poured.

HH: Curved-Sided Bowl
Mixing bowls can be found in two basic styles. A straight-sided bowl has a larger flat surface in the bottom before the side comes up at a right angle. A curved-sided bowl has a smaller flat surface at the center of the bottom before beginning a gradual curve that continues to the lip of the bowl. Curved-sided bowls work best for both stiffer doughs such as tortillas, crackers, and biscuits and thinner batters such as pancakes. Anchor Hocking 4-cup and 8-cup mixing-measures have nice curved sides, a pour spout, and a handle for comfort.

French Toast
(Day 1 Recipe)

1	egg, beaten
	OR 1 egg yolk, beaten with 1 tablespoon water
1/8 teaspoon	sea salt
dash	cinnamon (optional)
2 slices	your choice of purchased yeast-free bread
	or homemade bread

Nutritional Information/Serving	
Calories:	115
Protein (g):	7.8
Carbohydrate (g):	16.3
Fiber (g):	2
Total fat (g):	2.2
Saturated (g):	.78
Cholesterol (mg):	83
Sodium (mg):	275
Food Exchanges/Serving	
1 Br .4 LM .2 Fat	

1. Preheat griddle. Griddle is hot enough when water dances when sprinkled on surface. Lightly oil after preheating. I use a well-seasoned cast-iron griddle (see How to Season Cast Iron, page 59).

2. Beat egg (or yolk and water), salt, and cinnamon in shallow flat-bottom bowl. Dip bread slices to coat on both sides. Cook 2 minutes on each side until golden brown.

3. Serve with suggested Day 1 toppings, see pancake recipe (page 119).

Yield: 2 servings

USED FOR ANALYSIS: French Meadow Kamut Bread and whole egg

Dill "Stove-Top" Stuffing
(Day 1 Recipe)

1 tablespoon	sesame oil
1 cup	celery, diced
	OR 1 1/2 cups cabbage, finely chopped
	OR 1/2 cup celery, diced and 3/4 cup
	cabbage, finely chopped
1 teaspoon	sea salt
1 teaspoon	dill weed
1/4 cup	pecan pieces
2 cups	quick cooking Kamut or spelt flakes*
1 cup	Chicken Broth (page 130)
1 cup	water

Nutritional Information/Serving		
	Kamut	Spelt
Calories:	113	107
Protein (g):	3.4	3.3
Carbohydrate (g):	15.3	15.6
Fiber (g):	2.43	2.57
Total fat (g):	4.49	4.60
Saturated (g):	.45	.45
Cholesterol (mg):	0	0
Sodium (mg):	280	280
Food Exchanges/Serving		
Kamut: .9 Br .1 Veg .8 Fat		
Spelt: .8 Br .1 Veg .8 Fat		

1. In skillet over medium heat, sauté celery in oil until just tender. Stir often. (Omit this step if only using cabbage.)

2. Add salt, dill weed, and pecans and stir to evenly distribute spices.

3. Add flakes. Toast flakes over medium heat for approximately 5 minutes. Stir often.

4. Add liquids and cabbage, if using. Stir. Cover. Allow stuffing to cook on medium heat for 5 minutes or until flakes are done and liquid is absorbed. Stir and serve.

Yield: 4 cups   8 servings

*Recipe was developed using quicker-cooking brands of spelt or Kamut flakes, e.g., The Grain Place.

This recipe has been favorite a of my guests for Thanksgiving Dinner for years.

Dropped Biscuits

Spelt or Kamut Biscuits (Day 1 Recipe)

1 1/4 cups	spelt or Kamut flour
1/2 teaspoon	baking soda
scant 1/8 teaspoon	sea salt
1/8 teaspoon	unbuffered, corn-free vitamin C crystals
1/2 to 5/8* cup	water—use 1/2 cup for spelt use 5/8* cup for Kamut
1 tablespoon	sesame oil

*(5/8 cup = 1/2 cup + 2 tablespoons)

Amaranth Garbanzo Bean Biscuits (Day 2 Recipe)

1/2 cup	amaranth flour
1/4 cup	garbanzo bean flour
1/4 cup	arrowroot starch
3/8 teaspoon	baking soda
1/8 teaspoon	sea salt
1/8 teaspoon	unbuffered, corn-free vitamin C crystals
1/3 cup	water
2 teaspoons	sunflower or olive oil

Quinoa Biscuits (Day 3 Recipe)

3/4 cup	quinoa flour
1/4 cup	tapioca starch
3/8 teaspoon	baking soda (3/8 teaspoon = 1/4 teaspoon + 1/8 teaspoon)
scant 1/8 teaspoon	sea salt
1/8 teaspoon	unbuffered, corn-free vitamin C crystals
1 teaspoon	FOS (optional)
1/2 teaspoon	ground cinnamon (optional)—great for a dessert biscuit
1/3 cup	water
2 teaspoons	canola oil

Oat Biscuits (Day 3 Recipe)

1 cup	oat flour
1/2 teaspoon	baking soda
1/8 teaspoon	sea salt
1/8 teaspoon	unbuffered, corn-free vitamin C crystals
1/2 teaspoon	ground cinnamon (optional)—great for a dessert biscuit
1/3 cup	water
2 teaspoons	canola oil

continued . . .

Serve biscuits for breakfast or snacks, with casseroles or other meals, or as dessert topped with unsweetened pear or applesauce seasoned with cinnamon.

Let us train our minds to desire what the situation demands.

Seneca

Buckwheat Biscuits   (Day 4 Recipe)

1 1/4 cups	White Buckwheat Flour (page 105)
1/2 teaspoon	baking soda
1/8 teaspoon	sea salt
1/8 teaspoon	unbuffered, corn-free vitamin C crystals
5/8 cup	water (5/8 cup = 1/2 cup + 2 tablespoons)
1 tablespoon	safflower oil

Directions for Dropped Biscuits

1. Preheat oven to 400°F.
2. In a mixing bowl, whisk together your choice of dry ingredients. Make "well" in center.
3. Add water and oil. Stir with rubber spatula or fork until dough clumps into ball and flour is well mixed.
4. Drop batter from teaspoon onto lightly oiled stainless steel baking sheet. Bake for 10 minutes.

Yield: Amaranth Garbanzo Bean—10 / Buckwheat—12 / Kamut—12
Oat—9 / Quinoa—8 / Spelt—12

Directions for Spelt and Kamut Rolled Biscuits

Perform steps 1–3 as above except start with 1/4 cup additional flour (total 1 1/2 cups).

4. Knead dough lightly on a floured board using 1–2 tablespoons additional flour. Pat out to 1/2 inch thick using more flour if or as needed.
5. Cut with biscuit cutter or drinking glass (2 1/4 inch diameter). Form together remaining dough, pat out, and cut biscuits. Repeat to use all dough.
6. Bake on ungreased stainless steel baking sheet for 12 minutes.

Yield: 9 biscuits

HH: Dropped biscuits are the quickest bread form—they take only 5–6 minutes to prepare and 10 minutes to bake.

Nutritional Information per Rolled Biscuit		
	Kamut	Spelt
Calories:	106	106
Protein (g):	3.8	3.8
Carbohydrate (g):	22.2	21.7
Fiber (g):	2.17	4.34
Total fat (g):	2.06	2.06
Saturated (g):	.21	.21
Cholesterol (mg):	0	0
Sodium (mg):	94	94
Food Exchanges per Rolled Biscuit		
	1.1 Br .3 Fat	1.1 Br .3 Fat

Nutritional Information per Dropped Biscuit						
	Kamut	Spelt	Amaranth Garbanzo Bean	Oat	Quinoa	Buckwheat
Calories:	63	63	52	15	76	44
Protein (g):	2.2	2.18	1.4	.3	1.5	1.3
Carbohydrate (g):	12.8	12.8	8.4	1.1	12.5	7.2
Fiber (g):	1.25	2.50	.91	.17	.86	1.02
Total fat (g):	1.45	1.45	1.31	1.11	1.89	1.45
Saturated (g):	.16	.16	.11	.09	.08	.17
Cholesterol (mg):	0	0	0	0	0	0
Sodium (mg):	70	70	52	100	93	56
Food Exchanges per Dropped Biscuit						
	.7 Br .2 Fat	.7 Br .3 Fat	.5 Br .2 Fat	.1 Br .2 Fat	.8 Br .2 Fat	.4 Br .2 Fat

Crackers

Spelt or Kamut Crackers (Day 1 Recipe)

1 1/4 cup	spelt or Kamut flour
1/2 teaspoon	baking soda
1/4 teaspoon	sea salt
1/4 teaspoon	unbuffered, corn-free vitamin C crystals
1/3 to 1/2 cup	water— use 1/3 cup for Spelt Crackers / use 1/2 cup for Kamut Crackers
2 tablespoons	sesame oil

Teff Crackers (Day 1 Recipe)

1 1/8 cups	brown teff flour (1/8 cup = 2 tablespoons)
1 teaspoon	baking soda
1/4 teaspoon	sea salt
1/4 teaspoon	unbuffered, corn-free vitamin C crystals
2 tablespoons	hulled sesame seeds or 1 tablespoon additional flour
1/2 cup	water
2 tablespoons	sesame oil

Amaranth Crackers (Day 2 Recipe)

1 cup	amaranth flour
1/2 cup	arrowroot starch
1/3 cup	ground sunflower seeds (ground in food processor)
	OR add 3 tablespoons additional amaranth flour
1 teaspoon	baking soda
1/4 teaspoon	sea salt
1/4 teaspoon	unbuffered, corn-free vitamin C crystals
1/2 cup	water
2 tablespoons	sunflower or olive oil

Quinoa Crackers (Day 3 Recipe)

1 1/4 cups	quinoa flour
1/3 cup	tapioca starch flour or cornstarch
2 teaspoons	caraway seeds
1 teaspoon	baking soda
1/4 teaspoon	sea salt
1/4 teaspoon	unbuffered, corn-free vitamin C crystals
1/2 cup	water
2 tablespoons	canola oil

Rye Crackers (Day 3 Recipe)

1 1/3 cups	rye flour
2 teaspoons	caraway seeds
1/2 teaspoon	baking soda
1/4 teaspoon	sea salt
1/4 teaspoon	unbuffered, corn-free vitamin C crystals
1/2 cup	water
2 tablespoons	canola oil

Buckwheat Crackers (Day 4 Recipe)

1 1/3 cups	White Buckwheat Flour (page 105) (If not using pumpkin seeds, adjust this amount to 1 1/2 cups.)
1 teaspoon	baking soda
1/4 teaspoon	sea salt
1/4 teaspoon	unbuffered, corn-free vitamin C crystals
3 tablespoons	ground pumpkin seeds (ground in food processor) (Optional: See note with White Buckwheat Flour listing above.)
1/2 cup	water
2 tablespoons	safflower oil

1. Preheat oven to 350ºF.

2. In large mixing bowl, whisk together your choice of dry ingredients and seeds, if indicated. Make "well" in center.

3. Add water and oil. Stir with rubber spatula or fork until dough clumps into ball and flour is well mixed. If dough is rather sticky, add small amounts of additional flour up to 1 more tablespoon. Mix after each addition.

4. Spread 1 teaspoon of oil on 10x14 inch baking sheet with fingers to within one inch of edges. As dough is rolled out, it will push oil to edges.

HH: Before beginning cracker preparation, set up three work stations with the following items in each.

1. Mixing Area—recipe, ingredients, dry cup measures, measuring spoons, 1-cup liquid measure, table knife for leveling ingredients, bowl for mixing, bowl to catch extra flour when measuring, rubber spatula, whisk.

2. Rolling Area—baking sheet, rolling pin, pizza cutter and/or sharp knife, table fork and knife, flour and spoon which can be moved from mixing area when needed.

3. Baking Area—preheated oven, timer, cooling rack, metal spatula.

5. Transfer dough to center of baking sheet. Press dough out evenly in all four directions until it cannot be spread further with your fingers, maintain rectangular shape.

6. Lightly dust rolling pin with flour and roll dough out from center to edges. Be sure to press evenly in all directions to keep dough uniform thickness.

7. If needed, use dull back side of table knife to press edges of dough to maintain rectangular shape. Continue rolling and shaping until dough is about ¼ inch thick and fills baking sheet. To help reduce the possibility of extra-thin dough edge, use back side of table knife to gently push all four edges of dough to make edge thickness uniform with remaining dough.

8. Using a pizza cutter, cut dough into squares. Move pizza cutter slowly with a back and forth motion to help avoid tearing dough if cutter goes directly across a seed (see diagram). Cut (a) in half along length, (b) each half in half, and (c) each fourth in thirds to create 12 strips. Next cut (d) in half along dough width, (e) each half in half, and (f) each fourth in half to create 8 sections and 96 individual crackers. Then use a sharp knife to be sure each cut on the outer edge is completely separated.

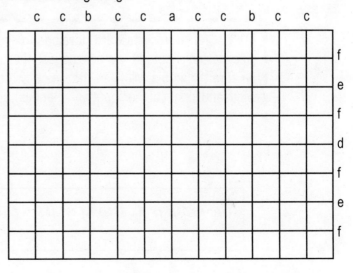

continued . . .

Crackers (continued)

9. Prick holes in each square with fork. Salt tops if desired.

10. Bake for first baking time according to chart (at right). Carefully remove outer circle of crackers if they are crispy. Return remaining crackers to oven for second baking time. **TURN OFF OVEN** and crisp crackers further during third baking time.

11. Place baking sheet on wire rack to cool. After cool, remove crackers and store in freezer. A wide-mouth quart jar works perfectly. No need to thaw, eat straight from freezer.

Yield: 96 crackers
(12 servings, 8 crackers each)

Cracker	1st	2nd	3rd
Amaranth	25 minutes	5 minutes	15 minutes
Buckwheat	25 minutes	5 minutes	15 minutes
Quinoa	23 minutes	5 minutes	15 minutes
Kamut	22 minutes	5 minutes	10 minutes
Rye	35 minutes	5 minutes	15 minutes
Spelt	17 minutes	5 minutes	10 minutes
Teff	20 minutes	5 minutes	20 minutes

Nutritional Information/Serving (8 crackers)							
	Kamut	Spelt	Teff	Amaranth	Quinoa	Rye	Buckwheat
Calories:	73	73	89	98	79	66	66
Protein (g):	2.2	2.2	2.2	2.3	1.4	2.3	1.8
Carbohydrate (g):	12.8	12.5	12.4	11.8	11.2	9	7.6
Fiber (g):	1.25	2.5	2.4	1.09	.9	1.9	1.32
Total fat (g):	2.58	2.58	3.39	4.74	3.01	2.78	3.58
Saturated (g):	.32	.32	.43	.47	.16	.16	.46
Cholesterol (mg):	0	0	0	0	0	0	0
Sodium (mg):	97	97	151	150	153	97	151

Food Exchanges/Serving (8 crackers)	
Kamut: .7 Br .4 Fat	Quinoa: .7 Br .4 Fat
Spelt: .7 Br .4 Fat	Rye: .6 Br .4 Fat
Teff: .8 Br .6 Fat	Buckwheat: .4 Br .1 VLM .6 Fat
Amaranth: .7 Br .1 VLM .1 LM .8 Fat	

HH: Cracker recipes were developed using a 10x14 inch stainless steel baking sheet with low side edges. If your baking sheet has sides, be sure rolling pin will fit all the way down onto surface on both the width and length of the sheet and that the handles clear the edge.

The brain is as strong as its weakest think.
Eleanor Doan

Soy Lasagna Noodles*
(Day 4 Recipe)

3/4 cup	soy flour (amount of flour to start)
1/4 teaspoon	sea salt
1/4 teaspoon	garlic powder
1/2 teaspoon	leaf oregano
1/4 teaspoon	basil*
1/4 cup	water
1/2 cup	soy flour (amount needed for rolling)

Nutritional Information/Recipe	
Calories:	466
Protein (g):	40.4
Carbohydrate (g):	35.0
Fiber (g):	2.65
Total fat (g):	22.04
Saturated (g):	3.20
Cholesterol (mg):	0
Sodium (mg):	548
Food Exchanges/Recipe	
2.1 Br 3.2 VLM 4 Fat	

1. In a bowl, whisk together 3/4 cup flour and seasonings.
2. Add water. Stir with rubber spatula or fork until dough clumps together into a moist ball.

Noodles for circular baking dishes:

3. Divide dough into eight (8) portions.
4. Lightly flour rolling pin and rolling surface. Pat dough portion into circular shape, then roll out noodle by pressing evenly from center out in all directions and working to keep noodle as round as possible. Keep dough well floured on both sides using approximately 1 tablespoon of flour per noodle. When needed, turn dough over by loosening with a spatula before flipping. Finished noodle will be thin and 4 1/2 inches in diameter, the size of a Grab-It bowl. Using a pastry brush, gently brush both sides of noodle to remove excess flour.

OR

Noodles for square or rectangular baking dishes:

3. Divide dough into four (4) portions.
4. Lightly flour rolling pin and rolling surface. Pat dough portion into rectangular shape, then roll out noodle by pressing from center out in all directions and working to keep noodle as rectangular as possible. Keep dough well floured on both sides using approximately 2 tablespoons of flour per noodle. When needed, turn dough over by loosening with spatula before flipping. Finished noodle will be thin and approximately 5x10 inches, one half the size of a Corning 10-inch casserole dish.
5. Place each noodle between layers of cellophane wrap or wax paper. Store in a cellophane or plastic bag in the freezer until needed for lasagna recipes on both Day 2 and 4.

Yield: 8 noodles (each 4 1/2 inches in diameter) OR 4 noodles (each 5x10 inches)

*Basil is usually eaten on Day 2, omit eating it on Day 2 just before and after eating basil in this recipe on Day 4.

Laughter is the sun that drives winter from the human face.
—*Victor Hugo*

*Your talent is God's gift to you.
What you do with it is your gift to God.*

Kamut or Spelt Muffins (Day 1 Recipe)

6 Muffins	12 Muffins	YIELD
1 1/4 cups	2 1/2 cups	Kamut or spelt flour
1 teaspoon	2 teaspoons	baking soda
1/8 teaspoon	1/4 teaspoon	sea salt
1/4 teaspoon	1/2 teaspoon	unbuffered, corn-free vitamin C crystals
2 tablespoons	1/4 cup	sesame oil

For Kamut:
1 cup – 1 Tbsp.	1 7/8 cups	pear juice or water (7/8 cup = 3/4 cup + 2 tablespoons)

For Spelt:
3/4 cup	1 1/2 cups	pear juice or water

Optional:
1/2 cup	1 cup	raspberries, fresh or frozen, thawed, drained

Teff Muffins (Day 1 Recipe)   YIELD: 6 muffins

1 cup	brown teff flour
1 teaspoon	baking soda
1/4 teaspoon	sea salt
1/4 teaspoon	unbuffered, corn-free vitamin C crystals
3/4 cup	water
2 tablespoons	sesame oil
1	egg (optional) OR 1 tablespoon ground flaxseed and 1/4 cup water

Special Note: I cannot tell any difference in taste between teff muffins without egg, with egg, or with flaxseed. However, muffins without egg seem to crumble when frozen and reheated. Flax variation crumbles a little less than those without egg. Also, flax and egg variations raise more when baking.

Optional:
1/2 cup	1 cup	raspberries, fresh or frozen, thawed, drained

Quinoa Applesauce Muffins (Day 3 Recipe)

6 Muffins	12 Muffins	YIELD
7/8 cup	1 3/4 cups	quinoa flour (7/8 cup = 3/4 cup + 2 tablespoons)
1/4 cup	1/2 cup	tapioca starch OR cornstarch
1 teaspoon	2 teaspoons	baking soda
1/4 teaspoon	1/2 teaspoon	sea salt
1 teaspoon	2 teaspoons	ground cinnamon (optional)
1/4 teaspoon	1/2 teaspoon	unbuffered, corn-free vitamin C crystals
1/2 cup	1 cup	unsweetened applesauce
1/3 cup	2/3 cup	water
1 tablespoon	2 tablespoons	canola oil

Quinoa Muffins (No Fruit) (Day 3 Recipe)

6 Muffins	12 Muffins	YIELD
1 cup	2 cup	quinoa flour
1/4 cup	1/2 cup	tapioca starch OR cornstarch
1 teaspoon	2 teaspoons	baking soda
1/4 teaspoon	1/2 teaspoon	sea salt
1 teaspoon	2 teaspoons	ground cinnamon (optional)
1/4 teaspoon	1/2 teaspoon	unbuffered, corn-free vitamin C crystals
3/4 cup	1 1/2 cups	water
2 tablespoons	1/4 cup	canola oil

Buckwheat Muffins (Day 4 Recipe)

6 Muffins	12 Muffins	YIELD
1 cup	2 cups	White Buckwheat Flour (page 105)
1 teaspoon	2 teaspoons	baking soda
1/4 teaspoon	1/2 teaspoon	sea salt
1/4 teaspoon	1/2 teaspoon	unbuffered, corn-free vitamin C crystals
7/8 cup	1 3/4 cups	water (7/8 cup = 3/4 cup + 2 tablespoons)
1/2 teaspoon	1 teaspoon	guar gum
2 tablespoons	1/4 cup	safflower oil
1/2 cup	1 cup	blueberries, fresh or frozen, thawed, drained (optional)

Variation: For a hint of orange flavor, add 2 teaspoons of alcohol-free orange extract with the liquid ingredients.

Optional for Teff Muffins: If using flaxseed egg substitute, whisk flaxseed with water in small saucepan. Bring to boil, reduce heat to medium-high, and boil for 1–2 minutes until consistency of egg white (however, color will not be like egg white). While boiling mixture, stir with whisk almost continuously. Set aside to cool.

1. Preheat oven (see chart below).

2. Oil and flour the bottom and sides of muffin cups.

3. In mixing bowl, whisk together your choice of dry ingredients (except guar gum—see special note).

> SPECIAL NOTE: Add guar gum to liquid ingredients and whisk well before adding to dry ingredients.

4. Add liquids, fruit sauce, egg (or egg substitute), and/or oil. Stir just to moisten dry ingredients. Gently smash larger lumps against side of bowl. Smaller lumps will bake out.

5. Optional: Fold in fruit.

6. Equally portion batter into prepared muffin cups (see chart for amount/cup). Bake according to chart.

7. Cool muffins in pan(s) on wire rack for 5 minutes. Take a sharp, thin knife around edges of muffins to loosen from sides. Turn out muffins. Best served warm. May be frozen. Reheat in microwave.

Muffin	Oven Temperature	Portion of Batter/Muffin Cup	Baking Time
Kamut/Spelt	350°F.	slightly more than 1/4 cup	20–25 minutes
Kamut/Spelt with Raspberries	350°F.	almost 1/3 cup	25–27 minutes
Teff	400°F.	slightly more than 1/4 cup	20 minutes
Quinoa Applesauce	375°F.	slightly more than 1/4 cup	20–22 minutes
Quinoa (No Fruit)	375°F.	slightly less than 1/4 cup	20–22 minutes
Buckwheat	375°F.	slightly more than 1/4 cup	23–25 minutes
Buckwheat with Blueberries	375°F.	almost 1/3 cup	24–25 minutes

Nutritional Information/Muffin						
	Kamut	Spelt	Teff w/o Egg or Egg Sub	Quinoa Applesauce	Quinoa (No Fruit)	Buckwheat
Calories:	165	161	147	126	149	95
Protein (g):	4.4	4.4	3.3	2.4	2.7	2
Carbohydrate (g):	30.3	28.7	21.3	21.4	20.9	11.5
Fiber (g):	2.5	4.99	4	1.86	1.72	1.63
Total fat (g):	5.17	5.17	5.21	3.44	5.88	5.05
Saturated (g):	.64	.64	.64	.16	.32	.52
Cholesterol (mg):	0	0	0	0	0	0
Sodium (mg):	258	259	302	305	305	300

USED FOR ANALYSIS: Figures not available for guar gum. See analysis figures to add for fruit on page 116.

Food Exchanges/Muffin	
Kamut: 1.3 Br .3 Fr .9 Fat	Quinoa Applesauce: 1.2 Br .1 LM .2 Fr .4 Fat
Spelt: 1.3 Br .2 Fr .9 Fat	Quinoa (No Fruit): 1.3 Br .1 LM .9 Fat
Teff: 1.3 Br .9 Fat	Buckwheat: .7 Br .9 Fat

The Nutritional Information and Food Exchanges given at right are for blueberries and raspberries added to the Buckwheat, Kamut, Spelt, and/or Teff Muffin recipes on pages 114–115. These figures should be ADDED TO the figures given for the individual muffins.

Nutritional Information/Muffin		
Fruit Only	Blueberries	Raspberries
Calories:	4.3	5
Protein (g):	0	.08
Carbohydrate (g):	1	1.25
Fiber (g):	.17	.58
Total fat (g):	.08	.08
Saturated (g):	0	0
Cholesterol (mg):	0	0
Sodium (mg):	0	0
Food Exchanges/Muffin		
	.1 Fr	.1 Fr

HH: To fix muffins without fruit for yourself as well as with fruit for your family, fill muffin cups for desired quantity without fruit then stir fruit into remaining batter for others to enjoy.

Oat Bran Muffins
(Day 3 Recipe)

6 Muffins	12 Muffins	YIELD
1 1/2 cups	3 cups	oat bran
1/4 cup	1/2 cup	raisins (optional)
1 1/2 teaspoons	1 tablespoon	baking powder (remember baking powder contains corn)
1/4 teaspoon	1/2 teaspoon	salt
3/4 cup	1 1/2 cups	unsweetened apple juice
2 tablespoons	1/4 cup	canola oil
1	2	eggs*

OR EGG SUBSTITUTE (my preference)

1 tablespoon	2 tablespoons	ground flax seed
3 tablespoons	3/8* cup	water

*(3/8 cup = 1/4 cup + 2 tablespoons)

Nutritional Information/Muffin		
	Without Raisins	With Raisins
Calories:	124	142
Protein (g):	5	5.2
Carbohydrate (g):	19.6	24.4
Fiber (g):	3.65	3.86
Total fat (g):	6.96	6.99
Saturated (g):	.87	.88
Cholesterol (mg):	31	31
Sodium (mg):	223	224
Food Exchanges/Muffin		
Without Raisins: .7 Br .1 LM .3 Fr 1 Fat		
With Raisins: .7 Br .1 LM .5 Fr 1 Fat		

Optional Step: If using flaxseed for egg substitute, whisk flaxseed with water in small saucepan. Bring to boil, reduce heat to medium high, and boil for 1–2 minutes until the consistency of egg white (however, color will not be like egg white). While boiling mixture, stir with whisk almost continuously. Set aside to cool.

1. Preheat oven to 425°F..
2. Oil and flour the bottom and sides of muffin cups.
3. In mixing bowl, whisk together dry ingredients.
4. Add apple juice, egg (or egg substitute), and/or oil. Stir just to moisten dry ingredients. Allow to set approximately 5 minutes to absorb liquid.
5. Optional: Fold in raisins.
6. Stir batter again and fill prepared muffin cups with 1/3 cup batter. Cups will be very full. Muffins do not raise and are rather heavy, but are delicious, moist, and filling. For the raisinless version, fill each muffin cup with slightly less than 1/3 cup batter. Bake 12–15 minutes.
7. Cool muffins in pan(s) on wire rack for 5 minutes. Take a sharp, thin knife around edges of muffins to loosen from sides. Turn out muffins. Best served warm. May be frozen. Reheat in microwave.

Special Notes: As a person with CRC, I cannot tolerate dried fruits, so I prepare the recipe without raisins. After filling muffin cups for desired quantity of muffins without raisins, stir some raisins into remaining batter for others to enjoy. If muffins are too sweet, replace 1/4–1/2 cup of apple juice with water. Give Oat Bran Muffins as Christmas gifts to neighbors and family.

*Eggs are assigned to Day 1. Omit them on Day 1 just before and after eating this version on Day 3.

Stuffing*
(Day 1 or 3 Recipe)

	neck and giblets from 1 roasting hen or turkey
2 1/2 cups	water
1/2 teaspoon	sea salt
4 cups	your choice of yeast-free purchased
	or homemade bread, cubed, slightly dried
1 1/4 cup	celery, diced (also include celery leaves)
1/2 cup	onion, diced*
1/2 cup	sesame oil
	OR 1/2 cup unsalted butter, melted (1 stick)*
1/4 teaspoon	sea salt
1 teaspoon	sage leaves, crushed*
1/2 teaspoon	thyme leaves*

Nutritional Information/Serving	
Calories:	233
Protein (g):	7.9
Carbohydrate (g):	17.7
Fiber (g):	2.54
Total fat (g):	14.56
Saturated (g):	2.19
Cholesterol (mg):	11
Sodium (mg):	335
Food Exchanges/Serving	
1 Br .5 VLM .2 Veg 2.8 Fat	

1. Remove fat and skin on neck and giblets. Bring first 3 ingredients to boil in large saucepan, reduce heat, cover, and simmer 1 hour or until tender.

2. Remove meat, cool to handle, and remove and dice meat . Yields approximately 3/4 cup. Measure broth and add water to yield 1 cup.

3. In large mixing bowl, mix together all ingredients, except broth and oil, to distribute spices evenly. Pour broth and oil or melted butter evenly over bread mixture and stir to moisten bread. Use hands to actually smash bread with fingers to break up the bread cubes into small crumbs. There may be some extra liquid at this point but it will be soaked up during baking.

4. Pour into an 8-inch square baking dish. Bake at 350ºF. for 35–40 minutes.

Yield: 8 servings

Special Notes: Stuffing may be cooked in microwave on full power for 15–25 minutes, turn pan one quarter turn every 5 minutes. Time depends on wattage of microwave. Be careful to not dry stuffing too much.

Also, stuffing can be placed inside the cavity of a roasting hen or turkey. Allow at least 1/2 hour more roasting time. Roast stuffed bird until internal temperature of stuffing is 180ºF.

*Realize that this recipe breaks rotation so you need to plan ahead and make modifications within your rotation to temporarily move onions, sage, thyme, and butter from Day 2 to Day 1 or 3 and move remaining ingredients to Day 3. I usually do not concern myself with the break since I usually only have this recipe for holiday meals.

USED FOR ANALYSIS: French Meadow Sour Dough Kamut Bread.

---

*The control center of your life
is your attitude.*

---

*The best thing about the future is
that it comes only one day at a time.*
Abraham Lincoln

Pancakes

Kamut® or Spelt Pancakes (Day 1 Recipe)

10 Dollar-size	30 Dollar-size	YIELD
1/2 cup	1 1/2 cups	Kamut® flour
	OR	
2/3 cup	2 cups	spelt flour
1/2 teaspoon	1 1/2 teaspoons	baking soda
3 pinches	scant 1/4 teaspoon	sea salt
1/4 teaspoon	1/2 teaspoon	unbuffered, corn-free vitamin C crystals
1/2 cup	1 1/2 cups	water
2 teaspoons	2 tablespoons	sesame oil
1/3 cup	1 cup	raspberries, fresh or frozen, thawed and drained (optional)

Teff Pancakes (Day 1 Recipe)

10 Dollar-size	YIELD
1/2 cup	brown teff flour
1/2 teaspoon	baking soda
2 pinches	sea salt
1/4 teaspoon	unbuffered, corn-free vitamin C crystals
1/2 cup	water
2 teaspoons	sesame oil
1/3 cup	raspberries, fresh or frozen, thawed and drained (optional)

Quinoa Pancakes (Day 3 Recipe)

12 Dollar-size	24 Dollar-size	YIELD
1/2 cup	1 cup	quinoa flour
3 tablespoons	1/4 cup + 2 tablespoons	tapioca starch or cornstarch
1/2 teaspoon	1 teaspoon	baking soda
3 pinches	scant 1/4 teaspoon	sea salt
1/4 teaspoon	1/2 teaspoon	unbuffered, corn-free vitamin C crystals
1/2 teaspoon	1 teaspoon	FOS (optional)
1/2 teaspoon	1 teaspoon	ground cinnamon (optional)
1/2 cup	1 cup	water
2 teaspoons	4 teaspoons	canola oil

Rice-Oat Pancakes (Day 3 Recipe)

12 Dollar-size	24 Dollar-size	YIELD
1/2 cup	1 cup	brown rice flour*
3 tablespoons	1/4 cup + 2 tablespoons	oat flour
1/2 teaspoon	1 teaspoon	baking soda
1/4 teaspoon	1/2 teaspoon	sea salt
1/4 teaspoon	1/2 teaspoon	unbuffered, corn-free vitamin C crystals
1 tablespoon	2 tablespoons	ground flax seed
1/2 cup	1 cup	water
2 teaspoons	1/4 cup	canola oil

*Rice is usually eaten on Day 1, omit rice on Day 1 just before and after eating this recipe on Day 3.

Buckwheat Pancakes (Day 4 Recipe)

7-8 Dollar-size	21-24 Dollar-size	YIELD
1/2 cup + 1 tbsp.	1 3/4 cups	White Buckwheat Flour (page 105)
1/2 teaspoon	1 1/2 teaspoons	baking soda
1/4 teaspoon	1/2 teaspoon	unbuffered, corn-free vitamin C crystals
2 pinches	scant 1/4 teaspoon	sea salt
1/2 cup	1 1/2 cups	water
2 teaspoons	2 tablespoons	safflower oil
1/4 cup	3/4 cup	blueberries, fresh or frozen, thawed & drained (optional)

1. Preheat griddle. Griddle is hot enough when water dances when sprinkled on surface. Lightly oil after preheating. I use a well-seasoned cast-iron griddle (see How to Season Cast Iron, page 59).
2. In mixing bowl, whisk together your choice of dry ingredients. Add water and oil. Stir with whisk until blended. Allow batter to set up to 30 seconds to thicken. Stir again.
3. Optional, add fruit and fold in.
4. Dip batter onto griddle using tablespoon. Cook on first side until pancakes bubble (some varieties smooth out) and are slightly dry around edges, approximately 1 1/2–2 minutes. Turn. Cook until dry on second side, approximately 1 1/2–2 minutes.
5. If batter thickens (especially common with Kamut, spelt, and buckwheat) add small amounts of additional water. Also, add additional oil to griddle as needed with repeated batches.
6. Serve plain, with flaxseed oil and/ or with allowed toppings for the rotation. Suggested toppings for:
   * Day 1—almond butter, heated Pear Sauce (page 230), or tahini
   * Day 3—heated applesauce, "Maple Syrup" (page 225), or filbert nut butter
   * Day 4—Rhubarb Jelly (page 229) or cashew butter

May be frozen. Reheat in microwave or toaster oven.

Nutritional Information/Serving						
	Kamut	Spelt	Teff	Quinoa	Rice-Oat	Buckwheat
Serving Amount	5	5	5	4	4	4
Calories:	167	210	200	146	126	136
Protein (g):	5.2	7	5	2.7	2.1	3.6
Carbohydrate (g):	30.7	40	32	23.3	20.8	20.2
Fiber (g):	2.99	7.98	6	1.72	1.31	2.86
Total fat (g):	5.29	5.54	5.54	4.36	3.82	5.43
Saturated (g):	.64	.64	.64	.21	.37	.61
Cholesterol (mg):	0	0	0	0	0	0
Sodium (mg):	386	386	373	288	390	389
Food Exchanges/Serving						
	1.6 Br .9 Fat	2.1 Br .9 Fat	2 Br .9 Fat	1.5 Br .1 LM .6 Fat	1.2 Br .6 Fat	1.2 Br .9 Fat

The Nutritional Information and Food Exchanges given below are for fruit added to the above Kamut, Spelt, Teff, and Buckwheat Pancake recipes. These figures should be ADDED TO figures given for the individual servings.

Nutritional Information/Serving								
Fruit Only	Calories	Protein (g)	Carbohydrate (g)	Fiber (g)	Total fat (g)	Saturated (g)	Cholesterol (mg)	Sodium (mg)
Raspberries per 5 Kamut/Spelt/Teff	10	.17	2.5	1.17	.17	0	0	0
Blueberries per 4 Buckwheat	6	0	1.5	.25	.13	0	0	0
Food Exchanges/Serving:	Raspberries: .2 Fr			Blueberries: .1 Fr				

Griddle Bread

Griddle bread is an excellent, easy-to-make substitute for bread and buns in sandwiches as well as a wonderful replacement for labor-intensive, time-consuming homemade tortillas. Because it is leavening-, preservative-, and sugar-free, griddle bread is very useful as a bread substitute for persons with CRC.

	Day 1	Day 2	Day 3	Day 4
1/3 cup	water			
1/4 cup	brown teff flour	amaranth flour (see directions on next page) garbanzo bean flour	quinoa flour	White Buckwheat Flour (page 105) OR legume flours (see below)
as needed	sesame oil	sunflower oil	canola oil	safflower oil
Optional Ingredients:				
1–2 pinches	sea salt			
3 "sprinkles"	ground cumin	cayenne (red) pepper	coriander	cayenne (red) pepper
1 tablespoon	hulled sesame seeds (add additional 1–2 teaspoons of water)	raw sunflower seeds		chopped pumpkin seeds

1. Preheat griddle. Griddle is hot enough when water dances when sprinkled on surface. Lightly oil after preheating. I use a well-seasoned cast-iron griddle (see How to Season Cast Iron on page 59). Recipe has also been tested using an electric, teflon-coated griddle set between 375° and 400°F.

2. Measure water in a glass 1-cup measure. Add flour and optional ingredients. Whisk together.

3. Stir batter and pour onto griddle in widening rings to create desired size. Use approximately 1/4 cup batter for 5" size. Cook for length of time indicated in chart. Turn and cook for length of time indicated for second side.

Flour	First Side	Second Side
brown teff	7 minutes	5 minutes
black bean, garbanzo bean, green lentil, red lentil	6 minutes	5 minutes
white buckwheat	5 minutes	5 minutes
quinoa	4 minutes	4 minutes

4. Serve immediately or cool slightly on cooling rack. Placing bread directly on a solid surface, such as a plate, to cool causes a moisture build up and an unpleasant texture. May be frozen. Thaw at room temperature.

Yield: two 5" OR one 8" griddle bread

Serving Suggestion: Large breads work well folded like tortillas for sandwiches such as Sloppy Joes, Fajitas, "salad" (i.e., poultry, egg, seafood, etc.), or nut or sesame butter. Or create a "veggie" sandwich by layering "greens" and thinly sliced veggies (i.e., cucumbers, zucchini, and/or sprouts). Use two 5" breads as a "sandwich" bun for your favorite meat or fish patty OR serve immediately with heated fruit sauce (pages 229–230) for breakfast as a flat pancake.

Special Notes:
- Optional ingredients may be interchanged to fit your taste and rotation.
- Chopping pumpkin seeds too fine creates a "meal" which changes consistency. May need to add additional water.
- For best results, mix ingredients and immediately pour onto preheated griddle. Some batters, such as quinoa, may be mixed in multiple batches and allowed to stand before making next bread, but restir batter before pouring onto griddle.
- If making multiple batches, scrape off residue and lightly reoil griddle surface (paper towel with small amount of oil works well).

continued . . .

Since griddle temperature ranges vary, cooking times may need to be adjusted slightly for good results. The following tips will help insure success.

- Make sure griddle is thoroughly preheated as described in step 1.
- Measure water and flour ingredients accurately (see page 53).
- Cook bread longer on first side until dry around edges (many varieties curl slightly).
- If air bubble forms when cooking first side, use spatula to break so batter falls to griddle and cooks.
- If bread is turned too soon and center surface is not done, return to first side for 1–2 additional minutes after second side is cooked.
- If consistently experiencing a doughy center after following above tips, use slightly more water per recipe (start with 1 teaspoon).

Directions for Amaranth Griddle Bread
(Day 2 Recipe)

1. Preheat griddle. Griddle is hot enough when water dances when sprinkled on surface. Lightly oil after preheating. I use a well-seasoned cast-iron griddle (see How to Season Cast Iron on page 59). I have not been successful with preparing this recipe on an electric, teflon-coated griddle.
2. Measure water in a glass 1-cup measure. Add flour and optional ingredients. Whisk together.
3. Stir batter. Pour onto griddle in widening rings to create desired size. Use approximately 1/4 cup for 5" size. Cover with a skillet lid that covers griddle or at least the batter. Cook covered for 6 minutes.
4. Turn, cover, and cook for 2 minutes. Then uncover and cook for 3 more minutes.
5. Serve immediately or cool slightly on cooling rack. Placing bread on a solid surface to cool, such as a plate, causes a moisture build up and an unpleasant texture. May be frozen. Thaw at room temperature.

Yield: two 5" OR one 8" griddle bread

Serve as a sandwich as described on previous page or serve immediately with heated fruit sauce or gravy. I prefer to serve this as a flat pancake for breakfast with Kiwi Sauce (page 229).

USED FOR ANALYSIS: Salt and spices not included in analyses.

Nutritional Information/Recipe							
	Teff	Amaranth	Garbanzo Bean	Quinoa	Buckwheat	Black Bean	Red/Green Lentil
Calories:	160	110	108	132	82	152	133
Protein (g):	5	4	6	4	3.1	10	10.8
Carbohydrate (g):	32	19	18	24	17.3	28	24
Fiber (g):	6	2	4	2.3	2.45	0	0
Total fat (g):	1	1.5	1	2	.76	1	0
Saturated (g):	0	0	0	0	.17	0	0
Cholesterol (mg):	0	0	0	0	0	0	0
Sodium (mg):	5	0	8	10	3	0	0
Food Exchanges/Recipe	Teff: 2 Br		Amaranth: 1.3 Br .2 LM			Garbanzo Bean: 1.2 Br	
Quinoa: 1.6 Br .1 LM		Buckwheat: 1 Br		Black Bean: 1.8 Br		Red or Green Lentil: 1.6 Br	

The Nutritional Information and Food Exchanges given below are for seeds added to the above Griddle Bread recipes. These figures should be ADDED TO figures given for the individual servings.

Nutritional Information/Recipe								
Seeds Only (1Tbls.)	Calories	Protein (g)	Carbohydrate (g)	Fiber (g)	Total fat (g)	Saturated (g)	Cholesterol (mg)	Sodium (mg)
Pumpkin Seeds	47	2.1	1.5	1.19	3.96	.75	0	2
Sesame Seeds	52	1.6	2.1	.82	4.47	.63	0	1
Sunflower Seeds	51	2	1.7	.54	4.46	.47	0	0
Food Exchanges/Recipe: Pumpkin: .3 VLM .8 Fat / Sesame: .2 VLM .9 Fat / Sunflower: .1 Oth Carb .2 VLM .9 Fat								

Tortillas

	Day 1			Day 2	Day 3	Day 4	
	Kamut	Spelt	Teff	Amaranth	Quinoa	Buckwheat	White Bean
flour (amount needed to start)	1 1/8 cups Kamut flour	1 1/4 cups spelt flour	1/2 cup brown teff flour	5/8 cup* amaranth flour	5/8 cup* quinoa flour	1/2 cup White Buckwheat flour	1/2 cup white bean flour
sea salt	1/2 teaspoon		1/4 teaspoon				
guar gum						1/2 teas.	
water	1/2 cup		1/4 cup				
oil			1/2 teas. sesame oil	1/2 teas. sunflower or olive oil	1/2 teas. canola oil	1/2 teas. safflower oil	1/2 teas. safflower oil
flour (amount for kneading)	1/2 cup						

*5/8 cup = 1/2 cup + 2 tablespoons

Special Note: Read Helpful Hints on Tortilla Preparation starting on page 124 before beginning.

1. Preheat nonstick, unoiled griddle or skillet. Griddle is hot enough when water dances when sprinkled on surface.
2. In mixing bowl, whisk together your choice of flour (use only first listing) and salt. (Also, add guar gum if required.) Make a "well" in center.
3. Add water and oil. Stir with rubber spatula or fork until dough clumps together into a moist ball.
4. With Amaranth, Quinoa, Buckwheat, and White Bean Tortillas this dough is too sticky for kneading, so add 1 tablespoon more flour and stir in thoroughly.
5. Scatter flour on rolling surface in amount indicated in Chart A. Transfer dough to floured surface and knead to work in as much of this additional flour as possible. Dough texture should resemble Play Doh. Add more flour if needed. Form dough into ball and cut into equal portions as indicated in Chart A. Flour cut surfaces of each portion with remaining flour.
   Special Note: If you have difficulty working additional flour into the delicate amaranth dough, first cut into equal dough portions then knead about 1/2 tablespoon of flour into each portion.

CHART A	Kamut	Spelt	Teff	Amaranth	Quinoa	Buckwheat	White Bean
rolling surface flour	1 Tbsp.	1–2 Tbsp.	1 Tbsp.	1–2 Tbsp.	1 Tbsp.	1 Tbsp.	2 Tbsp.
dough portion yield	8	8	4	3 or 4	4	4	3

6. Lightly flour rolling pin. Pat dough portion into circular shape then roll out tortilla by pressing evenly from center out in all directions and working to keep tortilla as round as possible. Keep dough well floured on both sides. See Chart B for approximate amount of flour needed per tortilla. Flip tortilla often, loosen with metal spatula before flipping. Feel surface occasionally for even thickness. Finished tortilla will be very thin. See Chart B for recommended final diameter of each tortilla.

CHART B	Kamut	Spelt	Teff	Amaranth	Quinoa	Buckwheat	White Bean
flour needed/tortilla	3/4 Tbsp.	3/4 Tbsp.	1 Tbsp.	1/2 Tbsp.	1/2 Tbsp.	1/2 Tbsp.	1/2 Tbsp.
final diameter/tortilla	7–8 inch	7–8 inch	6 inch	6" or 8"	7–8 inch	6–7 inch	6–7 inch

7. Using a pastry brush, gently brush both sides to remove excess flour.
   Special Note: Because of gluten present in Kamut and spelt flour, these tortillas are more durable so you may gently toss tortilla from hand to hand to remove excess flour.

continued . . .

<u>Special Note</u>: Amaranth Tortillas are very delicate and tear easily. If you have difficulty, only roll to 6 inches in diameter and/or only prepare three tortillas per recipe. This way the tortillas are thicker and should not tear as easily.

8. Cook each side of tortilla on preheated, unoiled griddle for cooking time indicated in Chart C.
   <u>Special Note</u>: For Amaranth Tortillas tiny air pockets form and cause a bubble or pebble effect on surface when cooking on second side.
   <u>Special Note</u>: For Quinoa Tortillas the edge will curl up when cooking on first side but will flatten out when cooking on second side.

9. Cool each tortilla on cooling rack as indicated in Chart C. Then place slightly cooled tortillas between two layers of clean towel.

CHART C	Kamut	Spelt	Teff	Amaranth	Quinoa	Buckwheat	White Bean
cooking time/each side	40 sec.	45 sec.	45 sec.	45 sec.*	45 sec.	40 sec.	45 sec.
time on cooling rack	1 min.	1–2 min.	1 min.	1–2 min.	1–2 min.	1 min.	1–2 min.

*50–55 seconds per side for thicker 6" amaranth tortillas

10. Serve either whole or cut in half. Use your imagination to create a simple deli-like sandwich—for example: slivered cooked meat, "greens," "Mayo," sprouts, sliced/shredded vegetables (i. e., cabbage, tomatoes, cucumbers, zucchini, carrots). Also, serve with Sloppy Joes, Enchiladas, Tacos, Burritos, Fajitas, "salad" (i.e., poultry, egg, seafood, etc.), or nut or sesame butter. Or create a "veggie" sandwich by layering "greens" and thinly sliced veggies as mentioned above.

May be frozen flat in cellophane or plastic bag. I prefer to freeze in cellophane bag with an outer sealable bag such as a ziplock bag.

Yield: As indicated in Chart A with approximate diameter defined in Chart B.

Special Note: For easier preparation of amaranth tortillas, you may add 1/2 teaspoon of guar gum and start with only 1/2 cup of flour. Guar gum is assigned to Day 4, omit on Day 4 before and after eating Amaranth Tortillas prepared with guar gum on Day 2.

USED FOR ANALYSIS: Amaranth Tortillas were analyzed for a yield of 4 tortillas per recipe. Buckwheat Tortilla figures do not include guar gum since no figures were available for this substance.

Nutritional Information/Tortilla							
	Kamut	Spelt	Teff	Amaranth 4/Recipe	Quinoa	Buckwheat	White Bean
Calories:	104	111	165	129	154	87	206
Protein (g):	4.3	4.6	5	4.5	4.5	3.09	14
Carbohydrate (g):	25	26.2	32	21.5	27.1	17.3	34
Fiber (g):	2.44	5.24	6	2.26	2.6	2.45	22
Total fat (g):	.61	.65	1.57	2.26	2.83	1.33	.76
Saturated (g):	0	0	.08	.08	.04	.22	.07
Cholesterol (mg):	0	0	0	0	0	0	0
Sodium (mg):	133	133	138	133	145	136	202
Food Exchanges/Tortilla							
	1.3 Br	1.4 Br	2.0 Br .1 Fat	1.5 Br .2 LM .1 Fat	1.8 Br .1 LM .1 Fat	1 Br .1 Fat	2.4 Br .1 Fat

Helpful Hints on Tortilla Preparation

A. Assemble Needed Equipment: Before beginning tortilla preparation, assemble needed equipment in each of the four preparation areas.

    1. Mixing Area Equipment:

medium-size, curved-sided bowl	table fork & knife
another small bowl	rubber spatula
set of dry measuring cups & spoons	recipe
clear 1-cup liquid measure	ingredients
whisk	

    2. Kneading and Rolling Area Equipment: [It is preferable that the rolling area be located within inches of the cooking area (see number 3 under Cooking Tips if this is not possible in your kitchen).]

clean rolling surface*	additional flour
rolling pin	pastry brush
table knife	solid metal spatula (a slotted spatula can tear the dough)

    3. Cooking Area Equipment:

preheated, nonstick, unoiled griddle or skillet. I prefer a well-seasoned cast-iron griddle (page 59).
an electric range with a heat setting between low and medium
another metal spatula (slotted or solid)
digital timer with memory feature that measures in seconds.
      But a touch pad timer on microwave oven is okay.

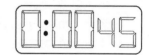

    4. Cooling Area Equipment:

cooling rack
clean cotton muslin towel placed on a second cooling rack (at least 16 by 22 inches, folded in half to place tortillas between layers to finish cooling)
large flat cellophane bags and/or plastic bags for storage

*Suggested rolling surfaces are:
clean, smooth kitchen counter (my preference)
smooth-surfaced, tempered-glass cutting board. The pebble-like acrylic cutting boards are not smooth enough to roll out tortillas.
clean, smooth, wooden bread board. Choose board with no knife cuts and that has never been used to cut meat. A wooden bread board is the worst sanitation problem you may have in your family kitchen.
cotton muslin rolling cloth may be acceptable

B. Mixing Tips:

    1. Measure accurately (see page 53 for accurate measuring). Until you become familiar with the proper feel of the dough, accurate measuring is your best guarantee of success.

    2. Recipe is designed to begin with less flour than needed to facilitate easier mixing and to prevent the formation of fewer dough particle crumbs.

C. Kneading Tips :

    1. The purpose of kneading is to work additional flour into dough making it easier to roll. Use any method you wish.

    2. If you have warm hands run them under cold water and dry them before you begin kneading. Hands that are too warm can cause dough to become sticky and difficult to handle.

    3. Keep surface well floured during entire process.

    4. Keep hands well floured. If hands become coated with dough, clean them off using back of table knife.

D. Rolling Tips:

1. Scrape rolling surface with metal spatula to remove any dough particles created during kneading. These particles tend to "mess things up" during rolling.

2. Wash hands and rinse with cold water.

3. Roll each tortilla separately on floured surface.

4. Pat each dough portion evenly flat as much as possible. If dough is still sticking to rolling surface knead additional flour into each portion before continuing.

5. Be sure both sides of dough are well floured before you begin rolling.

6. Using floured rolling pin, roll from center out in all directions until dough is evenly thin. Beginners may have more success with only a 6-inch tortilla. Keep tortilla circular, but it is not necessary to be perfect.

7. Keep dough well floured on both sides. When underneath side is sticking, flip dough to flour. Before flipping, use metal spatula to loosen edges and center of tortilla from rolling surface. To flip, place spatula under center of tortilla and your hand on top to support it. During this process, mend any cracked dough edges as they appear. Tiny cracks will become large ones if left unrepaired.

8. Before cooking tortilla, gently brush excess flour from top of dough using pastry brush or hand. Flip tortilla. If there are moist areas on dough surface, sprinkle flour on top surface (if areas are too moist, they will burn when cooking) and then brush excess flour away. A pastry brush is gentler than your hand. If edges are damaged, mend before cooking. I remove excess flour from tortilla surface because I do not like the taste of dry toasted flour on surface of cooked tortilla. Also, this excess flour will build up on griddle, burn, and cause an unpleasant taste and smell.

9. Before rolling next tortilla, clean flour off rolling surface with metal spatula. This excess flour usually does not work well to start another tortilla but can be used to flour moist areas on tortilla surface during rolling process. This means it is best to start each tortilla with a clean surface and small amount of fresh flour.

10. Clean off the build-up of raw dough on spatula as needed.

E. Cooking Tips:

1. Be sure your griddle or skillet is unoiled and preheated hot enough that water dances when sprinkled on surface.

2. Transfer tortilla carefully to griddle by first lifting left side of tortilla with metal spatula (Diagram A). Then replace spatula with your left hand (Diagram B). Next place spatula under right side of tortilla (Diagram C). This will give adequate support as you use your hand and spatula to lift tortilla over and gently drop it onto griddle (Diagram D). These directions are for a right-handed person. A left-handed person would do the opposite.

3. Follow these directions if your kitchen does not allow rolling area to be only inches away from range. First, place a protective pad (such as small metal cooling rack) that is able to withstand the griddle heat on counter surface near rolling area. Place hot griddle on protective pad, transfer tortilla as described above, and immediately return griddle to range.

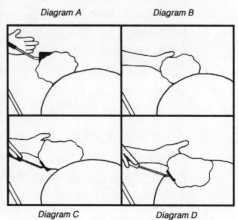

Diagram A   *Diagram B*

Diagram C   *Diagram D*

4. For timing, use digital timer which measures seconds and has memory feature. The memory feature is great because you set timer for 45 seconds, start it timing immediately after placing tortilla on griddle, then continue to roll out next tortilla. When timer dings, flip tortilla, stop timer, and then restart it for another 45 seconds that timer has automatically reset for you. When cooking something as delicate as tortillas for only 40–45 seconds per side and taking time to reprogram the timer, your tortilla is cooking 5–10 seconds while you are fumbling to reset it. Being hurried like this can cause mistakes and frustrations.

5. Cook first side for 45 seconds, flip tortilla, and cook for additional 45 seconds. If first side feels a little moist flip it back to first side for 5 seconds or less. (Buckwheat and Kamut Tortillas are best when cooked for only 40 seconds on each side.)

6. Clean off build-up of browned flour from spatula and griddle as needed.

F. Cooling Tips:

1. With spatula, transfer cooked tortilla to a cooling rack for time indicated in recipe. Then use hand to transfer partially cooled tortilla to between layers of cloth. This allows tortillas to finish cooling without becoming dry. Also, notice how durable yet pliable tortilla is after cooling.

2. If you cook tortilla too long on griddle, it may help to cool it completely between layers of cotton cloth rather than partially cool on rack.

3. If you allow a tortilla to cool too long and become dry, follow these directions. First, transfer too-dry tortilla between layers of cloth. Then, place next cooked tortilla directly on top of dry tortilla without allowing it to cool on cooling rack. This will help the dry tortilla to regain a little moisture.

G. Additional Tips:

1. After experience, dovetail your work. Begin the rolling process of next tortilla while one is cooking and another one is cooling.

2. When you get to this stage of success, set your timer for only 40 seconds. This will allow you 5 seconds to stop what you are doing, brush flour off hands, and get to range to attend to the cooking tortilla.

3. For the dovetail process, while first side is cooking, scrape and add flour to rolling surface. Pat out next tortilla and start rolling. After turning the cooking tortilla, put the cooling tortilla between layers of cloth and return to rolling process of next tortilla. After the second side has cooked, transfer cooked tortilla to cooling rack. The griddle is now empty, but leave it on range to stay hot while you finish rolling the next tortilla. Continue to prepare all tortillas.

4. With even more experience, learn to roll a faster way. Use the principle of rolling from center out, yet keep rolling pin moving by rolling back and forth. However, put the most pressure on dough when rolling from center out. Also, lift rolling pin off dough frequently and use your other hand to twist dough on rolling surface. This way you know immediately if underneath surface of the tortilla needs more flour.

5. VERY IMPORTANT: Do not make tortillas on days of high humidity. The dough will tend to be sticky and adding too much flour to make it workable will result in tough tortillas.

H. Tips on Preparing Multiple Batches:

1. When doubling recipe, divide dough in half in mixing bowl before kneading.

2. Tortilla preparation takes time just to set up and clean up kitchen. Prepare 4–8 tortillas of each desired flavor at one time. Remove the accumulated flour from griddle surface after preparing 4 tortillas. Just hold hot griddle over sink and quickly brush off with dry cloth.

3. Thoroughly clean rolling surface between each flavor of tortillas. First, clean off flour with a dry cloth, then use a wet cloth to clean.

HH: For easier cleanup, use a dry cloth to wipe dough particles and flour off the rolling surface and rolling pin before wiping with a wet cloth.

I. Tips on Storing, Freezing, Reheating, and Serving:

1. Prepare tortillas when you have time and energy to have them available for a quick meal—especially a meal away from home.

2. **To store**, place tortillas in a flat cellophane bag—one flavor per bag and usually no more than eight per bag. Use a self-adhesive label to mark flavor. Then seal each cellophane bag in sealable plastic bag. You may also place tortillas directly in a plastic bag. Whatever you choose, store them flat in freezer and in a safe place where other foods will not damage them.

3. **To thaw and/or reheat** as needed, begin by transferring desired amount from bag of frozen tortillas to another bag. Next, allow them to thaw:
    • at room temperature for approximately 30 minutes.
    • in microwave for 5–10 seconds.
    • on a splatter screen over top of a pan of steaming water for approximately 10–20 seconds.
    • in refrigerator for a few hours.
    Whatever way you choose, they will dry out if allowed to thaw outside a bag.

4. **Serve tortillas** whole folded over the ingredients or cut them in half easily with a pair of scissors. Buckwheat and Teff Tortillas sometimes crack when folded so cut them in half and layer the goodies between halves. Be creative. See recipe for many ideas.
    a. Tortillas make great sandwiches for meals eaten away from home. When you do this, pack tortillas separate from fillings so tortillas do not collect moisture from fillings and fall apart when eaten.
    b. Whatever filling you choose and however you serve them, tortillas are a special addition to any meal, especially for those who cannot tolerate yeasted breads. Simply fill, fold, and enjoy.

Special Note: If taking tortillas with you for a traveling meal and you are in a dry climate (e.g., Colorado, Arizona, etc.), definitely double bag tortillas and use sealable plastic bag as outer bag.

> *If things do not turn out as we wish,*
> *we should wish for them as they turn out.*
> *Aristotle*

> *We are all here for a spell;*
> *get all the good laughs you can.*
> *Will Rogers*

Oven Fried Chicken
(Day 1 Recipe)

1/2 cup	flour—brown teff, brown rice, Kamut, spelt
1/2 teaspoon	sea salt
1/2 teaspoon	ground cumin
	OR 1/4 teaspoon dill weed
8 pieces	chicken, skin removed

Nutritional Information/Serving		
	Average for 3.5 oz Breast	Average for 3.5 oz Thigh
Calories:	205	249
Protein (g):	32	27
Carbohydrate (g):	8	8
Fiber (g):	1.51	1.51
Total fat (g):	3.86	11.18
Saturated (g):	1.02	3.04
Cholesterol (mg):	85	95
Sodium (mg):	209	223
Food Exchanges/Serving		
Breast: .5 Br 4.4 VLM .3 Fat		
Thigh: .5 Br 3.7 VLM 1.8 Fat		

1. Preheat oven to 450ºF.
2. Oil baking dish(es) or see special note below.
3. Cut up chicken and remove skin. Rinse. Drain or pat dry leaving chicken a little moist.
4. In bowl, combine your choice of flour and seasonings. Add small amount (1–2 tablespoons) to small bowl with lid that seals, such as a Tupperware bowl.
5. Add 1 piece of chicken. Seal. Shake to coat. Place in baking dish, bone side down. Repeat for each piece, adding more mixture as needed.
6. Place in oven and reduce heat to 400ºF. Bake for 50–60 minutes until internal temperature is 180ºF.

Special Note: Chicken will be crispier on all sides if cooked on wire rack. If using wire rack, no need to oil pan in step 2. For crispier chicken, increase oven temperature to 450ºF. for final 10 minutes.

Yield: 8 pieces of chicken

Special Note: The taller the sides on the baking dish, the less likely to splatter in oven. Also, remove top rack in oven. For easier clean up, soak pan in warm, soapy water while eating.

Sondra's Thoughts: My favorite is brown teff flour with cumin. If preparing less than 8 pieces, use needed amount of flour and freeze the rest for next time.

Oven Fried Catfish
(Day 1 Recipe)

Preheat oven to 450ºF. Prepare flour/seasoning mixture as directed in recipe above. Cut an 1/2 pound catfish fillet in half. Rinse. Place moistened fillet in bag or bowl with sealable lid. Add small amount of flour mixture, close, and shake to coat. Place on wire rack in pan. Repeat for each piece. Bake as in step 6 above for 45 minutes until internal temperature is 180ºF. (More oven-fried fish recipes will appear in Canary Connect News, see page 271 for subscription information.) Mixture will coat approximately 3# of fillets.

Country Fried Chicken and Gravy
(Day 1 Recipe)

1	whole chicken fryer, 3–4 pound
1/2 cup	flour—brown rice, Kamut, spelt
1 tablespoon	sesame oil
to season	sea salt

Ingredients for gravy:

2 cups	water
2 tablespoons	flour—brown rice, Kamut, spelt
1/4 teaspoon	sea salt

Nutritional Information/Serving		
	Average for 3.5 oz Breast	Average for 3.5 oz Thigh
Calories:	225	269
Protein (g):	31.9	26.8
Carbohydrate (g):	9.44	9.44
Fiber (g):	.57	.57
Total fat (g):	5.63	12.95
Saturated (g):	1.33	3.35
Cholesterol (mg):	85	95
Sodium (mg):	142	156
Food Exchanges/Serving		
Breast: .6 Br 4.4 VLM .6 Fat		
Thigh: .6 Br 3.7 VLM 2.1 Fat		

1. Cut up chicken and remove the skin. (My preference is to boil back, neck, and wings, see page 130.)

continued on next page

Country Fried Chicken and Gravy
(Continued)

2. Preheat electric skillet to 350ºF. Add oil. Recipe was developed using stainless steel electric skillet; others may require more oil.

3. Pat chicken pieces dry and roll each piece in flour. Place in hot skillet with meaty side down. Sprinkle with salt. Cover with splatter screen. Brown for 8–10 minutes—the browner the chicken, the browner the gravy—but be careful not to dry chicken out or burn it. Turn using tongs or spatula. Cover with splatter screen and brown for another 8–10 minutes.

4. While second side is browning, whisk together gravy ingredients. Add to skillet. Loosen any stuck chicken pieces with spatula. Cover with lid. Reduce heat to between simmer and 200ºF. Simmer for 20–25 minutes. Check occasionally during cooking and loosen chicken that is sticking to pan.

Yield: 4 servings

Pheasant and Gravy
(Day 1 Recipe)

Prepare same as Country Fried Chicken and Gravy except for step 4. Transfer browned pheasant to shallow, covered casserole dish(es). Add gravy mixture. Cover and bake at 350ºF. for 1 hour or until tender. Also, I suggest you soak pheasant several hours or overnight in salt water to remove wild game taste.

Yield: 4 servings

Nutritional Information/Serving	
Calories:	354
Protein (g):	43.3
Carbohydrate (g):	18.9
Fiber (g):	1.14
Total fat (g):	10.52
Saturated (g):	2.82
Cholesterol (mg):	116
Sodium (mg):	200
Food Exchanges/Serving	
1.1 Br 5.9 VLM 1.2 Fat	

Easy Chicken Meal or Soup
(Day 1 Recipe)

1 serving	chicken breast or your favorite piece, skin removed
1 cup	celery, thick sliced
1 cup	cabbage, chopped in large pieces
1/4 teaspoon	sea salt
as desired	dill weed (optional)
1 1/2 cups	water

To Serve as a Meal:

1. Layer chicken, celery, and cabbage in 1-quart size slow cooker.* Sprinkle with salt and dill weed. Add water. Note: Cabbage will not be completely covered with water.

2. Cook for 4 hours on low.

3. Serve without broth as a meal. After meal, boil broth to make 1/2 cup. Freeze. Use chicken vegetable broth for Day 1 recipes such as Chicken Spaghetti/Pizza Sauce (page 150).

Nutritional Information/Serving	
Calories:	179
Protein (g):	28.6
Carbohydrate (g):	8.2
Fiber (g):	3.22
Total fat (g):	3.44
Saturated (g):	.95
Cholesterol (mg):	73
Sodium (mg):	714
Food Exchanges/Serving	
3.8 VLM 1.4 Veg .2 Fat	

To Serve as a Chunky Soup:

1. Debone and cut raw chicken meat into bite-size pieces. Partially frozen chicken is easier to debone and cut. Layer chicken bone, raw chicken meat, and rest of ingredients as described above. Cooking the bone with the vegetables adds more flavor.

2. Cook for 4 hours on low.

3. Remove any cooked meat from bone and add to soup.

Yield: a delicious, simple meal for 1

*Recipe designed to cook in 1-quart size slow cooker. Double, triple, or quadruple recipe to cook in standard-size slow cooker. Cook on low if cooker has two settings.

Roast Poultry and Broth

	Day 1	Day 3
Your choice of poultry	7–8 pound roasting hen OR 3-4 pound chicken fryer	12–15 pound turkey hen
sea salt, as indicated	1–2 teaspoons	1–2 tablespoons
water, as indicated	1–2 cups	2–3 cups

There are many ways to roast poultry. My preferences are a covered stainless-steel roasting pan or Reynolds Oven Cooking Bag.

1. Wash bird inside and out. Remove any pin feathers. Rub inside and outside of bird with salt. Tuck wings under back of bird or sew wing tips to breast. Tie legs together with heavy cotton string.
2. Place bird on rack in roasting pan. Add water. Cover and roast at 325–350ºF. See chart for roasting time.

7–8 pound roasting hen	2 1/2 to 3 hours
3-4 pound chicken fryer	1 3/4 to 2 hours
12–15 pound turkey hen	3 1/2 to 4 hours

Use a meat thermometer and roast until internal temperature reaches 180ºF. Be sure thermometer is inserted into thickest part of meat and is not touching a bone. If not browning to your liking, roast uncovered for the last 15–30 minutes.

OR

Insert bird into appropriate size Reynolds Oven Roasting Bag. Follow package directions except do not shake flour in the empty bag and add amount of water indicated above. Do not forget to make six 1/2-inch slits in top of bag.

3. After meal, strain leftover broth through fine-meshed strainer and chill. After chilling, remove solid fat layer on top. Remove remaining cooked meat from bones. Break carcass to fit into large kettle. Simmer carcass in small amount of water (usually 1 cup for chicken, 2 cups for turkey) for 1–2 hours until excess meat is so tender that it falls off the bones. Add this broth to broth reserved from roasting. Measure broth and add more water if needed to yield: 6–7 cups for roasting hen, 3–4 cups for chicken fryer, and 9–11 cups for turkey. Measure out and freeze broth in 1 cup servings. Broth is then ready for most recipes in this cookbook.

Chicken Broth
(Day 1 Recipe)

1. Simmer neck, wings, and back pieces of chicken fryer in 2 1/2 cups water, 1/2 teaspoon sea salt, and 1/4 teaspoon vitamin C crystals (optional). Cook until chicken is tender and water has reduced to approximately 1 cup.
2. Chill broth and meat separately. As the broth chills the fat will solidify on top. Remove solid fat layer and freeze broth. Remove cooked meat from bones and freeze. May wish to freeze in 1/2 cup portions ready to use in several recipes in this cookbook.
3. Recipes using chicken broth in this cookbook are based on a yield of 1 cup of broth for this recipe.

Millet or Quinoa Turkey Vegetable Stew
(Day 3 Recipe)

1 pound	ground turkey
1 teaspoon	sea salt
1 cup	Turkey Broth (page 130)
1 1/2 cups	water
1/4 cup	hulled millet grain OR whole quinoa, rinsed
1 1/2 cups	parsnips, peeled, sliced
2 cups	cauliflower, small florets
2 1/2 cups	carrots, peeled, sliced
1/2 cup	water (optional)
2 tablespoons	tapioca starch (optional)

Nutritional Information/Serving		
	Millet	Quinoa
Calories:	267	269
Protein (g):	23.1	23.2
Carbohydrate (g):	20.6	20
Fiber (g):	3.87	3.81
Total fat (g):	10.56	10.73
Saturated (g):	2.63	2.67
Cholesterol (mg):	77	77
Sodium (mg):	460	462
Food Exchanges/Serving		
Millet: .9 Br 3 VLM 1.2 Veg 1.5 Fat		
Quinoa: .9 Br 3.0 VLM 1.2 Veg 1.5 Fat		

1. Combine ground turkey and salt in 5-quart Dutch-oven kettle. Cook until meat is done. Stir often to chop meat and brown evenly.

2. Add turkey broth, 1 1/2 cups of water, millet or quinoa, and prepared vegetable. Heat to boiling, reduce heat, cover, and simmer for 15–20 minutes until millet or quinoa is done and vegetables tender. Stir occasionally. Add more water (or salt) if needed.

3. Optional—In small bowl, whisk together 1/2 cup of water and starch. Add to stew and cook to thicken. Serve with or without biscuits. May be frozen.

Yield: 6 1/2 cups   6 Servings

Special Note: I usually prepare this quick meal in winter using frozen vegetables. If fresh vegetables are used, may need to add more water.

Chicken or Turkey Loaf

	Chicken Rice Loaf (Day 1 Recipe)	Chicken Kamut or Spelt Loaf (Day 1 Recipe)	Turkey Oatmeal Loaf (Day 3 Recipe)
1 pound	ground chicken	ground chicken	ground turkey
Your choice of grain in amount indicated	2/3 cup cooked brown rice	1/2 cup Kamut or Spelt flakes	1/2 cup old fashioned rolled oats (regular, uncooked)
1/2 cup	celery, chopped	celery, chopped	carrots, shredded
liquid as indicated	1/4 cup water	1/2 cup water	1/2 cup water
1/2 teaspoon	sea salt		

1. In large mixing bowl, combine your choice of ingredients thoroughly.
2. Shape in 9 x 5-inch loaf pan, 9 muffin cups (1/3 cup of mixture each), or 6 custard cups (1/2 cup each).
3. Bake at 350°F. for 50–60 minutes in loaf pan, 20–25 minutes in muffin pans, or 35–45 minutes in custard cups.

Ingredients may be mixed early in day and stored in refrigerator to be cooked later.

Yield: 4 servings

USED FOR ANALYSIS: No figures were available for ground chicken. Turkey used for analysis.

Nutritional Information/Serving	
Calories:	231
Protein (g):	23.7
Carbohydrate (g):	7.71
Fiber (g):	1.35
Total fat (g):	11.24
Saturated (g):	2.85
Cholesterol (mg):	82
Sodium (mg):	358
Food Exchanges/Serving	
.4 Br 3.2 VLM .2 Veg 1.8 Fat	

Creamed Turkey on Rye Toast
(Day 3 Recipe)

1 pound	ground turkey
1/2 teaspoon	sea salt
1 cup	Turkey Broth (page 130)
1/2 cup	water
2 cups	carrots, diced or sliced thin
1/2 teaspoon	cilantro
1/4 cup	water
3 tablespoons	tapioca starch or cornstarch

Nutritional Information/Serving Sauce Only	
Calories:	235
Protein (g):	22.6
Carbohydrate (g):	10.8
Fiber (g):	1.43
Total fat (g):	10.73
Saturated (g):	2.75
Cholesterol (mg):	82
Sodium (mg):	638
Food Exchanges/Serving	
.3 Br 3.2 VLM .8 Veg 1.6 Fat	

1. In large skillet, cook ground turkey and salt. Stir often to chop meat and brown evenly.

2. Add broth, first measurement of water, carrots, and cilantro. Heat to boiling, reduce heat, cover, and simmer for 10–15 minutes or until carrots are tender. Taste and add more seasonings if desired.

3. In small bowl, whisk together second measurement of water and starch. Add and cook to thicken. Serve over toasted 100% sourdough rye bread or with any Day 3 biscuits. May be frozen, reheat slowly.

Yield: 4 cups   4 servings

Sesame Goulash
(Day 1 Recipe)

1 pound	ground chicken or 2 cups cooked chicken
1/2 teaspoon	sea salt (add as needed if use cooked chicken)
1 cup	elbow macaroni—Kamut, spelt, or rice
2 cups	cabbage, shredded
1 cup	celery, diced
1 cup	Chicken Broth (page 130)
1 2/3 cups	water
1/4 teaspoon	ground cumin or dill weed
1/2 teaspoon	sea salt
1/4 cup	flour—Kamut, spelt, or rice
1/4 cup	hulled sesame seeds
1/3 cup	water

Nutritional Information/Serving		
	Sesame Goulash	"Tuna Helper"
Calories:	330	301
Protein (g):	26.7	28.8
Carbohydrate (g):	33.7	35.9
Fiber (g):	10.47	11.95
Total fat (g):	10.53	4.92
Saturated (g):	1.94	.56
Cholesterol (mg):	58	12.76
Sodium (mg):	350	436
Food Exchanges/Serving		
Sesame Goulash: 1.8 Br 3 VLM .5 Veg 1.6 Fat		
"Tuna Helper": 2 Br 3 VLM .7 Veg .6 Fat		

1. Combine ground chicken with first measurement of salt in skillet. Cook until done, stir often to chop and brown evenly. If needed, drain off fat.

2. Add macaroni, vegetables, broth, 1 2/3 cups of water, cumin, and second measurement of salt. Bring to boil. Reduce heat. Cover. Simmer 10–12 minutes or until ingredients are tender.

3. While casserole is cooking, combine flour, sesame seeds, and 1/3 cup of water in blender. Blend on highest speed for 1–2 minutes until well blended. Stop at least once to scrape sides. Add to skillet and cook, stirring constantly until mixture thickens.

Yield: 6 cups   4 servings

USED FOR ANALYSIS: Cooked chicken and spelt macaroni and flour.

Pasta Primavera
(Day 1 Recipe)

1 ounce	spaghetti—Kamut, rice, or spelt OR Kamut angel hair
1 teaspoon	sesame or almond oil or 1/2 teaspoon of each
1	chicken breast
3 1/2 cups	your choice of fresh Day 1 vegetables (amounts may be adjusted). I prefer: 1 1/2 cups each chopped cabbage and fresh broccoli cuts with 1/2 cup slant-cut celery
as desired	sea salt, dill weed, ground cumin, and/or almonds

Method 1—Dry

1. Preheat electric skillet or wok to 350°F.

2. Remove skin and bone from chicken breast. Cut into thin strips. This step is easier when meat is slightly frozen.

3. In large saucepan, cook broken spaghetti or angel hair in salted, boiling water according to package directions. Stir occasionally to prevent sticking. Drain and set aside until finished with step 4.

4. While spaghetti is cooking, add oil and chicken to preheated skillet and cook, stirring almost continuously. Add prepared vegetables and almonds. Season as desired. Stir almost continuously until vegetables are cooked to your liking. My preference is crunchy.

5. Add spaghetti. Stir constantly until well mixed and at serving temperature. Serve immediately.

Method 2—With Sauce

Follow steps 1–4 as described in Method 1

5. Combine 1/4 cup of water, 1 tablespoon hulled sesame seeds, and 1 tablespoon of Kamut, rice, or spelt flour in blender. Blend on highest speed for 1–2 minutes until well blended. Stop at least once to scrape sides. Add rest of water and blend a couple seconds more.

6. Add spaghetti and sesame mixture to step 4. Stir constantly until sauce thickens and coats all ingredients. Serve immediately.

Yield: 2 1/2–3 cups   1 serving

Nutritional Information/Serving With Sauce	
Calories:	463
Protein (g):	43.9
Carbohydrate (g):	47.9
Fiber (g):	12.1
Total fat (g):	14.12
Saturated (g):	2.42
Cholesterol (mg):	85
Sodium (mg):	182
Food Exchanges/Serving	
1.7 Br 4.6 VLM 3.0 Veg 2.0 Fat	

"Tuna Helper"
(Day 1 Recipe)

1–7 1/2 oz. jar	Chuck's Seafood tuna
1/2 teaspoon	sea salt
1 cup	elbow macaroni—Kamut, spelt, or rice
2 cups	cabbage, shredded
1 cup	celery, diced
1 3/4 cups	water
1/4 teaspoon	dill weed
1 tablespoon	flour—Kamut, spelt, or rice
2 tablespoons	hulled sesame seeds
1/4 cup	water

1. Combine all ingredients except last three in large skillet or Dutch oven. Bring to boil. Reduce heat. Cover. Simmer 10–12 minutes or until ingredients are tender.

2. While casserole is cooking, combine flour, sesame seeds, and 1/4 cup of water in blender. Blend on highest speed for 1–2 minutes until well blended. Stop at least once to scrape sides. Add and cook on low, stirring constantly until mixture thickens.

Yield: 4 cups   3 servings

USED FOR ANALYSIS: Spelt macaroni and flour.
Analysis on previous page in Sesame Goulash square.

Chicken Noodle Casseroles
(Three Variations)
(Day 1 Recipe)

	With More Vegetables	With Extra Vegetables	
2 3 cups	2 4 cups	2 5 1/2 cups	SERVINGS YIELD
1/2 pound	1/2 pound	1/2 pound	ground chicken OR 1 cup cooked chicken
1/4 teaspoon	1/4 teaspoon	1/4 teaspoon	sea salt (omit when using cooked chicken)
1 1/3 cups	1 1/3 cups	1 1/3 cups	Vita-Spelt dry noodles, loosely packed OR Kamut rotini, loosely packed
1/2 cup	2 cups	4 cups	total measure of vegetables: your choice of diced celery, sliced bok choy, fresh or frozen broccoli cuts, and/or chopped cabbage
none	5/8 cup	1 1/4 cups	water (5/8 cup = 1/2 cup + 2 Tbsp.)
1 cup	1 cup	1 cup	Chicken Broth (page 130)
2 tablespoons	3 tablespoons	1/4 cup	hulled sesame seeds
2 tablespoons	3 tablespoons	1/4 cup	flour—spelt or Kamut
1/4 teaspoon	3/8 teaspoon	1/2 teaspoon	sea salt (3/8 tsp. = 1/4 tsp. + 1/8 tsp.)

1. Oven temperature—350ºF. Preheating not necessary.

2. Combine meat with first measurement of salt in skillet. Cook until done, stir often to chop and brown evenly. If needed, drain off fat. Transfer to covered casserole dish(es). If using cooked chicken, place in casserole dish(es) and omit first measure of sea salt.

3. In saucepan of boiling salted water, cook noodles for 4 minutes or rotini for 8 minutes. Stir occasionally. Drain and add to casserole dish(es).

4. Add vegetables and stir gently.

5. Combine 1/4 cup of liquid, seeds, flour, and second listing of salt in blender. Blend on highest speed for 1–2 minutes until well blended. Stop at least once to scrape sides. Add remaining liquid and blend a couple of seconds more.

6. Pour liquid mixture over ingredients in casserole dish(es). Lightly push any floating ingredients down into mixture. Cover. Bake 45–60 minutes or until vegetables are tender. Casserole may be mixed earlier in the day and refrigerated until baking time.

USED FOR ANALYSIS:

Cooked chicken and spelt pasta and flour.

First Variation: 1/2 cup celery

With More   1 cup broccoli
Vegetables: 1 cup cabbage

With Extra   1/2 cup bok choy
Vegetables: 1 1/2 cups broccoli
                 2 cups cabbage

Nutritional Information/Serving			
	First Variation	With More Veg	With Extra Veg
Calories:	365	423	481
Protein (g):	27.6	30.6	33.5
Carbohydrate (g):	38	45.9	54.1
Fiber (g):	12.08	14.81	17.52
Total fat (g):	11.04	13.94	16.47
Saturated (g):	1.93	2.27	2.61
Cholesterol (mg):	71	71	71
Sodium (mg):	356	487	639
Food Exchanges/Serving			
First Variation: 2.1 Br 3.0 VLM .2 Veg 2.0 Fat			
With More Vegetables: 2.3 Br 3.1 VLM .9 Veg 2.4 Fat			
With Extra Vegetables: 2.5 Br 3.3 VLM 1.6 Veg 2.9 Fat			

Chicken Rice Casseroles
(Three Variations)
(Day 1 Recipe)

	With More Vegetables	With Extra Vegetables	
2	2	2	SERVINGS
3 cups	4 cups	5 1/2 cups	YIELD
1/2 pound	1/2 pound	1/2 pound	ground chicken OR 1 cup cooked chicken
1/4 teaspoon	1/4 teaspoon	1/4 teaspoon	sea salt (omit when using cooked chicken)
1 cups	1 cups	1 cups	cooked rice
1/2 cup	2 cups	4 cups	total measure of vegetables: your choice of diced celery, sliced bok choy, fresh or frozen broccoli cuts, and/or chopped cabbage
none	5/8 cup	1 1/4 cups	water (5/8 cup = 1/2 cup + 2 Tbsp.)
1 cup	1 cup	1 cup	Chicken Broth (page 130)
2 tablespoons	3 tablespoons	1/4 cup	hulled sesame seeds
2 tablespoons	3 tablespoons	1/4 cup	brown rice flour
1/4 teaspoon	3/8 teaspoon	1/2 teaspoon	sea salt (3/8 tsp. = 1/4 tsp. + 1/8 tsp.)

Perform steps 1–2 and omit step 3 of Chicken Noodle Casserole (recipe on previous page).

4.   Add rice and vegetables to casserole dish(es), stir gently.

Continue with steps 5 and 6 of Chicken Noodle Casserole.

USED FOR ANALYSIS:

Cooked chicken and spelt pasta and flour.

First Variation: 1/2 cup celery

With More   1 cup broccoli
Vegetables: 1 cup cabbage

With Extra   1/2 cup bok choy
Vegetables: 1 1/2 cups broccoli
                       2 cups cabbage

HH: Prepare these casseroles in individual servings in separate casseroles dishes to the liking of each family member. For example: My husband will eat these casseroles if I prepare his with more noodles and meat yet with less vegetables. Also, serve in baking dishes to save washing plates.

Nutritional Information/Serving			
	First Variation	With More Veg	With Extra Veg
Calories:	297	356	417
Protein (g):	23.5	26.3	28.9
Carbohydrate (g):	27.4	35.4	43.7
Fiber (g):	3.03	5.25	7.43
Total fat (g):	10.15	12.73	15.31
Saturated (g):	2.12	2.48	2.85
Cholesterol (mg):	58	58	58
Sodium (mg):	347	479	631
Food Exchanges/Serving			
First Variation: 1.5 Br 3.0 VLM .2 Veg 1.6 Fat			
With More Vegetables: 1.7 Br 3.1 VLM .9 Veg 2.1 Fat			
With Extra Vegetables: 2.0 Br 3.3 VLM 1.6 Veg 2.5 Fat			

Cheerfulness is what greases the axles of the world.
Don't go through life creaking.
—H. W. Byles

Chicken Cabbage Rolls
(Day 1 Recipe)

1/2 pound	ground chicken
1 cup	celery, diced
1/4 teaspoon	sea salt
1 cup	cooked brown rice
2 cups	Chicken Broth (page 130)
2 tablespoons	hulled sesame seeds
1/4 cup	brown rice flour
1/4 teaspoon	sea salt
4–6	medium-size cabbage leaves

Nutritional Information/Serving	
Calories:	389
Protein (g):	27.1
Carbohydrate (g):	47.5
Fiber (g):	8.2
Total fat (g):	11.03
Saturated (g):	2.26
Cholesterol (mg):	58
Sodium (mg):	678
Food Exchanges/Serving	
1.9 Br 3.0 VLM 2.6 Veg 1.6 Fat	

Oven temperature—350ºF. Preheating not necessary. (This recipe requires a lot of preparation time and you may wish to make it in stages throughout the day as I do. Turn the oven on when you are ready to bake the cabbage rolls.)

1. Combine ground chicken, celery, and first listing of salt in skillet. Cook until meat is done, stir often to chop meat and brown evenly. If needed, drain off fat. Add cooked rice, stir, and set aside.

2. While meat and celery cook, boil 2 cups of Chicken Broth to make a concentrated broth of 1 1/2 cups.

3. Combine 1/4 cup of concentrated Chicken Broth, seeds, flour and second listing of salt in blender. Blend on highest speed for 1–2 minutes until well blended. Stop at least once to scrap sides. Add remainder of broth and blend a couple of seconds more. Pour mixture into saucepan that you used to boil broth. Heat slowly on low until thickened, stirring often with whisk to keep mixture smooth.

4. Add 2/3 cup of sauce to meat mixture, stir, and set aside. This should be enough to just moisten and hold mixture together. Mixture yields approximately 2 1/4 cups. Reserve rest of sauce for later.

5. Heat a large kettle of salted water until boiling.

6. Remove 4–6 medium-size cabbage leaves from head. Easiest way is to cut each leaf, one at a time, from center core and carefully remove beginning from core end. May need to loosen parts of each leaf from other leaves. Remove any bad places. Wash. Amount needed will vary depending on size.

7. Add to boiling water and boil on medium-high for 3–4 minutes to slightly cook and soften core.

8. Remove by grasping core end with tongs and place in colander to drain. Cool enough to handle. Leave water in pan in case you need to boil more leaves.

9. To stuff, lay cooled leaf on large plate so that curled edges are up and core end is toward you. Spoon desired amount of mixture (1/3–1/2 cup) onto leaf at least 1 inch from core or near widest part. Spread in log shape across center. Fold core on top of mixture then roll away from you to edge of leaf.

10. Transfer to shallow baking dish with lid. May be placed close together. Repeat to use all mixture.

11. Pour reserved sauce evenly over all rolls. Cover. Bake for 20–25 minutes until sauce bubbles and begins to turn golden brown around edges. (If ingredients are room temperature or colder at start, bake for 30–35 minutes.) Serve immediately, use 2 metal spatulas to remove to serving plates.

Special Note: Although this dish has a long preparation time, its wonderful flavor is well worth the effort. Double the recipe for an excellent meal for company. Prepare up to baking stage and refrigerate earlier in the day. Also, double the recipe and freeze half of it for later. To freeze, I recommend placing stuffed rolls on baking sheet until frozen solid, then transfer to cellophane or plastic bag. Freeze sauce separately in glass jar. Thaw rolls in baking dish, spread with thawed sauce and bake as before. What a wonderful meal to enjoy on a lazy day!

Yield: makes a complete meal for two

Tuna Cabbage Rolls
(Day 1 Recipe)

1 jar	Chuck's Seafood albacore tuna, flaked (7 1/2 ounces)
1 cup	celery, diced
1 cup	cooked brown rice
1/8 teaspoon	sea salt
1 1/2 cups	liquid (tuna broth, celery broth, and water)
2 tablespoons	sesame seeds
1/4 cup	brown rice flour
1/4 teaspoon	sea salt
4–6	medium-size cabbage leaves

Nutritional Information/Serving	
Calories:	405
Protein (g):	39.9
Carbohydrate (g):	47.5
Fiber (g):	8.2
Total fat (g):	6.86
Saturated (g):	1.13
Cholesterol (mg):	19
Sodium (mg):	554
Food Exchanges/Serving	
1.9 Br 4.5 VLM 2.6 Veg .9 Fat	

1. Drain tuna, reserving broth in 2-cup liquid measure. Steam celery in medium-size saucepan for 3–5 minutes to partially cook. Drain over 2-cup measure to reserve broth.

2. Add water to reserved tuna and celery broth to yield 1 1/2 cups. Combine 1/4 cup of this liquid, sesame seeds, rice flour, and second measure of salt in blender. Blend on highest speed for 1–2 minutes until well blended. Stop at least once to scrape sides. Add remainder of the liquid and blend a couple of seconds more. Pour mixture into saucepan that you used to steam celery. Heat slowly on low until thickened, stirring often with a whisk to keep mixture smooth. Remove from heat.

3. Remove 7/8 cup (2 tablespoons less than 1 cup) of white sauce from saucepan and reserve for later. Add tuna (flake it as you add it), celery, rice, and first measure of salt to saucepan, stir, and set aside. Tuna mixture yields approximately 2 1/2 cups.

Continue recipe starting with step 5 of Chicken Cabbage Rolls (previous page). However, allow 30–35 minutes baking time since filling is not hot.

Yield: makes a complete meal for two

Turkey Quinoa Pasta Stew
(Day 3 Recipe)

1 cup	Turkey Broth (page 130)
1 cup	water
2 cups	carrots, fresh or frozen, peeled and sliced
1 cup	cauliflower, fresh or frozen, sliced or small florets
1 cup	cooked turkey meat, diced
as needed	sea salt
1 cup	wheat-free quinoa pasta
2 tablespoons	tapioca starch
1/2 cup	water

Nutritional Information/Serving	
Calories:	343
Protein (g):	25.6
Carbohydrate (g):	46.4
Fiber (g):	5.57
Total fat (g):	5.41
Saturated (g):	1.23
Cholesterol (mg):	53
Sodium (mg):	108
Food Exchanges/Serving	
2.1 Br 2.9 VLM 2.3 Veg .4 Fat	

1. In saucepan, combine all ingredients except last 3. Simmer until vegetables are almost tender.

2. Cook pasta according to recipe Perfect Pasta (page 195).

3. Whisk together water and starch. Add to stew, stirring continuously until thickened. Then add cooked pasta and stir gently until pasta is just hot enough to serve. May serve with Quinoa Biscuits (page 108).

Yield: 4 1/2 cups   2 servings

Special Note: Prepare only amount to be served because quinoa pasta turns to mush when reheated.

Stir-Fry Meal

	Day 1	Day 2	Day 4
Your choice of meat, cut into thin strips	deboned chicken breast	minute steak	tenderized pork or venison cutlet
Your choice of vegetables	broccoli cuts cabbage, thinly sliced or shredded celery, slant cut bok choy, sliced sliced water chestnuts and/or bamboo shoots	onion, thinly sliced green pepper strips zucchini, sliced	leek, thinly sliced edible pea pods, blanched asparagus, blanched
Your choice of nuts or seeds	almonds pecans	sunflower seeds	cashew pieces toasted soybeans
Your choice of oil	sesame oil almond oil	sunflower oil olive oil	safflower oil soy oil
as desired	sea salt		
Your choice of seasonings	dill weed	cayenne (red) pepper garlic powder	paprika garlic powder (optional)

If using venison, soak strips in salted water for a few hours or overnight to remove wild game taste.

1. Preheat well-seasoned cast-iron skillet on medium (see How to Season Cast Iron on page 59) or electric skillet to 300°F. Add oil after preheating.

2. Prepare meat and vegetables in amounts desired. Meat will cut into strips easier if partially frozen.

3. Stir fry meat, stirring often to brown evenly. When not stirring, cover with splatter screen.

4. Add vegetables, nuts, and/or seeds. Sprinkle with salt and seasonings. Stir often to cook evenly. I prefer my vegetables crunchy. Serve immediately with Basic Rice (Day 1), Amaranth (Day 2), or Buckwheat Groats (Day 4).

Yield: Allow 3 ounces of meat, 2 cups of vegetables, and 1 teaspoon of oil per serving.

Venison or Ham and Bean Stew
(Day 4 Recipe)

1 pound	venison stew meat or raw roast cut into 1/2-inch cubes
	OR fresh ham steak, uncured, unsmoked, cut into 1/2-inch cubes
2 cloves	garlic, minced
1 tablespoon	safflower oil
1/2 teaspoon	sea salt
2 cups	Meat Broth (page 140) or water
1 cup	leek, sliced
4 cups	green beans, fresh or frozen
1/2 teaspoon	Watkins Salsa Seasoning Blend or other Mexican blend spices (optional)
1 teaspoon	chili powder (optional)
2 cups	Navy Beans and Broth (page 170)
1/4 cup	water
2 tablespoons	white bean flour

Nutritional Information/Serving		
	Venison	Ham
Calories:	339	339
Protein (g):	41.5	24.9
Carbohydrate (g):	25.8	25.8
Fiber (g):	9.32	9.32
Total fat (g):	7.76	15.71
Saturated (g):	1.91	4.73
Cholesterol (mg):	127	62
Sodium (mg):	509	488
Food Exchanges/Serving		
Venison: .9 Br 4.9 VLM 2.5 Veg .7 Fat		
Ham: .9 Br 2.3 LM 2.5 Veg 1.8 Fat		

1. Trim excess fat off meat. Cut, if needed, into 1/2-inch cubes. Soak venison in salted water for 2 hours or overnight to remove wild game taste. Drain.

Venison or Ham and Bean Stew
(continued)

2. Brown stew meat and sauté garlic in oil in 5-quart Dutch-oven kettle. Stir often to brown meat evenly and prevent garlic from burning. Season with salt.

3. Add liquid, leeks, green beans, and rest of seasonings. Bring to boil. Reduce heat, cover, and simmer 30 minutes until green beans are almost tender.

4. Add Navy Beans and Broth. Simmer 5 minutes until ingredients are tender and flavors are blended. Taste and add more spices, if desired.

5. Whisk together water and bean flour. Add to stew, stir, cook to thicken broth. May be frozen, thaw and reheat slowly.

Yield: about 6 1/2 cups   4 servings

Special Note: May use canned green beans. Drain and reserve bean broth for use in liquid measure. Add canned green beans in step 4 rather than step 3.

Beef Stew*
(Day 2 Recipe)

1 pound	beef stew meat
2 teaspoons	olive or sunflower oil
1/2 teaspoon	sea salt
1/4 teaspoon	summer savory
2 cups	Beef Broth (page 140) OR water
1/2 cup	onion, chopped
1 pint	tomato quarters or pieces
1 1/2 cups	eggplant, peeled, ½-inch cubed
3/4 cup	zucchini squash, peeled, ½-inch cubed
2 cups	potatoes, peeled, ½-inch diced
1/2 cup	green peppers, diced (optional)
1/2 cup	peas*, frozen or fresh (optional)
1/2 cup	water
1 tablespoon	potato starch

Nutritional Information/Serving	
Calories:	382
Protein (g):	23.7
Carbohydrate (g):	35.4
Fiber (g):	5.73
Total fat (g):	16.97
Saturated (g):	5.97
Cholesterol (mg):	69
Sodium (mg):	513
Food Exchanges/Serving	
1.2 Br 2.8 LM 2.4 Veg 1.6 Fat	

1. Trim any excess fat from meat. Cut into ½ inch cubes. In a 5-quart Dutch-oven kettle, brown meat in oil. Season with salt and savory. Stir occasionally to brown meat evenly.

2. Add liquid, onion, and eggplant. Bring to boil, reduce heat, and cover. Simmer for 20 minutes. Stir occasionally.

3. Add tomatoes and zucchini. Simmer 10 minutes more. Add potatoes and simmer an additional 10 minutes or until potatoes are almost done. If needed, add more liquid.

4. If using green peppers, add and stir. Continue to cook another 5 minutes.

5. If using peas, add now. Whisk water and potato starch together and add while stirring stew. Continue to cook to thicken, stirring continually.

6. Serve when potatoes are tender.

Yield: approximately 6 cups or 4 servings

Special Note: This recipe can be prepared with additional eggplant, zucchini, and water or with different vegetables as desired.

*If using peas, omit eating them on your Day 4 just before and after serving this recipe on Day 2.

Roast and Broth

	Day 2 Beef or Buffalo	Day 4 Pork	Day 4 Venison
2–3 pounds	roast (arm, blade, rump, chuck, etc.)	roast (shoulder or ham, uncured/unsmoked)	roast
1 teaspoon	sea salt		
Seasoning	1/2 teaspoon summer savory		
Your choice of vegetable (optional)	1 onion, chopped large	1 cup leek, chopped large	

If using venison, soak roast in salted water overnight to remove wild game taste.

Method 1

1. Sprinkle salt over meat on all sides. Place in standard-size slow cooker. Add summer savory to beef or buffalo. If desired, add onion or leek. Add water to cover roast or to within 1 inch of top of roast. Cook on low for 8–10 hours.

2. After meal, strain leftover broth through fine-meshed strainer and chill. After chilling, remove solid fat layer on top. Freeze broth in ice cube trays. After frozen, remove and package in a cellophane or plastic bag. OR freeze in glass jars in amounts needed for recipes. Freeze leftover meat in cellophane or plastic bags for recipes or sandwiches.

Method 2

Prepare roast in Reynolds cooking bags. Follow package directions except do not shake flour in the empty bag and add more liquid than the directions list.

Serving Suggestions:

Day 2—Serve with potatoes and salad. Use broth over potatoes, if desired.

Day 4—Serve with sweet potatoes, Basic Buckwheat, or buckwheat pasta; asparagus and/or green beans; and use broth over potatoes, pasta, and/or vegetables, if desired.

Pork and Bean Burritos
(Day 4 Recipe)

4	Day 4 tortillas or griddle breads
3 cups	green beans, fresh, frozen, or canned
1/2 pound	ground pork
2 cups	Mexican Medley Beans (page 168)

Nutritional Information/Serving	
Calories:	372
Protein (g):	23.4
Carbohydrate (g):	49.4
Fiber (g):	11.96
Total fat (g):	10.48
Saturated (g):	3.5
Cholesterol (mg):	38
Sodium (mg):	341
Food Exchanges/Serving	
2.2 Br 1.5 LM 1.8 Veg .9 Fat	

1. Prepare or thaw tortillas or griddle bread.

2. If using fresh or frozen green beans, cook in saucepan until tender in small amount of water. Season with salt to taste.

3. In skillet, cook meat with 1/4 teaspoon of salt until done. Stir often to chop and brown evenly.

4. Add beans and cooked, drained green beans. (Sauce should be fairly thick. If too thick, add bean liquid as needed.) Simmer 5 minutes to blend flavors. Taste and add more seasonings if needed. Sauce yields 5 cups.

5. Spread 1/2 cup of mixture lengthwise on center third of each tortilla. Fold tortilla from each side on top of mixture. Carefully transfer to casserole dish, folded side down. My preference is a 10-inch covered Corning shallow dish. Top with remaining mixture. Cover and bake at 350°F. until at serving temperature.

Yield: 4 burritos   4 servings

Pork Chop
(Day 4 Recipe)

In skillet, brown chops for 2–3 minutes on each side in small amount of safflower oil at 400°F. or medium high. Season with salt and/or garlic powder. Add 1 cup or more of water. Cover and simmer 15–20 minutes until tender. Check during simmer time, add more water if needed.

Breaded Pork Chop
(Day 4 Recipe)

1/4 cup	Jerusalem artichoke flour
1/4 teaspoon	paprika
1/4 teaspoon	sea salt
8	pork chops or boneless tenderized pork cutlet (3 oz.)

1. Preheat oven to 450°F.
2. Trim excess fat. Rinse and pat dry leaving them a little moist.
3. In bowl, combine flour and seasonings. Place approximately 1 tablespoon in container with sealable lid (like Tupperware) that is large enough to hold chop.
4. Add 1 chop to container. Seal. Shake to coat. Place meat in unoiled stainless steel baking dish. Repeat for each chop, adding more mixture as needed.
5. Place in oven and reduce heat to 400°F. Bake for 30–40 minutes or until internal temperature is 180°F. Baking time will depend upon thickness.

Nutritional Information/Serving	
Calories:	82
Protein (g):	12.3
Carbohydrate (g):	2.0
Fiber (g):	.36
Total fat (g):	2.8
Saturated (g):	.96
Cholesterol (mg):	35
Sodium (mg):	103
Food Exchanges/Serving	
.1 Br 1.7 LM	

Yield: 8 or more pork chops If you prepare less than 8 chops, use amount of mixture needed and freeze remainder.

Pork or Venison and Buckwheat Pasta Casserole
(Day 4 Recipe)

1 pint	green beans, home canned, drained but reserve juice
1/2 cup	water or Meat Broth (page 140)
2 ounces	100% Buckwheat Soba Noodles
1/2 cup	cooked pork or venison, leftover from roast
as needed	sea salt

1. In medium-size saucepan, heat reserved bean juice (add water to make 3/4 cup) and broth to boiling.
2. Break pasta into 2-inch lengths. Add noodles to boiling liquid. Turn heat down to medium-high. Cook for 10 minutes stirring often. Add water as needed when liquid is low or noodles begin to stick.
3. Add beans and meat (more water if needed). Reduce heat to medium. Cover and heat 5 minutes or longer until desired serving temperature. Stir often to prevent sticking. Taste and add salt as needed.

Nutritional Information/Serving		
	Pork	Venison
Calories:	352	330
Protein (g):	25.9	26.6
Carbohydrate (g):	57.8	57.8
Fiber (g):	5.22	5.22
Total fat (g):	4.67	1.93
Saturated (g):	1.62	.66
Cholesterol (mg):	34	48
Sodium (mg):	158	157
Food Exchanges/Serving		
Pork: 2.6 Br 1.7 LM 2.3 Veg .2 Fat		
Venison: 2.6 Br 1.8 VLM 2.3 Veg		

Yield: 2 1/2 cups

Special Note: I often prepare these two casseroles for quick lunch using frozen cooked meat. Cook noodles only 8 minutes before continuing with rest of recipe if you plan to use it for a meal away from home. Pack in wide-mouth stainless steel thermos where noodles will continue to cook.

Stuffed Green Peppers
(Day 2 Recipe)

1 pound	ground beef or buffalo
1 cup	Muir Glen brand organic tomato puree
1 cup	water
1/4 cup	onion, diced
2 cups	zucchini or eggplant, peeled, diced, fresh or frozen
1 1/2 cups	Garbanzo Beans and Broth, drained, unsalted (page 166)
1 3/4 teaspoons	sea salt
1/4 teaspoon	minced garlic
1/2 teaspoon	Watkins Salsa Seasoning Blend or other Mexican blend spices
as needed	green peppers, choose peppers with somewhat flat bottoms so they will stand up in the casserole dish after being stuffed

Nutritional Information/Serving	
Calories:	253
Protein (g):	19.7
Carbohydrate (g):	24.5
Fiber (g):	5.84
Total fat (g):	9.38
Saturated (g):	3.33
Cholesterol (mg):	47
Sodium (mg):	685
Food Exchanges/Serving	
.6 Br 2.0 LM 2.6 Veg .5 Fat	

1. In skillet, cook ground meat, until meat is done. Stir often to chop meat and brown evenly.

2. Add rest of the ingredients except green peppers. Bring to boil. Reduce heat, cover, and simmer 30 minutes. Stir occasionally. Taste and add more spices as desired.

3. While mixture is simmering, prepare peppers. Wash and cut off tops (stem end). Next, remove seeds and center bitter membranes. To remove membrane, first cut most of it out with a sharp knife and then use a teaspoon to scrape out remainder without cutting or damaging pepper. Rinse to remove seeds and loose pieces of membrane.

4. Steam peppers in steamer pan for 8–10 minutes. Remove and chill in ice water to stop the cooking process. Drain.

5. When sauce is ready, fill peppers. Place in covered casserole dish(es) tall enough to allow for height of peppers. Bake covered in 350ºF. oven 30 minutes or until peppers are tender and stuffing is serving temperature. Serve immediately. If needed, melt shredded cheese on top of peppers not served to person with CRC.

6. Freeze stuffed peppers before baking. OR freeze blanched peppers unstuffed when in season to enjoy year round.

Yield: 6 cups of stuffing, usually enough for 12 small- to medium-size peppers   6 servings

USED FOR ANALYSIS: 1 cup eggplant, 1 cup zucchini

Easy Steak Dinner
(Day 2 Recipe)

1 pound	beef round steak, cut into strips
1/3 cup	arrowroot or potato starch OR 1/2 cup garbanzo bean flour
1 teaspoon	sea salt
1/4 teaspoon	summer savory (optional)
2 cups	onion, sliced
2 cups	green pepper strips, fresh or frozen
2 cups	zucchini squash, peeled and sliced, fresh or frozen
1 quart	tomato quarters or pieces

1. Prepare ingredients as described above. Partially frozen meat will cut into thin strips easier. Layer beef strips in bottom of standard-size slow cooker. Add thickener and seasonings. Stir to coat meat.

continued . . .

Easy Steak Dinner
(continued)

2. Layer onions, green peppers, and zucchini on the top of the meat mixture. <u>Do Not Stir</u>. Pour tomato pieces and juice as evenly as possible over layers. <u>Again, Do Not Stir</u>.

3. Cover and cook on high for 4–5 hours or on low for 8–10 hours. Serve over boiled potatoes or cooked garbanzo beans. Wonderful served over brown rice or millet if not following rotation given in this book. May be frozen, reheat slowly. The appearance is not as pretty after freezing, but taste is still wonderful.

Yield: 4 servings

Nutritional Information/Serving		
	Steak	Rabbit
Calories:	251	311
Protein (g):	27	40.7
Carbohydrate (g):	26.5	26.5
Fiber (g):	5.54	5.54
Total fat (g):	4.32	4.61
Saturated (g):	1.37	1.3
Cholesterol (mg):	63	139
Sodium (mg):	600	605
Food Exchanges/Serving		
Steak: .5 Br 2.5 LM 3 Veg		
Rabbit: .5 Br 5.3 VLM 3 Veg .3 Fat		

Easy Rabbit Dinner
(Day 2 Recipe)

Prepare the same as Easy Steak Dinner (except omit savory) substituting deboned rabbit for steak. Substitute 1 rabbit for 1 pound of steak. In addition, soak rabbit several hours or overnight in salt water to remove wild game taste.

Yield: 4 servings

Squash and Meatballs
(Day 4 Recipe)

1	acorn or butternut squash (1 3/4–2 pounds)
1 pound	ground pork
1/2 cup	leek, sliced
1/4 teaspoon	garlic powder
1/2 teaspoon	sea salt

Nutritional Information/Serving		
	Acorn	Butternut
Calories:	315	296
Protein (g):	22.3	22
Carbohydrate (g):	19.5	14.6
Fiber (g):	5.56	3.72
Total fat (g):	16.95	16.89
Saturated (g):	6.26	6.24
Cholesterol (mg):	76	76
Sodium (mg):	333	333
Food Exchanges/Serving		
Acorn: 1.2 Br 2.9 LM .4 Veg 1.6 Fat		
Butternut: .6 Br 2.9 LM .4 Veg 1.6 Fat		

1. Oven temperature—350°F. Preheating not necessary.

2. Wash squash and cut in half lengthwise (core to core). Cut threads with scissors or curved, serrated grapefruit knife. Scoop out seeds with large spoon.

3. Rinse squash. Sprinkle salt inside squash cavity. Place cut sides down in casserole dish(es). (Use covered casserole dish deep enough to hold a squash half filled with meatballs.) Add approximately 1/4 cup of water to each casserole dish. Bake uncovered for 20 minutes.

4. Mix remaining ingredients thoroughly. Divide into 16–20 portions and form into balls. Brown in skillet. Do not crowd so turning is easier. Turn often to brown on all sides. Drain on paper towels.

5. Remove squash from oven. Turn over and fill each cavity with half of meatballs. If all meatballs will not fit inside squash cavity, place extra directly in casserole dish. Cover and bake another 30 minutes or until squash is tender and pork is at least 180°F.

6. To serve, remove porkballs. Cut each squash portion in half crosswise. Serve each portion with 1/4 of meatballs. Baste with delicious broth, if desired. Complete the meal with green beans.

Yield: 4 servings

Special Notes: May be frozen. Thaw and reheat, covered, in microwave (on medium power) or in slow oven (300°F.). If reheating in microwave, heat squash some before adding pork.

This dish can also be prepared in the microwave. Cook squash with cut side down for 3 minutes. Turn squash over and add meatballs. Cook covered for 5 minutes or longer. Microwave cooking time will vary depending on wattage of oven. When preparing this dish in the microwave, start meatballs first.

Steak or Cutlet with Gravy

	Day 2 (2 servings)	Day 4 (2 servings)	Day 4 (4 servings)
Your choice of meat	2/3 pound minute steak, beef or buffalo	2/3 pound pork cutlet	1 1/2 pounds venison (round) steak
as needed	garbanzo bean flour	bean flour (both navy and pinto bean flour have been tested)	
2 teaspoons	sunflower oil	safflower oil	
to season	sea salt summer savory	sea salt	

Ingredients for gravy:

flour, as indicated	2 tablespoons garbanzo bean flour	3 tablespoons bean flour	
2 cups	water		
1/4 teaspoon	sea salt		

If using venison, cut into small pieces. Cover with salted water and allow to soak for a few hours or overnight to remove excess blood and wild taste.

1. Preheat electric skillet to 350ºF. Add oil. Developed using stainless steel electric skillet; others may require more oil.

2. Roll meat in the flour. Place in hot skillet. Sprinkle with seasonings as desired. Cover with splatter screen. Brown for 2 minutes—the browner the meat, the browner the gravy—but be careful not to dry it out or burn it. Turn meat, cover with splatter screen, and brown for another 2 minutes.

3. While the second side is browning, whisk together gravy ingredients. After browning, add mixture to skillet. Loosen any stuck meat pieces with spatula. Cover and reduce heat to between simmer and 200ºF. Simmer for 15–20 minutes, however do check on it from time to time. Buffalo may need longer cooking time.

Easy Meal Banquet
(Day 4 Recipe)

2 medium-size   sweet potatoes, peeled
2   pork or lamb chops, trim off excess fat
2 servings   asparagus spears, fresh or frozen

1. Fill bottom of steamer pan with water to about 1/2 inch from bottom of steamer insert. Heat to boiling.

2. In steamer pan insert, lay peeled (whole) sweet potatoes and sprinkle with salt. Place pork chops on top of potatoes and sprinkle with salt. Place insert pan over boiling water. Cover. Steam on medium-high for 25 minutes.

3. Add asparagus spears and sprinkle with salt. Cover and continue to cook 10–15 minutes longer until tender. Dish onto plates arranging foods separately. This is not a stew.

Yield: 2 complete meal servings

Nutritional Information/Serving		
	Lamb	Pork
Calories:	270	265
Protein (g):	19.7	20.8
Carbohydrate (g):	37.2	37.2
Fiber (g):	3.38	3.38
Total fat (g):	5.49	4.33
Saturated (g):	1.89	1.42
Cholesterol (mg):	48	46
Sodium (mg):	61	68
Food Exchanges/Serving		
Lamb: 1.7 Br 1.8 LM 1.1 Veg		
Pork: 1.7 Br 2.2 LM 1.1 Veg		

USED FOR ANALYSIS: 1/2 lb. asparagus, sweet potato weight 4 1/2 oz. each, chop weight 4 oz. each.

Recipe idea from The Yeast Connection Cookbook by Crook & Jones, p. 281.

Stir-Fry Buckwheat and Vegetables
3 Variations
(Day 4 Recipe)

<u>Vegetarian Variation</u>

	Nutritional Information Vegetarian Variation	
Calories:		427
Protein (g):		18
Carbohydrate (g):		81.9
Fiber (g):		14.58
Total fat (g):		7.22
Saturated (g):		.98
Cholesterol (mg):		0
Sodium (mg):		569
Food Exchanges/Serving		
3.4 Br 4.8 Veg .9 Fat		

1 teaspoon	safflower oil
1 clove	garlic, minced
1/2 cup	leek, sliced
1/4 teaspoon	chili powder (optional)
1/8 teaspoon	Watkins Salsa Seasoning Blend or other Mexican blend spices (optional)
2 cups	total Day 4 vegetables
	I prefer: 1 1/2 cups asparagus, blanched or frozen
	1/2 cup edible pea pods, blanched or frozen
	OR frozen or fresh peas
1 1/2 cups	Basic Buckwheat Groats, chilled (page 96)
1/4 teaspoon	sea salt

1. In large stainless steel skillet (preferably electric), sauté garlic, leek, and seasonings in oil until soft.

2. Add vegetables and buckwheat. Sprinkle with salt. Cook at 300°F. or on medium until ingredients are serving temperature and vegetables tender. Using a sharp-edged spatula, stir frequently and almost constantly during end of cooking. This is necessary to keep buckwheat from sticking to skillet. Add more oil if desired.

3. Serve as complete vegetarian meal or as side dish with meal.

Yield: 3 cups, 1 complete vegetarian meal or 3–4 side dish servings

Special Note: I enjoy this recipe for a quick lunch. If desired, you may omit the spices and/or adjust amounts of other ingredients. I often do not measure most of the ingredients, just dump and cook.

<u>Shrimp* Variation</u>

Add desired amount of cooked, shelled, and deveined shrimp to above recipe.

*Shrimp is assigned to Day 2, omit eating it on Day 2 just before and after eating this recipe on Day 4.

<u>Red Meat Variation</u>

Add desired amount of leftover grilled venison or pork steak (cut into strips) to Vegetarian Variation. Also, you can use raw tenderized venison steak or pork cutlet, cut into strips. If so, stir fry in small amount of oil before adding the rest of the ingredients.

Preparation Suggestion: Raw meat will cut into strips easier if partially frozen. Also, soak venison strips in salted water for a few hours or overnight to remove wild game taste.

> *Reflect upon your present blessings, of which every man has many, not on your past misfortunes, of which all men have some.*
>
> Charles Dickens

Scalloped Potatoes and Ham*
(Day 4 Recipe)

1 pound	ham steak (unsmoked and uncured)
3 cups	potatoes,* peeled, thinly sliced
1 cup	leek, chopped or thinly sliced
3 tablespoons	potato starch*
2 tablespoons	chopped cashew, macadamia or Brazil nuts*
1 teaspoon	sea salt
2 cups	water

Nutritional Information/Serving	
Calories:	368
Protein (g):	20.4
Carbohydrate (g):	38.5
Fiber (g):	2.39
Total fat (g):	14.86
Saturated (g):	4.76
Cholesterol (mg):	62
Sodium (mg):	584
Food Exchanges/Serving	
1.8 Br .1 VLM 2.3 LM .7 Veg 1.8 Fat	

1. Oven temperature—350°F. Preheating not necessary.

2. Trim excess fat off ham steak and dice.

3. Prepare potatoes. I use my Black & Decker® Handy Shortcut™ Micro-Processor, using the slicer disk. Rinse and drain.

4. Layer potatoes, ham, and leeks in an oiled, covered, 2-quart casserole dish. I prefer to use a Corning 10-inch shallow casserole dish.

5. Combine potato starch, nuts, salt, and 1/4 cup water in blender. Blend on high for approximately 1–2 minutes until well blended. Stop at least once to scrape sides and bottom. Add rest of water and blend for a couple seconds. Pour over layered ingredients. Lightly push any floating ingredients down into mixture.

6. Cover and bake until potatoes are tender (45–50 minutes in shallow casserole dish or up to 1 1/2 hours in deeper dish).

Yield: approximately 3 cups   4 servings

USED FOR ANALYSIS: Macadamia nuts.

*Potatoes are assigned to Day 2, omit eating them on Day 2 just before and after eating this recipe on Day 4. Brazil and macadamia nuts are unassigned "Fun Foods," see explanation on page 24.

Meatballs and Gravy
(Day 4 Recipe)

1 pound	ground venison or pork
1/2 cup	leek, chopped or sliced
1/2 teaspoon	sea salt
1/4 teaspoon	garlic powder (optional)
1 1/2 cups	water
1/4 cup	white or pinto bean flour

Nutritional Information/Serving		
	Venison	Pork
Calories:	241	285
Protein (g):	39.6	23.5
Carbohydrate (g):	8.4	8.36
Fiber (g):	4.49	4.49
Total fat (g):	4.23	16.79
Saturated (g):	1.65	6.22
Cholesterol (mg):	136	76
Sodium (mg):	715	332
Food Exchanges/Serving		
Venison: .5 Br 5.2 LM .4 Veg .3 Fat		
Pork: .5 Br 2.9 LM .4 Veg 1.6 Fat		

1. Combine ground meat, leeks, salt, and garlic thoroughly.

2. Divide into 16–20 equal portions and form into balls.

3. Brown in skillet. Turn often to brown on all sides. Do not crowd in skillet so turning is easier. Drain on paper towels if needed. Rinse excess grease from skillet. Note: If meat is very lean you may need to brown in small amount of safflower oil.

4. Return browned meatballs to skillet.

5. Whisk together water and bean flour. Pour over meatballs. Cover and simmer 20 minutes. Serve gravy over peas for a creamed-peas taste and appearance.

Yield: 4 servings

Enchiladas
(Day 2 Recipe)

| 8 | Day 2 tortillas or griddle breads |

Filling Ingredients:

1 pound	ground beef or buffalo
1 cup	Muir Glen brand organic tomato puree
1 cup	water
1 cup	eggplant, peeled, cubed
1/4 cup	onion, diced
1/2 cup	green pepper, diced
1 teaspoon	sea salt
1/2 teaspoon	Watkins Salsa Seasoning Blend or other Mexican blend spices
1/4 teaspoon	minced garlic

Sauce Ingredients:

1 cup	Muir Glen brand organic tomato puree
1/4 cup	onion, diced
1/4 cup	green pepper, diced
1 teaspoon	sea salt
1/4 teaspoon	chili powder
1/8 teaspoon	Watkins Salsa Seasoning Blend or other Mexican blend spices
1/8 teaspoon	minced garlic

Topping Ingredients:

| as desired | shredded lettuce |
| as desired | diced fresh tomatoes |

Nutritional Information/Serving with Amaranth Tortillas and without Toppings	
Calories:	259
Protein (g):	16.5
Carbohydrate (g):	28.7
Fiber (g):	3.90
Total fat (g):	8.4
Saturated (g):	2.47
Cholesterol (mg):	35
Sodium (mg):	719
Food Exchanges/Serving	
1.5 Br 1.7 LM 1.4 Veg .4 Fat	

1. Prepare or thaw tortillas or griddle bread.

2. In skillet, cook meat until done. Stir often to chop meat and brown evenly.

3. Add rest of filling ingredients. Heat to boiling, reduce heat, cover, and simmer at least 30 minutes. Stir occasionally. Filling yields 4 cups.

4. While filling is simmering, combine sauce ingredients in mixer measure. Add enough water to yield 3 cups. Set aside.

5. Spread 1/2 cup of filling mixture lengthwise on center third of tortilla. Fold tortilla from each side on top of mixture. Carefully transfer enchilada to casserole dish, folded side down. My preference is a 10-inch covered Corning shallow dish. Crowd enchiladas to get 4 in one dish. Pour sauce evenly over enchiladas, 3/4 cup sauce each.

6. Bake in 350°F. oven for 30 minutes or until sauce bubbles and enchilada filling is hot.

7. While enchiladas are baking, prepare lettuce and tomatoes. Refrigerate until needed. Optional: stir small amount of Watkins Salsa Seasoning Blend into diced tomatoes.

8. To Serve: Cut each enchilada in half crosswise. Use 2 large metal spatulas to transfer enchiladas to dinner plates. Top with lettuce and tomatoes.

Keep your face to the sunshine and you cannot see the shadow.
—Helen Keller

Special Note: May freeze filling and sauce separately. Not recommended to freeze filled tortillas or griddle bread.

Yield: 8 enchiladas (4 cups of filling and 3 cups of sauce)   8 servings

12" Pizza Crust

	Day 1 Kamut®	Day 1 Spelt	Day 2 Amaranth	Day 4 Buckwheat
flour/starch	1 1/4 cup Kamut flour	1 1/4 cup spelt flour	1 cup amaranth flour 1/2 cup arrowroot starch	1 1/4 cup White Buckwheat flour (page 105)
baking soda	5/8 teaspoon			
unbuffered vitamin C crystals	3/8 teaspoon			
sea salt	scant 1/4 teaspoon			
water	1/2 cup	3/8 cup	1/2 cup	1/2 cup
oil	2 tablespoons sesame oil		2 tablespoons olive or sunflower oil	2 tablespoons safflower oil
sauce and toppings	as directed by recipe			

1. Have pizza sauce completely ready and warm. (Special Note: See notation at top of Chicken Pizza Sauce to begin crust first.)
2. Preheat oven to 350°F.
3. In medium-size mixing bowl, whisk together dry ingredients. Make a "well" in the center.
4. Add water and oil. Stir with rubber spatula, making sure all ingredients are moistened.
5. Place 1 teaspoon oil in center of 12-inch stainless steel pizza pan. Using fingers, spread oil on pizza pan to within 1 inch of edge. Make sure hands are lightly coated with oil before beginning next step.
6. With lightly oil coated fingers, touch dough. If dough seems a little too soft and is sticking to your fingers, mix between 1 teaspoon and 1 tablespoon more flour into dough before proceeding with next step.
7. Transfer to pizza pan. Press dough out in a circular shape, maintaining even thickness and pressing out from center in all directions. Push outer edge of dough circle up on outer edge of pizza pan. Dough will be about 3/8 inch thick. If it appears thin in spots, press surrounding dough toward the thin area to remedy.
8. Wash hands to remove oil.
9. Pour warm sauce onto crust and spread out to cover surface. Add desired toppings as directed on sauce recipes.
10. Bake at 350°F for 25–30 minutes.

Yield: one 12" pizza   8 slices

Recipe idea from Mastering Food Allergies *newsletter, May 1991.*

┌─────────────────────────┐
│ **HH**   │
│ See how to freeze and   │
│ reheat pizza on page 75.│
└─────────────────────────┘

Nutritional Information/Slice—Crust Only				
	Kamut	Spelt	Amaranth	Buckwheat
Calories:	110	110	113	81
Protein (g):	3.3	3.3	2	1.9
Carbohydrate (g):	19.2	18.7	16.6	10.8
Fiber (g):	1.87	3.74	1.27	1.53
Total fat (g):	3.87	3.87	4.13	3.88
Saturated (g):	.48	.48	.46	.41
Cholesterol (mg):	0	0	0	0
Sodium (mg):	152	152	153	154
Food Exchanges/Slice—Crust Only				
	1 Br .7 Fat	1 Br .7 Fat	1 Br .1 LM .7 Fat	.6 Br .7 Fat

Spaghetti or Pizza Meat Sauce
(Two Variations)
(Day 2 Recipe)

	With Vegetables	
4 cups	6 cups	YIELD
2 cloves	4 cloves	garlic, minced
1 teaspoon	1 teaspoon	olive oil
1 pound	1 pound	ground beef or buffalo
1/2 cup	1/2 cup	onion, chopped
1 cup	1 cup	green pepper, chopped
none	3 1/2 cups	your choice of Day 2 vegetables—eggplant, zucchini, okra
		I prefer: 2 1/2 cups eggplant, peeled, ½-inch cubed
		1 cup zucchini squash, peeled, ½-inch cubed
1/2 can	1/2 can	Muir Glen brand organic tomato puree (28 oz. can)
2 cups	2 cups	water
1 1/4 teaspoons	1 1/2 teaspoons	sea salt
1/4 teaspoon	1/4 teaspoon	summer savory
1 1/2 teaspoons	2 teaspoons	basil
1 tablespoon	1 1/2 tablespoons	leaf oregano
scan 1/4 teaspoon	1/4 teaspoon	crushed cayenne (red) pepper

Pizza Toppings:

as desired	green peppers, chopped or stripped
as desired	Spaghetti Squash (page 203)

1. In large skillet or kettle, sauté garlic in oil until soft. Add ground meat and cook until done. Stir often to chop and brown evenly.

2. Add rest of sauce ingredients. Heat to boiling, reduce heat, and cover. Simmer at least 1 hour. Stir occasionally. Taste and, if desired, add more seasonings.

3. For Spaghetti:
Serve with Spaghetti Squash or temporarily transfer buckwheat to Day 2 and serve with purchased 100% buckwheat soba noodles.

OR

For Pizza:
Prepare Amaranth Pizza Crust (page 148). Pour 2 cups of warm sauce onto crust and spread to cover surface. Sprinkle with desired amount of peppers. String spaghetti squash over top to give appearance of cheese. Bake according to pizza crust recipe.

Pizza Yield: 8 slices

Special Note: Vegetables used may be prepared and frozen when in season. May freeze sauce and prepared pizza.

USED FOR ANALYSIS: Pasta not included in spaghetti analysis. Toppings not included in pizza analysis.

Nutritional Information/Sauce Only/Cup		
	Regular	With Vegetables
Calories:	267	192
Protein (g):	23.8	16.6
Carbohydrate (g):	13.5	12.3
Fiber (g):	3.16	3.4
Total fat (g):	13.43	9.07
Saturated (g):	4.94	3.31
Cholesterol (mg):	71	47
Sodium (mg):	765	601
Food Exchanges/Sauce Only/Cup		
Regular: 3 LM 2.3 Veg .9 Fat		
With Vegetables: 2 LM 2.1 Veg .6 Fat		

Nutritional Information/Slice **Pizza with Amaranth Crust**		
	Regular	With Vegetables
Calories:	180	162
Protein (g):	8	6.2
Carbohydrate (g):	19.9	19.6
Fiber (g):	2.06	2.12
Total fat (g):	7.49	6.4
Saturated (g):	1.69	1.28
Cholesterol (mg):	18	12
Sodium (mg):	344	303
Food Exchanges/Sauce Only/Cup		
Regular: 1 Br .9 LM .6 Veg .9 Fat		
With Vegetables: 1 Br .6 LM .5 Veg .9 Fat		

Chicken Spaghetti/Pizza Sauce
(Day 1 Recipe)

1 cup	Chicken Broth (page 130) or water
1/2–1 cup	water (1/2 cup for Pizza Sauce, 1 cup for Spaghetti Sauce)
3 3/4–4 cups	Day 1 vegetables. My preference follows.
2 cups	cabbage, chopped fine or shredded
1 cup	broccoli cuts, fresh or frozen
3/4 cup	bok choy or celery, sliced
1 cup	cooked diced chicken
1/4 teaspoon	sea salt
3/4 teaspoon	ground cumin
	OR 1/2 teaspoon dill weed
1/4 cup	water
1 tablespoon	hulled sesame seeds
2 tablespoons	flour—Kamut, spelt, rice

For pizza, perform steps 1–4 of your choice of Day 1 crust recipe, set aside, then start this quick sauce.

For spaghetti, begin the meal preparation by boiling salted water and cooking your choice of Day 1 spaghetti (Kamut, spelt, or rice).

1. In medium-size saucepan, add broth, first listing of water, your choice of vegetables, chicken, and seasoning. Bring to boil, reduce heat, cover, and simmer for 3–5 minutes.

2. While vegetables are cooking, combine second listing of water, seeds, and flour in blender. Blend on highest speed for 1–2 minutes until well blended. Stop at least once to scrape sides.

3. Add to vegetable mixture and cook 2–5 minutes on low until sauce thickens and vegetables are cooked to your liking. Stir often.

For Spaghetti: Drain spaghetti, pour sauce over top, and serve immediately.

For Pizza: Complete crust preparation while sauce is cooking. Spread mixture evenly over crust. Bake according to crust recipe.

Yield: 3 1/2 cups Spaghetti Sauce   2 servings
      3 cups Pizza Sauce, enough for one 12 inch Pizza, 8 slices

Serving Suggestion: Sauce also delicious served over Day 1 biscuits.

USED FOR ANALYSIS: Vegetables listed as "My Preference" above. Analysis on next page.

Vegetarian Day 1 Spaghetti/Pizza Sauce
(Day 1 Recipe)

Use ingredients and follow directions for Chicken Spaghetti/Pizza Sauce recipe above except make the following changes:

- Omit chicken meat.
- Substitute water or vegetable broth in place of chicken broth.
- Increase vegetables to a total of 5 1/2 cups.
- Increase salt and other seasoning to your liking.
- I also prefer to add garlic powder to the vegetarian version even though it breaks rotation

Yield: 3 1/2 cups Spaghetti Sauce   2 servings
      3 cups Pizza Sauce, enough for one 12 inch Pizza, 8 slices

Serving Suggestion: Sauce also delicious served over Day 1 biscuits.

USED FOR ANALYSIS: 3 cups cabbage, 1 3/4 cups broccoli, 3/4 cup bok choy. Analysis on next page.

	Nutritional Information/Serving		Nutritional Information/Pizza Slice			
	Sauce Only		Chicken Sauce with Crust		Veggie Sauce with Crust	
	Chicken Sauce	Veggie Sauce	Kamut Crust	Spelt Crust	Kamut Crust	Spelt Crust
Calories:	218	114	164	164	138	138
Protein (g):	24.1	6.6	9.3	9.3	4.9	4.9
Carbohydrate (g):	15.7	19.7	23.1	22.6	24.1	23.6
Fiber (g):	4.43	6.23	2.98	4.85	3.43	5.3
Total fat (g):	7.7	3.26	5.8	5.8	4.69	4.69
Saturated (g):	1.66	.4	.9	.9	.58	.58
Cholesterol (mg):	58	0	14.5	14.5	0	0
Sodium (mg):	359	411	242	242	255	255
	Food Exchanges/Serving		Food Exchanges/Pizza Slice			
	Chicken Sauce	Veggie Sauce	Both Crusts:			
	.4 Br 2.9 VLM 1.4 Veg 1.2 Fat	.4 Br .1 VLM 2.1 Veg .5 Fat	1.1 Br .3 Veg 1 Fat		1.1 Br .5 Veg .8 Fat	

Amazing Spaghetti/Pizza Sauce
(Day 2 or Day 4 Recipe)

The color of this sauce resembles what you would expect had it been made with yellow or low-acid tomatoes. The flavor is wonderful so don't discount this recipe until you have tried it.

3 cloves	garlic, minced
1 cup	onion or leeks, chopped
1 tablespoon	oil—olive or sunflower for Day 2, safflower for Day 4
1 pound	ground meat: beef or buffalo for Day 2, pork or venison for Day 4
1 cup	green peppers, chopped OR sliced okra
2 cups	zucchini squash, peeled, 1/2-inch cubed
1 3/4 cups	Pumpkin Puree or cooked butternut squash (page 209), OR 1–15 oz. can of pumpkin
2 1/2 cups	water
1 1/4 teas.	sea salt
4 1/2 teas.	leaf oregano
2 teaspoons	basil
1/4 teaspoon	crushed cayenne (red) pepper

Nutritional Information—Sauce Only/Cup			
	Beef	Pork	Venison
Calories:	169	192	166
Protein (g):	13.7	13.4	23
Carbohydrate (g):	8.7	8.7	8.7
Fiber (g):	2.21	2.21	2.21
Total fat (g):	9.11	11.73	4.56
Saturated (g):	3.03	3.86	1.25
Cholesterol (mg):	40	44	78
Sodium (mg):	421	420	639
Food Exchanges—Sauce Only/Cup			
Beef: 1.7 LM .9 Veg .8 Fat			
Pork: 1.7 LM .9 Veg 1.3 Fat			
Venison: 3 LM .9 Veg .5 Fat			

1. In large skillet or Dutch oven, sauté garlic and onion or leeks in oil until soft. Add your choice of meat and cook until done. Stir often to chop meat and brown evenly. Add remaining ingredients. Heat to boiling. Reduce heat and cover. Simmer at least one hour, stirring occasionally.

2. Add additional water if needed. Taste and, if desired, add more seasonings. Freeze leftovers. Reheat slowly.

3. For Spaghetti: serve on Day 2 with Spaghetti Squash (page 203) or on Day 4 with purchased 100% Buckwheat Soba noodles.

4. For Pizza: For Day 2, prepare Amaranth Pizza Crust. For Day 4, prepare Buckwheat Pizza Crust (page 148). Follow directions in crust recipe. Add green peppers and spaghetti squash as explained on pizza recipe on page 149.

Nutritional Information/Slice With Pork and Buckwheat Pizza Crust—Toppings Not Included	
Calories:	129
Protein (g):	5.3
Carbohydrate (g):	13
Fiber (g):	2.08
Total fat (g):	6.81
Saturated (g):	1.38
Cholesterol (mg):	11
Sodium (mg):	259
Food Exchanges/Slice	
.6 Br .4 LM .2 Veg 1 Fat	

Sauce Yield: 7 cups   7 servings

Vegetarian Pizza
(Day 2 Recipe)

1/2 recipe	sauce only from Vegetarian Lasagna (page 152) except reduce salt to 1 teaspoon/recipe
4 ounces	amaranth greens, washed and drained OR spinach leaves*
12-inch	Amaranth Pizza Crust (page 148)
as desired	green peppers, chopped
as desired	Spaghetti Squash (page 203)

1. Prepare sauce according to Vegetarian Lasagna recipe with addition of 4 pinches of crushed red pepper. Keep warm.

2. Prepare Amaranth Pizza Crust. Spread thin layer of sauce on crust. Layer greens to cover (1 or more layer). Pour on remaining sauce and spread to cover greens and crust.

3. Sprinkle with desired amount of peppers. String spaghetti squash over top to give appearance of cheese. Bake according to pizza crust recipe.

Yield: one 12-inch pizza, cut into 8 servings

Special Note: Prepare a single recipe of sauce and freeze half to prepare a quick pizza later.

*If using spinach, plan ahead to omit it on Day 3 before and omit all foods from Goosefoot Family (beet, chard, quinoa, spinach) from Day 1 just before and Day 3 just after enjoying spinach in this recipe on Day 2 (see table with Vegetarian Lasagna (page 153).

Nutritional Information/Slice Toppings Not Included in Analysis		
	Sauce Only	With Amaranth Crust
Calories:	33	146
Protein (g):	1.3	3.3
Carbohydrate (g):	5.7	22.2
Fiber (g):	1.58	2.85
Total fat (g):	.98	5.11
Saturated (g):	.14	.59
Cholesterol (mg):	0	0
Sodium (mg):	146	299
Food Exchanges/Slice		
Sauce Only: 1 Veg .2 Fat		
With Crust: 1 Br .1 LM 1 Veg .9 Fat		

Taco Pizza Sauce
(Day 2 Recipe)

Sauce Ingredients/2 Pizzas

1 pound	ground beef or buffalo
1 cup	Muir Glen brand organic tomato puree
1 cup	water
1/4 cup	onion, chopped
2 cups	eggplant, peeled, chopped
1/2 teaspoon	sea salt
1/4 teaspoon	garlic, minced
3/4 teaspoon	Watkins Salsa Seasoning Blend or other Mexican blend spices

Topping Ingredients/1 Pizza

1/2 cup	onions, diced
4–5 cups	lettuce, shredded
2 cups	tomatoes, fresh, diced
as desired	Guacamole and/or Picante Sauce (page 227)

Nutritional Information/Slice Analysis Includes Tomato & Lettuce Toppings		
	Sauce & Toppings Only	With Amaranth Crust
Calories:	68	181
Protein (g):	6.2	8.2
Carbohydrate (g):	4	20.5
Fiber (g):	1.08	2.35
Total fat (g):	3.16	7.29
Saturated (g):	1.21	1.67
Cholesterol (mg):	18	18
Sodium (mg):	90	143
Food Exchanges/Slice		
Sauce & Toppings Only: .8 LM .7 Veg .2 Fat		
With Crust: 1 Br .9 LM .7 Veg .9 Fat		

1. Prepare Guacamole and Picante Sauce. Chill.

2. In skillet, cook meat until done, stir often to chop and brown evenly. Add remaining sauce ingredients. Bring to boil, reduce heat, cover, and simmer 30 minutes. Stir occasionally. Taste and, if desired, add more spices.

3. While sauce is simmering, prepare Amaranth Pizza Crust (page 148). Pour 2 cups of warm sauce onto crust and spread to cover. Sprinkle with additional onions. Bake according to pizza crust recipe.

4. While pizza is baking, prepare tomatoes, lettuce, and onions. Refrigerate until needed. Optional, stir 1/8 teaspoon of Watkins Salsa Seasoning Blend or other Mexican blend spices into tomatoes.

5. Cut pizza. Garnish as desired with toppings.   Yield: 4 cups sauce (two 12" pizzas/ 8 pieces each)

Vegetarian Lasagna*
(Day 2 Recipe)

5 cloves	garlic, minced
1 cup	onion, chopped
1 tablespoon	olive oil
1/2 can	Muir Glen brand organic tomato puree (28 oz. can)
2 cups	water
3 cups	eggplant, peeled, chopped
1 cup	green pepper, chopped
4 teaspoons	leaf oregano
2 teaspoons	basil
1 1/2 teaspoons	sea salt
as desired	amaranth greens, washed and drained (page 32) OR spinach leaves*
1 recipe	Soy Lasagna Noodles (page 113)**
1 pound	soft tofu, drained, thinly sliced lengthwise (12 slices)**

Nutritional Information/Serving	
Calories:	327
Protein (g):	24
Carbohydrate (g):	32
Fiber (g):	7.97
Total fat (g):	14.74
Saturated (g):	2.11
Cholesterol (mg):	0
Sodium (mg):	990
Food Exchanges/Serving	
.5 Br 1.1 VLM 3.6 Veg 2.7 Fat	

To prepare sauce:

1. In a large kettle sauté garlic and onion in oil until soft.

2. Add remaining ingredients from list through salt. Heat to boiling, reduce heat, cover, and simmer at least 1 hour. Stir occasionally. Taste and add more seasonings, if desired. Sauce yields 4 1/2–5 cups, add more water if needed.

To prepare lasagna:

3. Oven temperature—350°F. Preheating not necessary.

4. Layer ingredients in following order. (Amounts given are for Corning 10-inch square covered casserole dish. Divide ingredients evenly to prepare in 4 or 6 covered Corning Grab-It Bowls.)

   - 1 cup sauce, spread evenly
   - 2–3 layers of greens
   - 1 layer of Soy Lasagna Noodles
   - 6 slices of tofu
   - 1 1/2 cups sauce, spread evenly

   - 1 layer of Soy Lasagna Noodles
   - 2–3 layers of greens
   - 6 slices of tofu
   - 2 cups sauce, spread evenly

5. Cover. Bake for 60–70 minutes until sauce bubbles and ingredients are fork tender. Remove, allow to set 5 minutes. Cut in desired portions, serve with spatula. May be frozen. For best quality, thaw and reheat slowly in covered dish. If preparing recipe in individual bowls, freeze unbaked, thaw completely, and bake as usual.

Special Notes: Can substitute uncooked whole-wheat or spelt noodles. Also can replace 1 layer of tofu with mozzarella cheese.

USED FOR ANALYSIS: 4 oz. of amaranth greens

*If using spinach, plan ahead to omit it on Day 3 before and omit all foods from Goosefoot Family (beet, chard, quinoa, spinach) from Day 1 just before and Day 3 after enjoying spinach in this recipe on Day 2 (see table below).

**Soy is assigned to Day 4. Omit eating it on Day 4 just before and after eating this recipe on Day 2.

Yield: 4 servings

Day 1	Day 2	Day 3	Day 4
		omit spinach	
omit all Goosefoot Family	enjoy Pizza or Lasagna with spinach leaves	omit all Goosefoot Family	

Tofu Lasagna*
(Day 2 Recipe)

3 cloves	garlic, minced
3/4 cup	onion, chopped
1 teaspoon	olive oil
1 pound	ground beef or buffalo
1 1/2 teaspoons	sea salt
1/2 can	Muir Glen brand organic tomato puree (28 oz. can)
2 cups	water
1 1/2 teaspoons	basil
1 tablespoon	oregano
1/2 teaspoon	summer savory
1 pound	soft tofu, drained, thinly sliced*
1 medium	eggplant, peeled, thinly sliced

Nutritional Information/Serving	
Calories:	395
Protein (g):	34.2
Carbohydrate (g):	25.8
Fiber (g):	8.3
Total fat (g):	19.2
Saturated (g):	5.79
Cholesterol (mg):	71
Sodium (mg):	911
Food Exchanges/Serving	
1.1 VLM 3 LM 3.7 Veg 2.0 Fat	

To Prepare Sauce:

1. In large skillet or kettle, sauté garlic and onion in oil until soft. Add ground meat cook until done. Stir often to chop meat and brown evenly.

2. Add remaining ingredients except tofu and eggplant. Heat to boiling, reduce heat, cover, and simmer at least 30 minutes. Stir occasionally. Taste and, if desired, add more seasonings. Sauce yields 4 1/2 cups, add water if needed.

To Prepare Lasagna:

3. Oven temperature—350°F. Preheating not necessary.

4. Layer ingredients in following order. (Amounts given are for Corning 10-inch square covered casserole dish. Divide ingredients evenly to prepare in 4 or 6 covered Corning Grab-It Bowls.)
   - 1 cup of sauce, spread evenly over bottom of dish
   - thin slices of eggplant to cover sauce (can be straight from freezer)
   - thin slices of tofu to cover eggplant
   - 1 1/2 cups of sauce, spread evenly over tofu
   - thin slices of eggplant to cover sauce
   - thin slices of tofu to cover eggplant
   - 2 cups of sauce to cover everything completely

5. Cover. Bake for 50–60 minutes or until sauce bubbles and ingredients are fork tender. Remove and allow to set 5 minutes. Cut in desired portions and serve with spatula. May be frozen. For best quality, thaw and reheat slowly in covered dish. If preparing in individual bowls, freeze unbaked, thaw completely, and bake as usual.

Yield: 4 servings

*Tofu is assigned to Day 4, omit eating soy on Day 4 just before and after eating this recipe on Day 2.

Special Note: If desired, add Soy Lasagna Noodles (page 113) or dry, uncooked whole-wheat or spelt noodles. Layer noodles in place of eggplant for first layer and with eggplant for second layer.

Happiness is not a state to arrive at, but a manner of traveling.
—*Margaret Lee Runbeck*

Low Carbohydrate Lasagna
(Day 2 Recipe)

Use sauce ingredients from Tofu Lasagna (page 154)—except use
only 1 1/2 cups of water

3 layers	summer squash, sliced approximately 1/4 inch thick
3–6 layers	amaranth greens, washed and drained (page 32)
	OR spinach leaves (see * explanation on Vegetarian Lasagna on page 153)

Nutritional Information/Serving	
Calories:	199
Protein (g):	17.5
Carbohydrate (g):	13.1
Fiber (g):	3.69
Total fat (g):	9.2
Saturated (g):	3.35
Cholesterol (mg):	47
Sodium (mg):	607
Food Exchanges/Serving	
2 LM 2.3 Veg .6 Fat	

1. Prepare sauce as in steps 1 and 2 in Tofu Lasagna, except use only 1 1/2 cups of water. Sauce yields 4 cups.

2. Oven temperature—350ºF. Preheating not necessary.

3. Layer ingredients in following order. (Amounts given are for Corning 10-inch square covered casserole dish. Divide ingredients evenly to prepare in 4 or 6 covered Corning Grab-It Bowls.)

   • 3/4 cup of sauce, spread evenly over bottom of dish

   • 1 layer of squash slices to cover sauce (can be straight from freezer)

   • 1–2 layers of greens

   • 1 cup of sauce, spread evenly

   • repeat squash, greens, and 1 cup sauce layers 2 more times using remaining sauce on top of final layer

4. Bake and serve as described in step 5 in Tofu Lasagna.

Yield: 6 servings

Italian Tofu*
(Day 4 Recipe)

1 cup	Muir Glen brand organic tomato puree*
1 cup	liquid (green bean broth and/or water)
2 cups	green beans, fresh, frozen, or drained canned (reserve drained liquid)
1/4 teaspoon	sea salt
1/4 teaspoon	minced garlic
1/4 teaspoon	basil*
1/2 teaspoon	leaf oregano
1 pinch	crushed cayenne (red) pepper*
8 ounces	tofu

Nutritional Information/Serving	
Calories:	153
Protein (g):	12.7
Carbohydrate (g):	18.2
Fiber (g):	5.12
Total fat (g):	5.56
Saturated (g):	.82
Cholesterol (mg):	0
Sodium (mg):	317
Food Exchanges/Serving	
1.1 VLM 3 Veg 1.1 Fat	

1. In saucepan, combine all ingredients except tofu. Simmer until green beans are tender and flavors are blended. Yields approximately 2 1/2 cups.

2. Drain and dice tofu. Gently stir into step 1. Heat just long enough to bring tofu to serving temperature.

Yield: 2 servings

*These foods are assigned to Day 2. Omit eating them on Day 2 just before and after serving this recipe on Day 4.

Baked Fish for Day 1, 2, 3, or 4

	Day 1	Day 2	Day 3	Day 4
Your choice of fish fillets	halibut sole tuna steak	cod (scrod) pollack red snapper	flounder salmon steak	haddock mahi mahi ocean perch
Your choice of seasonings	dill weed ground cumin	basil garlic oregano savory rosemary and/or thyme	fennel ginger caraway seeds and/or canola seeds	tarragon garlic oregano
Your choice of foods	sliced celery sliced water chestnuts bamboo shoots almonds pecans sesame seeds	sliced onion green pepper strips sliced zucchini sunflower seeds	sliced apples thinly sliced carrots thinly sliced parsnips	leeks peas cashews lentil or pea sprouts
Your choice of oil, if desired	sesame oil almond oil	olive oil, butter, or Clarified Butter (pg. 226)	canola oil (for flounder)	safflower oil soy oil
Your choice of garnish (after cooking)	fresh parsley	squeeze of fresh lemon	fresh spinach	squeeze of fresh orange

1. Using your choice of ingredients:
   * Place fish fillet in covered casserole dish.
   * Sprinkle with salt and seasonings.
   * Add choice of other foods.
   * Drizzle with 1/2 teaspoon of oil per serving (if desired).
2. Add 1–2 tablespoons of water to dish. Cover and bake for 30 minutes at 350°F. until fish is flaky. Time will depend on thickness of fillet, if fillet is frozen or thawed, and amount of other foods used.
3. After cooking, garnish as desired and serve immediately.

Yield: 1 pound of fish equals 5 servings.

Spicy Baked Fish
(Day 2 Recipe)

1/2 pound	cod (scrod) or pollack fillet (2 servings)
2 cups	canned tomato quarters or pieces, drained OR 1 cup fresh peeled tomato quarters
1/4 teaspoon	sea salt
1/2 teaspoon	leaf oregano
1/4 teaspoon	basil
1/4 teaspoon	minced garlic
2 cups	zucchini squash, peeled, sliced or diced OR 1 cup sliced okra
1/2 cup	onion, sliced or chopped (optional)

Place fish fillets in a shallow covered casserole dish. Combine tomatoes and seasonings. Add rest of vegetables, stir, pour evenly over fish. Cover and bake 45 minutes until fish is flaky and vegetables tender.

Suggestion: Save tomato juice to drink or freeze to add to a soup.

Yield: 2 servings

Nutritional Information/Serving	
Calories:	148
Protein (g):	23
Carbohydrate (g):	12
Fiber (g):	3.42
Total fat (g):	1.33
Saturated (g):	.24
Cholesterol (mg):	49
Sodium (mg):	341
Food Exchanges/Serving	
2.9 VLM 2.2 Veg	

Rainbow Trout
(Baked or Grilled)
(Day 3 Recipe)

<u>To bake:</u>
- Rainbow Trout is cooked with head and tail intact.
- Rinse trout thoroughly. Sprinkle inside with small amount of sea salt.
- Place in shallow covered casserole dish that is large enough to keep fish flat.   Cover and bake at 350ºF. for 20 minutes or until trout is flaky and skin removes easily.

<u>To Grill:</u>
- Prepare trout same as for baking except place trout in aluminum foil. Fold ends and edges of foil around trout to make a folded seal.
- Place on preheated counter-top electric grill on highest setting. Grill 10 minutes on first side, turn, and grill 7 minutes on second side.

<u>To remove skin and bones:</u>
- Using the edge of a fork, break through skin along back bone.
- Use two (2) table forks like tongs to pull skin off top of trout.
- Slide fork under meat to remove top fillet without bone. Fillet may come off in more than one piece.
- Carefully use fingers to pull bone up from tail. Look closely and remove any remaining small bones from bottom fillet.
- Turn fish over and remove skin from bottom fillet.
- Serve immediately with small amount of flaxseed oil or break rotation and sprinkle with garlic powder and use Clarified Butter (page 226) instead of oil.

HH: Counter-top Grill
   An electric **thermostat-controlled** counter-top grill is a handy to grill fish filets, steaks, pork chops, etc. Look for a model that disassembles and reassembles easily for cleaning.

Grilled Fish for Day 1, 3, or 4

	Day 1	Day 3	Day 4
Your choice of fish fillet for grilling	fresh tuna steak halibut steak	fresh salmon steak	mahi mahi
Your choice of seasonings	dill weed ground cumin		tarragon garlic
Your choice of oil	sesame oil	canola oil	safflower or soy oil
Your choice of garnish (after cooking)	fresh parsley	fresh spinach fresh parsley	squeeze of fresh orange

Baste both sides of fish fillet with small amount of oil. Sprinkle both sides with salt. Cook on small electric grill with thermostatic control OR in electric skillet (see Orange Roughy recipe for details, page 160). Garnish.
Yield: 1 pound of fish equals 5 servings.

Grilled Shrimp
(Day 2 Recipe)

Prepare jumbo shrimp as described in Fresh Shelled Shrimp recipe (page 158). Heat and brown shrimp to serving temperature on small electric grill with thermostatic control. Turn often to prevent burning. Serve with squeeze of fresh lemon, Clarified Butter (page 226), and/or Picante Sauce (page 227).

Fresh Shelled Shrimp
(Cooking Directions)
(Day 2 Recipe)

1. In large saucepan or kettle, bring salted water to boil. Reduce heat to medium-high. Add rinsed shrimp. Cook 2–3 minutes until shrimp turns gentle pink color.

2. Drain and chill in ice water until shrimp is cold throughout. Peel and devein. To peel, pinch tail and break shell to remove it. To devein, make shallow cut lengthwise down back. Remove sand vein with point of knife and rerinse shrimp.

> **HH:** Cook 1–2 pounds of shrimp at one time. Freeze in portions ready to use in many recipes.

Shrimp Cocktail
(Day 2 Recipe)

1/4 pound	Fresh Shelled Shrimp per serving
as desired	Picante Sauce (page 227)

Prepare shrimp and Picante Sauce. Chill. Serve in stem cocktail glass for romantic dinner at home. Or take chilled sauce with you and order Shrimp Cocktail as appetizer for romantic outing.

Salmon Millet Dinner
(Day 3 Recipe)

1/2 cup	hulled millet
1 1/4 cups	water
1/2 teaspoon	sea salt
4 cups	Day 3 vegetables, fresh or frozen
	I prefer: 2 cups cauliflower florets, fresh or frozen,
	2 cups carrots, sliced
1 jar	Chuck's Seafood Salmon, flaked (7 1/2 ounces)

Nutritional Information/Serving	
Calories:	444
Protein (g):	24.8
Carbohydrate (g):	16.6
Fiber (g):	6.29
Total fat (g):	7.26
Saturated (g):	1.6
Cholesterol (mg):	39
Sodium (mg):	449
Food Exchanges/Serving	
3.7 Br 1.8 LM 2.1 Veg	

1. Rinse and drain millet. Add all ingredients in order given to a 2 1/2 quart saucepan. Bring to boil. Cover. Reduce heat to between low and medium. Simmer for 15 minutes. Do not peek during cooking time.

2. Stir and serve. May be frozen. Thaw and reheat in slow oven or microwave.

Yield: 5 cups   3 servings

Salmon Patties
(Day 3 Recipe)

1 jar	Chuck's Seafood Salmon, flaked (7 1/2 ounces)
1/2 cup	shredded carrots
1/4 cup	tapioca starch or cornstarch
1/4 teaspoon	sea salt
1 teaspoon	canola oil

Nutritional Information/Serving	
Calories:	240
Protein (g):	21.3
Carbohydrate (g):	168
Fiber (g):	.72
Total fat (g):	8.77
Saturated (g):	1.81
Cholesterol (mg):	58
Sodium (mg):	356
Food Exchanges/Serving	
.8 Br 2.7 VLM .4 Veg .4 Fat	

1. Preheat electric skillet to 350ºF. Add oil to preheated skillet.

2. In bowl, combine all ingredients except oil. Mix thoroughly. Divide and patty into 6 portions.

3. Cook for 3–5 minutes on each side until golden brown. Serve immediately.

Yield: 2 servings, 6 patties

Shrimp Tofu Lasagna*
(Day 4 Recipe)

4 cloves	garlic, minced
1 cup	leeks, sliced
2 teaspoons	safflower oil
1/4 cup	chopped macadamia or Brazil nuts*
1/3 cup	kudzu starch
2 cups	liquid (water and/or green bean broth)
1 teaspoon	sea salt
1 1/2 teaspoons	basil**
1 tablespoon	leaf oregano
3 cups	Your choice of Day 4 vegetables:
	cooked green beans (fresh, frozen, or canned—drained)
	asparagus cuts and tips (fresh or frozen)—my preference
1 pound	Fresh Shelled Shrimp**, diced (2 cups) (page 158)
1 pound	soft packed tofu, drained, thinly sliced lengthwise (12 slices)
2 layers	Soy Lasagna Noodles (page 113)

Nutritional Information/Serving	
Calories:	445
Protein (g):	37.9
Carbohydrate (g):	32.2
Fiber (g):	5.87
Total fat (g):	21.0
Saturated (g):	3.02
Cholesterol (mg):	111
Sodium (mg):	795
Food Exchanges/Serving	
1 Br 3.3 VLM 1.8 Veg 3.8 Fat	

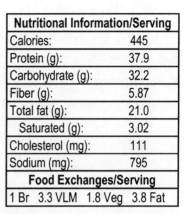

To Prepare Sauce:

1. In medium saucepan, sauté garlic and leeks in oil until soft.

2. Combine nuts, kudzu, and small amount liquid in blender. Blend on highest speed for 1–2 minutes until well blended, stop at least once to scrape sides and bottom of blender jar. Add this mixture and rest of liquid to step 1. Cook on medium, stirring almost constantly, until thickened.

3. In large (8-cup) measure or bowl, combine thickened sauce, seasonings, vegetables, and shrimp. Sauce yields 5 1/2 cups.

To prepare Lasagna:

4. Oven temperature—350ºF. Preheating not necessary.

5. Layer ingredients in following order. (Amounts given are for Corning 10-inch square covered casserole dish. Divide ingredients evenly to prepare in 4 or 6 covered Corning Grab-It Bowls.)

   - 1 cup sauce, spread evenly
   - 1 layer of lasagna noodles
   - 6 slices of tofu
   - 1 1/2 cups sauce, spread evenly

   - 6 slices of tofu
   - 1 layer of lasagna noodles
   - 3 cups sauce, spread evenly

6. Cover. Bake for 50–60 minutes until sauce bubbles and ingredients are fork tender. Remove and allow to set 5 minutes. Cut into desired serving portions and serve with spatula. May be frozen. For best quality, thaw and reheat slowly in covered dish. If preparing in individual bowls, freeze unbaked, thaw completely, and bake as usual.

Yield: 4 servings

USED FOR ANALYSIS: Asparagus cuts and tips.

Special Notes:
Can substitute dry, uncooked whole-wheat or spelt noodles for Soy.
Using an 8-cup measure to mix ingredients allows confirmation of the sauce yield. Add additional liquid and/or vegetables if needed to yield 5 1/2 cups.

---

*Brazil and macadamia nuts are unassigned "Fun Foods" in this rotational diet, see explanation on pages 24.

**Realize these foods are assigned to Day 2. Avoid eating on Day 2 just before and after serving this recipe on Day 4.

Orange Roughy
(Day 4 Recipe)

Preheat electric skillet to 250ºF. Add small amount of safflower oil (or break rotation and use Clarified butter). Add fillets and sprinkle with sea salt and tarragon. Cover with splatter screen (information on page 198) to prevent splattering. Cook until flaky. Turn often to prevent burning. Total cooking time is 5–8 minutes—time depends upon thickness of fillets and whether fillets are frozen or thawed.

Yield: 1 pound of fish equals 5 servings

Serving Suggestion: Serve with Cream of Asparagus Soup (page 177).

Tuna Noodle Casseroles
Three Variations   (Day 1 Recipe)

	With More Vegetables	With Extra Vegetables	
2 3 cups	2 4 cups	2 5 1/2 cups	SERVINGS YIELD
1 1/3 cups	1 1/3 cups	1 1/3 cups	Vita-Spelt dry noodles, loosely packed OR Kamut rotini, loosely packed
1/2 cup	2 cups	4 cups	total measure of vegetables: your choice of diced celery, sliced bok choy, fresh or frozen broccoli cuts, and/or chopped cabbage
1 jar	1 jar	1 jar	Chuck's Seafood tuna, flaked (7 1/2 oz.)
1 cup	1 5/8 cups	2 1/4 cups	water (5/8 cup = 1/2 cup + 2 Tbsp.)
2 tablespoons	3 tablespoons	1/4 cup	hulled sesame seeds
2 tablespoons	3 tablespoons	1/4 cup	flour—spelt or Kamut
1/4 teaspoon	3/8 teaspoon	1/2 teaspoon	sea salt (3/8 tsp. = 1/4 tsp. + 1/8 tsp.)

1. Oven temperature—350ºF. Preheating not necessary.

2. In saucepan of boiling salted water, cook noodles for only 4 minutes or Kamut rotini for only 8 minutes. Stir occasionally. Drain and add to casserole dish(es).

3. Add vegetables and tuna, stir gently.

4. Combine 1/4 cup of water, seeds, flour, and salt in blender. Blend on highest speed for 1–2 minutes. Stop at least once to scrape sides. Add rest of water and blend a couple of seconds more.

5. Pour liquid mixture over ingredients in casserole dish(es). Lightly push any floating ingredients down into mixture. Cover. Bake 40–60 minutes or until vegetables are tender. Casserole may be mixed earlier in day and refrigerated until baking time.

Special Note: Spelt noodles contain whole egg.

USED FOR ANALYSIS:

Spelt pasta and flour.

First Variation: 1/2 cup celery

With More Veg   1 cup each broccoli and cabbage

With Extra Veg   1/2 cup bok choy, 1 1/2 cups broccoli, and 2 cups cabbage

Nutritional Information/Serving			
	First Variation	With More Veg	With Extra Veg
Calories:	380	439	497
Protein (g):	39.9	43	45.9
Carbohydrate (g):	38.0	45.9	54.1
Fiber (g):	12.08	14.81	17.52
Total fat (g):	7.23	9.77	12.3
Saturated (g):	.81	1.15	1.49
Cholesterol (mg):	32	32	32
Sodium (mg):	360	491	533
Food Exchanges/Serving			
	2.1 Br 4.5 VLM .2 Veg 1.3 Fat	2.3 Br 4.6 VLM .9 Veg 1.7 Fat	2.5 Br 4.7 VLM 1.6 Veg 2.2 Fat

Tuna Rice Casseroles
Three Variations (Day 1 Recipe)

	With More Vegetables	**With Extra Vegetables**	
2 3 cups	2 4 cups	2 5 1/2 cups	SERVINGS YIELD
1 cup	1 cup	1 cup	cooked rice
1/2 cup	2 cups	4 cups	total measure of vegetables: your choice of diced celery, sliced bok choy, fresh or frozen broccoli cuts, and/or chopped cabbage
1 jar	1 jar	1 jar	Chuck's Seafood tuna, flaked (7 1/2 oz.)
1 cup	1 5/8 cups	2 1/4 cups	water (5/8 cup = 1/2 cup + 2 Tbsp.)
2 tablespoons	3 tablespoons	1/4 cup	hulled sesame seeds
2 tablespoons	3 tablespoons	1/4 cup	brown rice flour
3/8 teaspoon	1/2 teaspoon	3/4 teaspoon	sea salt (3/8 tsp. = 1/4 tsp. + 1/8 tsp.)

1. Oven temperature—350ºF. Preheating not necessary.
2. Combine rice, veggies, and tuna in covered casserole dish(es).
3. Continue with steps 4 and 5 of Tuna Noodle Casserole (page 160).

USED FOR ANALYSIS:

Spelt pasta and flour.

First Variation: 1/2 cup celery

With More Veg: 1 cup each broccoli and cabbage

With Extra Veg 1/2 cup bok choy, 1 1/2 cups broccoli and 2 cups cabbage

Nutritional Information/Serving			
	First Variation	With More Veg	With Extra Veg
Calories:	312	372	433
Protein (g):	35.9	38.6	41.2
Carbohydrate (g):	27.4	35.4	43.7
Fiber (g):	3.03	5.25	7.43
Total fat (g):	5.97	8.56	11.14
Saturated (g):	.99	1.36	1.73
Cholesterol (mg):	19	19	19
Sodium (mg):	351	482	635
Food Exchanges/Serving			
	1.5 Br 4.5 VLM .2 Veg .9 Fat	1.7 Br 4.6 VLM .9 Veg 1.4 Fat	2.0 Br 4.7 VLM 1.6 Veg 1.8 Fat

Tuna Rice Dinner
(Day 1 Recipe)

1/2 cup	brown rice, long-grain, short-grain, or basmati
1 1/2 cups	water
1/2 teaspoon	sea salt
1 jar	Chuck's Seafood Tuna, flaked, 7 1/2 ounce
4 cups	Day 1 vegetables I prefer 2 cups each broccoli cuts and chopped cabbage.

1. Rinse and drain rice. Add rice, salt, and tuna to a 2 1/2 quart saucepan. Do not stir. Cover. Bring to boil. Reduce heat to between low and medium and simmer for 35 minutes or until rice is almost tender. Do not peek during cooking time.

2. Carefully add vegetables so as not to disturb steam pockets. Continue to cook for approximately 15 minutes until vegetables and rice are tender. Stir and serve. May be frozen. Thaw and reheat in slow oven or microwave.

Yield: 5 cups   3 servings

Nutritional Information/Serving	
Calories:	236
Protein (g):	26.1
Carbohydrate (g):	29.4
Fiber (g):	4.57
Total fat (g):	1.62
Saturated (g):	.39
Cholesterol (mg):	13
Sodium (mg):	420
Food Exchanges/Serving	
1.4 Br 2.8 VLM 1.2 Veg	

Scrambled Eggs with Bok Choy
(Day 1 Recipe)

1. Wash bok choy stalks and leaves. Slice stalks into small portions. Cut leaves with scissors or tear into small portions.
2. Using your preferred skillet for scrambling eggs, sauté prepared bok choy in small amount of Day 1 oil until tender.
4. Add slightly beaten eggs and your choice of Day 1 seasonings (dill weed, ground cumin, sea salt). Cook as for scrambled eggs. Serve immediately.

Denver Eggs
(Day 1 Recipe)

2 cups	cabbage, finely chopped
1 cup	celery, diced
1/2 cup	bok choy, prepare as described in recipe above
4	eggs, slightly beaten
1 cup	leftover cold cooked rice
as desired	ground cumin or coriander, dill weed, sea salt

Nutritional Information/Serving	
Calories:	241
Protein (g):	14.6
Carbohydrate (g):	24.1
Fiber (g):	3.8
Total fat (g):	9.76
Saturated (g):	2.91
Cholesterol (mg):	374
Sodium (mg):	191
Food Exchanges/Serving	
1 Br 1.7 LM 1.2 Veg .9 Fat	

1. Preheat cast-iron skillet (my preference) or any skillet you prefer for preparing stir fry. Add small amount of Day 1 oil.
2. Add vegetables and sprinkle with desired spices. Stir fry until desired doneness. I prefer mine crispy.
3. Add rice to vegetables and mix. Add eggs by pouring evenly over mixture. Cook while stirring quickly until eggs are done and rice is heated. Serve immediately.

Yield: 2 servings

Egg (Cheese-Free) Soufflé*
(Day 3 Recipe)

2	extra-large eggs, separated *
1 teaspoon	canola oil
1/4 cup	tapioca starch, packed
1/8 teaspoon	sea salt
1 tablespoon	water
3/4 teaspoon	homemade baking powder (on next page)

Nutritional Information/Serving	
Calories:	166
Protein (g):	7.3
Carbohydrate (g):	14.7
Fiber (g):	0
Total fat (g):	8.07
Saturated (g):	1.96
Cholesterol (mg):	2.47
Sodium (mg):	212
Food Exchanges/Serving	
.8 Br 1.1 LM 1.0 Fat	

1. Preheat oven to 350ºF.
2. Using 2 separate bowls, separate eggs. Place yolks in larger mixing bowl and whites in smaller bowl. Set bowl of egg whites in sink containing warm water. Stir occasionally to bring whites to room temperature.
3. Oil bottom and sides of 9-inch square glass baking dish with 1 teaspoon of oil.
4. Scoop tapioca starch into a 1/4 cup measure, rounding it. Tap edge of measure with knife a few times to aid in packing it. Level off. Place in small bowl, stir with whisk to unpack it. Set aside.
5. Beat egg whites until stiff. Set aside.
6. Beat yolks with whisk. Add salt, water, tapioca starch, and stir well. Add baking powder and stir. Fold in stiff egg whites.

continued . . .

Egg (Cheese-Free) Soufflé*

(Continued)

7. Pour into prepared baking dish. Bake for 15 minutes or until a toothpick inserted in the center comes out clean. Serve immediately. Soufflé raises to be approximately 1 1/4 inches high and then falls to be about 3/4 to 1 inch high. Use sharp knife to cut edges away from side of dish and to cut into 4 squares. Use a wide, sharp spatula to scrap bottom of dish when serving. This makes a delicious grain-free breakfast or serve with vegetables for light lunch or brunch.

Yield: 2 Servings

*Eggs are assigned to Day 1. Omit eggs on Day 1 just before and after enjoying on Day 3.

Recipe idea from Deb Buhr of Sumner, Iowa.

Homemade Baking Powder

(Used in Above Recipe)

1 teaspoon	baking soda
2 teaspoons	tapioca starch
2 teaspoons	cream of tartar

Mix all ingredients well and store in airtight container until needed for above recipe.

Yield: 5 teaspoons

Breakfast Brunch Squares*

(Day 1 Recipe)

2 3/4 cups	your choice of bread, cubed
	Purchased yeast-free, organic, 100% Kamut, spelt, or rice* bread
	Kamut or Spelt Yeast-Free Bread (page 102)
2 cups	broccoli cuts, fresh or frozen
1/4 cup	hulled sesame seeds
1/4 cup	flour—Kamut, spelt, brown rice
3/4 teaspoon	sea salt
1 cup	water
4	eggs

Nutritional Information/Serving	
Calories:	274
Protein (g):	15.22
Carbohydrate (g):	34.6
Fiber (g):	5.64
Total fat (g):	9.21
Saturated (g):	2.01
Cholesterol (mg):	187
Sodium (mg):	618
Food Exchanges/Serving	
1.8 Br .2 VLM .8 LM	
.5 Veg 1.3 Fat	

1. Preheat oven to 350ºF.

2. Oil bottom and sides of 8-inch stainless steel square baking pan with 1 teaspoon of sesame oil. Glass is not recommended because it tends to stick.

3. Evenly layer cubed bread and broccoli cuts in prepared pan.

4. Combine sesame seeds, flour, and salt with approximately 1/3 cup of water in blender. Blend on highest speed for 1–2 minutes until well blended. Stop at least once to scrap sides. Add remaining water and eggs. Blend on low speed only a couple of seconds more. Pour liquid mixture evenly over broccoli and bread cubes. Lightly push any floating broccoli or bread cubes down into the mixture.

5. Bake for 45–50 minutes until egg mixture is set. Cut into squares and remove from pan with stiff metal spatula.

Yield: 4 servings

*Ener-G brand rice bread has a few ingredients that break rotation. I personally do not concern myself with this break.

USED FOR ANALYSIS: French Meadow brand Kamut bread

Basic Bean Cookery

Many people shy away from cooking beans, but they are one of the easiest foods to prepare. Beans take a long time to <u>cook,</u> either on the stove or in a slow cooker, yet the actual preparation time that <u>you</u> spend is very, very low in comparison with many other foods

Beans are generally sorted by machine and occasionally you will find some shriveled ones as well as stones and dirt clods in your purchased beans. Try to purchase beans that contain no or very few shriveled ones. To save time later, sort through them and discard any shriveled beans, large stones, dirt clods, or other debris before storing. Beans store well in a tightly covered glass jar in a cool dry place.

Many people mention experiencing intestinal gas after eating beans. While this is a common experience, there are preparation and cooking steps which can help alleviate the problem. Following are general rules of thumb for cooking beans, especially to diminish intestinal gas.

Step 1: Measure beans according to recipe or amount you wish to cook.

Step 2: Rinse beans thoroughly to remove surface mold, dirt, and other debris. Add enough water to cover beans and use a spoon or your hand to stir them around. If beans and debris float to the top, skim off and discard. Drain and discard water. Add fresh water and repeat procedure two or three times until the rinse water is clear.

Step 3: Place rinsed beans in a large container. (For 2 cups of dried beans, I use an 8-cup measuring cup.) Fill with water to allow beans to more than double in size. Place container in refrigerator and allow beans to soak for 8–12 hours. Washing beans in preparation for soaking can easily be accomplished in five minutes or less while preparing your evening meal the night before you plan to cook beans.

If you forget to presoak beans, use the following procedure:
- Place beans in a large saucepan, Dutch oven, or kettle. Cover with water.
- Bring to a boil and cook for approximately two minutes.
- Remove from heat, cover, and let stand for one hour.
- Drain water and thoroughly rinse beans.
- Continue with normal cooking steps.

If you soak too many beans, drain and freeze them in a cellophane or plastic bag. To cook, simply pull from freezer and cook as directed.

Step 4: To cook beans, drain off soaking water. Again thoroughly rinse beans to remove the filmy (starchy) substance that formed when the beans were soaked. Repeat two or three times until rinsing water is clear.

Step 5: Follow individual recipe directions regarding required size of slow cooker, cooking temperature, amount of water, and seasonings. **NOTE: It is IMPORTANT to <u>not</u> add salt at this time.**

Step 6: Cook beans until tender but not mushy. Three methods of testing for doneness are described by Marjorie Hurt Jones in <u>Mastering Food Allergies</u> newsletter ("Bean Cookery," <u>Mastering Food Allergies</u>, Vol. IV, No. 3, issue 33 [March 1989[, 1). Test beans should be discarded once the test is completed.

1. Remove three or four beans on a spoon and blow on them. If the skins burst, the beans are done.
2. Put a sample bean in your mouth and press it against the roof of your mouth. If you are able to break it up with your tongue without using your teeth, the beans are done.
3. Bite into a bean. If it is tender without firm resistance, the beans are done.

If beans finish cooking earlier than you plan to serve them (e.g., an hour or so early), turn slow cooker setting to low or off for a while. Turn heat on near serving time to reheat beans to serving temperature.

Step 7: IMPORTANT! Add salt listed in recipe within the last ten or fifteen minutes of cooking. For additional assistance in alleviating intestinal gas, add appropriate proportion of salt to only the amount of cooked beans to be served at meal. Freeze leftover cooked beans unsalted. Add salt during last few minutes of reheating. Experiment with this procedure to see if it will aid you in incorporating beans into your diet.

Three additional methods to use to aid in alleviating intestinal gas are:
1. Begin soaking beans earlier in the day. After two hours, drain and rinse beans and add new soaking water. Repeat procedure every two hours or so throughout the day. Continue to soak beans overnight as described in Step 3.
2. Add kombu to beans while cooking.
3. Start cooking beans by simmering on stove top for 30 minutes with no seasonings added. Drain and rinse beans thoroughly. Transfer to slow cooker and follow recipe directions.

Notice that my recipes for lentils and split peas call for presoaking. While these two legumes do not need to be presoaked before cooking as beans do, I presoak to aid in eliminating intestinal gas.

If you prefer to cook beans on the stove top, use the following method.
1. Place soaked, rinsed, and drained beans in a large kettle or Dutch oven.
2. Cover with approximately three to four inches of water.
3. Bring to a boil, reduce heat, and simmer for appropriate time according to the following chart.

Bean Cookery Chart

Type of Legume	Simmering Time	Type of Legume	Simmering Time
Anasazi Beans	1 1/2 – 2 1/2 hours	Lima Beans	45 minutes – 1 1/2 hours
Adzuki Beans	1 1/2 – 2 1/2 hours	Mung Beans	2 – 3 hours
Black Turtle Beans	1 1/2 – 3 hours	Navy Beans	2 – 3 hours
Black-eyed Peas	1 – 1 1/2 hours	Northern Beans	2 – 3 hours
Garbanzo Beans (Chickpeas)	2 – 3 hours	Pinto Beans	1 1/2 – 2 hours
Kidney Beans	2 – 3 hours	Soybeans	2 1/2 – 3 hours
Lentils, Green	1 – 2 hours	Split Peas	1 – 2 hours
Lentils, Red (do not soak)	25 minutes		

Many factors affect the cooking time of beans. These factors include the variety, maturity, age, and moisture content of the beans as well as altitude. Even the kind of water you use can affect the cooking time (e.g., beans take longer to cook when hard water is used).

HH: Any bean recipe prepared in a 1 quart slow cooker may be doubled or tripled for a standard-size slow cooker.

Happiness is found along the way—not at the end of the road.
—Sol Gordonr

Garbanzo Beans and Broth*
(Day 2 Recipe)

2 cups	garbanzo beans
5 cups	water
5–6	bay leaves* (optional)
1/4 cup	chopped onion
1/2 teaspoon	minced garlic
1 teaspoon	sea salt

Nutritional Information/1 Cup	
Calories:	215
Protein (g):	11.5
Carbohydrate (g):	36.2
Fiber (g):	6.61
Total fat (g):	3.39
Saturated (g):	.36
Cholesterol (mg):	0
Sodium (mg):	337
Food Exchanges/Serving	
2.2 Br 1.3 VLM .2 Veg	

1. Rinse, soak, rerinse, and drain beans (see Bean Cookery, page 164).
2. Add all ingredients except salt to standard-size slow cooker. Cook on low for 10–12 hours or on high for 4 1/2–5 hours until beans are tender but not mushy.
3. Remove bay leaves. Just before serving, add salt and stir.

Yield: 6 1/2 cups

Serving suggestions:
1. Serve as side dish with meal or use in Day 2 recipes.
2. Drain and serve on lettuce salad. Use broth in place of water in Zucchini Salad Dressing.
3. Temporarily transfer garbanzo beans to Day 4 and use in Beans and Beans (page 171).

*Bay leaf belongs to Laurel Family with avocado and cinnamon. Eating bay leaf on Day 2 breaks rotation since cinnamon is used on Day 3. Make your own decision regarding this break. I personally use it without any concern regarding when I have or plan to consume cinnamon.

Black Beans and Sauce*
(Day 4 Recipe)

1 cup	black turtle beans
1 3-inch	kombu
2 cups	water
1/4 cup	fresh minced cilantro (optional)*
1/3 cup	green or red peppers, diced (optional)*
1/2 cup	leek, sliced or diced
1/2 teaspoon	sea salt

Nutritional Information/Serving	
Calories:	191
Protein (g):	12.4
Carbohydrate (g):	35
Fiber (g):	12.41
Total fat (g):	.8
Saturated (g):	.2
Cholesterol (mg):	0
Sodium (mg):	309
Food Exchanges/Serving	
1.7 Br 1.4 VLM .5 Veg	

1. Rinse, soak, rerinse, and drain beans (see Bean Cookery, page 164).
2. Add all ingredients except salt to 1-quart size slow cooker or double this recipe and cook in a standard-size slow cooker. Cook on low for 8 hours or until beans are tender but not mushy.
3. Add salt just before serving and stir. Serve as side dish or use in recipe below.

Yield: 3 1/2 cups

Tofu and Asparagus in Black Bean Sauce*
(Day 4 Recipe)

1 clove	garlic, minced
1/2 teaspoon	safflower oil
1–1 1/2 cups	asparagus cuts and tips, fresh or frozen
7/8 cup	Black Beans and Sauce,* 1/4 of above recipe (7/8 cup = 3/4 cup + 2 Tbls.)
1/4 pound	tofu, soft or firm, drained, cubed (optional)

directions on next page

Tofu and Asparagus in Black Bean Sauce*
(continued)

1. In skillet, sauté garlic in oil until soft.

2. Add asparagus and a small amount of salted water. Cook covered until almost tender. See cooking directions on page 200.

3. Add beans and tofu, stir gently. Cover and heat to serving temperature. Stir gently occasionally during heating process.

Yield: 2 1/2 cups, complete vegetarian meal for 1

*Green pepper is assigned to Day 2. Omit them on Day 2 just before and after eating this recipe on Day 4. Also, cilantro (Mustard Family) is assigned to Day 3. I personally do not concern myself with this minor break in rotation.

Nutritional Information/Serving		
	With Tofu	Without Tofu
Calories:	345	260
Protein (g):	24.8	15.7
Carbohydrate (g):	43.1	40.9
Fiber (g):	16.56	15.20
Total fat (g):	11.9	5.67
Saturated (g):	1.47	.68
Cholesterol (mg):	0	0
Sodium (mg):	285	277
Food Exchanges/Serving		
With Tofu: 1.5 Br 1.1 VLM 2.5 Veg 2 Fat		
Without Tofu: 1.5 Br 2.5 Veg .9 Fat		

Sondra's Thoughts: I desire the combination of black turtle beans and asparagus more often that I can tolerate soy, so I often omit tofu and serve the beans and asparagus with or without a pork chop.

Lentil Casserole
Variations: Lamb, Pork, Vegetarian
(Day 4 Recipe)

1/2 cup	dry lentils, rinse and drain
1 package	frozen green beans, 10 oz. (or more)
1/2 cup	sliced leeks or chopped onions
2/3 cup	water
	OR 3/4 cup for vegetarian variation
1/4 teaspoon	cayenne (red) pepper
2	lamb or pork chops, trim excess fat (omit for vegetarian variation)
1 teaspoon	rosemary (with lamb version)
1/4–1/2 teas.	sea salt

Nutritional Information/Serving			
	Vegetarian	Pork 3 oz. chop	Lamb 3 oz. chop
Calories:	232	309	313
Protein (g):	13.7	25.9	25
Carbohydrate (g):	41	41	41
Fiber (g):	10.41	10.41	10.41
Total fat (g):	1.59	4.38	5.26
Saturated (g):	.08	1.05	1.40
Cholesterol (mg):	0	35	36
Sodium (mg):	294	416	411
Food Exchanges/Serving			
Vegetarian: 1.3 Br 1.3 VLM 3.5 Veg			
Pork: 1.3 Br 1.3 VLM 1.7 LM 3.5 Veg			
Lamb: 1.3 Br 1.3 VLM 1.4 LM 3.5 Veg			

May be prepared in oven using a covered casserole or in a standard-size slow cooker.

1. Layer lentils, green beans, and leeks in casserole dish or slow cooker. Sprinkle with cayenne. Add water.

2. Layer chops on top of lentil mixture. Sprinkle lamb chops with rosemary. Cover.

3. Bake in oven at 350ºF. for 1 3/4 hours OR cook in slow cooker on high for 4–5 hours, on low for 8–9 hours, or until lentils and meat are tender.

4. Temporarily remove chops. Add at least half of salt and stir. Return chops and sprinkle with additional salt. Cover. Cook for additional 10 minutes. May need to add small amount of water for vegetarian version.

Serves 2

Recipe may be doubled and prepared in a standard-size slow cooker or cut in half and prepared in a Crockette-size slow cooker.

Adapted from a recipe submitted by CCN reader Katie R., MN. She layers dry lentils, frozen lima beans, and seasoned tator tots in a tall casserole, then arranges the chops in a teepee on top and oven bakes it covered.

Mexican Medley Beans
(Day 4 Recipe)

1/4 cup	black turtle beans (these help with color)
1/4 cup	kidney beans
1/4 cup	pinto beans
1/4 cup	adzuki beans
1/4 cup	navy beans
	OR 1 1/4 cups of any combination of dry beans
2 cups	water
1 3-inch	kombu
1/2 cup	leek, diced
1/4 teaspoon	minced garlic
1 teaspoon	chili powder
1/4 teaspoon	Watkins Salsa Seasoning Blend or other Mexican blend spices
1/2 teaspoon	sea salt

Nutritional Information/Cup	
Calories:	264
Protein (g):	16.3
Carbohydrate (g):	49.3
Fiber (g):	13.03
Total fat (g):	1.02
Saturated (g):	.23
Cholesterol (mg):	0
Sodium (mg):	329
Food Exchanges/Serving	
2.4 Br 1.7 VLM .6 Veg	

1. Rinse, soak, rerinse, and drain beans (see Bean Cookery, page 164).

2. Add all ingredients except salt to a 1-quart size slow cooker. Cook on low for 10–12 hours or until beans are tender but not mushy.

3. Just before serving, add salt and stir.

Special Note: Sauce thickens if beans are allowed to cool in refrigerator and then reheated. After reheating, flavors are even better.

Yield: 3 1/4 cups

Tomato-Free Vegetarian Chili*
(Day 4 Recipe)

3/4 cup	Mexican Medley Beans (recipe above)
1 pint	green beans, drain and reserve broth
1 cup	zucchini squash, peeled, cubed* (optional)
	OR 1/2 cup okra, sliced* (optional)

Combine ingredients in saucepan. Add green bean broth to get the consistency you prefer. Simmer for 20 minutes to cook squash and blend flavors. Taste and add more seasonings if desired.

Yield: 2–2 1/2 cups   1 serving

*If using zucchini squash or okra, omit eating them on Day 2 just before and after eating this dish on Day 4.

Nutritional Information/Serving		
	With Squash	With Okra
Calories:	270	267
Protein (g):	16.8	16.1
Carbohydrate (g):	53.4	53
Fiber (g):	14.21	13.8
Total fat (g):	1.31	1.2
Saturated (g):	.29	.28
Cholesterol (mg):	0	0
Sodium (mg):	270	268
Food Exchanges/Serving		
With Squash: 1.8 Br 3.7 Veg		
With Okra: 1.8 Br 3.3 Veg		

HH: Freeze unsalted basic cooked beans in amounts needed for many recipes or to serve as a side dish. Mark on the label the amount of salt needed. When reheating, add salt measure within last 10 minutes before serving.

Tomato-Free Chili
(Day 4 Recipe)

1/2 cup	black turtle beans (these help with color)
1/2 cup	kidney beans
1/2 cup	pinto beans
1/2 cup	adzuki beans
1/2 cup	navy beans
	OR 2 1/2 cups of any combination of dry beans
5 cups	water
2 3-inch	kombu
1/2 cup	leek, diced
1/2 teaspoon	minced garlic
2 teaspoons	chili powder
1 teaspoon	Watkins Salsa Seasoning Blend or other Mexican blend spices
1 1/2 teaspoons	sea salt
1 pound	ground pork or venison

Nutritional Information/Cup		
	Venison	Pork
Calories:	274	294
Protein (g):	28	20.9
Carbohydrate (g):	35	34.8
Fiber (g):	9.27	9.27
Total fat (g):	2.58	8.16
Saturated (g):	.9	2.93
Cholesterol (mg):	61	34
Sodium (mg):	563	393
Food Exchanges/Serving		
Venison: 1.8 Br 1.2 VLM 2.3 LM .2 Veg .1 Fat		
Pork: 1.8 Br 1.2 VLM 1.3 LM .2 Veg .7 Fat		

1. Rinse, soak, rerinse, and drain beans (see Bean Cookery, page 164).

2. Add all ingredients except meat and salt to a standard-size slow cooker. Cook on low for 10–12 hours or until beans are tender but not mushy.

3. In skillet, cook meat until done. Stir often to chop and brown evenly. Add to cooked beans and cook on low for one additional hour. Just before serving, add salt and stir.

Special Note: Sauce thickens if allowed to cool. Add more water as needed when reheating.

Yield: 9 cups

Tomato-Free "Veggie" Chili*
(Day 4 Recipe)

1 cup	Tomato-Free Chili (recipe above)
1 pint	green beans, home canned, drained and reserve broth
1/2 cup	zucchini squash, peeled, cubed* (optional) OR 1/2 cup okra, sliced* (optional)

Combine ingredients in saucepan. Add green bean broth to get the consistency that you prefer. Simmer for 20 minutes to cook squash and blend flavors. Taste and add more seasonings if desired.

Yield: 3 cups 1 serving

*If using zucchini squash or okra, omit eating them on Day 2 just before and after eating this dish on Day 4.

Nutritional Information/Serving				
	Venison/Zucchini	Venison/Okra	Pork/Zucchini	Pork/Okra
Calories:	338	343	357	362
Protein (g):	31.8	31.9	24.7	24.7
Carbohydrate (g):	49.3	50.1	49.3	50.8
Fiber (g):	12.93	13.3	12.93	13.3
Total fat (g):	3.03	3.02	8.61	8.6
Saturated (g):	1	1	3.03	3.03
Cholesterol (mg):	61	61	34	34
Sodium (mg):	572	592	402	402
Food Exchanges/Serving				
	1.8 Br 2.3 LM 3.0 Veg .1 Fat	1.8 Br 2.3 LM 3.0 Veg .1 Fat	1.8 Br 1.3 LM 3 Veg .7 Fat	1.8 Br 1.3 LM 3 Veg .7 Fat

Ham and Beans
(Day 4 Recipe)

1 pound	fresh ham hocks, uncured, unsmoked
2 cups	navy beans
4 cups	liquid (pork broth and/or water)
1/2 cup	leek, sliced
1 1/4 teaspoons	sea salt

Nutritional Information/Cup	
Calories:	340
Protein (g):	24.3
Carbohydrate (g):	37.4
Fiber (g):	11.27
Total fat (g):	10.49
Saturated (g):	3.7
Cholesterol (mg):	45
Sodium (mg):	518
Food Exchanges/Serving	
2.4 Br .7 VLM 1.6 LM .2 Veg 1.2 Fat	

1. In saucepan, simmer pork in 1–2 cups unsalted water for 2 hours or until meat is very tender. Remove meat and cool to touch. Strain broth through fine-meshed strainer and chill. After chilling, remove the fat that is solid on the top. Remove meat from bones and cut into bite-size pieces. Chill to use in step 4.
2. Rinse, soak, rerinse, and drain beans (see Bean Cookery, page 164).
3. Transfer beans and leeks to standard-size slow cooker. Add liquid. Cook 2 1/2–3 hours on high or 6 1/2–7 hours on low, until beans are tender but not mushy. Add cooked pork meat about midway through cooking of beans.
4. Just before serving, add salt and stir.

Yield: 7 cups

Navy Beans and Broth
(Day 4 Recipe)

2 cups	navy beans
3 1/2 cups	water
1 teaspoon	sea salt

Nutritional Information/Serving	
Calories:	108
Protein (g):	6.8
Carbohydrate (g):	19.5
Fiber (g):	5.97
Total fat (g):	.48
Saturated (g):	.13
Cholesterol (mg):	0
Sodium (mg):	329
Food Exchanges/Serving	
1.3 Br .4 VLM	

1. Rinse, soak, rerinse, and drain beans (see Bean Cookery, page 164).
2. Transfer beans to standard-size slow cooker. Add water. Cook 2 1/2–3 hours on high or 6 1/2–7 hours on low, until beans are tender but not mushy.
3. Just before serving, add salt and stir.

Yield: 6 1/2 cups

Serving Suggestions: Serve as side dish or use in Day 4 recipes.

Baked Beans
(Day 4 Recipe)

2 cups	navy beans
3 1/2 cups	water
1 cup	leek, chopped or sliced
1 1/2 teaspoons	basil
1 teaspoon	paprika
1 tablespoon	safflower oil
1 1/2 teaspoons	sea salt

Nutritional Information/Serving	
Calories:	133
Protein (g):	7.6
Carbohydrate (g):	22.5
Fiber (g):	6.78
Total fat (g):	1.71
Saturated (g):	.24
Cholesterol (mg):	0
Sodium (mg):	270
Food Exchanges/Serving	
1.4 Br .4 VLM .2 Veg .2 Fat	

1. Rinse, soak, rerinse, and drain beans (see Bean Cookery, page 164).
2. Add all ingredients except salt to standard-size slow cooker. Stir. Cook for 10–12 hours on low or 5–6 hours on high until beans are tender but not mushy. Stir beans occasionally during cooking time.
3. Just before serving, add salt and stir.

Yield: 6 cups   12 servings

Lentil or Split Pea Soup*
(Day 4 Recipe)

1 cup	lentils or green split peas
2–3	bay leaves* (optional)
2 cups	water
1/4 cup	leek, chopped
1/8 teaspoon	minced garlic (optional)
1/4 teaspoon	sea salt

Nutritional Information/Cup		
	Lentil	Split Pea
Calories:	203	200
Protein (g):	15.3	13.8
Carbohydrate (g):	35.8	36.5
Fiber (g):	8.16	6.23
Total fat (g):	.76	.76
Saturated (g):	.12	.12
Cholesterol (mg):	0	0
Sodium (mg):	183	183
Food Exchanges/Serving		
Lentil: 1.7 Br 1.7 VLM .4 Veg		
Split Pea: 1.6 Br 1.6 VLM .4 Veg		

Method 1

1. Rinse, soak, rerinse, and drain beans (see Bean Cookery, page 164).

2. Add rest of ingredients except salt to 1-quart size slow cooker. Cook on low (see chart below) until tender but not mushy .

Lentils	5–5 1/2 hours
Green split peas	6 1/2–7 hours

3. Add salt and remove bay leaves just before serving.

Yield: Lentil Soup, 3 cups   Split Pea Soup, 3 1/2 cups

Method 2

1. Follow step 1 from Method 1.

2. Combine all ingredients except salt in a 5-quart Dutch-oven Vision cookware kettle. Cook, covered, in a 700 watt microwave oven on full power for 7–10 minutes, or until boiling. Then cook on medium power for 5–7 minutes or until lentils or split peas are tender. Microwave cooking time will vary with different brands and wattage's of microwaves. After cooking, remove bay leaves and add salt.

Serving Suggestion: Add cooked, crumbled fresh pork side (unsmoked and uncured bacon) to cooked lentils and serve as breakfast cereal. Add leftover cooked roast pork to split peas during last hour of cooking or when reheating.

Special Note: Lentils do not need to be soaked overnight, but I prefer it.

*Bay leaf belongs to Laurel Family with avocado and cinnamon. Eating bay leaf on Day 2 breaks rotation since cinnamon is used on Day 3. Make your own decision regarding this break. I personally use it without any concern regarding when I have or plan to consume cinnamon.

Beans and Beans*
(Day 4 Recipe)

1 cup	Navy Beans and Broth (unsalted)
	OR 1 cup Garbanzo Beans and Broth*
	(unsalted) (page 166)
2 cups	green beans, cooked or canned

Nutritional Information/Serving		
	Navy	Garbanzo
Calories:	91	144
Protein (g):	5.41	7.7
Carbohydrate (g):	18.1	26.5
Fiber (g):	6.37	6.68
Total fat (g):	.54	1.99
Saturated (g):	.13	.25
Cholesterol (mg):	0	0
Sodium (mg):	206	210
Food Exchanges/Serving		
Navy: .7 Br 1.7 Veg		
Garbanzo: 1.1 Br 1.8 Veg		

Combine beans in saucepan. Simmer for 10 minutes to blend flavors. Add rounded 1/8 teaspoon salt, stir, and serve as a side dish or complete meal.

*If using garbanzo beans, omit eating them on Day 2 just before and after enjoying this recipe on Day 4.

Yield: 3 cups   2 servings

Kidney Beans for Chili
(Day 2 Recipe)

1 1/2 cups   kidney beans
3 cups   water

1. Rinse, soak, rerinse, and drain beans (see Bean Cookery, page 164).
2. Transfer beans to standard-size slow cooker. Add water. Cook on low for 7–8 hours until tender but not mushy.

Yield: 4 cups cooked beans and 1 1/2 cups liquid to use in Chili, recipe below

*Kidney beans are assigned to Day 4. Omit kidney beans on Day 4 just before or after eating Chili on Day 2.

Nutritional Information/Cup	
Calories:	233
Protein (g):	15.5
Carbohydrate (g):	42.3
Fiber (g):	13
Total fat (g):	.74
Saturated (g):	.11
Cholesterol (mg):	0
Sodium (mg):	8
Food Exchanges/Serving	
2.1 Br 2.1 VLM	

Chili*
(Day 2 Recipe)

1 pound   ground beef or ground buffalo
1/2 cup   onion, chopped
1/2 can   Muir Glen brand organic tomato puree (28 ounces)
4 cups   cooked kidney beans, drained (recipe above)*
2 cups   liquid (kidney bean broth and water)
2 cups   eggplant, peeled, diced
1/2 cup   green pepper, chopped
2 teaspoons   chili powder
1 teaspoon   Watkins Salsa Seasoning Blend or other Mexican blend spices
1 1/2 teaspoons   sea salt

Nutritional Information/Serving	
Calories:	488
Protein (g):	39
Carbohydrate (g):	55.6
Fiber (g):	16.62
Total fat (g):	13.25
Saturated (g):	4.95
Cholesterol (mg):	71
Sodium (mg):	914
Food Exchanges/Serving	
2.1 Br 3 VLM 2.4 Veg .7 Fat	

1. In large kettle or skillet, cook meat and onions until done. Stir often to chop and brown evenly.
2. Add remaining ingredients except salt. Heat to boiling, reduce heat, cover, and simmer at least 30 minutes. Stir occasionally. Add more water if needed. Just before serving, add salt to taste and, if desired, add more seasonings.

Yield: 8 cups   4 servings

*Kidney beans are assigned to Day 4. Omit them on Day 4 just before and after enjoying Chili on Day 2.

Egg Drop Soup*
(Day 3 Recipe)

1 cup   Turkey Broth (page 130)
1 cup   water
2   eggs, beaten*
1/2 cup   carrots, peeled, diced small or thinly sliced
1/8 teaspoon   sea salt
1/2 cup   spinach, fresh leaves, torn small

Nutritional Information/Serving	
Calories:	161
Protein (g):	12.4
Carbohydrate (g):	7.6
Fiber (g):	2.19
Total fat (g):	9
Saturated (g):	2.76
Cholesterol (mg):	374
Sodium (mg):	429
Food Exchanges/Serving	
1.7 LM 1 Veg .9 Fat	

1. In saucepan, heat turkey broth and water to simmer (just at boiling point).
2. While stirring broth, gradually pour beaten egg in by a thin stream. Add salt and carrots. Simmer until carrots are warm or tender. My preference is slightly crispy.
3. Garnish each bowl with 1/4 cup fresh spinach. Serve with muffin, biscuit, or crackers.

Yield: 2 cups   1 serving

*Eggs are assigned to Day 1. Omit eggs on Day 1 just before and after eating this soup on Day 3.

Garbanzo Bean and Potato Soup
(Day 2 Recipe)

1 cup	Garbanzo Beans and Broth (page 164)
1 cup	potatoes, peeled, diced
2 tablespoons	green pepper, chopped
1/4 teaspoon	summer savory
1/8 teaspoon	sea salt

In saucepan, combine ingredients. Simmer for 15 minutes or until potatoes are done. For crunchy peppers add them during last couple minutes of cooking.

Yield: 2 cups   2 servings

Recipe idea from The Yeast Connection Cookbook *by Crook & Jones, p. 188.*

Nutritional Information/Serving	
Calories:	176
Protein (g):	7.13
Carbohydrate (g):	34.1
Fiber (g):	4.42
Total fat (g):	1.79
Saturated (g):	.2
Cholesterol (mg):	0
Sodium (mg):	311
Food Exchanges/Serving	
2 Br .2 Veg	

Minestrone Soup
(Day 2 Recipe)

3 cloves	garlic, minced
2 teaspoons	olive oil
1 quart	tomato quarters or pieces (unsalted)
1 cup	onion, chopped
1 1/2 cups	Garbanzo Beans and Broth, drained, reserve broth (unsalted) (page 164)
2 cups	liquid (approximately 3/4 cup of bean broth and 1 1/4 cups water)
1/2 teaspoon	leaf oregano
1/2 teaspoon	basil
1/2 teaspoon	marjoram
1 3/4 teaspoons	sea salt

Nutritional Information/Serving		
	Version I	Version II
Calories:	115	114
Protein (g):	4.9	4.8
Carbohydrate (g):	20.2	19.8
Fiber (g):	4.15	3.81
Total fat (g):	2.78	2.75
Saturated (g):	.37	.36
Cholesterol (mg):	0	0
Sodium (mg):	591	592
Food Exchanges/Serving		
Version I: .5 Br 2.1 Veg .3 Fat		
Version II: .5 Br 1.9 Veg .3 Fat		

Vegetables of your choice: (recipe has been tested with the following)

Version I	2 cups each eggplant and zucchini squash, each peeled, 1/2-inch cubed
OR Version II	1 cup each chopped green peppers and sliced okra plus 2 cups amaranth greens, torn into small pieces

1. In 5-quart Dutch-oven kettle, sauté garlic in oil until soft. Add remaining ingredients except salt. Heat to boiling, reduce heat, and cover. Simmer 3 hours. Stir occasionally. Just before serving, add salt (about 1/4 teaspoon per 1 cup) and stir. May be frozen.

2. Serve as complete meal or complement soup with Baked Cod and kiwi fruit.   Yield: 6 1/2 cups

Sondra's Thoughts: I have prepared this in slow cooker, but flavor was not as good as with above method.

Garbanzo Bean Soup
(Day 2 Recipe)

1 cup	Garbanzo Beans and Broth (page 164)
1 tablespoon	green pepper, chopped
1/8 teaspoon	summer savory and/or basil

Combine ingredients in saucepan. Simmer for 10 minutes to blend flavors. For crunchy peppers add them during last couple minutes of cooking.

Yield: 1 cup   1 serving

Nutritional Information/Serving	
Calories:	217
Protein (g):	11.5
Carbohydrate (g):	36.7
Fiber (g):	6.77
Total fat (g):	3.41
Saturated (g):	.36
Cholesterol (mg):	0
Sodium (mg):	337
Food Exchanges/Serving	
2.2 Br .3 Veg	

Vegetable Shrimp Soup
(Day 2 Recipe)

2 pints	tomato juice (unsalted)
	OR 2 cups of tomato juice and
	2 cups of water
1 cup	zucchini squash, peeled, diced
1 cup	eggplant, peeled, diced
1 cup	potatoes, peeled, diced
	OR 1 cup Garbanzo Beans and Broth
	(unsalted) (page 164)
1/2 teaspoon	summer savory
1/4 teaspoon	sea salt
1/2 pound	Fresh Shelled Shrimp (page 158)

Nutritional Information/Serving		
	With Potatoes	With Beans
Calories:	168	194
Protein (g):	16	18.6
Carbohydrate (g):	27	28.8
Fiber (g):	4.48	6.01
Total fat (g):	.96	2.04
Saturated (g):	.22	.33
Cholesterol (mg):	108	108
Sodium (mg):	339	339
Food Exchanges/Serving		
With Potatoes: .6 Br 1.7 VLM 3.3 Veg		
With Beans: .7 Br 1.7 VLM 3.4 Veg		

Combine all ingredients except shrimp in saucepan. Heat to boiling, reduce heat, cover. Simmer until potatoes and eggplant are almost done (20–25 minutes) . Add shrimp and simmer 5 minutes longer.

Yield: 6 cups   3 servings

Vegetable Beef Soup
(Day 2 Recipe)

1 pint	tomato juice (unsalted)
2 cups	Beef Broth (page 140)
1 cup	zucchini squash, peeled, diced
1 cup	eggplant, peeled, diced
1 cup	cooked roast beef, diced
1 cup	potatoes, peeled, diced
	OR 1 cup Garbanzo Beans and Broth
	(unsalted) (page 164)
1/2 teaspoon	summer savory
1/4 teaspoon	sea salt

Nutritional Information/Serving		
	With Potatoes	With Beans
Calories:	195	222
Protein (g):	17.4	20.4
Carbohydrate (g):	20.2	21.9
Fiber (g):	3.18	4.71
Total fat (g):	5.51	6.59
Saturated (g):	2.02	2.13
Cholesterol (mg):	47	47
Sodium (mg):	338	338
Food Exchanges/Serving		
With Potatoes: .6 Br 2 LM 2 Veg		
With Beans: .7 Br 2 LM 2.1 Veg		

Combine all ingredients in saucepan. Heat to boiling, reduce heat, cover, and simmer 25–30 minutes or until potatoes and eggplant are done.

Yield: 6 cups   3 servings

Nightshade Beef Soup
(Day 2 Recipe)

2 cups	tomato juice (unsalted)
2 cups	Beef Broth (page 140)
2 cups	eggplant, peeled, diced
1 cup	cooked roast beef, diced
1 cup	potatoes, peeled, diced
	OR 1 cup Garbanzo Beans and Broth
	(unsalted) (page 164)
1 cup	green peppers, diced
1/2 teaspoon	summer savory
1/4 teaspoon	sea salt

Nutritional Information/Serving		
	With Potatoes	With Beans
Calories:	205	232
Protein (g):	17.5	20.4
Carbohydrate (g):	22.8	24.4
Fiber (g):	3.92	5.45
Total fat (g):	5.57	6.64
Saturated (g):	2.03	2.14
Cholesterol (mg):	47	47
Sodium (mg):	338	338
Food Exchanges/Serving		
With Potatoes: .6 Br 2 LM 2.3 Veg		
With Beans: .7 Br 2 LM 2.4 Veg		

Combine all ingredients in saucepan. Heat to boiling, reduce heat, cover, and simmer 25–30 minutes or until potatoes and eggplant are done.

Yield: 6 cups   3 servings

Quick Bean Soup
(Day 4 Recipe)

1/2 cup	Navy Beans and Broth (page 170)
1 pint	green beans and broth, home canned or purchased
1/2 cup	cooked roast pork
1/2 cup	water or Pork Broth (page 140)

Combine and simmer to blend flavors and heat to serving temperature.

Yield: 3 cups   1 serving

Special Note: Makes a quick and easy meal using *plan*overs.

Nutritional Information/Serving	
Calories:	352
Protein (g):	24
Carbohydrate (g):	26.6
Fiber (g):	6.82
Total fat (g):	17.9
Saturated (g):	6.58
Cholesterol (mg):	65
Sodium (mg):	195
Food Exchanges/Serving	
.7 Br 2.1 LM 3 Veg 3 Fat	

Chicken Collard Soup
(Day 1 Recipe)

6 cups	Chicken Broth (page 130)
2 cups	water
2 cups	collard greens, approximately 5 medium-size leaves, torn
4 cups	cabbage, diced
2 cups	cooked chicken, diced
1/2 teaspoon	dill weed

Combine all ingredients in large saucepan. Bring to boil, reduce heat, cover, and simmer for 15–20 minutes or until vegetables are tender.

Yield: 8 cups

Nutritional Information/Cup	
Calories:	74
Protein (g):	10.2
Carbohydrate (g):	2.6
Fiber (g):	.93
Total fat (g):	2.47
Saturated (g):	.66
Cholesterol (mg):	29
Sodium (mg):	33
Food Exchanges/Serving	
1.4 VLM .5 Veg .4 Fat	

Chicken Rice or Turnip Soup
(Day 1 Recipe)

2 cups	Chicken Broth (page 130)
1/2 cup	cooked brown rice OR turnips, peeled and diced
1/2 cup	celery, diced
1/2 cup	cooked chicken, diced
1/8 teaspoon	sea salt
1/8 teaspoon	dill weed

Combine ingredients in saucepan. Bring to boil, reduce heat, cover and simmer 10–15 minutes or until vegetables are tender.

Yield: 2 cups   1 serving

Nutritional Information/Serving		
	Rice	Turnip
Calories:	214	151
Protein (g):	21.4	20.2
Carbohydrate (g):	18.9	6.3
Fiber (g):	2.21	2.49
Total fat (g):	5.44	4.85
Saturated (g):	1.45	1.32
Cholesterol (mg):	58	58
Sodium (mg):	382	422
Food Exchanges/Serving		
Rice: 1 Br 2.8 VLM .3 Veg .7 Fat		
Turnip: 2.8 VLM 1 Veg .7 Fat		

Chicken Broccoli Soup
(Day 1 Recipe)

1 cup	Chicken Broth (page 130)
1/2 cup	water
1/2 cup	cooked chicken, diced
1 cup	broccoli cuts, fresh or frozen
1/8 teaspoon	sea salt
1/8 teaspoon	dill weed

Combine all ingredients except broccoli in saucepan, bring to boil. Reduce heat, add broccoli, cover, and simmer 5 minutes or until broccoli is tender. Serve immediately.   Yield: 2 1/4 cups   1 serving

Nutritional Information/Serving	
Calories:	149
Protein (g):	21.7
Carbohydrate (g):	4.62
Fiber (g):	2.64
Total fat (g):	5.01
Saturated (g):	1.34
Cholesterol (mg):	58.1
Sodium (mg):	350
Food Exchanges/Serving	
2.8 VLM 1 Veg .7 Fat	

Cream of Broccoli or Cauliflower Soup

	Cream of Broccoli Soup (Day 1 Recipe)	Cream of Cauliflower Soup (Day 3 Recipe)
1 cup	water	
3/8 teaspoon	sea salt	
2 cups	broccoli cuts, fresh or frozen	cauliflower florets
2 tablespoons	chopped macadamia or Brazil nuts*	
2 tablespoons	flour—rice, Kamut, or spelt	tapioca starch or cornstarch
1 cup	water	
seasoning, as indicated	1/4 teaspoon dill weed	1/2 teaspoon cilantro

1. In saucepan, bring water and salt to boil, reduce heat. Add broccoli or cauliflower, cover, and simmer 5 minutes.

2. While vegetable cooks, combine flour, nuts, and 1/3 cup of water in blender. Blend on highest speed for 1–2 minutes until well blended. Stop at least once to scrape sides and bottom of blender jar. Add rest of water and between 1/2–3/4 of cooked mixture. Blend 20 seconds on low.

3. Pour into saucepan. Add dill weed or cilantro. Heat to thicken. Stir almost constantly. Serve with crackers, biscuit, or muffin for quick light lunch or as side dish with meal.

Yield: 2 3/4 cups   2 servings

Nutritional Information/Serving				
	Cream of Broccoli		Cream of Cauliflower	
	Macadamia	Brazil	Macadamia	Brazil
Calories:	119	118	114	112
Protein (g):	4.04	4.6	2.7	3.2
Carbohydrate (g):	13.3	13.3	13.4	13.3
Fiber (g):	3.54	3.61	2.39	2.47
Total fat (g):	6.76	6.38	6.38	6.00
Saturated (g):	1.02	1.52	.95	1.45
Cholesterol (mg):	0	0	0	0
Sodium (mg):	430	430	435	435
Food Exchanges/Serving				
Broccoli/Macadamia: .4 Br .1 VLM 1 Veg 1.2 Fat				
Broccoli/Brazil: .4 Br .2VLM 1 Veg 1.2 Fat				
Cauliflower/Macadamia: .4 Br .1 VLM 1 Veg 1.2 Fat				
Cauliflower/Brazil: .4 Br .2 VLM 1 Veg 1.2 Fat				

Tuna Broccoli Chowder*

(Day 1 Recipe)

Prepare Cream of Broccoli Soup with addition of 1 jar (7 1/2 oz.) of Chunk's Seafood tuna at Step 3. Increase salt to at least 1/2 teaspoon.

Yield: 3 2/3 cups   2 servings

Nutritional Information/Serving		
Tuna Broccoli	Macadamia	Brazil
Calories:	259	257
Protein (g):	35.5	36
Carbohydrate (g):	13.3	13.3
Fiber (g):	3.54	3.61
Total fat (g):	7.29	6.91
Saturated (g):	1.19	1.69
Cholesterol (mg):	19.1	19.1
Sodium (mg):	611	611
Food Exchanges/Serving		
Both: .4 Br 4.4 VLM 1 Veg 1.2 Fat		

Nutritional Information/Serving		
Salmon Cauliflower	Macadamia	Brazil
Calories:	261	260
Protein (g):	23.7	24.3
Carbohydrate (g):	13.4	13.3
Fiber (g):	2.39	2.47
Total fat (g):	12.82	12.45
Saturated (g):	2.59	3.09
Cholesterol (mg):	58	58
Sodium (mg):	515	515
Food Exchanges/Serving		
Mac.: .4 Br .1 VLM 2.7 LM 1 Veg 1.2 Fat		
Braz.: .4 Br .2 VLM 2.7 LM 1 Veg 1.2 Fat		

Salmon Cauliflower Chowder*

(Day 3 Recipe)

Prepare Cream of Cauliflower Soup with addition of 1 jar (7 1/2 oz.) of Chunk's Seafood salmon at Step 3. Increase salt to at least 1/2 teaspoon.

Yield: 3 2/3 cups   2 servings

*Brazil and macadamia nuts are unassigned "Fun Foods," see explanation on page 24.

Chicken Broccoli Chowder*
(Day 1 Recipe)

2 cups — Chicken Broth (page 130), separated
1/4 teaspoon — sea salt
2 cups — broccoli cuts, fresh or frozen
2 tablespoons — flour—rice, Kamut, or spelt
2 tablespoons — chopped macadamia or Brazil nuts*
1 cup — cooked chicken, diced
1/4 teaspoon — dill weed

Prepare Cream of Broccoli Soup except replace water with broth and add chicken at Step 3. Serve with crackers or muffin for complete light lunch.

Yield: 3 cups   2 servings

*Brazil and macadamia nuts are unassigned "Fun Foods", see explanation on page 24.

Nutritional Information/Serving		
	Macadamia	Brazil
Calories:	243	241
Protein (g):	23	23.7
Carbohydrate (g):	13.3	13.3
Fiber (g):	3.54	3.61
Total fat (g):	11.46	11.08
Saturated (g):	2.32	2.82
Cholesterol (mg):	58	58
Sodium (mg):	340	340
Food Exchanges/Serving		
Macadamia: .4 Br 2.9 VLM 1 Veg 1.9 Fat		
Brazil: .4 Br 3 VLM 1 Veg 1.9 Fat		

HH: Many recipes call for a small amount (such as 2 tablespoons) of chopped nuts—Brazil, macadamia, cashew, walnuts, almonds. Too save time, chop 1–2 or more cups of each kind (amount depends on your personal usage). Store chopped nuts in freezer in glass jars. I keep mine in the door of the refrigerator freezer compartment so they are handy to use. Also see General Tip #7 on page 12 about digestion and tolerance of nuts/seeds.

Cream of Asparagus Soup*
(Day 4 Recipe)

2 cloves — garlic, minced
1/2 cup — leek, sliced or chopped
2 teaspoons — safflower oil
3 cups — asparagus cuts and tips, fresh or frozen (10 oz. pkg.)
1 cup — water
1/2 teaspoon — sea salt
2 tablespoons — chopped macadamia nuts* or cashews
2 teaspoons — kudzu starch
1 cup — water
1/8 teaspoon — tarragon

Nutritional Information/Serving	
Calories:	175
Protein (g):	5.9
Carbohydrate (g):	17.4
Fiber (g):	5.38
Total fat (g):	11.21
Saturated (g):	1.44
Cholesterol (mg):	0
Sodium (mg):	543
Food Exchanges/Serving	
.1 Br .1 VLM 2.8 Veg 2.1 Fat	

1. In medium-size saucepan, sauté garlic and leeks in oil until soft.
2. Add asparagus, 1 cup water, and salt. Bring to boil. Cover and reduce heat. Simmer for 15 minutes or until asparagus is tender.
3. While asparagus is cooking, combine nuts, kudzu, and 1/4 cup water in blender. Blend on highest speed for 1–2 minutes until smooth and well blended. Add remaining water and between 1/2 to 3/4 of cooked mixture to blender. Blend about 20 seconds on lowest speed.
4. Pour into saucepan. Add tarragon. Heat to thicken. Stir almost constantly. Serve with Orange Roughy for complete light meal.

Yield: 3 cups   2 servings

*Macadamia nuts are unassigned "Fun Foods", see explanation on page 24.

Turkey Parsnip Soup
(Day 3 Recipe)

3 1/2 cups	water
1 cup	Turkey Broth (page 130)
1 1/2 cups	cooked turkey, diced
1 1/2 cups	carrots, peeled, sliced thin or diced
3/4 cup	parsnips, peeled, sliced thin or diced
1/4 teaspoon	sea salt
as desired	fresh spinach leaves, torn (optional)

Nutritional Information/Serving	
Calories:	251
Protein (g):	32
Carbohydrate (g):	17
Fiber (g):	4.59
Total fat (g):	5.54
Saturated (g):	1.78
Cholesterol (mg):	80
Sodium (mg):	374
Food Exchanges/Serving	
.4 Br 4.4 VLM 1.1 Veg .5 Fat	

1. Combine ingredients except spinach in large saucepan. Bring to boil, reduce heat, cover, and simmer for 10–15 minutes or until vegetables are tender.

2. Garnish each bowl with fresh spinach.

Yield: 4 1/2 cups without spinach

Turkey Kale Soup
(Day 3 Recipe)

3 1/2 cups	water
1 cup	Turkey Broth (page 130)
1 1/2 cups	cooked turkey, diced
2 cups	kale, torn, packed
1 cup	parsnips, peeled, sliced thin or diced
	OR turnips* or rutabaga, peeled, diced
2 teaspoons	cilantro (omit with turnip or rutabaga variations)
1/4 teaspoon	sea salt

Nutritional Information/Serving	
Calories:	258
Protein (g):	33
Carbohydrate (g):	17.6
Fiber (g):	4.5
Total fat (g):	5.72
Saturated (g):	1.8
Cholesterol (mg):	80
Sodium (mg):	363
Food Exchanges/Serving	
.9 Br 4.4 VLM 1.1 Veg .5 Fat	

Combine ingredients in large saucepan. Bring to boil, reduce heat, cover, and simmer for 15–20 minutes or until vegetables are tender.

*Turnips are assigned to Day 1. Omit them on Day 1 before and after using them in this soup on Day 3.

Special Note: Using the turnip or rutabaga variations keeps this a two food family soup. Using parsnips (my preference) makes it a three food family soup.

Yield: 5 cups   2 servings

Turkey Quinoa Soup
(Day 3 Recipe)

4 cups	water
1 cup	Turkey Broth (page 130)
1/4 cup	whole quinoa, rinse and drain 2–3 times
1 1/2 cups	cooked turkey, diced
1 1/2 cups	carrots, peeled, sliced thin or diced
1/4 teaspoon	sea salt
as desired	fresh spinach leaves, torn (optional)

Nutritional Information/Serving	
Calories:	293
Protein (g):	34.4
Carbohydrate (g):	23
Fiber (g):	3.4
Total fat (g):	6.62
Saturated (g):	1.88
Cholesterol (mg):	79.8
Sodium (mg):	373
Food Exchanges/Serving	
1 Br 4.4 VLM 1.1 Veg .5 Fat	

1. Bring ingredients, except spinach, to boil in large saucepan. Reduce heat, cover, and simmer for 15 minutes or until carrots and quinoa are tender. Taste and add more salt if desired.

2. Garnish each bowl with fresh spinach.

Yield: 5 cups without spinach   2 servings

Turkey Barley Soup
(Day 3 Recipe)

5 cups	water
1 cup	Turkey Broth (page 130)
1/4 cup	pearled barley
1 1/2 cups	cooked turkey, diced
1 1/2 cups	carrots, peeled, sliced thin or diced
1/2 teaspoon	sea salt
as desired	fresh spinach leaves, torn (optional)

Nutritional Information/Serving	
Calories:	302
Protein (g):	34.1
Carbohydrate (g):	27.8
Fiber (g):	5.57
Total fat (g):	5.68
Saturated (g):	1.82
Cholesterol (mg):	80
Sodium (mg):	638
Food Exchanges/Serving	
1 Br 4.4 VLM 1.1 Veg .5 Fat	

1. Bring water, broth, and barley to boil in large saucepan. Reduce heat, cover, and simmer for 50 minutes.

2. Add remaining ingredients except spinach. Simmer until carrots and barley are tender, approximately 10–15 minutes. Taste and add more salt if desired.

3. Garnish each bowl with fresh spinach.

Yield: 5 1/2 cups without spinach   2 servings

Turkey Soup
(Day 3 Recipe)

3 cups	water
1 cup	Turkey Broth (page 130)
1 1/2 cups	cooked turkey, diced
2 cups	carrots, sliced thin or diced
1/4 teaspoon	sea salt
as desired	fresh spinach leaves, torn (optional)

Nutritional Information/Serving	
Calories:	226
Protein (g):	31.9
Carbohydrate (g):	11.1
Fiber (g):	1.86
Total fat (g):	5.44
Saturated (g):	1.77
Cholesterol (mg):	80
Sodium (mg):	378
Food Exchanges/Serving	
4.4 VLM 1.5 Veg .5 Fat	

1. Combine all ingredients except spinach in large saucepan. Bring to boil, reduce heat, cover and simmer for 10–15 minutes or until carrots are tender. Taste and add more salt, if desired

2. Garnish each bowl with fresh spinach.

Yield: 4 cups without spinach   2 servings

Turkey Quinoa Pasta Soup
(Day 3 Recipe)

1 cup	Turkey Broth (page 130)
1 cup	water
1 cup	carrots, fresh or frozen, peeled and sliced
1/2 cup	cauliflower, fresh or frozen, sliced or small florets
1/2 cup	cooked turkey meat, diced
as needed	sea salt
1/2 cup	wheat-free quinoa pasta

Nutritional Information/Serving	
Calories:	312
Protein (g):	25.6
Carbohydrate (g):	39.4
Fiber (g):	5.57
Total fat (g):	5.41
Saturated (g):	1.23
Cholesterol (mg):	53
Sodium (mg):	107
Food Exchanges/Serving	
1.7 Br 2.9 VLM 2.3 Veg .4 Fat	

1. In saucepan, combine ingredients except pasta. Simmer until vegetables are almost tender.

2. Cook pasta (see Perfect Pasta recipe, page 195) and add. Serve immediately. Do not overcook.

Yield: 3 cups   1 serving

Special Note: Prepare only amount to be served because quinoa pasta turns to mush when reheated.

Sandwich Ideas

	Day 1	Day 2	Day 3	Day 4
Bread Options:				
Griddle breads	Teff	Amaranth Garbanzo Bean	Quinoa	Lentil, Black Bean, Buckwheat
Tortillas	Kamut, Spelt, Teff	Amaranth	Quinoa	Buckwheat White Bean
Flat breads	Simun's Flat Breads	Nu-World Amaranth Flat Bread Simun's Flat Breads	Simun's Flat Breads	Simun's Flat Breads
Bread	Kamut or Spelt Sour Dough Bread EnerG Foods rice bread		Rye Sour Dough Bread	
You may also use a pancake of the Day (especially for kids). Cut griddle bread in fourths for smaller sandwich.				
Filling Options:				
Meats	chicken ground meat patty	roast beef or buffalo minute steak ground meat patty Sloppy Joes	turkey ground meat patty	roast pork or venison pork cutlet roast lamb ground meat patty
Fish	Halibut Medallions Day 1 fish fillet	Day 2 fish fillet	Day 3 fish fillet	Day 4 fish fillet
Vegetarian	almond butter tahini	Garbanzo Bean Patty	filbert butter	Black Bean Patty Lentil Patty Lentil Sloppy Joes grilled sliced tofu cashew butter
"Salads"	Chicken, Tuna, Egg	Shrimp	Salmon, Turkey	Tofu and Cucumber
Spread Options:				
"Mayos"	Almond	Sunflower	Filbert	Macadamia, Cashew
Other spreads		butter or ghee, Quick Catsup, Creamy Italian Dressing		
Topping Options:				
Vegetables	chard shredded cabbage cabbage leaves sliced celery sliced radish sliced water chestnuts	sliced tomato sliced cucumber lettuce sliced zucchini sliced onion green pepper strips	spinach shredded carrots kale sliced avocado	sliced cucumber sorrel sliced leeks
Sprouts	cabbage, radish	sunflower greens	barley, millet	alfalfa, buckwheat, mung bean, clover, lentil
Chopped nuts or seeds	pecan, almond, sesame seeds	pumpkin seeds sunflower seeds	walnuts filberts	cashews
Seasoning Options:	dill weed, cumin, dry mustard	onion or garlic powder, chili powder, oregano, cayenne pepper, basil, sage, savory	caraway seed fennel	tarragon, oregano, garlic powder, chili powder

Fajitas

	Day 1	Day 2	Day 4
Your choice of bread	Day 1 tortilla or griddle bread	Day 2 tortilla or griddle bread	Day 4 tortilla or griddle bread
Your choice of meat, cut into thin strips	1/2 cup deboned chicken breast (1/2 breast is usually enough)	8 ounces beef or buffalo–round steak (pounded to tenderize) or minute steak (about 1 cup)	6 ounces tenderized pork or venison cutlets (about 1 cup)
Your choice of vegetables	3/4 cup cabbage, thinly sliced or shredded 1/2 cup celery, sliced thin	1/2 cup onion, thinly sliced 1 cup green pepper strips 1 1/2 cups zucchini squash, cut into strips	1 cup leek, thinly sliced 1 cup green pepper strips* 1 1/2 cups zucchini squash, cut into strips*
Your choice of oil	sesame oil	sunflower or olive oil	safflower oil
Your choice of seasoning, as desired	sea salt dill weed cumin parsley	sea salt summer savory	sea salt tarragon
Your choice of garnish, as desired		fresh tomato, diced, seasoned with small amount of Watkins Salsa Seasoning Blend or other Mexican blend spices Guacamole (page 227) Picante Sauce (page 227)	fresh tomato*, diced, seasoned with small amount of Watkins Salsa Seasoning Blend or other Mexican blend spices
YIELD	1 1/2 cups filling, ample for 2 fajitas	3 cups filling, ample for 4 fajitas	3 cups filling, ample for 4 fajitas

If using venison, soak strips in salted water for few hours or overnight to remove wild taste.

1. Prepare or thaw tortillas or griddle bread.
2. Prepare tomato, Guacamole, and/or Picante Sauce if desired.
3. Preheat electric skillet to 300°F.
4. Prepare meat and vegetables as described above. Meat will cut into strips easier if partially frozen.
5. Add oil to preheated electric skillet. Stir fry meat, stirring often to brown evenly. Cover with splatter screen when not stirring.
6. Add vegetables and sprinkle with salt and desired seasoning. Stir often to cook evenly. I prefer my vegetables crunchy.
7. Serve immediately. The easiest way to serve fajitas is to spread 3/4 cup of filling in center of bread lengthwise but about 1 inch from one side as Diagram A shows. Fold the 1-inch edge side over first, then fold the 1/3 side edges over the filling as Diagram B shows. Lift and hold with both hands. Eat and enjoy.

*These foods are assigned to Day 2. Avoid eating them on Day 2 just before and after serving this recipe on Day 4.

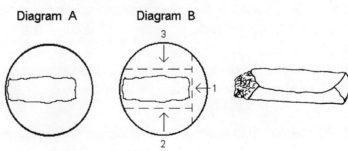

Diagram A   Diagram B

Lentil Patties
(Day 4 Recipe)

1 cup	dry green lentils
2 1/2 cups	water
1/2 cup	leeks, sliced
1/2 teaspoon	cayenne pepper* (optional or use other desired spices/herbs)
2 tablespoons	whole flaxseeds
2 tablespoons	green lentil flour
1/2 cup	pumpkin seeds, ground
as desired	sea salt and safflower oil

Nutritional Information/Small Pattie	
	Lentil
Calories:	74
Protein (g):	5.5
Carbohydrate (g):	12.2
Fiber (g):	3.18
Total fat (g):	.7
Saturated (g):	.12
Cholesterol (mg):	0
Sodium (mg):	3
Food Exchanges/Serving	
.5 Br .5 VLM .4 Veg .1 Fat	

1. Rinse and drain lentils. Presoaking not necessary. However, if have difficulty digesting legumes, soak overnight, rerinse, and drain like other legumes and use 1/2 cup less water for cooking.

2. In a medium-size saucepan, combine lentils, water, leeks, and cayenne. Bring to boil on high. Reduce heat to medium. Cover and simmer 30–35 minutes or until lentils are tender. Stir occasionally.

Method to use if lentils are tiny baby lentils

3. Transfer 2/3 of cooked lentils to blender. Blend until smooth.

4. To remaining lentils, add flaxseeds and cook for 3 minutes, stirring almost constantly. Remove from heat. Add blended lentils, flour, and pumpkin seeds to saucepan. Stir to combine. May need to add small amount of additional water (such as 1–2 tablespoons).

OR

Method to use if lentils are large enough to mash with potato masher

3. Add flaxseeds and cook for 3 minutes, stir almost constantly. Remove from heat.

4. Mash beans with hand potato masher. Add flour and pumpkin seeds. Stir to combine.

5. To Form Patties: Level pack mixture into 1/4 or 1/2 cup measure. Transfer measured amount to stainless steel baking sheet. Flatten to form round 2 1/2-inch or 4-inch patty. Repeat to use all. (If desired, may line baking sheet with cellophane or wax paper as well as cover patties with another sheet.) Place baking sheet in freezer. After frozen, transfer patties to cellophane or plastic bag and keep frozen.

6. To Cook Patties: Add small amount of oil to griddle/skillet. Oil amount depends upon type of griddle/skillet. I prefer a seasoned cast-iron griddle (see page 59) and only use 1/2 teaspoon or less of oil per large patty. Cook and season with sea salt as with any ground meat patty. Turn often to brown and heat evenly. Total cooking time with preheated cast-iron griddle is usually 15 minutes for frozen patty. If desired, cook patty immediately (measure and form patty directly on lightly oiled griddle) for about 10 minutes total cooking time.

Serving Suggestions: Serve as sandwich with Lentil Griddle Bread (page 129). Garnish with thinly sliced zucchini (moved from Day 2) or cucumbers, sprouts, and/or Day 4 "Mayo." Larger-size is great to serve on a Buckwheat "Hamburger" Bun. Move tomatoes to Day 4 and serve patties with Quick Catsup, Picante Sauce, etc.

Sondra's Thoughts: I prefer to make small patties and serve on griddle bread. I cut the bread into fourths to make 2 small sandwiches. I prefer to make a double batch and freeze extras for a later quick meal.

Yield in Patties: 6 large/12 small

USED FOR ANALYSIS: Analysis does not include flaxseed since figures were unavailable.

*Cayenne is assigned to Day 2. Omit eating it on Day 2 before and after serving this recipe on Day 4.

Garbanzo Bean or Black Bean Patties

(Garbanzo Bean–Day 2 / Black Bean–Day 4 Recipe)

1 1/2 cups	Garbanzo Beans & Broth (page 166) or Black Beans & Sauce (page 166), unsalted, drained, reserve broth

OR

1–15 oz. can Eden brand organic garbanzo beans or black beans, drained, reserve broth

as indicated	2/3 cup garbanzo bean broth OR 1/2 cup black bean broth (amounts in Eden brand beans)
2 tablespoons	whole flaxseed
1/4 cup	ground seeds—sunflower seeds for garbanzo, pumpkin seeds for black bean
2 tablespoons	garbanzo bean flour or black bean flour
1/4 teaspoon	garlic powder*
1/4 teaspoon	onion powder*

1. Drain beans and measure broth as listed. Add water if needed to yield required amount.

2. In small saucepan, combine 1/4 cup bean broth and flaxseed. Bring to boil. Reduce heat and simmer for 3 minutes stirring almost constantly. Set aside.

3. In medium-size bowl, mash beans with remaining broth using hand potato masher or blender.

4. Combine all ingredients and stir to blend.

Nutritional Information/Small Pattie		
	Garbanzo	Black Bean
Calories:	73	55
Protein (g):	3.6	3.3
Carbohydrate (g):	8.9	9.5
Fiber (g):	1.79	3.07
Total fat (g):	2.93	.60
Saturated (g):	.3	.11
Cholesterol (mg):	0	0
Sodium (mg):	2	25
Food Exchanges/Serving		
Garbanzo: .5 Br .7 VLM .5 Fat		
Black Bean: .4 Br .6 VLM .3 Veg .1 Fat		

5. To Form Patties: Level pack mixture into 1/4 or 1/2 cup measure. Transfer measured amount to stainless steel baking sheet. Flatten to form round 2 1/2-inch or 4-inch round patty. Repeat to use all. (If desired, may line baking sheet with cellophane or wax paper as well as cover patties with another sheet.) Place baking sheet in freezer. After frozen, transfer patties to cellophane or plastic bag and keep frozen.

6. To Cook Patties: Add small amount of oil to griddle/skillet. Oil amount depends upon type of griddle/skillet. I prefer a seasoned cast-iron griddle (see page 59) and only use 1/2 teaspoon or less of oil per large patty. Cook and season with sea salt as with any ground meat patty. Turn often to brown and heat evenly. Total cooking time with preheated cast-iron griddle is usually 15 minutes for frozen patty. If desired, cook patty immediately (measure and form patty directly on lightly oiled griddle) for about 10 minutes total cooking time.

Serving Suggestions: Serve as sandwich with Garbanzo or Black Bean Griddle Bread (page 120). Garnish Day 2 patties with thinly sliced zucchini, sunflower greens (sprouts), lettuce greens, and/or Sunflower "Mayo." Garnish Day 4 patties with thinly sliced cucumbers, sprouts, and/or your choice of Day 4 "Mayo." Larger size is great with Amaranth or Buckwheat "Hamburger" Bun. Also, patties are delicious served with Quick Catsup, Picante Sauce, etc.

Sondra's Thoughts: I prefer to make small patties and serve on griddle bread. I cut the bread into fourths to make 2 small sandwiches. I like to make a double batch and freeze extras for a later quick meal. I usually prepare these patties with home cooked beans and have found that they mash easier if the beans are warm. Since I season the beans during cooking as indicated in the recipes, I omit the listed onion powder and use about half the amount of garlic powder listed above.

Yield in Patties: 4 large/8 small

USED FOR ANALYSIS: Analysis does not include flaxseed since figures were unavailable.

*These spices are assigned to Day 2. Omit eating them on Day 2 before and after serving the black bean version on Day 4.

Lentil Sloppy Joes
(Day 4 Recipe)

1 cup	dry green lentils
2 1/2 cups	water
1/2 cup	sliced leeks or chopped onions*
1/2 teaspoon	leaf oregano*
1/4 teaspoon	garlic powder*
1/8 teaspoon	cayenne powder*
1-6 oz. can	Muir Glen organic tomato paste*
1/2 teaspoon	sea salt

Nutritional Information/Serving	
Calories:	64
Protein (g):	4.7
Carbohydrate (g):	11.6
Fiber (g):	2.47
Total fat (g):	.18
Saturated (g):	.02
Cholesterol (mg):	0
Sodium (mg):	98
Food Exchanges/Serving	
.4 Br .4 VLM .6 Veg	

1. Rinse and drain lentils. Presoaking not necessary. However, if have difficultly digesting legumes, soak overnight like other legumes and use 1/2 cup less water for cooking.

2. In a medium-size sauce pan, combine all ingredients except tomato paste and salt. Bring to boil on high. Reduce heat to medium. Cover and simmer 30–35 minutes or until lentils are tender. Stir occasionally.

3. Add tomato paste and salt and simmer uncovered approximately 10 minutes or until desired temperature and consistency. Stir almost constantly. Taste and add more seasoning if desired.

4. Serve on your choice of Day 4 "hamburger" buns, tortillas, or Griddle Breads. Garnish with sprouts, thinly sliced cucumber, and/or tomato slices.

Yield: 3 cups   12 servings (1/4 cup each)

*Onion, tomato, and these three spices are assigned to Day 2. Omit eating them on Day 2 before and after serving this recipe on Day 4.

Sloppy Joes
(Day 2 Recipe)

1 pound	ground beef or buffalo
1/3 cup	onion, chopped
3/4 teaspoon	sea salt
1/2 teaspoon	oregano
1/4 teaspoon	garlic powder
1/8 teaspoon	cayenne (red) pepper
1–6 oz. can	Muir Glen organic tomato paste
1 can	water (use tomato paste can)

Nutritional Information/Serving	
Calories:	98
Protein (g):	9.6
Carbohydrate (g):	3.57
Fiber (g):	.64
Total fat (g):	4.88
Saturated (g):	1.91
Cholesterol (mg):	28
Sodium (mg):	195
Food Exchanges/Serving	
1.2 LM .7 Veg .3 Fat	

1. In skillet, combine meat, onion, salt, and spices. Cook until done. Stir often to chop and brown meat evenly.

2. Add tomato paste and water, blend ingredients. Cook, stirring often, until serving temperature and desired consistency. Taste and, if desired, add more seasonings.

3. Serve on your choice of Day 2 "hamburger" bun, tortillas, or griddle breads. Garnish with sprouts, thinly sliced cucumber, and/or sliced tomato.

Yield: 2 1/2 cups   10 servings (1/4 cup each)

> *Few of us do as much as we want to for others. But there is always one gift we can bestow—a smile.*
>
> —*Marjorie Holms*

Tacos
(Day 2 Recipe)

1 pound	ground beef or buffalo
1–6oz. can	Muir Glen brand organic tomato paste
1 can	water (use tomato paste can)
1/3 cup	onion, chopped
1/2 teaspoon	sea salt
1/4 teaspoon	minced garlic
1/2 teaspoon	Watkins Salsa Seasoning Blend or other Mexican blend spices
as needed	Day 2 tortillas or griddle bread

Toppings

| as needed | fresh diced tomatoes, shredded lettuce, diced onions, Guacamole, and/or Picante Sauce (page 227) |

Nutritional Information 1/4 Cup Taco Meat	
Calories:	111
Protein (g):	10.9
Carbohydrate (g):	4.57
Fiber (g):	.78
Total fat (g):	5.41
Saturated (g):	2.12
Cholesterol (mg):	31.4
Sodium (mg):	159
Food Exchanges/Serving	
1.4 LM .9 Veg .3 Fat	

1. If desired, prepare onions, Guacamole, and/or Picante Sauce. Chill.

2. Prepare or thaw tortillas or griddle bread.

3. In skillet, cook meat until done. Stir often to chop and brown evenly. Add remaining ingredients except for breads and toppings. Simmer 30 minutes. Stir occasionally. Taste and, if desired, add more spices.

4. While meat mixture is simmering, prepare tomatoes and lettuce. Refrigerate until needed. Optional: Stir 1/8 teaspoon of Watkins Salsa Seasoning Blend into diced tomatoes.

5. To serve—layer meat mixture, lettuce, tomatoes, onions, Guacamole, and/or Picante Sauce in amount desired on 1/2 of tortilla or griddle bread. Fold, lift, and hold with both hands. Eat and enjoy.

Yield: 2 1/4 cups of taco meat

> **SPECIAL NOTE:** Garden Valley Naturals brand organic roasted garlic tomato salsa may be substituted for Picante Sauce and fresh tomatoes.

Lentil Tacos
(Day 4 Recipe)

1 cup	dry green lentils
2 1/2 cups	water
1/2 cup	sliced leeks or chopped onion*
1/2 teaspoon	minced garlic
3/4 teaspoon	Watkins Salsa Seasoning Blend or other Mexican blend spices
1–6 oz. can	Muir Glen brand organic tomato paste*
1/2 teaspoon	sea salt
as needed	Day 4 tortillas or griddle bread
as needed	Toppings: See list in Taco recipe above.

Nutritional Information 1/4 Cup Lentil Taco Mixture	
Calories:	72
Protein (g):	5.6
Carbohydrate (g):	12.8
Fiber (g):	2.73
Total fat (g):	.17
Saturated (g):	.02
Cholesterol (mg):	0
Sodium (mg):	101
Food Exchanges/Serving	
.5 Br .5 VLM .7 Veg	

1. Using all ingredients except breads and toppings, follow directions for steps 1–3 from Lentil Sloppy Joe recipe (see previous page).

2. To serve—layer lentil mixture, lettuce, tomatoes, onions, Guacamole, and/or Picante Sauce in amount desired on 1/2 of tortilla or griddle bread. Fold, lift, and hold with both hands. Eat and enjoy.

Yield: 3 cups of lentil mixture

*Onion and tomato are assigned to Day 2. Omit eating them on Day 2 before and after serving this recipe on Day 4.

Tuna Salad
(Day 1 Recipe)

1/2 jar	Chuck's Seafood albacore tuna, flaked. (3 3/4 ounces)
1/3 cup	celery, diced
1	egg, hard boiled, diced (optional)
few sprigs	fresh parsley, torn or cut into small pieces (optional)
2–3 tablespoons	Almond "Mayo" (page 188)
to taste	sea salt

Yield: 3/4 cup without egg   1 cup with egg Enough for 2 tortillas.

> *The ability to beat the odds lies within us all.*

Egg Salad
(Day 1 Recipe)

2	eggs, hard boiled, diced
1/3 cup	celery, diced
few sprigs	fresh parsley, torn or cut into small pieces (optional)
2 tablespoons	Almond "Mayo" (page 188)
to taste	sea salt

Yield: 1 cup Enough for 2 tortillas

Chicken Salad
(Day 1 Recipe)

1/2 cup	cooked chicken, diced
1	egg, hard boiled, diced
1/3 cup	celery, diced
few sprigs	fresh parsley, torn or cut into small pieces (optional)
3 tablespoons	Almond "Mayo" (page 188)
to taste	sea salt

Yield: 1 cup Enough for 2 tortillas

> *The darkest hour is only 60 minutes long.*

Shrimp Salad
(Day 2 Recipe)

1 cup	Fresh Shelled Shrimp (page 158)
3/4 cup	cucumber, peeled or unpeeled, diced
1/2 cup	green pepper, diced
1/4 cup	Sunflower "Mayo" (page 188)
1/4 teaspoon	sea salt

Yield: 2 cups Enough for 4 tortillas.

Salmon Salad
(Day 3 Recipe)

1/2 jar	Chuck's Seafood salmon, flaked (3 3/4 ounces)
1/3 cup	shredded carrots
1	egg, hard boiled, diced* (optional)
few sprigs	fresh parsley, torn or cut into small pieces (optional)
2–3 tablespoons	Filbert "Mayo" (page 188)
to taste	sea salt

Yield: 3/4 cup without egg   1 cup with egg Enough for 2–3 sandwiches.

Turkey Salad*
(Day 3 Recipe)

1/2 cup	cooked turkey, diced
1	egg, hard boiled, diced*
1/3 cup	shredded carrots
few sprigs	fresh parsley, torn or cut into small pieces (optional)
3 tablespoons	Filbert "Mayo" (page 188)
to taste	sea salt

Yield: 1 cup Enough for 2–3 sandwiches

Tofu and Cucumber Salad Sandwich
(Day 4 Recipe)

1/2 pound	soft tofu, drained
2 cups	cucumber, diced
2 tablespoons	Macadamia** or Cashew "Mayo" (page 188)
1/8 teaspoon	sea salt
1/8 teaspoon	unbuffered, corn-free vitamin C crystals
1/4 teaspoon	tarragon

Yield: 2 cups (4 sandwiches)

<u>Directions for Above "Salad" Recipes:</u>

Combine your choice of ingredients and chill. Serve as salad on bed of greens as indicated:

Day 1	**Day 2**	**Day 3**	**Day 4**
Swiss chard	lettuce	spinach	sorrel

Serve as sandwich with greens mentioned above on a tortilla or griddle bread assigned to that Day or with Day 1 or 3 purchased yeast-free breads.

*Eggs are assigned to Day 1. Omit eggs on Day 1 just before and after enjoying this recipe on Day 3.

**Macadamia nuts are an unassigned "Fun Food," see explanation on page 24.

Nutritional Information/Recipe								
	Tuna	Tuna with Egg	Egg	Chicken	Shrimp	Salmon	Salmon with Egg	Turkey	Tofu Cucumber
Calories:	188	275	180	260	260	206	293	265	246
Protein (g):	33	39.4	12.7	27	33.6	22	28	27.6	20.2
Carbohydrate (g):	3.5	5.1	4.6	5.1	10.6	5.3	6.7	6.7	11.6
Fiber (g):	1.27	1.61	1.27	1.61	2.26	1.42	1.66	1.66	4.5
Total fat (g):	4.09	10.24	12.36	14.41	9.42	10.47	16.86	13.9	15.7
Saturated (g):	.52	2.05	3.08	3.18	1.23	1.94	3.45	2.97	2.36
Cholesterol (mg):	19	206	374	245	221	58	246	240	0
Sodium (mg):	138	219	196	215	852	143	223	192	347

Food Exchanges/Serving	
Tuna: 4.3 VLM .2 Veg .6 Fat	Salmon: 2.7 LM .5 Veg .8 Fat
Tuna with Egg: 4.3 VLM .8 LM .2 Veg 1.3 Fat	Salmon with Egg: 3.5 LM .5 Veg 1.6 Fat
Egg: 1.7 LM .2 Veg 1.5 Fat	Turkey: 2.9 VLM .8 LM .5 Veg 2 Fat
Chicken: 2.8 VLM .8 LM .2 Veg 2.0 Fat	Tofu Cucumber: 2.3 VLM .9 Veg 3.2 Fat
Shrimp: 4.2 VLM .8 Veg 1.2 Fat	

"Mayo"

AMOUNT	INGREDIENT	DAY 1	DAY 2	DAY 3	DAY 4
1/2 cup	raw nut or seed—	almonds	hulled sunflower seeds	filberts	macadamia or unsalted cashews
1 tablespoon	flour or starch—	Kamut, spelt, or rice	arrowroot starch or potato starch	tapioca starch or corn starch	kudzu
1/4 teaspoon		sea salt			
1 teaspoon		unbuffered, corn-free vitamin C crystals			
1 cup		water			
as indicated or desired	seasoning (optional)—	1/2 teaspoon dry mustard	1/4 teaspoon garlic powder	caraway seed, fennel, cilantro	tarragon

1. Blend nuts or seeds in blender on highest speed for 1–2 minutes until they become a fine powder. Stop at least once to scrape sides and bottom of blender jar. Be careful not to create a "butter." If needed to make it smoother, add flour or starch and blend on highest speed 1 minute longer.

2. Add remaining ingredients. Blend on highest speed for a minute longer, stopping once or twice to scrape sides and bottom of blender jar.

3. Pour mixture into small saucepan. Add desired seasoning. Cook over medium heat, stirring constantly with whisk until mixture is thick yet smooth.

4. Chill. If too thick, add a tablespoon more water. Taste and add more seasoning if desired. If necessary, may be stored in glass jar in refrigerator for a week.

Yield: 1 1/3 cups (21 1/3 tablespoons)

Special Note: Flour and starch options may be interchanged. Seasoning options may be interchanged.

Recipe idea is from The Yeast Connection Cookbook by Crook and Jones, page 208.

Creamy Italian Salad Dressing
(Day 2 Recipe)

1 1/3 cups	Sunflower "Mayo" (recipe above)
2 teaspoons	leaf oregano
1 teaspoon	basil
1/4 teaspoon	garlic powder
1/4 teaspoon	sea salt

Prepare "Mayo." Add seasonings. Stir. Chill. Add small amount of water if too thick.

Yield: 1 1/3 cups

HH: Freeze "mayos" or Creamy Italian Dressing in glass jars or small single serving amounts (in ice cube trays or by spoonfuls on a baking sheet). Once the single servings are frozen, remove and keep frozen in a cellophane or plastic bag. Thaw in refrigerator for a few hours or overnight.

Nutritional Information/Tablespoon						
	Almond	Sunflower	Filbert	Macadamia	Cashew	Creamy Italian
Calories:	21	21	22	24	20	21
Protein (g):	.7	.8	.41	.26	.5	.8
Carbohydrate (g):	1	1	.81	.76	1.4	1.1
Fiber (g):	.34	.22	.24	.17	.1	.3
Total fat (g):	1.75	1.67	1.98	2.32	1.49	1.68
Saturated (g):	.17	.18	.15	.35	.29	.18
Cholesterol (mg):	0	0	0	0	0	0
Sodium (mg):	25	25	25	25	26	50
Food Exchanges/Tablespoon						
	.1 VLM .3 Fat	.1 VLM .3 Fat	.1 VLM .4 Fat	.5 Fat	.1 VLM .3 Fat	.3 Fat

Creamy Veggie Salad Dressing

	Day 1	Day 2	Day 3
Yield	1/3 cup	1 cup	1cup
vegetable	1/3 cup cabbage, shredded, packed	1 cup zucchini squash, peeled, diced	1 cup carrot, peeled, shredded
water	1/4 cup	1/2 cup	1/2 cup
oil	1 teaspoon sesame	1 1/2 teas. sunflower	1 1/2 teas. canola
unbuffered vitamin C crystals	1/4 teaspoon	1/2 teaspoon	1/2 teaspoon
sea salt	1 pinch	2 pinches	2 pinches
optional ingredients	1/4 teas. dry mustard 1/2 teas. hulled sesame seeds	as desired garlic and/or onion powder	1/2 teaspoon caraway seed

Combine all ingredients, except Day 2 or 3 optional ingredients, in blender. Blend on highest speed for 1–2 minutes until smooth. Stop once or twice to scrape sides and bottom of blender jar. Pour into jar or bottle. Add caraway seed to Day 3 dressing and shake. Chill.

Sondra's Thoughts: Do not prepare Day 1 dressing in advance because if it is stored longer than one day the taste turns sour. Add garlic and/or onion powder just before serving only to amount of zucchini dressing to be used. Day 2 and 3 dressings may be stored in glass jar in refrigerator for a week.

Recipe idea from The Yeast Connection Cookbook *by Crook & Jones, p. 207.*

Nutritional Information/Serving				
	Day 1	Day 2	Day 3	Oil & Spice/C
Serving Size	complete recipe	1/4 cup	1/4 cup	complete recipe
Calories:	55	20	27	40
Protein (g):	.6	.4	.3	0
Carbohydrate (g):	1.6	1	2.8	0
Fiber (g):	.61	.4	.72	0
Total fat (g):	5.35	1.75	1.76	4.54
Saturated (g):	.76	.21	.13	.32–.64
Cholesterol (mg):	0	0	0	0
Sodium (mg):	58	28	36	0
Food Exchanges/Serving				
	.2 Veg 1 Fat	.3 Veg .3 Fat	.4 Veg .3 Fat	.9 Fat

HH: You may prepare zucchini salad dressing with frozen zucchini. First freeze prepared zucchini in 1 cup servings. Combine ingredients in blender. Blend a few seconds, stir, and allow to thaw for a minute or so. Repeat process until zucchini is thawed and blended smooth.

HH: Blender with Glass Jar:

I recommend the KitchenAid brand because it comes with a glass jar and has a very heavy duty motor that works well for chopping and grinding nuts. Another advantage is that the jar base is wider than most other brands. If you cannot purchase a KitchenAid, the next brand I would recommend is Oster because of its durability over some less-expensive brands. In addition, you may wish to have a second glass blender jar.

HH: Day 1 and 3 dressings may be frozen. Freeze in ice cube trays, 1 tablespoon per cube. Remove frozen cubes and keep frozen in cellophane or plastic bag. Thaw just the amount to be used.

Lemon/Oil Dressing
(Day 2 Recipe)

Because of the vinegar component, the person with CRC usually cannot use commercial salad dressings. An easy, rather tasty, substitute salad dressing may be prepared by mixing 1 teaspoon of sunflower oil with 1/2 teaspoon of freshly squeezed lemon juice (or use Santa Cruz brand organic 100% lemon juice). Recently I have found one vinegar-free commercial dressing—Annie's Wild Herbal Organics Green Garlic Vinaigrette.

It is difficult to always have fresh lemon on hand, so use the following recipe method.

Lemon Juice—Tips on Preparing and Storing

Wash lemons, cut in half crosswise, and squeeze juice using a hand juicer. Remove large pulp pieces and seeds. Pour into any dish with sides that will allow juice to be only 1/4–1/2 inch thick. Freeze, cut into 1-inch squares, and keep frozen in a bag. A square thaws very quickly to mix with oil for use in salad dressing. Save time and prepare several lemons at a time. Optional method is to peel lemons as you would an orange and run them through a juicer.

Easy Oil & Spice/C Dressing

In a small bowl, whisk together your choice of oil and herbs/spices with water and corn-free, unbuffered vitamin C crystals until vitamin C dissolves. (If desired, you may substitute between 1/2 and 1 teaspoon of freshly squeezed lemon or orange juice for vitamin C crystals.)

	Day 1	**Day 2**	**Day 3**	**Day 4**
1 teaspoon oil	sesame	sunflower	canola	safflower
1 tablespoon	water			
1/8 teaspoon	corn-free, unbuffered vitamin C crystals			
optional seasonings	2 pinches dill weed	2 sprinkles onion powder 2 pinches basil	2 pinches cilantro 1 pinch caraway seed	2 pinches tarragon
Serve on your choice: All-in-One Salad, 4 cups of "greens" salad, or side salads				

Nutritional analysis for Easy Oil & Spice/C Dressing is found on the previous page.

Chef Salad

Day 2 Choices	Day 3 Choices
lettuce, assorted variety, torn	spinach, torn
cucumbers and/or zucchini squash, sliced	carrots, shredded
tomato wedges	cauliflower, sliced or florets
green peppers, rings, strips, or diced	walnuts or filberts, chopped
red onions, rings or diced	eggs, hard-cooked, diced (floated from Day 1)
sunflower seeds	salmon, flaked
garbanzo beans, drained	cooked turkey, diced or strips
shrimp, diced, chilled	Day 3 Creamy Veggie Dressing
cooked roast beef, diced or strips	Day 3 Easy Oil & Spice/C Dressing
Day 2 Creamy Veggie Dressing	Filbert "Mayo"
Day 2 Easy Oil & Spice/C Dressing	
Creamy Italian Dressing	

Clean and prepare your choice of vegetables and protein ingredients in amount desired. Assemble as desired. Top with your choice of dressing. Serve with of your choice crackers, biscuits, or muffins for a complete light meal on a hot summer day.

All-in-One Salads

	Day 1	Day 2	Day 3	Day 4
Your choice of pasta, grain/nongrain, or beans:				
1/2 cup cooked pasta (recipe on page 195)	Kamut, rice, or spelt		wild rice, rye, or quinoa	mung bean
1/2 cup cooked grain/nongrain	rice	amaranth	millet or quinoa	buckwheat
1 cup cooked drained beans		garbanzo beans lima beans		navy beans kidney beans
Your choice of meat (I prefer to omit meat if using beans):				
1/2 jar Chuck's Seafood	tuna		salmon	
1/2 cup cooked diced meat	chicken	shrimp, roast beef, or buffalo	turkey	roast pork
2 hard boiled eggs	chicken eggs		turkey eggs	
Your choice of vegetables and spices:				
1/2 cup		cooked diced potatoes		frozen peas, thawed
2 cups your choice of fresh vegetables, bite-size pieces	celery broccoli cabbage bok choy	green pepper zucchini cucumber onion	cauliflower carrots	pea pods bean sprouts cucumber leeks
fresh "greens" (optional)	Swiss chard	lettuce	spinach	sorrel
sea salt as desired and/or other seasonings as desired	dill weed ground cumin parsley	cayenne pepper paprika	caraway cilantro	basil tarragon
Your choice of dressing:				
1/4–1/2 cup "Mayo"	Almond	Sunflower or Creamy Italian	Filbert	Macadamia or Cashew
1/3 cup Creamy Veggie Dressing	Cabbage	Zucchini	Carrot	
1 recipe Oil & Spice/C Dressing	Sesame	Sunflower	Canola	Safflower

1. Prepare your choice of ingredients and dressings. In bowl, gently toss all ingredients except "greens" and dressing. Add dressing and mix to coat all ingredients. Chill.

2. Serve on a bed of "greens" or tear leaves and mix into salad along with more dressing just before serving. Makes a complete easy meal or serve with crackers, muffin, or biscuit.

Sondra's Thoughts: Rice pasta does not have as much flavor as other listed pastas, so I prefer to add a little extra dry mustard to Almond "Mayo" before adding to salad. Because of their distinctive individual flavors, I do not combine salmon and quinoa. Often, I choose either a pasta/grain/bean option or meat option rather than have both.

Yield: 2 1/2–3 cups, serves 1 complete meal

HH: To cut up only the amount you need, snip and measure parsley and other fresh herbs all in one step by clipping them with kitchen scissors over a clear liquid measure.

Coleslaw
(Day 1 Recipe)

1 cup	cabbage, shredded or finely chopped
1/4 cup	celery, diced
1/4 cup	Almond "Mayo" (page 188)
as desired	sea salt, fresh parsley, dill weed

Combine and chill.

Yield: 1 cup   2 servings

Special Note: If desired, you may use 1/2 recipe of Day 1 Easy Oil & Spice/C Dressing (page 190) on this salad.

Nutritional Information/Serving	
Calories:	54
Protein (g):	2.0
Carbohydrate (g):	4.5
Fiber (g):	1.61
Total fat (g):	3.62
Saturated (g):	.35
Cholesterol (mg):	0
Sodium (mg):	70
Food Exchanges/Serving	
.5 Veg .6 Fat	

Kidney Bean Salad*
(Day 2 Recipe)

Bean Preparation

1 cup	kidney beans
2 cups	water

Follow steps 1–3 of Kidney Beans for Chili (page 172). This will yield 3 1/4 cups cooked beans and broth or 2 1/2 cups drained kidney beans—enough for a double batch of Kidney Bean Salad. Freeze extra beans with liquid. When ready to use, thaw and drain to prepare salad.

Salad Preparation

1 1/4 cups	cooked, drained kidney beans*
1 cup	cucumber, peeled or unpeeled, diced
1/2 cup	green peppers, diced
1/4 cup	Sunflower "Mayo" (page 188)
1/4 teaspoon	onion powder
1/4 teaspoon	sea salt

Combine all ingredients and chill.

Yield: 2 1/2 cups   5 servings

*Kidney beans are assigned to Day 4, omit them on Day 4 just before and after eating this salad on Day 2.

Nutritional Information/Serving	
Calories:	84
Protein (g):	5
Carbohydrate (g):	13.4
Fiber (g):	4.02
Total fat (g):	1.58
Saturated (g):	.18
Cholesterol (mg):	0
Sodium (mg):	130
Food Exchanges/Serving	
.6 Br .6 VLM .2 Veg .2 Fat	

Potato Salad
(Day 2 Recipe)

2 cups	potatoes, peeled, diced
1/2 teaspoon	sea salt
2/3 cup	green or red pepper, diced
2/3 cup	cucumber
1/2 teaspoon	onion powder
	OR 2 tablespoons finely diced onion
1/3 cup	Sunflower "Mayo" (page 188)

In saucepan, cook diced potatoes in small amount of water with salt on medium until tender. Drain and chill. Add rest of ingredients. Stir and chill. Sprinkle with paprika if desired.

Yield: 2 1/2 cups   5 servings.

Nutritional Information/Serving	
Calories:	82
Protein (g):	2.1
Carbohydrate (g):	14.9
Fiber (g):	1.4
Total fat (g):	1.88
Saturated (g):	.21
Cholesterol (mg):	0
Sodium (mg):	243
Food Exchanges/Serving	
.7 Br .2 Veg .3 Fat	

Cucumber and Pea Salad
(Day 4 Recipe)

1 cup	peas, fresh or frozen, thawed and drained
1 cup	cucumber, sliced
1/2 cup	leek, sliced
1/8 teaspoon	sea salt
1/3 cup	Macadamia* or Cashew "Mayo" (page 188)
	OR 1 recipe of Day 4 Easy Oil & Spice/C Dressing
as desired	fresh sorrel

Nutritional Information/Serving	
Calories:	71
Protein (g):	2.5
Carbohydrate (g):	8.8
Fiber (g):	2.57
Total fat (g):	3.2
Saturated (g):	.49
Cholesterol (mg):	0
Sodium (mg):	107
Food Exchanges/Serving	
.3 Br .5 Veg .7 Fat	

Gently toss together prepared vegetables. Add your choice of salad dressing. Mix and chill. If desired, serve on a bed of sorrel leaves.

Yield: 2 cups 4 servings

*Macadamia nuts are unassigned "Fun Foods," see explanation on page 24.

7 Layer Salad
(Day 4 Recipe)

4 cups	lettuce, washed, drained, torn into small pieces*
1 cup	frozen peas, thawed
1/4 cup	leeks, fresh, sliced
1/2 cup	cucumbers, peeled, diced
1/2 cup	green pepper, diced*
1 pound	fresh pork side (unsmoked, uncured bacon)—
	about 8 10-inch long, 1/4-inch thick slices
1/3–1/2 cup	Macadamia Nut "Mayo" (page 188)

Nutritional Information/Serving	
Calories:	78
Protein (g):	3.5
Carbohydrate (g):	9.7
Fiber (g):	3.25
Total fat (g):	3.37
Saturated (g):	.51
Cholesterol (mg):	0
Sodium (mg):	41
Food Exchanges/Serving	
.4 Br .7 Veg .7 Fat	

1. Prepare vegetables and "Mayo" as described above.

2. Cook fresh pork side with sea salt as you would normal bacon. It does take slightly longer to cook because of the thickness. Drain on paper towel. Cool enough to handle and crumble into small pieces.

3. To Assemble Salad: I prefer to use a 10-inch square, covered, Corning casserole dish. Layer ingredients evenly in casserole dish in following order: lettuce, peas, leeks, cucumbers, green peppers, cooked fresh pork side.

4. Pour "Mayo" over top of salad. Cover and refrigerate a few hours to blend flavors.

Yield: 4 servings

*These foods are assigned to Day 2. Omit them on Day 2 before and after enjoying this recipe on Day 4.

USED FOR ANALYSIS: Nutritional analysis done without fresh side since figures were not available.

Sprout Salad
(Day 4 Recipe)

1 can	unsweetened pineapple chunks (20 oz.)
1 pkg.	alfalfa sprouts (4 oz.)
1/4 cup	raw pumpkin seeds

Nutritional Information/Serving	
Calories:	83
Protein (g):	2.5
Carbohydrate (g):	13.5
Fiber (g):	2.4
Total fat (g):	3.18
Saturated (g):	.54
Cholesterol (mg):	0
Sodium (mg):	3
Food Exchanges/Serving	
.2 VLM .6 Fr .3 Veg .5 Fat	

Combine all ingredients and chill for a few hours to blend flavors.

Yield: 6 servings

Thank you to Elva W. of Iowa for developing this quick and easy salad recipe. The pineapple provides wonderful flavor and lessens the "green" taste of sprouts.

Apple Salad
(Day 3 Recipe)

1	small apple, peeled and diced (approximately 2/3 cup)
1–2 tablespoons	walnuts, chopped
2 tablespoons	Filbert "Mayo" (page 188)

Combine, chill, and serve.

Yield: 2/3 cup   2 servings

Vegetable/Apple Salad
(Day 3 Recipe)

1	medium apple, peeled and diced (approximately 1 cup)
1/2 cup	shredded carrot
2 tablespoons	walnuts, chopped
3 tablespoons	Filbert "Mayo" (page 188)

Combine, chill, and serve.

Yield: 1 1/2 cups   2 servings

Nutritional Information/Serving		
	Apple	Veggie/Apple
Calories:	62	115
Protein (g):	.9	1.9
Carbohydrate (g):	6.8	13.3
Fiber (g):	1.08	2.39
Total fat (g):	4.03	7.06
Saturated (g):	.34	.6
Cholesterol (mg):	0	0
Sodium (mg):	25	48
Food Exchanges/Serving		
Apple: .3 Fr .4 Fat		
Veggie/Apple: .1 Br .4 Fr .4 Veg .6 Fat		

Variation 1: Add 1–2 tablespoons small flaked coconut.

Variation 2: Add 1 cup of fresh torn spinach leaves and more "Mayo."

Variation 3: Substitute 1/4 cup of diced celery for half of the carrots. However, do remember to avoid eating celery on Day 1 just before and after eating this variation on Day 3.

Quinoa Salad
(Day 3 Recipe)

1 cup	Basic Quinoa (page 96), chilled
1/2 cup	apple, finely diced
1/3 cup	carrot, shredded
few springs	fresh parsley (optional)

Combine all ingredients. Chill and serve.

Yield: 1 1/3 cups firmly packed   1 serving

Three Color Salad
(Day 3 Recipe)

3/4 cup	Basic Quinoa (page 96), chilled
1 cup	shredded carrots
about 1 cup	fresh spinach, washed, torn, loosely packed

Combine all ingredients. Chill.   Serve within 24 hours.

Nutritional Information/Recipe		
	Quinoa	3 Color
Calories:	206	179
Protein (g):	6	6.9
Carbohydrate (g):	41.2	35.1
Fiber (g):	4.5	6.25
Total fat (g):	2.72	2.26
Saturated (g):	.30	.25
Cholesterol (mg):	0	0
Sodium (mg):	154	189
Food Exchanges/Recipe		
Quinoa: 1.8 Br .4 LM .4 Fr .6 Veg		
3 Color: 1.3 Br .3 LM 3 Veg		

This is a complete meal which is Quick & Easy with Advanced Preparation (using *plan*over Basic Quinoa). It is also an excellent recipe to use for a meal away from home, such as lunch at work. The Basic Quinoa may be cooked days beforehand, frozen, and thawed or it may be cooked the night before or a few hours before to allow time for chilling. You can use more or less of each of the three ingredients to create a combination that you enjoy. This is one of my favorite recipes for using leftover Basic Quinoa.

Day 2 Mixed Vegetable Salad

2 cups	your choice of Day 2 diced vegetables: zucchini, cucumber, green pepper
1/2 teaspoon	onion powder OR 2 tablespoons finely diced onion
1/3 cup	Sunflower "Mayo" or Creamy Italian Dressing (page 188)
	OR 1 recipe of Day 2 Easy Oil & Spice/C Dressing (page 188)

Combine ingredients, chill, and serve.

Yield: 2 cups

Day 4 Mixed Vegetable Salad

2 cups	cucumber and/or zucchini slices*
as desired	sprouts
1 recipe	Day 4 Easy Oil & Spice/C Dressing (page 190)

Combine ingredients, chill, and serve.

Yield: 2 cups

*Zucchini are assigned to Day 2. Omit it on Day 2 before and after using it in this Day 4 salad.

Perfect Pasta
Tips and Techniques

FOR MIO AMORE AMARANTH AND ANCIENT HARVEST WHEAT-FREE QUINOA PASTA:*

1. In saucepan, bring 1 1/2 cups of salted water to boil. Add 1/2 cup pasta. Bring back to boil if needed. Immediately remove from heat, cover, and let stand for 8–10 minutes.

2. If serving hot, drain and serve immediately or add to soup/stew and serve immediately. If using in cold salad, drain and immediately chill in ice water. Drain and gently toss in salads.

FOR MIO AMORE WILD RICE AND MIO AMORE RYE PASTA:

1. In saucepan, bring 1 1/2 cups of salted water to boil. Add 1/2 cup pasta. Bring back to boil if needed. Reduce heat to medium-high and gently boil for 7–8 minutes until tender. Stir occasionally.

2. If serving hot, drain and serve immediately or add to soup/stew and serve immediately. If using in cold salad, drain and immediately chill in ice water. Drain and gently toss in salads.

FOR FOLLOWING PASTAS, FOLLOW PACKAGE DIRECTIONS FOR COOKING:

Eden Foods Kudzu & Sweet Potato Pasta	100% Buckwheat Soba Noodles
Eden Foods Mung Bean Pasta	Various Kamut, Rice, and Spelt pastas

Yield:
Amaranth—1/2 cup = 1/2 cup	Mung Bean—1.2 oz. (1/2 pkg.) = 1 cup
Buckwheat—2 oz. (1/4 pkg.) = 2/3 cup	Quinoa—1/2 cup = 1 cup
Kamut, Rice, Spelt—1/2 cup = 1 cup	Rye—1/2 cup = scant 1 cup
Kudzu/Swt Pot—1.2 oz. (1/3 pkg.) = scant 1 cup	Wild Rice—1/2 cup = 2/3 cup

*Special Note: Overcooking these gluten-free pastas makes them mushy.

FYI: Ancient Harvest Wheat-free Quinoa Pasta ingredients: corn and quinoa flour
Mio Amore Amaranth Pasta ingredients: organic amaranth flour, organic flax meal
Mio Amore Rye Pasta ingredients: organic rye flour, agar agar, locust bean gum

NUTRITIONAL INFORMATION AND FOOD EXCHANGES: VEGETABLES

Food Item	Amount	Calories	Protein (g)	Carbohydrate (g)	Fiber (g)	Total Fat (g)	Sat. Fat (g)	Cholesterol (mg)	Sodium (mg)	Food Exchanges
Amaranth greens	1/2 cup	4	0.4	0.6	0.19	0.05	0.01	0	3	.2 Veg
Asparagus pieces	1/2 cup	15	1.5	3.1	1.41	0.13	0.03	0	1	.7 Veg
Bok choy	1/2 cup	5	0.5	0.8	0.35	0.07	0.01	0	23	.2 Veg
Broccoli pieces	1/2 cup	12	1.3	2.3	1.32	0.15	0.02	0	12	.5 Veg
Brussels sprouts	1/2 cup	19	1.5	4.0	2.18	0.13	0.03	0	11	.5 Veg
Cabbage	1/2 cup	9	0.5	1.9	0.71	0.09	0.01	0	6	.4 Veg
Carrots	1/2 cup	24	0.6	5.6	1.43	0.10	0.02	0	19	.8 Veg
Cucumber slices	1/2 cup	7	0.4	1.4	0.35	0.07	0.02	0	1	.2 Veg
Cauliflower	1/2 cup	11	0.9	2.0	0.84	0.22	0.04	0	7	.8 Veg
Celery	1/2 cup	10	0.5	2.2	0.90	0.08	0.02	0	52	.3 Veg
Collard greens	1/2 cup	6	0.3	1.3	0.42	0.04	0.01	0	3	.2 Veg
Eggplant	1/2 cup	11	0.4	2.5	1.03	0.07	0.01	0	1	.5 Veg
Green snap/string beans	1/2 cup	17	1.0	3.9	1.87	0.07	0.01	0	3	.5 Veg
Green pepper	1/2 cup	14	0.5	3.2	0.87	0.10	0.01	0	1	.5 Veg
Kale	1/2 cup	17	1.1	3.4	1.01	0.23	0.03	0	14	.5 Veg
Leeks	1/2 cup	32	0.8	7.4	1.30	0.16	0.02	0	10	1.5 Veg
Lettuce, looseleaf	1 cup	10	0.7	2.0	0.71	0.17	0.02	0	5	.4 Veg
Okra slices	1/2 cup	15	0.9	3.3	1.15	0.08	0.02	0	2	.5 Veg
Onions	1/2 cup	30	0.9	6.9	1.34	0.13	0.02	0	2	1.3 Veg
Parsnips	1/2 cup	57	0.9	13.6	3.09	0.21	0.03	0	7	.9 Br
Pea pods/snow peas, edible	1/2 cup	30	2.0	5.5	1.89	0.15	0.03	0	3	1.2 Veg
Peas, green, frozen	1/2 cup	62	4.1	11.4	4.40	0.22	0.04	0	70	.8 Br
Potato, small baked, flesh only	1 each	65	1.4	15.1	1.05	0.07	0.02	0	4	.9 Br
Potato, peeled/boiled/diced	1/2 cup	67	1.3	15.6	1.01	0.08	0.02	0	4	.9 Br
Spinach	1 cup	12	1.6	2.0	1.51	0.20	0.03	0	44	.5 Veg
Sweet potato, small peeled, after baking	1 each	62	1.0	14.6	1.80	0.07	0.02	0	6	.8 Br
Tomato, medium whole	1 each	26	1.1	5.7	1.27	0.41	0.06	0	11	1.0 Veg
Zucchini squash	1/2 cup	9	0.8	1.9	0.78	0.09	0.02	0	2	.5 Veg

NUTRITIONAL INFORMATION AND FOOD EXCHANGES: MEATS

Food Item	Amount	Calories	Protein (g)	Carbohydrate (g)	Fiber (g)	Total Fat (g)	Sat. Fat (g)	Cholesterol (mg)	Sodium (mg)	Food Exchanges
Beef, cooked	1/2 cup	164	21.8	0	0	7.88	2.96	71	208	3.0 LM
Chicken, cooked	1/2 cup	124	19.1	0	0	4.70	1.30	58	49	2.8 VLM .7 Fat
Egg, extra large	1 each	86	7.3	0.7	0	5.80	1.80	247	73	1.1 LM .6 Fat
Pork, cooked	1/2 cup	191	18.8	0	0	12.32	4.53	66	42	2.5 LM 1.2 Fat
Salmon, pink, drained/no salt/can	2 oz. wt.	79	11.2	0	0	3.44	0.87	31	43	1.4 LM
Shrimp	1/2 cup	77	14.8	0.7	0	1.26	0.24	111	108	2.1 VLM
Tuna, light in water, drained/no salt/can	2 oz. wt.	74	16.8	0	0	0.28	0.09	10	28	2.3 LM
Turkey, cooked	1/2 cup	119	20.5	0	0	3.49	1.16	53	49	2.9 VLM .4 Fat

NUTRITIONAL INFORMATION AND FOOD EXCHANGES: PASTA

Food Item	Dry Amount	Cooked Amount	Calories	Protein (g)	Carbohydrate (g)	Fiber (g)	Total Fat (g)	Sat. Fat (g)	Cholesterol (mg)	Sodium (mg)	Food Exchanges
Amaranth pasta, Mio Amore*	1/2 cup	1/2 cup									
Brown rice pasta, Pastariso	1/2 cup	1 cup	210	5	42	unknown	2	unknown	2	1	2.6 Br
Buckwheat noodles, soba 100%	2 oz. wt. (1/4 pkg.)	2/3 cup	200	5.0	41.0	3.00	1.50	0	0	30	2.5 Br
Kamut pasta	1/2 cup	1 cup	150	6	34.5	5.25	0.75	0	0	0	1.9 Br
Kudzu & sweet potato pasta, Eden Foods	1.2 oz. (1/3 pkg.)	scant 1 cup	114	0	28.2	0	0	0	0	0	1.4 Br
Mung bean pasta, Eden Foods	1.2 oz. (1/2 pkg.)	1 cup	114	0	28.2	0	0	0	0	3	1.4 Br
Quinoa pasta, Ancient Harvest (corn & quinoa)	1/2 cup	1 cup	135	3.0	26.3	1.88	1.50	0	0	4	1.7 Br
Rye pasta, Mio Amore	1/2 cup	scant 1 cup	120	5.3	26.0	6.00	5.33	0.67	0	17	1.5 Br
Spelt pasta	1/2 cup	1 cup	152	5.6	29.4	9.80	1.40	0	0	1	1.9 Br
Wild rice pasta, Mio Amore	1/2 cup	2/3 cup	176	5.6	30.4	2.40	5.60	1.60	0	0	2.2 Br

*Values for Mio Amore amaranth pasta are currently unavailable. Figures will be included in a future issue of Canary Connect News.

Stir-Fry Vegetables

	Day 1	Day 2	Day 3	Day 4
Your choice of vegetables	broccoli cuts cabbage, thinly sliced or shredded celery, slant cut sliced water chestnuts and/or bamboo shoots bok choy, sliced collards, torn into small pieces	zucchini squash, slant cut onion, sliced into rings green peppers, strips amaranth greens, torn into small pieces cherry tomato*	cauliflower florets Brussels sprouts, sliced, blanched, or frozen carrot, slant cut kale, torn into small pieces spinach*, torn into small pieces	asparagus cuts, blanched leek, sliced edible pea pods, blanched green peas, fresh or frozen Jerusalem artichoke*, sliced thin
Your choice of nuts or seeds	almonds pecans	sunflower seeds pumpkin seeds	filberts walnuts (chopped coarse)	roasted soy beans cashews pumpkin seeds
Your choice of oil	sesame oil almond oil	olive oil sunflower oil	canola oil walnut oil	safflower oil soy oil
Your choice of seasonings	sea salt dill weed ground cumin	sea salt garlic powder savory basil marjoram cayenne (red) pepper	sea salt caraway seed fennel coriander	sea salt tarragon garlic powder

*Add cherry tomato, spinach, and Jerusalem artichoke near end of cooking time just prior to serving.

1. Preheat well-seasoned cast-iron skillet on medium (see How to Season Cast Iron on page 59) or electric skillet to 300°F.

2. Prepare vegetables in amounts desired.

3. Add oil to preheated skillet (cast-iron skillet will require less oil). Add vegetables and nuts or seeds. Sprinkle with seasonings. Stir often to cook vegetables evenly. I prefer my vegetables crunchy. Serve immediately.

HH: Splatter Screens

This fine-mesh screen, approximately 11–12 inches in diameter, has a circular frame and a handle and usually costs under $3. Use a splatter screen to prevent oil or liquids from splattering out onto stove top, as a lid for dry heat cooking to prevent moisture from building up in cooking food, and to reheat muffins and thaw or heat tortillas (see page 75).

HH: Cutting Board

Cutting boards can be used for several food preparation purposes such as chopping vegetables and rolling out noodles, tortillas, pie crust, biscuit dough, etc. A 12x13" pebble-like-surfaced acrylic cutting board is recommended for chopping vegetables. An over-the-sink style is handy for limited kitchen space. To use the cutting board to roll out doughs, a 16x20" smooth-surfaced, tempered-glass cutting board is best.

A wooden cutting board is the worst sanitation problem in a family kitchen. Since wood is porous, any liquids or juices from food products, especially meats, can seep down into the board's surface.

Broccoli
(Day 1 Vegetable)

Use this method to prepare fresh broccoli cuts or spears for casseroles, stir fry, or as vegetable side dish.

1. Cut off florets part of broccoli. Remove leaves from stalk and floret portion. Peel stalk portion with vegetable peeler or paring knife to remove fibrous outer bark. The outer bark is a little darker green and you can see the fibers in this woody covering. The inner tender stalk is lighter green and has a smooth, even texture.
2. FOR BROCCOLI CUTS: Cut stalk into medallion (disk) pieces and floret portion into bite-size pieces.
3. FOR BROCCOLI SPEARS: Cut both stalk and floret portion into strips.
4. Soak pieces in salted water for 5 minutes to kill any bugs present. Drain, rinse again.

Bok Choy
(Day 1 or Day 3 Vegetable)

Also known as Chinese cabbage, bok choy has broad white or greenish-white stalks with loose, dark green leaves and is an excellent source of vitamins A and C. In appearance it looks like a cross between celery (stalk) and collards (leaves). Bok choy has a pungent smell and taste, especially when eaten raw, but becomes milder when cooked. (Graphic shows only an individual stalk and leaf.) For more information on bok choy, see issue #3 of <u>Canary Connect News</u>, Veggie Corner: Bok Choy (see page 271).

Recipe Ideas:

1. Add to recipes for stir-fry, stews, soups, and casseroles.
2. Use in place of other Day 1 vegetables in recipes such as Chicken Spaghetti/Pizza Sauce (page 150) or Chicken or Tuna Noodle Casseroles (pages 134 and 160).
3. Enjoy in scrambled eggs or serve raw in salads.

Kale/Cauliflower
(Day 3 Recipe)

1. Use amount of kale and cauliflower you wish to prepare. After a little experimenting, you will learn what proportions are most enjoyable for you.
2. Wash kale thoroughly. Remove center leaf rib and tear into small pieces.
3. Place kale in saucepan with small amount of salted water. Cover and cook for approximately 10–15 minutes.
4. Add cleaned and prepared cauliflower florets to pan and cook covered approximately 10 minutes more until both vegetables are tender. Check water level during cooking time to be sure pan does not boil dry. Serve immediately.

This is an excellent vegetable side dish to serve with any Day 3 Quick & Easy meal. Kale and cauliflower are in the same food family (Mustard Family [#36]) and make a nice blend of flavors.

HH: Save cooking water from vegetables and meats to use as broth in soups and casseroles. Freeze in amounts commonly used in recipes.

Fresh Asparagus
(Day 4 Vegetable)

Preparation of Asparagus Spears:

Asparagus spears are tender from the top down until they get close to the ground where they begin to develop a woody, fibrous texture. The woody portion of the spear is tough and tasteless and should be removed before cooking. To remove this woody portion:

- Hold on to spear at top.
- With paring knife in other hand, place knife blade against "ground" end of asparagus on side of spear away from you and place your thumb on side of spear toward you (opposite the blade).
- Apply gentle pressure with knife against spear as you move up spear a small distance at a time. You will feel the difference in texture as you move past the woody part and into the tender part of the spear. This will happen when your knife blade cuts easily into the spear.
- Cut off and discard woody portion.
- Cut tender portion into approximately 6-inch lengths for spears and 1-inch lengths for cuts and tips.
- Wash pieces thoroughly to remove sand and dirt.

Cooking Asparagus:

Arrange asparagus spears in top portion of steamer pan or in a steamer basket. Sprinkle with salt as desired. Cook covered over steaming water for 10–15 minutes or until tender. Time will depend on diameter of spears. Cook cuts and tips as above or in saucepan with small amount of salted water for 10 minutes or until tender.

Tips on Freezing Asparagus

Prepare cuts or spears as described above.

To Blanch:

- Fill bottom of steamer pan with water to about 1/2 inch from the bottom of steamer insert. Heat water to boiling.
- Add cuts or spears to steamer pan insert . Cover and immediately begin timing. Cook over boiling water for 3–5 minutes. Time will depend upon diameter of asparagus spears.

3 minutes for small stalks	4 minutes for medium stalks	5 minutes for large stalks

- Immediately drain and chill in ice water until cold.

To Freeze:

- Drain well.
- Place in cellophane or plastic bag and freeze.

           OR

Individually freeze on baking sheet before placing in bag. See explanation on page 49 in the Canning and Freezing section.

HH: Stainless Steel Steamer Pan

   Used for steaming vegetables and heating some leftovers, this pan is especially useful for persons who cannot tolerate using a microwave oven. To allow the use of Grab-It bowls for thawing and reheating leftovers, be sure steamer insert has an inside diameter of at least 7 3/4 inches and a height of at least 3 1/4 inches. I recommend a steamer pan over a collapsible steamer basket since it is easier to clean.

Garlic
(Day 2 Vegetable)

Many of my recipes use garlic. Fresh garlic is my preference over dehydrated minced garlic or garlic powder in many recipes. However, if time is at a premium, you may substitute dehydrated minced garlic or garlic powder for fresh minced garlic. (I do not recommend using garlic salt.) See the garlic product bottle for suggested amount to substitute for each clove of garlic.

Mincing Fresh Garlic:

1. Separate clove of garlic from bud (head).
2. Peel and rinse clove.
3. Hold clove between index finger and thumb on cutting board. Using a sharp paring knife, slice garlic as thin as possible.
4. Cut each thin slice into very narrow strips.
5. Using a French knife, rock blade back and forth to finely mince garlic strips. To rock the French knife, use fingers of left hand to hold tip of blade firmly on cutting board. With right hand lift blade from board to rock up and down several times across garlic. Stop several times to remove garlic from blade. Gather garlic into pile on cutting board and repeat rocking procedure. (Rocking procedure described is for a right-handed person. Reverse if you are left handed.)
6. Gather minced garlic into thin layer in central area of cutting board. Place flat side of French knife over garlic and gently smash pieces. This will help to release the garlic flavor.

HH: Knives

A set of good quality knives, or at least a paring and a French knife, is an important asset to make food preparation easier and faster.

French Knife

Although I am chemically sensitive, I purchased a full set of white-handled Cutco cutlery and was able to tolerate the materials immediately. Explore your available options and choose a brand that will work well for you. You may wish to build your knife set over a period of time instead of investing in a complete set immediately.

Leeks—Lily Family
(Day 4 Vegetable)

1. Remove and discard any wilted and dried portions from leek top and any portion that feels flabby.
2. Wash leek under running water to remove as much of the dust and sand as possible.
3. Cut the leek in half lengthwise. Wash each half thoroughly under running water or in basin of water. In order to wash out sand and dirt trapped between layers, you can carefully separate them since the root end is still intact.
4. Cut off root end. Rinse cut end by carefully holding leek together.
5. Lay cut side of leak down on cutting board. Slice thin or thick depending on use.
6. Freeze unneeded portion in cellophane or plastic bag for later use.

Yield: 1 medium leek yields approximately 1 cup of sliced leeks

---

HH: When a recipe calls for leeks or onions, chop or slice complete vegetable and freeze unused portion for later use. (No blanching required.)

Steamed Greens

This recipe may be used to prepare cooked "greens"—chard, spinach, collards, amaranth, and kale.

AMARANTH

1. Wash greens. Trim away any bad leaves. If leaf is very large, remove center rib (i.e., collards, chard). Always remove center rib on kale since it is tough. Also, removing the stem and leaf rib will remove the stronger, more pungent flavor of the green.

2. Tear leaves into small pieces.

3. In saucepan, bring small amount of water to a boil. Add prepared greens. Sprinkle with salt or any other herb or seasoning.

4. Cover pan and cook on medium as chart indicates. Check water level during cooking time to be sure pan does not boil dry.

5. If desired, drizzle with flaxseed oil just before serving. Serve immediately

Chard Day 1	Collards Day 1	Amaranth Day 2	Spinach Day 3	Kale Day 3
10–15 min.	15 min.	10–15min.	10 min.	25 min.

Bare Bones Collard Rolls

(Day 1 Recipe)

3-4 medium	collard leaves
your choice	Chuck's brand tuna, cooked rice, cooked diced chicken meat, or other Day 1 ingredients as desired*
seasoning	dill weed, ground cumin, or dry mustard

1. Heat and/or prepare filling.

2. For each roll, wash 2–3 medium to large collard leaves. Trim any bad spots from leaves. Remove leaf rib, especially thick part.

3. In saucepan or skillet large enough to hold leaves with minimal folding (fold no more than once), bring small amount of salted water to boil.

4. Place leaves in pan, cover, and cook on medium for approximately 15 minutes until leaves are tender. Check water level about every 5 minutes.

Collards, a non-heading cabbage with broad, smooth, dark green leaves and fairly long stems, have a strong, somewhat bitter flavor, but are somewhat milder than other varieties of greens. They are an excellent source of vitamins A and C, iron, calcium, magnesium, and potassium. For more information on collards and other "greens," see issue #2 of <u>Canary Connect News</u>, "Greens" Cookery—Getting Started (see page 271).

5. <u>To Prepare Roll</u>: Remove leaves using two slotted spoons or spatulas for support as you lift and transfer them onto plate. If leaves were folded, unfold on plate surface.

6. Spoon desired amount of your choice of filling in center of leaves. Sprinkle with seasonings. Carefully pick up edge of 2–3 leaves using fingertips (move quickly to avoid being burned). Roll leaves around filling. Transfer finished roll to serving plate and continue making additional rolls. Serve immediately. Extra rolls may be frozen and heated later in microwave.

*Collards may also be floated to Day 3 and filled with your choice of Chuck's brand salmon, cooked diced turkey meat, millet, or other Day 3 foods and spices. If you are not following the rotational diet given in this book, your filling choice are limitless—to mention a few: meats, grains/nongrains (i.e. buckwheat groats), Cascadian Farm organic Cajun Vegetarian Meal, etc.

Spaghetti Squash—How to Cook and Serve
(Day 2 Vegetable)

1. Wash spaghetti squash, remove stem, and place in 9 X 13-inch baking dish. Add approximately 1/2-inch of water.

2. Bake at 350ºF. for approximately 1 1/2–2 hours until shell yields to gentle pressure. During cooking time turn squash by a one-quarter or one-half turn every 30 minutes. Add more water as needed so pan does not become dry.

3. Remove from oven and allow to cool approximately 10 minutes.

4. Cut in half lengthwise. The knife will cause cooked squash to fold over seeds in center so use a fork or spoon to gently push this back to expose the seeds. With scissors, cut the strands that attach to the seeds then remove seeds from center with a large spoon.

5. With 2 table forks, start picking at the cooked squash. It will separate from shell into strands that resemble spaghetti pasta. Place desired amount on plate and top with sauce. Spaghetti squash has a somewhat sweet flavor.

Special Notes: You can also bake squash in microwave on full power for approximately 30 minutes. Turn squash one quarter turn every 5 minutes.

> **HH:** Bake as many squash as oven will hold at one time. Then freeze squash for many meals throughout the year

Spaghetti Squash—Tips on Freezing and Reheating

To Freeze: Transfer long stands of cooked spaghetti squash with forks onto stainless steel baking sheets. I usually pile strands together in stacks approximately 6 inches long and 1 inch high. Place sheets in freezer until squash is frozen at least enough to hold together. Use a metal spatula to loosen squash from baking sheet and transfer to cellophane or plastic bags. Return to freezer.

To Reheat: Thaw squash at room temperature for a couple hours or in the refrigerator for several hours or overnight. Drain. Heat in a covered casserole dish in microwave on half power until warm. Or heat in a 300ºF. oven in a covered casserole dish until warm. Serve with hot sauce.

For Pizza: Thaw and drain squash as described above under Reheat. Spread a thin layer on completed pizza to resemble cheese-like appearance (I love the appearance and flavor). Do not place too much squash on pizza or the flavor will seem too sweet and not spicy enough.

Parsnips
(Day 3 Vegetable)

Parsnips are an old-fashioned vegetable being rediscovered now that complex carbohydrates are growing in popularity. Add parsnips to winter stews and soups (such as Millet or Quinoa Turkey Vegetable Stew and Turkey Parsnip Soup) and/or try the following delicious recipe.

Steamed or Whipped Parsnips
(Day 3 Vegetable)

Choose young, tender parsnips. Scrub, peel, and slice. In saucepan, steam with small amount of water and salt approximately 15 minutes until tender. (If only have large parsnips, remove pithy center at top before cooking.) If desired, whip as you would mashed potatoes. I prefer to use a Braun hand blender. Serve plain or season with flaxseed oil and/or caraway seeds.

Amazing Cheese-Free "Mac & Cheese"
(Non-rotating Recipe)*

2 cups	macaroni (elbow, shells, penne, twists)—Kamut, rice, Mio Amore rye, spelt, whole wheat
1 cup	raw cashew, Brazil, or macadamia nuts
2 tablespoons	lemon juice (fresh squeezed or use Santa Cruz brand organic 100% lemon juice)
1 teaspoon	sea salt
1 teaspoon	onion powder
1/2 teaspoon	garlic powder
1/2 cup	diced red peppers or pimientos
2 cups	water

Nutritional Information/Serving	
Calories:	394
Protein (g):	9.0
Carbohydrate (g):	41.2
Fiber (g):	7.44
Total fat (g):	25.48
Saturated (g):	3.69
Cholesterol (mg):	0
Sodium (mg):	536
Food Exchanges/Serving	
1.9 Br .4 VLM .1 Veg 4.9 Fat	

1. Oven temperature—350ºF. Preheating not necessary.

2. Bring 2 quarts water (no salt) to boil in large saucepan. Add your choice of pasta and boil until tender. Follow package directions or see Perfect Pasta (page 195).

3. While pasta is cooking, blend nuts in blender to finely chop. Add remaining ingredients except use only 1/4 cup water. Blend until smooth. Stop to scrape sides and bottom of blender jar as needed. Add remaining water and blend a couple of seconds longer.

4. Drain and rinse cooked pasta. Transfer to covered casserole dish. My preference is a 10-inch covered Corning shallow baking dish. Pour sauce over macaroni. If macaroni floats, push down into sauce.

5. Cover and bake 30 minutes. Uncover and bake another 15–25 minutes until sauce thickens. Remove from oven, cover, and allow to set for 5 minutes, if needed, to completely thicken. Leftovers (if any exist) may be frozen.

Yield: almost 5 cups for all pastas, except rye yields 4 cups   4 servings

Special Note: A baking time beyond 45 minutes is usually needed for rye pasta and/or when using Brazil or macadamia nuts.

*This amazing, delicious recipe does not fit the rotation as outlined in this cookbook. I personally enjoy this recipe on Day 1 without concern regarding the Day 2 foods in the recipe. Brazil and macadamia nuts are unassigned "Fun Foods," see explanation on page 24. Cashews are assigned to Day 4 but can easily be considered a "Fun Food" since there are only a few other members of the Cashew Family.

USED FOR ANALYSIS: Kamut pasta and macadamia nuts used for analysis.

Recipe idea from Vegetarian Cooking School Cookbook by Vierra.

"Mac & Cheese" Lower Fat Version

As you can see, the above delicious recipe is high in fat, but it is oh so good! Just days before this cookbook when to the press, I retested the recipe with Kamut pasta using only 1/2 cup of macadamia nuts. It was still good but watery, so just after removing the casserole from the oven I immediately stirred 1 tablespoon of Kamut flour into a very small amount of water. I poured and stirred the mixture evenly around the casserole of cooked "Mac & Cheese." Immediately the flour mixture thickened the sauce. Future testing of this lower-fat version with other pastas will be done and reported in future issues of Canary Connect News newsletter (see page 271 for subscription information).

Nutritional Information/Serving	
Calories:	284
Protein (g):	8
Carbohydrate (g):	40.9
Fiber (g):	6.73
Total fat (g):	13.18
Saturated (g):	1.85
Cholesterol (mg):	0
Sodium (mg):	535
Food Exchanges/Serving	
2 Br .2 VLM .1 Veg 2.5 Fat	

Spiced Baked Potatoes
(Day 2 Recipe)

2 teaspoons	sunflower oil
2 cups	potatoes, peeled, diced
2 tablespoons	potato starch
1/4 teaspoon	sea salt

Your choice of these seasoning combinations.

1/2 teaspoon	garlic powder
1/4 teaspoon	cayenne (red) pepper
OR	
1/4 teaspoon	garlic powder
1/4 teaspoon	Mexican oregano
1/8 teaspoon	marjoram
OR	
1/4 teaspoon	garlic powder
1/2 teaspoon	chili powder
1/4 teaspoon	Watkins Salsa Seasoning Blend

If your mouth has been watering over the "Shake and Bake" ads for coated/baked potatoes and/or your kids have been clamoring to try them, this recipe has the flavor without the preservatives and large amount of oil. Try the spice combinations listed or create your own "flavor." Let us know of special combinations you develop and we'll share them in Canary Connect News (see page 269).

Nutritional Information/Serving	
Calories:	117
Protein (g):	1.5
Carbohydrate (g):	23.2
Fiber (g):	1.18
Total fat (g):	2.38
Saturated (g):	.29
Cholesterol (mg):	0
Sodium (mg):	138
Food Exchanges/Serving	
1.2 Br .4 Fat	

1. Preheat oven to 425°F.
2. Add oil to 9-inch square stainless steel baking pan. Spread evenly.
3. Prepare potatoes. Cover with water.
4. In a small bowl combine potato starch, salt, and your choice of seasonings.
5. Drain potatoes and immediately add to a one-gallon size plastic food bag. Add spice mixture. While holding bag closed with as little air in bag as possible, quickly toss to evenly coat potatoes.
6. Pour potatoes into prepared pan. Spread out evenly. Bake for 30–40 minutes until potatoes are done. Serve immediately.

Yield: 4 servings

SPECIAL NOTE: Leftovers may be refrigerated or frozen. Reheat in slow oven or microwave. However, they are best when served immediately.

Fried Potatoes
(Day 2 Recipe)

3 medium-size	potatoes OR *plan*over, peeled, baked potatoes
1/4 cup	onions, finely diced
1/2 cup	green peppers
2 teaspoons	sunflower oil
sprinkle	ground cayenne (red) pepper
as needed	butter or Clarified Butter (page 226)

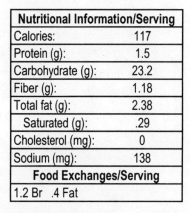

1. Wash and peel potatoes. Cut lengthwise twice (like quartered apples) then cut quarters into 1/4-inch thick slices. Should yield approximately 2 cups. Steam in steamer pan for only 1–2 minutes.
2. Preheat electric skillet to 350ºF. Add oil, potatoes, onions, green peppers, and cayenne pepper. Cover with splatter screen. Cook for approximately 10 minutes, stirring potatoes every 2 minutes. Use a metal spatula to loosen browned potato from skillet. Add butter or Clarified Butter about half way through cooking process. Be careful not to burn potatoes or vegetables but only brown them and make potatoes crispy.

Yield: 3–4 servings

Cream of Potato Soup*
(Day 2 Recipe)

2 cups	potatoes, peeled, diced
1/4 cup	onions, chopped
1/2 teaspoon	sea salt
2 tablespoons	potato starch
2 tablespoons	chopped Brazil or macadamia nuts*
3 cups	liquid (potato broth and water)

Nutritional Information/Serving	
Calories:	255
Protein (g):	4.2
Carbohydrate (g):	48.5
Fiber (g):	2.88
Total fat (g):	5.98
Saturated (g):	1.46
Cholesterol (mg):	0
Sodium (mg):	542
Food Exchanges/Serving	
2.4 Br .2 VLM .3 Veg 1.2 Fat	

1. In medium-size saucepan, cook potato, onion, and salt in small amount of water until potatoes are almost done. Drain. Reserve liquid.

2. Combine potato starch, nuts, and 1/4 cup of liquid in blender. Blend on highest speed for 1–2 minutes until well blended. Stop once or twice to scrape sides and bottom. Add remaining liquid and blend a few seconds longer.

3. Pour mixture into saucepan used to cook potatoes. Cook over low to medium heat until mixture thickens. Stir constantly with a whisk to keep mixture smooth.

4. Add potatoes and continue cooking until tender. Taste and add more salt if desired.

Yield: 5 cups   2 servings

Creamed Potatoes*
(Day 2 Recipe)

3 cups	potatoes, diced
3 tablespoons	onion, finely diced
3 tablespoons	green peppers, finely diced
1/2 teaspoon	sea salt
2 tablespoons	potato starch
2 tablespoons	chopped Brazil or chopped macadamia nuts*
1 1/4 cups	liquid (potato broth and water)

Nutritional Information/Serving	
Calories:	215
Protein (g):	3.7
Carbohydrate (g):	42.8
Fiber (g):	2.65
Total fat (g):	4.05
Saturated (g):	.99
Cholesterol (mg):	0
Sodium (mg):	364
Food Exchanges/Serving	
2.2 Br .1 VLM .2 Veg .8 Fat	

Prepare same as Cream of Potato Soup (recipe above). Cook green peppers in step 1. If mixture is too thick, add a small amount of water.

Yield: 3 1/3 cups   3 servings

*Brazil and macadamia nuts are unassigned "Fun Foods," see explanation on pg. 24.

HH: Scrub the skins of all vegetables and fruits before peeling or cutting to avoid spreading mold which may have accumulated on the surface during the growth or storage process.

HH: Food Processor

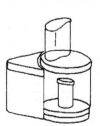

A large food processor is very helpful if you will be doing an extensive amount of canning or freezing. However, for the basic recipe needs in this cookbook, the Black and Decker® Handy Shortcut is easier to clean than a larger model. Since the container holds two cups you often can use it as your measuring guide in recipes, such as for Scalloped Potatoes (on next page).

Scalloped Potatoes*
(Day 2 Recipe)

2 cups	potatoes, peeled, thinly sliced, and rinsed
2 tablespoons	onions, diced or thinly sliced
1/2 teaspoon	summer savory
1 tablespoon	potato starch
1 tablespoon	chopped Brazil or macadamia nuts*
1/2 teaspoon	sea salt
1 cup	water

Nutritional Information/Serving	
Calories:	130
Protein (g):	2.3
Carbohydrate (g):	26.7
Fiber (g):	1.71
Total fat (g):	2.05
Saturated (g):	.5
Cholesterol (mg):	0
Sodium (mg):	381
Food Exchanges/Serving	
1.4 Br .1 VLM .1 Veg .4 Fat	

1. Oven temperature—350°F. Preheating not necessary.
2. Oil 1 1/2-quart covered casserole dish with sunflower oil.
3. Wash, peel, and thinly slice potatoes. Rinse and drain potatoes.
4. Layer potatoes, onions, and summer savory in oiled casserole dish.
5. Combine potato starch, nuts, salt, and 1/4 cup water in blender. Blend on high for approximately 1–2 minutes until well blended. Stop at least once to scrape sides and bottom. Add remaining water and blend for a couple seconds. Pour blended mixture into casserole dish and stir gently.
6. Bake covered for 1 1/2 hours or until potatoes are tender.

Yield: 3 cups   3 servings

*Brazil and macadamia nuts are unassigned "Fun Foods," see explanation on pg. 24.

Italian Tomato Vegetable Casserole
(Day 2 Recipe)

1 cup	Muir Glen brand organic tomato puree
1 cup	water
1 1/2 cups	eggplant, peeled, 1/2 inch diced
1 1/2 cups	zucchini squash, peeled, 1/2 inch diced
1/4 cup	onion, chopped
1/2 teaspoon	sea salt
1/4 teaspoon	minced garlic
1/2 teaspoon	basil
1 teaspoon	leaf oregano

Nutritional Information/Serving	
Calories:	54
Protein (g):	2.8
Carbohydrate (g):	12.8
Fiber (g):	3.67
Total fat (g):	.21
Saturated (g):	.04
Cholesterol (mg):	0
Sodium (mg):	386
Food Exchanges/Serving	
2.5 Veg	

In saucepan, combine all ingredients. Bring to boil, reduce heat, and cover. Simmer 20 minutes or until vegetables are tender and flavors are well blended. Leftovers may be frozen.

Yield: 3 1/2 cups   3 servings

Italian Nightshade Casserole
(Day 2 Recipe)

1 cup	Muir Glen brand organic tomato puree
1 cup	water
2 cups	eggplant, peeled, 1/2 inch diced
1/2 cup	green pepper
1/2 teaspoon	sea salt
1/4 teaspoon	minced garlic
1/2 teaspoon	basil
1 teaspoon	leaf oregano

Nutritional Information/Serving	
Calories:	48
Protein (g):	2.2
Carbohydrate (g):	11.6
Fiber (g):	3.29
Total fat (g):	.16
Saturated (g):	.02
Cholesterol (mg):	0
Sodium (mg):	384
Food Exchanges/Serving	
2.2 Veg	

In saucepan, combine all ingredients. Bring to boil, reduce heat, and cover. Simmer 20 minutes or until vegetables are tender and flavors are well blended. Leftovers may be frozen.

Yield: 2 1/2 cups   3 servings

Zucchini or Okra with Tomato
(Day 2 Recipe)

2 cups	canned tomato quarters or pieces
2 cups	zucchini squash, peeled, sliced
	OR 1 cup sliced okra
1/2 cup	onions, chopped (optional)
1/8 teaspoon	sea salt
1/4 teaspoon	summer savory
1/4 teaspoon	leaf oregano (optional)
1/8 teaspoon	basil (optional)
1/8 teaspoon	minced garlic (optional)

Nutritional Information/Serving		
	Zucchini	Okra
Calories:	64	60
Protein (g):	3.2	2.6
Carbohydrate (g):	13.9	13.4
Fiber (g):	3.81	3.4
Total fat (g):	.71	.6
Saturated (g):	.11	.09
Cholesterol (mg):	0	0
Sodium (mg):	156	154
Food Exchanges/Serving		
Zucchini: 2.6 Veg Okra: 2.1 Veg		

In saucepan, combine all ingredients. Heat to boiling, reduce heat, and cover. Simmer for 15 minutes to blend flavors and cook the squash or okra.   Yield: 2 cups   2 servings

Serving Suggestion: Serve over baked or boiled potatoes as substitute for gravy or butter. May be frozen.

Italian Eggplant
(Day 2 Recipe)

1/2 cup	Muir Glen brand organic tomato puree
1 cup	water
1/4 cup	green pepper, finely chopped
1/4 cup	onion, finely chopped
1/4 teaspoon	sea salt
1/4 teaspoon	minced garlic
1/2 teaspoon	basil
3/4 teaspoon	leaf oregano
2 cups	eggplant, peeled, diced OR 6 3-inch peeled, and sliced eggplant (1/2 inch thick)

1. Oven temperature—350°F. Preheating not necessary.

2. Combine tomato puree, water, green pepper, onion, and seasoning in small bowl or 2 cup measure.

3. Layer eggplant in covered, shallow baking dish. I use a 10-inch square Corning casserole dish. Note: Some slices may need to be cut in half to fit in dish. (Freeze extra eggplant for later use.)

4. Pour tomato mixture evenly over eggplant. Bake covered for 30–40 minutes or until sauce bubbles and eggplant is tender. Time will depend upon whether eggplant is fresh or frozen.

Yield: 4 vegetable servings

Serving suggestion: If needed, during last 5 minutes of baking time, remove eggplant to be served to person with CRC to another dish and sprinkle mozzarella and/or Parmesan cheese on remainder for family or guests.

Special Note: Can be prepared in microwave, but I believe the flavor blends better when oven baked.

PASTA SAUCE VERSION: For a fast, even easier version of Italian Eggplant, combine 3/4 cup each of Millina's Finest brand organic tomato and basil pasta sauce and water to replace all sauce ingredients in recipe. Follow steps 1, 3, and 4 as directed above.

HH: Freeze diced and/or sliced eggplant when in season to enjoy this dish year round.

Nutritional Information/Serving		
	Regular	Pasta Sauce Version
Calories:	28	28
Protein (g):	1.2	1.2
Carbohydrate (g):	6.6	5.9
Fiber (g):	1.99	1.78
Total fat (g):	.12	.07
Saturated (g):	.02	.01
Cholesterol (mg):	0	0
Sodium (mg):	145	87
Food Exchanges/Serving		
Both Versions: 1.2 Veg		

Butternut Squash, Sweet Potatoes, or Yams*
How to Prepare for Delicious Pie

To Prepare Sweet Potatoes or Yams:

1. Select firm potatoes with no sign of mold. Wash and scrub thoroughly. Peel, cut into small pieces.
2. Steam or cook in small amount of water until very tender. Drain, reserve liquid.
3. Using a hand blender (Braun), blender, or potato masher, blend until you get a creamy mixture. Add drained liquid if needed to blend or to get the texture of pumpkin. Measure into 1 cup portions and freeze in glass jars to be ready to prepare a pie in minutes. Use any extra liquid in soups.

To Prepare Butternut Squash:

1. Select ripe butternut squash. Ripe squash has a medium tan color whereas unripe squash is off white in color, sometimes with green lines.
2. Wash squash, cut in half lengthwise. Scoop out seeds and strings (use serrated grapefruit knife).
3. Place cut side down in shallow baking dish. Add a small amount of water. Bake in oven at 350ºF. for 30–60 minutes or until very tender. Baking time will depend on size of squash.

OR

3. Cook in microwave on full power for 5 minutes; turn one quarter turn; cook for 3–5 minutes longer until very tender. Cooking time will vary depending on size of squash and difference in microwaves.
4. Allow squash to cool at least enough to handle. Scoop out soft squash. Stir, no need to blend. Measure out into 1 cup portions and freeze in glass jars (as well as extra) to prepare a pie in minutes.

Special Note: Four small butternut squash yield approximately 3 cups. Purchase several butternut squash when in season, bake, and freeze filling in 1- or 2-cup portions all ready to make a quick pie.

*Sweet potato, yams, and butternut squash are assigned to Day 4. For sweet potatoes and yams, omit eating them on Day 4 just before and after enjoying this pie on Day 3. For butternut squash, omit butternut squash on Day 4 before and all members of the squash family from Day 2 before and Day 4 after enjoying this pie on Day 3.

Pumpkin Puree
(Day 2 or 4 Vegetable)

Method 1—for Small or Large Pumpkins

1. Wash pumpkin, remove stem, and cut in half through equator. Cut threads with scissors. Scoop out seeds and threads.
2. Rinse pumpkin. Place cut sides down in large casserole dish(es). Add water to casserole dish(es) to depth of 1/4 inch. Bake at 350ºF. for 45–60 minutes until pulp of pumpkin is fork tender. Add more water to dish(es) if needed so they do not become dry.
3. Remove from oven and allow pumpkin to cool enough so you can handle it.
4. Use a large spoon to remove pulp from shell. If desired, blend pumpkin. Measure pumpkin in desired amounts. Freeze in measured amounts, as well as extra, in glass jars.

Method 2—for Small Pumpkins (such as Sugar Pumpkins)

This method is for pumpkins that weigh approximately 2 1/2 to 2 3/4 pounds and are of a size that will fit in a large slow cooker.

1. Wash pumpkin and remove stem. Place pumpkin in slow cooker with approximately 6 cups of water. Water should cover approximately 3/4 of height of pumpkin. Cook on high for 3 1/2–4 hours until pumpkin is tender when pushed in with a spoon.
2. Remove carefully with two large spoons and set on cutting board to cool.
3. Remove pulp as described in step 3 of Method 1.

YIELD: a 2 3/4 lb. sugar pumpkin yields approximately 3 cups of pumpkin puree

Butternut Squash or Sweet Potato/Yam Pie
A delicious substitute for Pumpkin Pie

1	egg, lightly beaten*
1 cup	Butternut Squash, Sweet Potato, or Yams for pie* (page 209)
1/4 teaspoon	sea salt
3/4 teaspoon	cinnamon
1/4 teaspoon	ginger*
1/8 teaspoon	cloves*
1/2 cup	unsweetened apple juice

1. Prepare Oatmeal Pie Crust (page 211).

2. Preheat oven to 350°F.

3. In medium-size bowl, mix egg, prepared squash (or sweet potato or yam), and spices to distribute spices evenly as you would when preparing a normal pumpkin pie. (I prefer butternut squash.)

4. Add apple juice and mix.

5. Mixture should yield 1 3/4 cups. Pour mixture into prebaked and cooled Oatmeal Pie Crust and bake 45–50 minutes or until knife inserted into center of pie comes out clean. Cool. Serve with Vanilla Rice Dream, a non-diary dessert, if desired. (Realize Rice Dream also breaks rotation.)

6. These pies freeze well for future desserts. Before freezing, cut pie into serving pieces and loosen for ease in thawing just amount desired.

Yield: 1 pie   8 servings

TO PREPARE THIS PIE IN OTHER CRUSTS such as Quinoa Pie Crust (page 212), double recipe and bake 65–70 minutes.

*Realize these ingredients break rotation but careful planning can allow you to eat this recipe occasionally—especially for holidays.

- Eggs are assigned to Day 1. Omit eggs on Day 1 just before and after enjoying this pie on Day 3.
- Sweet potato, yams, and butternut squash are assigned to Day 4. For sweet potatoes and yams, omit eating them on Day 4 just before and after enjoying this pie on Day 3. For butternut squash, omit butternut squash on Day 4 before and all squash from Day 2 before and Day 4 after enjoying this pie on Day 3.
- Ginger is an unassigned "Fun Food," see explanation on page 24.
- Cloves are assigned to Day 2. Omit cloves on Day 2 just before and after enjoying this pie on Day 3.

Special Note:

Several pumpkin pie recipes, with many variations for each recipe, appear in issue #4 of <u>Canary Connect News</u> (see page 271 for ordering information). These recipes include unsweetened as well as stevia, honey, and brown rice sweetened versions. A dairy-free whipped topping recipe will appear in issue #8. A great additional to the Holidays.

Nutritional Information/Serving—Filling Only		
	Butternut Squash	Sweet Potato or Yam
Calories:	29	43
Protein (g):	1	1.1
Carbohydrate (g):	5.4	8.2
Fiber (g):	1	.72
Total fat (g):	.61	.65
Saturated (g):	.18	.19
Cholesterol (mg):	23	23
Sodium (mg):	76	78
Food Exchanges/Serving		
Butternut: .2 Br .1 LM .1 Fr .1 Fat		
Sweet Potato/Yam: .3 Br .1 LM .1 Fr .1 Fat		

Oatmeal Pie Crust

(Day 3 Recipe)

1 1/2 cups	old fashioned rolled oats (regular, uncooked)
1/2 teaspoon	sea salt
1/4 cup	canola oil
1 tablespoon	water

Nutritional Information/Serving (Crust Cut in 8 Pieces)			
	Crust Only	w/Butternut Squash Filling	w/Sweet Potato or Yam Filling
Calories:	15	144	158
Protein (g):	2.3	3.3	3.4
Carbohydrate (g):	9.5	14.9	17.7
Fiber (g):	1.49	2.5	2.2
Total fat (g):	7.69	8.3	8.34
Saturated (g):	.64	.82	.84
Cholesterol (mg):	0	23	23
Sodium (mg):	134	210	212
Food Exchanges/Serving			
Crust Only: .6 Br 1. Fat			
With Butternut Squash Filling: .8 Br .1 LM .1 Fr 1.6 Fat			
With Sweet Potato/Yam Filling: .9 Br .1 LM .1 Fr 1.6 Fat			

1. Preheat oven to 450ºF.

2. Combine oats and salt. Stir to distribute salt evenly.

3. Add oil gradually while stirring to evenly coat oats.

4. Pour water as evenly as possible over mixture and stir again.

5. Pour into an 8-inch pie pan. Use hands to press oat mixture evenly onto bottom and sides of pie pan, making crust as firm and compact as possible. Do not allow crust to be closer than 1/8 inch from lip of pie pan to prevent oil from crust from bubbling over edge of pie pan during baking.

6. Bake for 10 minutes, then cool for 10 minutes while allowing oven temperature to cool down to 350ºF. to bake Butternut Squash, Sweet Potatoes, or Yam Pie.

Special Note: This recipe was developed for use with Butternut Squash or Sweet Potato/Yam Pie recipe (page 210). It has not been tested with other pie fillings. This crust does not form together like regular pie crusts. However, it will surprisingly do so after the filling is baked in the crust.

Recipe idea from Rotational Bon Appetité! by Hayes & Maynard, p. 38.

Teff Pear Cake

(Day 1 Recipe)

1 cup	brown teff flour
1 teaspoon	baking soda
1/4 teaspoon	sea salt
1/4 teaspoon	unbuffered, corn-free vitamin C crystals
1/2 cup	pear juice
1/4 cup	Pear Sauce (page 230)
2 tablespoons	sesame oil

Nutritional Information/Serving	
Calories:	125
Protein (g):	2.6
Carbohydrate (g):	19.7
Fiber (g):	3.28
Total fat (g):	3.95
Saturated (g):	.49
Cholesterol (mg):	0
Sodium (mg):	228
Food Exchanges/Serving	
1Br .2 Fr .7 Fat	

1. Preheat oven to 400ºF.

2. Oil and flour the bottom and sides of a 9-inch pie pan.

3. In mixing bowl, whisk together dry ingredients. Add juice, sauce, and oil. Stir just to moisten dry ingredients.

4. Transfer to prepared pan. Spread evenly. Bake 20 minutes. Cool slightly. Cut into 8 wedges. Serve warm with additional heated Pear Sauce.

Yield: 8 servings

Pie Crust

	Kamut (Day 1)	**Spelt** (Day 1)	**Amaranth** (Day 2)	**Quinoa** (Day 3)	**Buckwheat** (Day 4)
flour	1 cup Kamut	1 1/8* cups spelt	3/4 cup amaranth	3/4 cup quinoa	3/4 cup White Buckwheat (page 105)
starch/gum if needed			1/4 cup arrowroot starch	1/4 cup tapioca starch	3/4 teaspoon guar gum
optional ingredients				1/2 teaspoon cinnamon	
ice water	1/4 cup				
oil	1/4 cup sesame	1/4 cup sesame	3 tablespoons olive oil	3 tablespoons canola	3 tablespoons safflower
sea salt	1/4 teaspoon rounded		1/4 teaspoon		

*1/8 cup = 1 cup + 2 tablespoons

1. Chill a curved-sided medium-size bowl and whisk.
2. Combine your choice of dry ingredients in separate bowl, set aside.
3. In chilled bowl whisk together ice cold water, oil, and salt until mixture is slightly thick and opaque (whitish creamy color). Note: if water and oil are not cold, mixture will not become slightly thick and opaque. Oils which get cloudy and thick in refrigerator—such as olive and sesame—will become more opaque and thick.
4. Add flour mixture all at once to oil mixture and stir with rubber spatula or fork until dough clumps together into a ball and is well mixed. Some doughs, such as buckwheat, will be a little sloppy and soft at first, just continue stirring for few seconds longer.
5. Oil bottom and sides of 8- or 9-inch pie pan or 8-inch square baking dish to use with Tofu "Cheesecake" recipes (page 223). With oiled fingers, transfer dough to pan. Press dough firmly into bottom and sides (bottom only for cheesecakes) as evenly thin as possible. If you get oil on outside of pan when spreading dough (as I do), before baking wipe outside of pan with damp cloth.
6. Chill until filling is prepared and ready to bake.
7. Bake according to filling recipe. If need a prebaked crust, bake in preheated 400°F. for 15 minutes or until done. Allow to cool before filling.

Recipe idea from Mastering Food Allergies *newsletter, September 1990.*

Nutritional Information/Slice (Crust Cut into 8 Pieces)					
	Kamut	Spelt	Amaranth	Quinoa	Buckwheat
Calories:	124	132	100	110	76
Protein (g):	2.6	3	1.5	1.5	1.2
Carbohydrate (g):	15.3	16.9	10.7	12.6	6.5
Fiber (g):	1.5	3.38	.89	.93	.92
Total fat (g):	7.19	7.24	5.63	5.86	5.4
Saturated (g):	.97	.97	.68	.36	.53
Cholesterol (mg):	0	0	0	0	0
Sodium (mg):	67	67	67	71	68
Food Exchanges/Slice					
	.8 Br 1.3 Fat	.9 Br 1.3 Fat	.7 Br .1 LM 1 Fat	.8 Br 1 Fat	.4 Br 1 Fat

Special Note: Fresh Strawberry Pie recipe appears in issue #2 of Canary Connect News newsletter (see ordering information on page 271)

Apple Oat or Quinoa Crisp
(Day 3 Recipe)

Amount for:

Grab-It Bowl:	Pie Pan:	
1 serving	4 servings	YIELD
1/2 cup	2 cups	apples, fresh or frozen, peeled, sliced
1/4 teaspoon	1 teaspoon	ground cinnamon
sprinkle	sprinkle	nutmeg
1 teaspoon	4 teaspoons	maple granules* (optional)

Ingredients for **OAT** crisp topping:

1/4 cup	1 cup	old fashioned rolled oats (regular, uncooked)
1 tablespoon	1/4 cup	oat bran
2 pinches	1/8 teaspoon	sea salt
1/8 teaspoon	1/2 teaspoon	ground cinnamon
sprinkle	sprinkle	nutmeg*
1 teaspoon	4 teaspoons	maple granules* (optional)
1 1/4 teaspoons	5 teaspoons	canola oil

Ingredients for **QUINOA** crisp topping:

2 tablespoons	1/2 cup	quinoa flour
1 pinch	4 pinches	sea salt
1/8 teaspoon	1/2 teaspoon	ground cinnamon
sprinkle	sprinkle	nutmeg*
1 teaspoon	4 teaspoons	maple granules* (optional)
scant 1 teaspoon	1 tablespoon	canola oil
scant 1 teaspoon	1 tablespoon	water

Nutritional Information/Serving		
	Oat	Quinoa
Calories:	171	130
Protein (g):	4.2	2.1
Carbohydrate (g):	25.3	20.7
Fiber (g):	4.36	2.62
Total fat (g):	7.43	4.58
Saturated (g):	.72	.27
Cholesterol (mg):	0	0
Sodium (mg):	71	58
Food Exchanges/Serving		
Oat: .9 Br .4 Fr 1.4 Fat		
Quinoa: .8 Br .1 LM .4 Fr .7 Fat		

1. Preheat oven to 425ºF.

2. Prepare apple slices; toss lightly with spices and maple granules. Layer in oiled Corning Grab-It bowl or 8-inch pie pan.

3. In mixing bowl, whisk together dry topping ingredients.

4. FOR OAT: Gradually add oil while stirring mixture. May use hands to completely blend in oil so that all the oatmeal is evenly moistened.

    FOR QUINOA: Add oil and water. Stir with fork or rubber spatula to coat flour mixture evenly with liquids. You may desire to use a pastry blender.

5. Sprinkle crisp mixture evenly over apples. Bake for 18–20 minutes or until apples are tender. Cooking time will depend on whether fresh or frozen apple slices are used.

Special Notes: I prefer to use eating apples rather than baking apples because an eating apple like red delicious will be more naturally sweet. This dessert will teach you that cinnamon, rather than sugar, is the key to apple crisp. Freeze leftovers for future cravings for a sweet treat.

To make this a real treat, serve with a small scoop of Vanilla Rice Dream non-dairy dessert. However do realize that rice is normally eaten on Day 1.

*Maple and nutmeg are unassigned "Fun Foods" on this rotational diet, see explanation on page 24.

USED FOR ANALYSIS: Maple granules were not included in nutritional analysis.

Carob Cake Brownies
(Day 4 Recipe)

1 1/2 cups	White Buckwheat Flour (page 105)
1/3 cup	carob powder (after measuring, sift to remove lumps)
1 1/2 teaspoons	baking soda
1/4 teaspoon	sea salt
3/4 teaspoon	guar gum
1/2 teaspoon	unbuffered, corn-free vitamin C crystals

Your choice of sweetener

> 1/4 teaspoon stevia, white powder concentrate
> 2 tablespoons honey
> 1/4 cup honey (reduce water by 1 tablespoon)

1 1/4 cups	water
2 tablespoons	safflower oil (may use 1/4 cup of oil, if desired)
1/2 teaspoon	alcohol-free peppermint extract (optional)

> **HH:** Sift carob powder by placing measurement of powder into a fine-mesh strainer. (Have a bowl under it.) Then stir powder to work it through the mesh and into bowl.

1. Preheat oven to 350°F.
2. Oil and flour 8-inch square baking dish. If using stainless steel, only need to oil dish.
3. In a large mixing bowl, whisk together dry ingredients. Make a "well" in the center.
4. Add liquid ingredients. Using an electric mixer, mix on lowest speed until dry ingredients are moistened. Then blend on mix speed for 20 seconds until you have a creamy, cake-like batter.
    OR without electric mixer, stir to moisten dry ingredients and then beat by hand for 30 seconds to make a creamy, cake-like batter.
5. Pour into prepared pan and spread evenly. Bake for 25–30 minutes until toothpick comes out clean when inserted into center. The top will be a little dry and cracked just like regular chocolate brownies.
6. Cool in pan on cooling rack. Cover with towel. If desired, spread with Carob Icing (below). Cut 4x4. May be frozen. These brownies are even liked by people who eat sweets and do not like buckwheat.

Yield: 16 servings
USED FOR ANALYSIS: Analysis done with 2 tablespoons of oil.

Carob Icing
(Day 4 Recipe)

1/4 cup	carob powder, sifted
2 teaspoons	kudzu starch

Your choice of sweetened and water combination

> 1/16 teaspoon stevia, white powder concentrate (1/2 of 1/8 teaspoon) with 1/2 cup water
> 2 tablespoons honey with 3/8 cup water (1/4 cup + 2 tablespoons)
> 1/4 cup honey with 1/4 cup water

1/4 teaspoon	alcohol-free peppermint extract (optional)

In small saucepan, whisk together dry ingredients. Add liquid ingredients and blend. Cook on medium heat until thickened, stirring with whisk almost constantly. Spread on slightly cooled brownies.

Yield: 1/2 cup

Nutritional information on next page.

> **Special Note:** For more cake recipes—Quinoa Carob, Rice Carob, Cherub (Angel) Food Cake—and birthday celebration ideas, see issue #3 of Canary Connect News newsletter. Also, issue #7 has a easy dairy-free, sugar-free ice cream recipe with several variations. (See ordering information on page 271.)

Nutritional Information/Serving			
	Brownies without icing	Brownies with icing	Orange cake w/o glaze	Orange with glaze
Sweetened with	stevia/honey/more honey	stevia/honey/more honey	stevia/honey/more honey	stevia/honey/more honey
Calories:	54 / 62 / 70	61 / 77 / 94	55 / 59 / 63	62 / 70 / 74
Protein (g):	1.3 / 1.3 / 1.3	1.3 / 1.4 / 1.4	1.3 / 1.3 / 1.3	1.4 / 1.4 / 1.4
Carbohydrate (g):	8.4 / 10.6 / 12.7	10.1 / 14.5 / 18.8	8.6 / 9.7 / 10.8	10.3 / 12.5 / 13.6
Fiber (g):	1.76 / 1.77 / 1.77	2.40 / 2.42 / 2.43	.96 / .96 / .96	.98 / .99 / .99
Total fat (g):	2 / 2 / 2	2.01 / 2.01 / 2.01	2 / 2 / 2	2.01 / 2.01 / 2.01
Saturated (g):	.22 / .22 / .22	.22 / .22 / .22	.22 / .22 / .22	.22 / .22 / .22
Cholesterol (mg):	0 / 0 / 0	0 / 0 / 0	0 / 0 / 0	0 / 0 / 0
Sodium (mg):	127 / 127 / 127	127 / 128 / 128	153 / 153 / 153	153 / 153 / 153
Food Exchange/Serving			
Stevia	.4 Br .1 Oth Carb .3 Fat.	.5 Br .1 Oth Carb .3 Fat	.4 Br .2 Fr .3 Fat	.4 Br .2 Fr .3 Fat
Honey	.4 Br .2 Oth Carb .3 Fat	.5 Br .4 Oth Carb .3 Fat	4 Br .1 Oth Carb .2 Fr .3 Fat	.4 Br .1 Oth Carb .2 Fr .3 Fat
More Honey	.4 Br .3 Oth Carb .3 Fat	.5 Br .6 Oth Carb .3 Fat	.4 Br .1 Oth Carb .2 Fr .3 Fat	.4 Br .2 Oth Carb .2 Fr .3 Fat

Orange Buckwheat Cake
(Day 4 Recipe)

Analysis for Carob & Orange Cakes done without guar gum.

1 1/2 cups — White Buckwheat Flour (page 105)
1 1/2 teaspoons — baking soda
1/4 teaspoon — sea salt
Your choice of sweetener: 1/16 teaspoon stevia, white powder concentrate
1 OR 2 tablespoons honey
1 1/4 cups — orange juice, freshly squeezed or made from concentrate
3/4 teaspoon — guar gum
2 tablespoons — safflower oil
1/2 teaspoon — alcohol-free orange flavoring

1. Preheat oven to 350ºF.
2. Oil and flour 8-inch square baking dish. If using stainless steel, only need to oil the dish.
3. In large mixing bowl, whisk together flour, soda, salt, and stevia. Make a "well" in the center.
4. To help eliminate lumps, whisk guar gum into orange juice. Add oil and orange flavoring. Mix.
5. Add liquids to dry ingredients. Stir to moisten evenly. Beat by hand for 20 strokes until you have a creamy, cake-like batter. Do not use an electric mixer.
6. Pour into pan and spread evenly. Bake until center bounces back when lightly tapped or toothpick comes out clean when inserted into center. Usual baking time is 20–22 minutes for stevia version and 25–30 minutes for honey versions.
7. Cool cake and serve plain or ice with Orange Glaze (below). Cut cake 4x4. May be frozen. This cake is liked even by people who eat sweets and do not like buckwheat.

Yield: 16 servings

Glaze for Orange Buckwheat Cake (Stevia or Honey Sweetened)

3/4 cup — orange juice, freshly squeezed or made from concentrate
1/32 teaspoon — stevia (1/4 of 1/8 teaspoon) OR 1 tablespoon honey
1 tablespoon — kudzu starch
1/4 teaspoon — unbuffered, corn-free vitamin C crystals (optional)

In small saucepan, whisk together all ingredients except vitamin C. While stirring almost constantly with whisk, gently boil over low for 3–5 minutes. Add vitamin C and stir. Spread on slightly cooled cake.

Almond-Sesame Granola Bars
(Day 1 Recipe)

2 cups	quick-cooking spelt or Kamut flakes*
1/4 cup	almonds or pecans
2 tablespoons	hulled sesame seeds
1/2 teaspoon	sea salt
2/3 cup	Pear Sauce Sweetener (page 230)
2 tablespoons	almond or sesame oil
1 teaspoon	alcohol-free almond extract (optional)

Nutritional Information/Serving			
	spelt	Kamut	oat
Calories:	161	167	150
Protein (g):	4.3	4.5	4.4
Carbohydrate (g):	22.8	22.5	22
Fiber (g):	3.89	3.74	3.31
Total fat (g):	7.38	7.28	6.2
Saturated (g):	.67	.67	.71
Cholesterol (mg):	0	0	0
Sodium (mg):	134	134	138
Food Exchanges/Serving			
spelt: .8 Br .2 VLM .5 Fr 1.4 Fat			
Kamut: .9 Br .2 VLM .5 Fr 1.4 Fat			
oat: 1 Br .3 Fr .9 Fat			

1. Preheat oven to 350°F.
2. Oil 8-inch square baking pan with 1/2 teaspoon oil.
3. To coarsely chop, pour flakes into chopper cup of Black & Decker® Handy Shortcut™ food processor (cup holds 2 cups). Chop for 10 seconds. Stop, stir with knife or handle of spoon. Chop for 5 seconds more. Add to mixing bowl.
4. Place nuts in chopper and chop for 15–20 seconds to desired size.
5. Add nuts, salt, and sesame seeds to mixing bowl. Toss to distribute ingredients evenly.
6. In separate bowl, combine Pear Sauce Sweetener, oil, and extract. Pour evenly over flake mixture. Mix thoroughly with rubber spatula to evenly coat flake mixture.
7. Transfer to pan and spread evenly. Press mixture firmly in pan with metal spatula. Use both hands, one on top of the other to press firmly.
8. Bake 25 minutes. Cool completely. Cut 4x2. Enjoy for breakfast, dessert, or snack. May be frozen. I individually bag bars in cellophane bags. No need to thaw, just unwrap and enjoy. These granola bars do crumble a little, but for the most part they hold together.

Yield: 8 servings

*Recipe was developed using the quicker-cooking brands of spelt or Kamut flakes, e.g., The Grain Place.

Oat Granola Bars
(Day 3 Recipe)

2 cups	old fashioned rolled oats
2 tablespoons	walnuts
1/2 cup	oat bran
1/4 cup	small flaked unsweetened coconut (optional)
1/2 teaspoon	sea salt
2 teaspoons	cinnamon
1/3 cup	undiluted apple juice concentrate
2 tablespoons	walnut or canola oil

Analysis for Oat Granola Bars listed above was done without coconut.

Perform Steps 1–4 as directed in granola bar recipe above.

5. Add nuts, oat bran, coconut, salt, and cinnamon to mixing bowl. Toss to evenly distribute.
6. Measure apple juice concentrate in 1-cup glass measure. Add water slowly until liquid totals 1/2 cup. Add oil and stir. Pour evenly over oat mixture. Mix thoroughly with rubber spatula to evenly coat flake mixture.

Perform Steps 7–8 to finish preparing, baking, and serving as directed in granola bar recipe above.

Yield: 8 servings

Amaranth Carob Cookies*
(Day 2 Recipe)

1 cup	amaranth flour
1/2 cup	arrowroot starch
1/4 cup	carob powder, sift after measuring*
3/4 teaspoon	baking soda
1/2 teaspoon	unbuffered, corn-free vitamin C crystals
1/4 teaspoon	sea salt
1/2 teaspoon	stevia, white powder concentrate*
1/2 cup	water
2 tablespoons	olive oil or sunflower oil

Nutritional Information/Cookie	
Calories:	56
Protein (g):	1
Carbohydrate (g):	8.6
Fiber (g):	1.13
Total fat (g):	1.85
Saturated (g):	.2
Cholesterol (mg):	0
Sodium (mg):	83
Food Exchanges/Cookie	
.5 Br .1 Oth Carb .3 Fat	

1. Preheat oven to 350ºF.
2. Oil cookies sheets.
3. In mixing bowl, whisk together dry ingredients. Make "well" in the center.
4. Add water and oil. Stir with rubber spatula to moisten dry ingredients.
5. Lightly oil fingers. Form dough into 1-inch balls. Place on cookie sheet approximately 2 inches apart. Flatten with fork or bottom of glass.
6. Bake 10 minutes. Immediately remove cookies to cooling rack to cool.

Yield: 18 cookies

*Stevia and carob are assigned to Day 4, omit them on Day 4 just before and after eating these cookies on Day 2.

Amazing Sugarless Cookies
(Day 1 Recipe)

1 cup	brown rice flour
1 teaspoon	baking soda
1/4 teaspoon	sea salt
1/4 teaspoon	unbuffered, corn-free vitamin C crystals
1 cup	whole raw almonds, chop in food processor (optional)
1/3 cup	brown rice syrup
2 tablespoons	almond oil
1 teaspoon	alcohol-free almond extract (optional)
2/3 cup	almond butter

Nutritional Information/Cookie	
Calories:	80
Protein (g):	2.2
Carbohydrate (g):	6.7
Fiber (g):	1.02
Total fat (g):	5.47
Saturated (g):	.51
Cholesterol (mg):	0
Sodium (mg):	51
Food Exchanges/Cookie	
.3 Br .1 Oth Carb .4 VLM 1 Fat	

1. Preheat oven to 350ºF.
2. In mixing bowl, whisk together dry ingredients and almonds.
3. Measure out brown rice syrup in glass measuring cup. Add oil and almond extract. Mix.
4. Add almond butter and rice syrup mixture to dry ingredients and mix thoroughly. Batter will be a little stiff and slightly sticky.
5. Roll dough into 1-inch balls. Place balls onto cookie sheet about 2 1/2 inches apart. Flatten each ball with fork or bottom of drinking glass to 1/4 inch thickness and 2 inch diameter. Dip fork or glass in water frequently to prevent dough from sticking.
6. Bake cookies for 8–10 minutes. Cookies do not brown much. In fact, they seem to lighten during baking. Cool on cookie sheet just long enough to completely set up and allow successful transfer of cookies to cooling rack. Leftover cookies freeze nicely in a wide-mouth pint glass canning jar.

Yield: 3 dozen (2 1/2 dozen if almonds are omitted)

Special Note: These have been named Amazing Sugarless Cookies because everyone who eats them is so amazed that they are sugar-free. These cookies make a great hit at any social gathering.

Oatmeal Cookies
(Day 3 Recipe)

7/8 cup	oat flour OR 1 cup rolled oats blended into oat flour (7/8 cup = 3/4 cup + 2 tbls.)
1/4 cup	tapioca starch
1 teaspoon	baking soda
1/4 teaspoon	unbuffered vitamin C crystals
1/4 teaspoon	sea salt
1/2–1 teas.	ground cinnamon
1/2 cup	Brazil or macadamia nuts*
	OR 2 tablespoons walnut or canola oil
3/4 cup	apple juice concentrate, 3/1
1 1/2 cups	rolled oats
3/4 cup	chopped walnuts OR an additional 1/2 cup rolled oats

Nutritional Information/Cookie	
Analysis Done Using Canola Oil	
Calories:	84
Protein (g):	1.9
Carbohydrate (g):	10.8
Fiber (g):	1.08
Total fat (g):	3.98
Saturated (g):	.38
Cholesterol (mg):	0
Sodium (mg):	78
Food Exchanges/Cookie	
.4 Br .2 Fr .3 Fat	

1. Preheat oven to 350ºF.

2. If using rolled oats rather than oat flour, blend one cup rolled oats in blender on high to make 7/8 cup of oat flour.

3. In large mixing bowl, whisk together all dry ingredients except rolled oats and nuts.

4. If using Brazil or macadamia nuts: Add to blender and blend to create nut butter, being sure to make it as smooth as possible. Add apple juice to blender and blend on high a few seconds longer.

5. Add step 4 and nut mixture OR oil and apple juice to dry ingredients. Stir with rubber spatula until mixture forms a "sloppy" dough. Add rolled oats and nuts and stir to form a soft batter.

6. Drop dough by rounded teaspoons onto cookie sheets approximately two inches apart. Bake 10 minutes. Immediately remove cookies to cooling rack to cool.

YIELD: 24 cookies

*Brazil and macadamia nuts are unassigned "Fun Foods," see explanation on page 24..

SPECIAL NOTE: Preparing recipe with nuts yields cookies that hold together slightly better than those prepared with oil.

> *The time to relax is when you don't have time for it.*
> —Sydney J. Harris

Sunflower Seed Butter
(Day 2 Recipe)

3 cups	raw, hulled sunflower seeds
2 tablespoons	sunflower oil

Nutritional Information/Tbls.	
Calories:	84
Protein (g):	3.1
Carbohydrate (g):	2.5
Fiber (g):	.82
Total fat (g):	7.55
Saturated (g):	.8
Cholesterol (mg):	0
Sodium (mg):	0
Food Exchanges/Tablespoon	
.1 Oth Carb .3 VLM 1.5 Fat	

1. Chill sunflower seeds in freezer at least overnight. Leave seeds in freezer until ready to process.

2. Assemble Champion Juicer for homogenizing. Use funnel for easier insertion of seeds.

3. In bowl, stir sunflower seeds and oil to evenly coat seeds. Run approximately 1/4 cup of seeds through at a time. The Champion Juicer manufacturer recommends to discontinue making seed butter if juicer body becomes excessively warm.

4. Store in wide-mouth, glass pint jar. Spread on crackers or tortillas and use in Carob Sunflower Candy (recipe on next page).

Yield: 2 cups

Carob Sunflower Candy*

(Day 2 Recipe)

1 1/3 cups	Sunflower Seed Butter (page 218)
1/3 cup	carob powder* (after measuring, sift to remove lumps)
1/4 teaspoon	stevia,* white powder concentrate
1/3 cup	water
1/2 cup	ground sunflower seeds

Nutritional Information/Serving	
Calories:	49
Protein (g):	1.7
Carbohydrate (g):	2
Fiber (g):	.73
Total fat (g):	4.09
Saturated (g):	.43
Cholesterol (mg):	0
Sodium (mg):	0
Food Exchanges/Serving	
.8 Fat	

1. In bowl, whisk together carob powder and stevia. Add water and mix until smooth. Add sunflower seed butter and mix thoroughly. Mixture will be sticky at first but will become firmer as you mix.

2. Divide batter in half. Form into two balls. Cut each ball into eight wedges. Shape each wedge into a ball and cut each into thirds yielding 48 portions. Shape each portion into a ball. Roll each in ground sunflower seeds. Chill and serve. May be frozen for one month.

Yield: 48 servings   Great to serve in place of fudge at holiday times.

*Carob powder and stevia are assigned to Day 4, omit them on Day 4 just before and after eating this recipe on Day 2.

Zucchini Amaranth Cookies

(Day 2 Recipe)

1/2 cup	amaranth flour
1/4 cup	arrowroot starch
1/2 teaspoon	baking soda
1/4 teaspoon	sea salt
1/4 teaspoon	unbuffered, corn-free vitamin C crystals
1/8 teaspoon	allspice
1/4 cup	Kiwi Sauce (page 229) OR pineapple sauce
1 tablespoon	olive oil
3/4 cup	zucchini squash, peeled, shredded

Nutritional Information/Cookie	
Calories:	42
Protein (g):	.8
Carbohydrate (g):	7
Fiber (g):	1.55
Total fat (g):	1.21
Saturated (g):	.12
Cholesterol (mg):	0
Sodium (mg):	79
Food Exchanges/Cookie	
.3 Br .1 Fr .1 Veg .2 Fat	

1. Preheat oven to 375ºF.

2. In mixing bowl, whisk together dry ingredients.

3. Add fruit sauce and oil to dry ingredients. Stir thoroughly but do not beat. Mixture will be stiff.

4. Add squash. Mix.

5. Drop by teaspoon onto oiled cookie sheet. Flatten each cookie a little with fork. Do not make cookies more than 1 inch in diameter. Bake 18–20 minutes on upper rack of oven. Cool completely on cookie sheet to continue baking. Cookies freeze well. Thaw at room temperature for 15 minutes or so before serving. Do not thaw in microwave or they will become soggy and taste undone.

Yield: 15 cookies

Special Note: Prepare only this small batch at one time because batter should not set before baking. The idea is to bake them crispy on the outside yet soft but not doughy on the inside. The trick is to make them small, flatten just enough, and bake as long as possible without burning them on the bottom.

HH: Freeze squash when in season. Premeasure shredded squash (3/4 cup) and package. Then thaw and drain thoroughly before preparing these cookies.

Pear Custard*
(Day 1 Recipe)

1/4 cup	almonds
2/3 cup	water
2	eggs
1/4 teaspoon	sea salt
2/3 cup	pear juice
1/2 teaspoon	alcohol-free almond extract
sprinkle	cinnamon
sprinkle	nutmeg* (optional)

Nutritional Information/Serving	
Calories:	105
Protein (g):	4.6
Carbohydrate (g):	7.1
Fiber (g):	.84
Total fat (g):	6.83
Saturated (g):	1.12
Cholesterol (mg):	94
Sodium (mg):	166
Food Exchanges/Serving	
.3 VLM .4 LM .3 Fr 1.1 Fat	

1. Preheat oven to 350°F.
2. Blend almonds in blender on highest speed into fine powder. Add small amount of water and blend on highest speed for 1–2 minutes until well blended, stopping at least once to scrap sides and bottom of blender jar.
3. Beat egg in small bowl with whisk. Add rest of ingredients and nut milk. Stir.
4. Pour into 4 custard cups. Place cups in an 8-inch square glass baking dish. Add room temperature water to baking dish so that water is 1 inch deep in pan.
5. Bake 40–45 minutes or until knife comes out clean when inserted in center of custard. Serve warm or cold. I prefer warm.

Yield: 4 servings (1/2 cup each)

*Nutmeg is an unassigned "Fun Food," see explanation on page 24.

Lemon Pudding*
(Day 2 Recipe)

1 quart	Mountain Sun brand organic Lemonade*
3 tablespoons	freshly squeezed lemon juice
	(approximate amount of juice from 1 lemon)
1/2 cup	arrowroot
1 teaspoon	alcohol-free lemon flavor (optional)
as desired	grated lemon rind

Nutritional Information/Serving	
Calories:	85
Protein (g):	.1
Carbohydrate (g):	21.1
Fiber (g):	.29
Total fat (g):	.02
Saturated (g):	0
Cholesterol (mg):	0
Sodium (mg):	22
Food Exchanges/Serving	
.4 Br .5 Oth Carb .5 Fr	

Combine ingredients in large saucepan. Stir with whisk to dissolve arrowroot. Cook over medium heat until thickened. Stir with whisk almost constantly, especially toward end. Portion into individual bowls. Chill.

Yield: 4 1/4 cups   8 servings

*Mountain Sun brand lemonade contains wild honey, omit eating honey on Day 4 just before and after enjoying this recipe on Day 2. According to Mountain Sun, they add approximately 12% (by weight) honey to their juices. Using this information, I calculated that this lemonade contains about 1 tablespoon of honey per 1 cup of juice.

Thanks to Elva W. of Iowa for her assistance in developing this recipe.

> *If you have tried to do something and failed, you are vastly better off than if you had tried to do nothing and succeeded.*

Quinoa Pudding I
(Day 3 Recipe)

1 cup	Basic Quinoa (page 96)
1/2 cup	unsweetened applesauce
1/2 cup	water
2 tablespoons	chopped walnuts
3/4 teaspoon	ground cinnamon
1 teaspoon	alcohol-free vanilla flavoring

Combine all ingredients in small saucepan. Simmer on low heat for 5–10 minutes to combine flavors. If desired, add more water. Serve warm or cold.

Yield: 1 1/2 cups   3 servings

Quinoa Pudding II
(Day 3 Recipe)

1 cup	Quinoa Cereal I or II (page 98)
1/4 cup	unsweetened applesauce
1–2 tablespoons	walnuts, chopped
1/2 teaspoon	ground cinnamon
1 teaspoon	alcohol-free vanilla flavoring

Combine all ingredients in small saucepan. Simmer on low heat for 5–10 minutes to combine flavors. Serve warm or cold.

Yield: 1 1/4 cups   2 servings

Nutritional Information/Serving		
	Pudding I	Pudding II
Calories:	96	102
Protein (g):	2.6	2.9
Carbohydrate (g):	15.9	17.4
Fiber (g):	1.97	2.04
Total fat (g):	3.4	3
Saturated (g):	.32	.26
Cholesterol (mg):	0	0
Sodium (mg):	50	139
Food Exchanges/Serving		
Pudding I: .6 Br .1 LM .3 Fr		
Pudding II .8 Br .1 LM .3 Fr		

Carob Pudding
(Day 4 Recipe)

1/2 cup	chopped macadamia or Brazil nuts*
1/4 cup	kudzu starch
2 cups	water
1/8 teaspoon	stevia, white powder concentrate OR 2 tablespoons honey
1/4 cup	carob powder (after measuring, sift to remove lumps)
1/4 teaspoon	alcohol-free peppermint extract (optional)

1. Blend nuts, starch, and small amount of water in blender on highest speed for 1–2 minutes until well blended. Stop at least once to scrap sides and bottom of jar. Add rest of water, blend a few seconds longer.

2. Pour nut milk into saucepan, add remaining ingredients. Blend with whisk. Cook over medium heat, stirring almost constantly with whisk, until thickened. Pour into custard cups. Chill.

Yield: 2 1/4 cups   4 servings

Nutritional Information/Serving		
	with stevia	with honey
Calories:	171	203
Protein (g):	1.7	1.7
Carbohydrate (g):	15.1	23.9
Fiber (g):	3.45	3.47
Total fat (g):	12.4	12.4
Saturated (g):	1.85	1.85
Cholesterol (mg):	0	0
Sodium (mg):	3	4
Food Exchanges/Serving		
Stevia: .5 Br .3 Oth Carb .2 VLM 2.5 Fat		
Honey: .5 Br .7 Oth Carb .2 VLM 2.5 Fat		

*Brazil and macadamia nuts are unassigned "Fun Foods," see explanation on page 24.

Millet Pudding I
(Day 3 Recipe)

1 cup	sliced or diced apple, peeled
1/4 cup	water
1/2 teaspoon	cinnamon
1–2 tablespoons	walnuts, chopped
1 cup	Millet Cereal I (page 98)
2 teaspoons	tapioca starch
1 teaspoon	alcohol-free vanilla flavoring

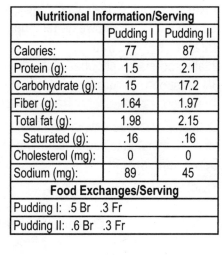

Nutritional Information/Serving		
	Pudding I	Pudding II
Calories:	77	87
Protein (g):	1.5	2.1
Carbohydrate (g):	15	17.2
Fiber (g):	1.64	1.97
Total fat (g):	1.98	2.15
Saturated (g):	.16	.16
Cholesterol (mg):	0	0
Sodium (mg):	89	45
Food Exchanges/Serving		
Pudding I: .5 Br .3 Fr		
Pudding II: .6 Br .3 Fr		

1. Layer apples, water, cinnamon, walnuts, and millet in a 1-quart Visions saucepan. Do not stir. Cover. Bring to boil over medium heat. The glass Visions cookware allows you to see when water begins to boil.

2   Turn heat down to low and simmer for 15 minutes or until apples are tender.

3. Dissolve tapioca starch in 1 tablespoon of water and vanilla. Add, stir, and cook to thicken.

4. Serve warm or cold for breakfast or dessert. However, it is best warm. May be frozen.

Yield: 1 2/3 cups   3 Servings.

Millet Pudding II
(Day 3 Recipe)

1 cup	sliced or diced apple, peeled
3/4 cup	water
1/2 teaspoon	cinnamon
1–2 tablespoons	walnuts, chopped
1 cup	Basic Millet, prepared without caraway (page 96)
1 teaspoon	alcohol-free vanilla flavoring

Prepare same as Millet Pudding I except omit step 3. Add vanilla and stir before serving.

Yield: 1 3/4 cups   3 Servings

HH: Since I enjoy these puddings warm for breakfast, I cook and freeze extra millet on a previous Day 3. Thaw cooked millet over night in refrigerator. It does not need to be completely thawed—just enough to chunk up with a fork. Also, I use frozen sliced apples (page 228). Once you have prepared this recipe a couple of times, no need to measure apples, cinnamon, and walnuts. You will know what it looks like in the pan. Quick and easy breakfast.

The smiles that count are those that shine when it rains.

Tears are the safety valve of the heart when pressure is laid on it.
—*Albert Smith*

Carob Tofu "Cheesecake"
(Day 2 or 4 Recipe*)

2 pounds	soft tofu, drained
1/4 cup	carob powder (after measuring, sift to remove lumps)
3/8 cup	honey (3/8 cup = 1/4 cup + 2 tablespoons)
1/2 teaspoon	sea salt
2 tablespoons	dacopa (optional)

Blueberry Tofu "Cheesecake"
(Day 2 or 4 Recipe*)

2 pounds	soft tofu, drained
1 cup	frozen blueberries, no need to thaw except to remove ice crystals
1/4 cup	honey
1/2 teaspoon	sea salt

1. Preheat oven to 350°F.

2. Combine your choice of ingredients in large mixing bowl. Using electric mixer or Braun hand mixer, blend ingredients until thoroughly mixed and tofu is smooth.

3. Pour into 8-inch square baking dish with unbaked Buckwheat Pie Crust pressed only in bottom of dish. Spread batter evenly.

4. Bake for 60–65 minutes or until filling is done and knife comes out clean when inserted into center. Chill. Cut 4x4 to yield 16 servings. Both versions may be frozen and thawed for future desserts. However, crust usually separates from cheesecake and is a little watery.

Special Note: Sift carob powder is by placing in fine-mesh strainer. (Have bowl underneath.) Then stir powder to work it through mesh and into bowl.

*Ingredients are easily "floated" between Days 2 and 4. See explanation on page 24.

Nutritional Information/Serving						
	Carob Tofu "Cheesecake"			Blueberry Tofu "Cheesecake"		
	Filling Only	w/Buckwheat Crust	w/Amaranth Crust	Filling Only	w/Buckwheat Crust	w/Amaranth Crust
Calories:	74	113	124	62	100	113
Protein (g):	4.7	5.3	5.4	4.6	5.2	5.4
Carbohydrate (g):	9.1	12.4	14.5	6.2	9.4	11.5
Fiber (g):	1.34	1.8	1.78	.82	1.28	1.26
Total fat (g):	2.72	5.42	5.54	2.77	5.47	5.59
Saturated (g):	.4	.66	.74	.4	.66	.74
Cholesterol (mg):	0	0	0	0	0	0
Sodium (mg):	71	106	105	71	105	104
Food **Exchanges** **Per Serving**	.4 Oth Carb .6 VLM .5 Fat	.2 Br .4 Oth Carb .6 VLM 1 Fat	.3 Br .4 Other Carb .6 VLM 1 Fat	.2 Oth Carb .6 VLM .1 Fr .6 Fat	.2 Br .2 Oth Carb .6 VLM .1 Fr 1.1 Fat	.4 Br .2 Oth Carb .6 VLM .1 LM .1 Fr 1.1 Fat

> *True enjoyment comes from activity of the mind and exercise of the body; the two are ever united.*
>
> —*Humboldt*

Spritzer Beverages

	Grapefruit (Day 2)	Cranberry (Day 4)	Orange (Day 4)	Cranberry Orange (Day 4)
1 bottle	carbonated, unflavored mineral water, chilled (12 ounces)			
juice concentrate— unsweetened, chilled	1/4 cup grapefruit	1/2 cup cranberry	1/4 cup orange	1/4 cup orange 1/2 cup cranberry
Total Yield: 2 servings	1 3/4 cups	2 cups	1 3/4 cups	2 1/4 cups

Combine your choice of ingredients and serve immediately.

Yield: 2 1/4 cups

Special Note: At publication the only brand of unsweetened 100% cranberry juice I have used is R.W Knudsen. See Appendix C: Resources for another brand available from Walnut Acre Organic Farms. I prefer to mix in 1/4 teaspoon of stevia per quart of unsweetened cranberry juice. Also, partially frozen cranberry juice added to mineral water makes an interesting slush.

Nutritional Information/Serving				
	Grapefruit	Cranberry	Orange	Cranberry Orange
Calories:	55	15	56	71
Protein (g):	.5	.1	.9	1
Carbohydrate (g):	13.5	3.5	13.6	17
Fiber (g):	.3	0	.28	.28
Total fat (g):	0	0	.07	.07
Saturated (g):	0	0	.01	.01
Cholesterol (mg):	0	0	0	0
Sodium (mg):	0	6	1	7
Food Exchanges/Serving				
	.9 Fr	.3 Fr	1 Fr	1.3 Fr

Carob Shake

(Day 4 Recipe)

1/4 cup	Ener-G Pure Soy Quick
1/4 cup	carob powder
2 cups	water
1/16 teaspoon	stevia, white powder concentrated (1/16 tsp. = 1/2 of 1/8 tsp.)

Combine all ingredients in blender. Blend on highest speed until dissolved. Taste for desired sweetness. If needed, add more stevia (add only a few grains at a time) and blend a little longer. Chill. Shake or stir before drinking.   Yield: 2 cups   2 servings

Nutritional Information/Serving	
Calories:	101
Protein (g):	7.2
Carbohydrate (g):	15.4
Fiber (g):	7.39
Total fat (g):	2.21
Saturated (g):	.24
Cholesterol (mg):	0
Sodium (mg):	6
Food Exchanges/Serving	
.5 Br .5 Oth Carb .2 Fat	

Pau D'Arco Tea

To prepare, boil 4 cups of water in stainless steel saucepan. Add 1 heaping tablespoon of bulk tea and an optional teaspoon of fresh basil for a sweeter flavor. Remove from heat, cover, and allow to steep for 20 minutes or longer. Pour steeped tea through fine mesh strainer to remove leaves and store in refrigerator. Drink 3–6 cups of unsweetened tea evenly and slowly throughout each day, warm or cold on an empty stomach. (For more information, see page 16.)

Dacopa Beverage

(Day 2 or 4)

Dacopa is hot beverage similar to coffee. Made from dahlia root, it is a member of the Composite Family (#80). See Appendix C for sources for this beverage.

HH: If you miss having a hot beverage to sip during or between meals, use your creativity to find alternatives which fit your diet. Try steeping assigned herbs and spices to learn if you enjoy them as a tea. Or add alcohol-free extracts to warm water. (For more options, see the "Question & Answer" Exchange in issues #2 and #4 of Canary Connect News, see Appendix G, page 271.)

Nut Milks

	Almond (Day 1)	Brazil "Fun Food"	Cashew (Day 4)	Filbert (Day 3)	Macadamia "Fun Food"
1/4 cup nuts	almonds	chopped Brazil	cashew pieces	filberts	macadamia
water	1 cup				

1. Blend nuts/seeds in blender on highest speed until they become a fine powder, approximately 1–2 minutes. (Brazil and macadamia nuts will only become finely chopped.) Stop once or twice to scrape sides and bottom of blender jar.
2. Add 1/4 cup water and blend on highest speed approximately 1 minute until well blended. Stop at least once to scrape sides and bottom of blender jar. Add remaining water and blend a couple of seconds longer. Chill. Add salt if desired. Stir before serving. Use milks to flavor hot cereals and serve with cold cereals.

Yield: slightly over 1 cup

HH: Prepare 1 or 2 cups at a time to save time. After blending, pour immediately into ice cube trays. After frozen, remove and transfer to cellophane or plastic bags.

Nutritional Information/Serving = 2 Tablespoons						
	Almond	Brazil	Cashew	Filbert	Macadamia	Sesame
Calories:	24	29	25	27	29	13
Protein (g):	.8	.6	.7	.6	.4	.4
Carbohydrate (g):	.8	.6	1.4	.7	.6	.5
Fiber (g):	.39	.26	.13	.31	.22	.2
Total fat (g):	2.12	2.9	1.99	2.64	3.09	1.12
Saturated (g):	.2	.71	.39	.19	.46	.16
Cholesterol (mg):	0	0	0	0	0	0
Sodium (mg):	1	0	1	0	0	0
Food Exchanges/Serving = 2 Tablespoons						
Almond: .1 VLM .4 Fat Brazil: .1 VLM .6 Fat Cashew: .2 VLM .4 Fat						
Filbert: 1 VLM .5 Fat Macadamia: .1 VLM .6 Fat Sesame: .1 VLM .2 Fat						

Sesame Milk
(Day 1 Recipe)

2 tablespoons   hulled sesame seeds
1 cup   water

Prepare same as nut milk recipe above.

Nutritional information in chart above.

FYI: Mill Milk - oat milk is a commercial, dairy-free milk substitute product (see Resources, page 253).

Pancake or French Toast "Maple Syrup"
(Day 3 Recipe)

1 teaspoon   alcohol-free maple extract
2–4 ounces   100% pure vegetable glycerine
as desired   NutriFlora FOS

Combine ingredients and serve over pancakes or French toast. *Gene D. of Ohio enjoys this recipe and says it tastes "about like the real thing." The idea is not his own—he found it in some information from the Candida Research and Information Foundation and added the FOS for more sweetness. Thank you, Gene, for sharing!*

This recipe was shared in Canary Connect News, *Issue #4. Thought it was a nice addition to this section.*

No nutritional information was available for these ingredients.

Quick Catsup*
(Day 2 Recipe)

1-6oz. can	Muir Glen brand tomato paste
1/2 cup	water
1/8 teaspoon	sea salt
rounded 1/2 teaspoon	onion powder
rounded 1/2 teaspoon	leaf oregano
3/8 teaspoon	unbuffered, corn-free vitamin C crystals
scant 1/8 teaspoon	garlic powder
scant 1/8 teaspoon	ground cloves
scant 1/8 teaspoon	ground cumin*
scant 1/8 teaspoon	dry mustard*

Nutritional Information/Tablespoon	
Calories:	14
Protein (g):	.9
Carbohydrate (g):	2.7
Fiber (g):	.48
Total fat (g):	.01
Saturated (g):	0
Cholesterol (mg):	0
Sodium (mg):	29
Food Exchanges/Tablespoon	
.5 Veg	

Combine ingredients and chill. This is thick catsup. Dilute with more water if desired. Freeze in ice cube trays. After frozen, remove and store frozen in cellophane or plastic bag. Thaw as needed.

Yield: almost 1 cup

*These seasonings are assigned to Days 1 and 3. However, since they are in such small amounts, I personally do not concern myself with this minor break in rotation.

> *Things do not change—we do.*
> *Henry David Thoreau*

> *Laughter is by definition healthy.*
> *—Doris Lessing*

Clarified Butter
(Day 2 Recipe)

To make clarified butter, heat 1/4 to 1 pound of unsalted butter in pan or skillet to a slow boiling point until it foams well. Remove from heat and allow it to cool until milk solids fall to bottom of pan or float to top. Carefully skim off floating white milk solid residue and discard. Gently pour clear yellow liquid into a storage container and discard residue on bottom.

HINTS: Using a pan or skillet that will allow melting butter to have a little depth works best to facilitate the separation process. Do not start with too much butter as it will begin to burn on the bottom of pan before it can completely melt and uniformly reach a boiling stage.

Store in a container with a tight-fitting lid. To maintain freshness and prevent possible mold formation, keep container tightly closed. Always use a clean utensil. Store in refrigerator. Since clarified butter is partially saturated, it is firm when cold yet it will soften quickly at room temperature. (I recommend that you only soften the amount you wish to use.)

While this recipe is relatively simple to make, clarified butter is also available commercially at health-food stores and through mail-order sources under the product name Ghee.

1/4 pound yields approximately 2/3 cup.

Recipes: Beverages and Miscellaneous

Guacamole*
(Day 2 Recipe)

1	ripe avocado*
2 tablespoons	onion, chopped
2 tablespoons	green pepper, chopped
1/4 teaspoon	chili powder
1/8 teaspoon	minced garlic
2 pinches	sea salt
2 pinches	unbuffered, corn-free vitamin C crystals
1	tomato, diced

Nutritional Information/Serving	
Calories:	61
Protein (g):	1
Carbohydrate (g):	4
Fiber (g):	1.8
Total fat (g):	5.26
Saturated (g):	.84
Cholesterol (mg):	0
Sodium (mg):	26
Food Exchanges/Serving	
.2 Fr .3 Veg 1 Fat	

1. Cut avocado in half, remove pit, and scoop flesh into a blender.
2. Add remaining ingredients except tomato. Blend until smooth. Transfer to bowl, and stir in tomatoes. Cover and chill. Serve as a dip with crackers.

OR

Do not stir in tomatoes and serve with Enchiladas, Tacos, Taco Pizza, or Beef Fajitas.

Yield: approximately 2/3 cup without tomato   6 servings

<u>Special Notes</u>:

For chunky guacamole, place all ingredients except tomatoes in a Black & Decker® Handy Shortcut™ Micro-Processor using knife blade.

Guacamole may be frozen without tomato. Since freezing causes avocado to darken slightly, stir in a pinch of unbuffered, corn-free vitamin C crystals to lighten.

*Avocado belongs to the Laurel Family with bay leaf and cinnamon. Eating avocado on Day 2 breaks rotation since cinnamon is used in recipes on Days 1 and 3. Make your own decision about eating avocado on Day 2.

Picante Sauce
(Day 2 Recipe)

1/2 can	Muir Glen brand tomato puree (14 ounces)
1 cup	water
1/4 cup	green pepper, finely chopped
2 tablespoons	onion, finely chopped
1 teaspoon	chili powder
1 teaspoon	leaf oregano
1/2 teaspoon	sea salt
1/2 teaspoon	minced garlic
1/2 teaspoon	Watkins Salsa Seasoning Blend or other Mexican blend spices

Nutritional Information/Serving	
Calories:	21
Protein (g):	1
Carbohydrate (g):	5.2
Fiber (g):	1.19
Total fat (g):	.07
Saturated (g):	.01
Cholesterol (mg):	0
Sodium (mg):	154
Food Exchanges/Serving	
1 Veg	

1. In saucepan, combine all ingredients. Bring to boil, reduce heat to medium-high. Cover with splatter screen (information on page 198) and boil gently for 10 minutes or longer to blend flavors and reduce sauce to 2 cups. Stir often, especially at end.
2. Chill and serve with Enchiladas, Tacos, Taco Pizza, Beef Fajitas, etc.
3. Freeze leftovers in ice cube trays, 1 tablespoon per cube. After frozen, remove and store frozen in a cellophane or plastic bag. Thaw as needed.

Yield: 2 cups   8 servings (1/4 cup each)

Yogurt Delights
(Day 2 Recipe)

Choose one of the following to add to plain sugar-free yogurt. My favorite brand is 7-Stars original plain Organic Yogurt.

Delight I
Add alcohol-free vanilla extract to plain yogurt.

Delight II
Avoid eating blueberries on Day 4 just before and after Day 2 to enjoy blueberries with yogurt. Thaw blueberries (do not drain), add to yogurt, and stir. I prefer to smash blueberries before adding. Other fruits could be used, use guideline to temporarily or permanently move foods (page 23).

Delight III
Stir desired amount of puffed amaranth into yogurt. Eat immediately.

Delight IV
Stir desired amount of peeled, sliced cucumbers into yogurt.

Delight V
Enjoy a combination of above suggestions

Apples—How to Freeze
(Day 3 Recipe)

Sliced or diced apple is a wonderful sweetener for Day 3 cereals and puddings. However, often a whole apple is not needed, especially when sweetening only a single bowl of cereal. Follow this simple method to freeze apples for a quick sweetener for Day 3 cereals and desserts.

To Prepare:
- Dissolve 1/4 teaspoon of vitamin C crystals in medium-size bowl of water.
- Wash, peel, core, and rinse apples. Slice or dice. Soak in vitamin C water until ready to blanch. Drain just before blanching.

To Blanch:
- Fill bottom of steamer pan with water to about 1/2 inch from bottom of steamer insert. Add 1/4 teaspoon of vitamin C crystals. Heat water to boiling.
- Add 2 cups of prepared apples to steamer insert. Cover and immediately begin timing. Steam for 2 minutes.
- Immediately drain and chill in ice water until cold.

To Freeze:
- Drain well.
- Place the amount desired for recipe in cellophane or plastic bag and freeze.

OR

Individually freeze on baking sheet before placing in bag. See explanation on page 49 in Canning and Freezing section.

Nutritional Information Per 2 Tablespoons Peeled Apple	
Calories:	8
Protein (g):	0
Carbohydrate (g):	2
Fiber (g):	.26
Total fat (g):	.04
Saturated (g):	.01
Cholesterol (mg):	0
Sodium (mg):	0
Food Exchanges/2 Tablespoons	
.1 Fr	

Raspberry Pear Jam
(Day 1 Recipe)

2 cups	frozen raspberries
2 cups	Pear Sauce (page 230)
	OR 1 1/3 cups Pear Sauce Sweetener (page 230)
2 tablespoons	flour—brown rice, spelt, or Kamut

Combine fruits and flour in deep saucepan. Cook on medium-high for 5–10 minutes until thickened. Stir almost constantly with whisk to prevent burning. Freeze leftovers in small wide mouth jar or in ice cube trays, 1/2 tablespoon per cube. After frozen, remove from trays and store frozen in cellophane or plastic bag until ready to use.

Nutritional Information/Tablespoon	
Calories:	29
Protein (g):	.3
Carbohydrate (g):	7.4
Fiber (g):	1.53
Total fat (g):	.26
Saturated (g):	.01
Cholesterol (mg):	0
Sodium (mg):	0
Food Exchanges/Tablespoon	
.4 Fr	

Yield: 1 1/3 cups

Rhubarb Jelly
(Day 4 Recipe)

2 cups	diced rhubarb
1/4 cup	honey
	OR 1/4 cup water and 1/4 teaspoon stevia, white powder concentrate
1/8 teaspoon	sea salt
1/2 teaspoon	kudzu starch

1. Combine all ingredients except kudzu in saucepan. Cover and cook on low for 15 minutes or until rhubarb is tender. Stir occasionally during cooking process.

2. Add kudzu and continue to cook, stirring constantly, until thickened. Cool. This jelly is delicious for breakfast or snack on toasted Buckwheat Yeast-Free Bread (page 104) .

3. Freeze stevia version in ice cube trays, 1 tablespoon per cube. When frozen, remove from trays and store frozen in cellophane or plastic bags. Thaw as needed. Usually 1/2 or 1 cube is perfect for one serving. The honey version may be frozen in a jar since it does not freeze as solid.

Yield: 1 cup   16 servings

Nutritional Information/Tablespoon		
	with stevia	with honey
Calories:	4	20
Protein (g):	.1	.2
Carbohydrate (g):	.8	5.1
Fiber (g):	.27	.29
Total fat (g):	.03	.03
Saturated (g):	.01	.01
Cholesterol (mg):	0	0
Sodium (mg):	18	18
Food Exchanges/Tablespoon		
with stevia: .2 Fr		
with honey: .2 Oth Carb .2 Fr		

Kiwi Sauce
(Day 2 Recipe)

METHOD 1:

Wash and peel. Use a serrated knife. Blend on low speed in blender adding 1 kiwi at a time. Or place in bowl and blend with a Braun hand blender.

METHOD 2:

Wash and peel as in method 1. Run fruit through Champion Juicer assembled for homogenizing.

Special Note: 3 kiwi yield approximately 1/2 cup.

Nutritional Information/Kiwi	
Calories:	46
Protein (g):	.8
Carbohydrate (g):	11.3
Fiber (g):	1.44
Total fat (g):	.33
Saturated (g):	.01
Cholesterol (mg):	0
Sodium (mg):	4
Food Exchanges/Kiwi	
1 Fr	

Tips on Freezing Kiwi Sauce

Freeze in ice cube trays, 1 tablespoon per cube. After frozen, remove and store frozen in a cellophane or plastic bag until ready to use.

Pear Sauce or Applesauce
(Pear is Day 1 / Apple is Day 3)

METHOD 1

1. Wash fresh, ripe fruit. (Be careful not to over ripen pears.) Peel, core, quarter, rinse, and drain.
2. Run fruit through Champion Juicer set up for homogenizing. This will make sauce very quickly. To prevent fruit from darkening, add between 1/4–1 teaspoon of unbuffered, corn-free vitamin C crystals to 8 cups of applesauce. It is best to add it before fruit darkens. I prefer to stir in 1/4 teaspoon as soon as I have made about 2 cups of sauce. Add more as needed, stir after each addition.
3. FOR APPLESAUCE: Transfer to saucepan. Cover with splatter screen and cook on medium to thicken to desired consistency. Stir often to prevent sticking.

METHOD 2

1. Wash fresh, ripe fruit. (Be careful not to over ripen pears.) Peel, core, quarter, rinse, and drain.
2. Transfer to saucepan. To prevent fruit from darkening, add between 1/4–1 teaspoon unbuffered, corn-free vitamin C crystals for 8–10 cups of fruit quarters. It is best to add 1/4 teaspoon as soon as you have about 2 cups of quarters ready to cook. Add more as needed, stir after each addition.
3. It is not necessary to add water during cooking since the fruit will create its own juice as it cooks. Cook on low until soft. Stir often to prevent sticking.
4. Blend in blender OR press through a canning sieve or food mill.
5. FOR APPLESAUCE: Return to saucepan, cover with splatter screen, and cook on medium to thicken to desired consistency.
   FOR PEAR SAUCE: Pear sauce is complete. However some recipes call for Pear Sauce Sweetener, refer to that recipe below.

FYI: 25 pounds of pears yields approximately 7 quarts of Pear Sauce

Tips on Freezing Fruit Sauce

An easy way to freeze fruit sauce is to use ice cube trays, approximately 1 tablespoon per cube. After frozen, remove from trays and store frozen in a cellophane or plastic bag.

Pancake Fruit Sauce

For pancake topping, dilute fruit sauce with water and heat before serving (2 tablespoons fruit sauce to 1 tablespoon water is a nice consistency). This allows more sauce for the pancakes with less sweetness.

Nutritional Information/Serving			
	1/4 cup Pear Sauce	2/3 cup Pear Sweetener	1/4 cup Applesauce
Calories:	55	220	26
Protein (g):	.4	1.5	.1
Carbohydrate (g):	14.1	56.3	6.9
Fiber (g):	2.2	8.9	.73
Total fat (g):	.37	1.49	.03
Saturated (g):	.02	.08	0
Cholesterol (mg):	0	0	0
Sodium (mg):	0	0	1
Food Exchanges/Serving			
	.9 Fr	3.7 Fr	.5 Fr

Pear Sauce Sweetener

After preparing Pear Sauce, transfer to saucepan, cover with splatter screen, and cook on medium to thicken. Recipes are developed with ratio of 1 cup of Pear Sauce cooked down to yield 2/3 cup of Pear Sauce Sweetener. Stir often to prevent sticking, especially at end. Also, reduce heat to low towards end. Cook 16 cups of Pear Sauce in a large Dutch-oven kettle to yield 10 2/3 cups. Then freeze in glass jars in portions needed for recipes. Sauce will darken as it becomes thicker.

BIBLIOGRAPHY

"About Amaranth." Pamphlet from Nu-World Amaranth, Inc., PO Box 2202, Naperville, IL 60567.

"About Amaranth—and Us." Pamphlet from Nu-World Amaranth, Inc., PO Box 2202, Naperville, IL 60567.

"Amaranth." Pamphlet from Nu-World Amaranth, Inc., PO Box 2202, Naperville, IL 60567.

"Amaranth—The Grain with a Future." Pamphlet from Nu-World Amaranth, Inc., PO Box 2202, Naperville, IL 60567.

Beaman, Chris. Flax Oil Recipe Booklet. Colorado Springs, CO: Omega Logic Books, 1988. *(Available from Allergy Resources, Inc., PO Box 444, Guffey, CO 80820.)*

Bell, Louise, M.Sc., R.P.Dt., Miriam Hoffer, R.P.Dt., and J. Richard Hamilton, M.D., F.R.C.P. "Recommendations for Foods of Questionable Acceptance for Patients with Celiac Disease," Journal of the Canadian Dietetic Association, 42, no. 2 (April 1981). Abstract. *(Available from The National Buckwheat Institute, PO Box 440, Penn Yan, NY 14527.)*

"Buckwheat Backgrounder." Pamphlet from The National Buckwheat Institute, PO Box 364, Penn Yan, NY 14527.

Burton, Gail. The Candida Control Cookbook. New York, NY: New American Library Books, a Division of Penguin Books USA, Inc., 1989.

Campbell, J.A., Ph.D. "Diet Therapy of Celiac Disease and *Dermatitis herpetiformis*," World Review Nutritional Dietetics, 51: 189-233. *(Available from The National Buckwheat Institute, PO Box 440, Penn Yan, NY 14527.)*

_____. "Food for Celiacs," Journal of the Canadian Dietetic Association, 43, no 1 (January 1982). Abstract. *(Available from The National Buckwheat Institute, PO Box 440, Penn Yan, NY 14527.)*

Candida Albicans - Booklet of Reprints. San Diego, CA: Price-Pottenger Nutrition Foundation. *(Price-Pottenger Nutrition Foundation, PO Box 2614, LaMesa, CA 91943-2614)*

Chevalier, Denise (Ed.) Growing and Marketing Your Organic Produce. Iowa City, IA: Iowa Organic Growers and Buyers Association, PO Box 2935, Iowa City, IA 52244-2935.

Collier's Encyclopedia, 1963 ed. S.v. "Arrowroot," 2: 704.

Collier's Encyclopedia, 1963 ed. S.v. "Tapioca," 22: 66.

"Composting." Information sheet from Earth Day 1990, PO Box AA, Stanford, CA 94309.

Connolly, Pat and Associates of the Price-Pottenger Nutrition Foundation. The Candida Albicans Yeast-Free Cookbook. New Canaan, CT: Keats Publishing, Inc., 1985. *(Keats Publishing, Inc., 27 Pine Street [Box 876], New Canaan, CT 06840)*

"A Consumers Guide to Organically Grown Produce." Pamphlet from Albert's Organics, Inc., Los Angeles, CA.

Crook, William G., M.D. Chronic Fatigue Syndrome and the Yeast Connection. Jackson, TN: Professional Books, Inc., 1992. *(Professional Books, Inc., Box 3246, Jackson, TN 38303)*

_____. The Yeast Connection. New York, NY: Vintage Books, a Division of Random House, 1986. *(Available from Professional Books, Inc., Box 3246, Jackson, TN 38303.)*

_____. The Yeast Connection and the Woman. Jackson, TN: Professional Books, Inc., 1995. *(Professional Books, Inc., Box 3246, Jackson, TN 38303)*

_____ and Marjorie Hurt Jones, R.N. The Yeast Connection Cookbook. Jackson, TN: Professional Books, 1989. *(Professional Books, Inc., Box 3246, Jackson, TN 38303)*

Dadd, Debra Lynn. Nontoxic, Natural, and Earthwise. Los Angeles, CA: Jeremy P. Tarcher, Inc., 1990.

Donovan, Ann, C.N. "Spelt." Colorado Springs, CO: By the author, 1991. *(Ann Donovan, C.N., 627 N. Weber, Colorado Springs, CO 80903)*

Dumke, Nicolette M. Allergy Cooking with Ease. Lancaster, PA: Starburst Publishers, 1992. *(Available from Allergy Adapt, Inc., 1877 Polk Avenue, Louisville, CO 80027.)*

_____. "Stevia the Herbal Sweetener," Mastering Food Allergies, VI, no. 4, issue #54 (April 1991): 1. *(See Mastering Food Allergies address in Appendix D, Newsletter section.)*

Eibensteiner, Karl E. "Dinkle (Spelt) Rediscovered." Port Coquitlam, B.C., Canada: Lentia Enterprises, Ltd. *(Available from Nature Farm Foods, Inc., 328 E. Second Street, Sumner, IA 50674.)*

Erasmus, Udo. <u>Fats and Oils</u>. Vancouver, B.C., Canada: Alive Books, 1986.

"Flours." Information sheet from Blooming Prairie Warehouse, 2340 Heinz Road, Iowa City, IA 52240.

"Fresh Flax Oil." Pamphlet from Allergy Resources, Inc., PO Box 444, Guffey, CO 80820.

Friedman, Harold M., M.D., Robert E. Tortolani, M.D., John Glick, M.D., and Richard T. Burtis, M.D. "Spelt is Wheat," <u>Allergy Proceedings</u>, 15, no. 4 (July-August 1994): 217-218.

"From the Cradle of Civilization to Your Table in Only 6000 Years!" Information sheet from the Kamut® Association of North America, 295 Distribution Street, San Marcos, CA 92069 (September, 1992).

Fukuyasu, T., T. Oshida, and K. Ashida. "Effect of Oligosaccharides on Growth of Piglets and on Bacterial Flora, Putrefactive Substances and Volatile Fatty Acids in Their Feces," <u>Bulletin of Animal Hygiene</u>, 26 (1987): 15-22. Abstract. *(Copy available from Canary Connect, see Appendix G.)*

Futrell, Sue. "Farming Sustainably: Where Farmers and Producers Can Go for Answers," <u>Blooming Prairie Prairie News</u>, 2340 Heinz Road, Iowa City, IA 52240 (May/June 1992): A-97.

Golos, Natalie and Frances Golos Golbitz. <u>Coping with Your Allergies</u>. New York, NY: A Fireside Book, Published by Simon and Schuster, Inc., 1986.

_____. <u>If This Is Tuesday, It Must Be Chicken</u>. New Canaan, CT: Keats Publishing, Inc., 1983. *(Keats Publishing, Inc., 27 Pine Street [Box 876], New Canaan, CT 06840)*

Golos, Natalie and William J. Rea, M.D. <u>Success in the Clean Bedroom</u>. Rochester, NY: Pinnacle Publishers, 1992.

Goulart, Frances Sheridan. <u>Cooking with Carob: The Healthful Alternative to Chocolate</u>. Charlotte, VT: Garden Way Associates, Inc., 1980. *(Garden Way Associates, Inc., Dept. F157, Charlotte, VT 05445)*

"Grains." Information sheet from Blooming Prairie Warehouse, 2340 Heinz Road, Iowa City, IA 52240.

Greenberg, Ron, M.D. and Angela Nori. <u>Freedom from Allergy Cookbook</u>. Vancouver, B.C., Canada: Blue Poppy Press, 1988.

Grimmett, Charlene. <u>Beat the Yeast Cookbook</u>. Aurora, IL: By the author, 1985. *(Charlene Grimmett, PO Box 1971, Aurora, IL 60507)*

Harris, Gardiner. "Low Stomach Acidity," <u>Medical Nutrition</u> (Spring 1989): 39-40.

Hayes, Stephanie, R.D. and Barbara Maynard, R.D. <u>Rotational Bon Appetite!</u> Dallas, TX: WJR and Associates, P.A. dba Environmental Health Center-Dallas, 1986. *(Environmental Health Center–Dallas, 8345 Walnut Hill Lane, Suite 205, Dallas, TX 75231)*

Hidaka, H., T. Eida, T. Takizawa, T. Tokunaga, and Y. Tahiro. "Effects of Fructooligosaccharides on Intestinal Flora and Human Health," <u>Bifidobacteria</u> <u>Microflora</u>, 5, no. 1 (1986): 37-50. Abstract. *(Copy available from Canary Connect, see Appendix G.)*

"A History of Buckwheat." Pamphlet from Birkett Mills, PO Box 440A, Penn Yan, NY 14527.

Hoff, Dena. "Why Organic?" Information sheet from Blooming Prairie Warehouse, 2340 Heinz Road, Iowa City, IA 52240.

"Honey: From Nature's Food Industry." Information packet from the National Honey Board, 421 21st Avenue, Suite #203, Longmont, CO 80501.

Hosoya, N., D. Dhorranintra, and H. Hidaka. "Utilization of [U-^{14}C] Fructooligosaccharides in Man as Energy Resources," <u>Journal of Clinical Biochemical Nutrition</u>, 5 (1988): 67-74. Abstract. *(Copy available from Canary Connect, see Appendix G.)*

"I Just Don't Have Time for Stress!" Perpetual calendar. Marshalltown, IA: Thoughtful Books Sta-Kris, Inc., 1991. *(Thoughtful Books Sta-Kris, Inc., PO Box 1131, Marshalltown, IA 50158)*

"IOFS: Iowans for Organic Food Standards." Pamphlet from Iowans for Organic Food Standards, PO Box 2935, Iowa City, IA 52244-2935.

Johnston, Ingeborg M., C.N., and James R. Johnston, Ph.D. <u>Flaxseed (Linseed) Oil and the Power of Omega-3: How to Make Nature's Cholesterol Fighters Work for You</u>. New Canaan, CT: A Good Health Guide, Keats Publishing, Inc., 1990. *(Keats Publishing, Inc., 27 Pine Street [Box 876], New Canaan, CT 06840)*

Jones, Marjorie Hurt, R.N. <u>The Allergy Self-Help Cookbook</u>. Emmaus, PA: Rodale Press, 1984. *(Available from MAST Enterprises, Inc., 2615 N. Fourth Street #616, Coeur d'Alene, ID 83814.)*

_____. "Balance in Your Diet: Tough But Possible," <u>Mastering Food Allergies</u>, V, no. 9, issue #49 (October 1990): 1. *(See <u>MFA Collection</u> address in Appendix D, Newsletter section.)*

_____. "Bean Cookery," <u>Mastering Food Allergies</u>, IV, no. 3, issue #33 (March 1989): 1.

_____. "Between Us: Leavening Agents," <u>Mastering Food Allergies</u>, VII, no. 2, issue #62 (February 1992): 5.

_____. "Buckwheat Basics: Rediscovering an Old Treasure," <u>Mastering Food Allergies</u>, VIII, no. 2, issue #72 (March-April 1993): 1.

_____. *"Candida—A Different Approach,"* <u>Mastering Food Allergies</u>, IV, no. 7, issue #37 (July-August 1989): 3.

_____. "FOS—A 'Good for You' Sweetener," <u>Mastering Food Allergies</u>, VII, no. 10, issue #70 (November 1992): 1.

_____. "Kamut®—Another Ancient Grain," <u>Mastering Food Allergies</u>, VII, no. 1, issue #61 (December-January 1992): 1.

_____. "Leaky Gut: A Common Problem with Food Allergies," <u>Mastering Food Allergies</u>, VIII, no. 5, issue #75 (September-October, 1993): 1.

_____ "Leaky Gut—What Is It?," Mastering Food Allergies, X, no. 4, issue #86 (July-August 1995): 7.

_____. "New Foods and How to Use Them," <u>The Human Ecologist</u>, no. 52 (Winter 1991): 1. *(<u>The Human Ecologist</u>, PO Box 49126, Atlanta, GA 30359-1126)*

_____. "Spelt, Wonderful Spelt," <u>Mastering Food Allergies</u>, V, no. 7, issue #47 (July-August 1990): 1.

_____. "Superfood #5: Spelt," <u>Mastering Food Allergies</u>, V, no. 3, issue #43 (March 1990): 1.

_____. <u>Super Foods</u>. Coeur d'Alene, ID: Mast Enterprises, Inc., 1990. *(Mast Enterprises, Inc., 2615 N. Fourth Street #616, Coeur d'Alene, ID 83814)*

Jordan, C.L., M.D. and Associates. "The Total Person: The Concept of Health-Chiropractic," <u>Allergy Connections</u>, 1, no. 4 (Winter 1992): 1. *(<u>Allergy Connections</u>, PO Box 154, Pewaukee, WI 53072)*

Kamen, Betty, Ph.D. "FOS: A Healthful Sweetener (No Kidding!)," <u>Let's Live Magazine</u>, 60, no. 10 (October 1992): 32-34. *(<u>Let's Live Magazine</u>, PO Box 74908, Los Angeles, CA 90004)*

<u>Kamut®'s Effectiveness for People with Wheat Allergies Scientifically Confirmed</u>. Press release from the Kamut® Association of America, 295 Distribution Street, San Marcos, CA 92069 (November 15, 1991).

Lee, William H., R.Ph., Ph.D. <u>The Friendly Bacteria</u>. New Canaan, CT: A Good Health Guide, Keats Publishing, Inc., 1988. *(Keats Publishing, Inc., 27 Pine Street [Box 876], New Canaan, CT 06840)*

Levin, Alan Scott, M.D. and Merla Zellerbach. <u>The Type 1/Type 2 Allergy Relief Program</u>. Los Angeles, CA: Jeremy P. Tarcher, Inc., 1983.

Mandell, Marshall, Ph.D. and Lynne Waller Scanlon. <u>5-Day Allergy Relief System</u>. New York, NY: Pocket Books, a Division of Simon and Schuster, Inc., 1979.

"Manitok Wild Rice," <u>Blooming Prairie Price Guide Supplement and Prairie News</u>, 2340 Heinz Road, Iowa City, IA 52240 (November-December 1991): 70.

McCormick, Angela. "How to Start a Food Buying Club," <u>Allergy Connections</u>, 1, no. 3 (Fall 1991): 9. *(<u>Allergy Connections</u>, PO Box 154, Pewaukee, WI 53072)*

McKellar, R.C. and H.W. Modler. "Metabolism of Fructooligosaccharides by *Bifidobacterium sp.*," <u>Applied Microbiology Biotechnology</u>, 31 (1989): 537-541. Abstract. *(Copy available from Canary Connect, see Appendix G.)*

Meehan, Beth Ann. "Linus Pauling's Rehab," <u>Discover Magazine</u>, 14, no. I (January 1993): 54.

Mitsuoka, T. *"Bifidobacteria* and Their Role in Human Health," <u>Journal of Industrial Microbiology</u>, 6 (1990): 263-268. *(Copy available from Canary Connect, see Appendix G.)*

_____. "Effects of Long-term Intake of Neosugar (Fructooligosaccharides) on Intestinal Flora and Serum Lipids," <u>Proceedings of the 3rd Neosugar Conference</u>, Tokyo (1986). Abstract. *(Copy available from Canary Connect, see Appendix G.)*

_____, H. Hidaka, and T. Eida. "Effect of Fructooligosaccharides on Intestinal Microflora," <u>Die Nahrung</u>, 31, no. 5-6 (1987): 427-436. Abstract. *(Copy available from Canary Connect, see Appendix G.)*

Modler, H.W., R.C. McKellar, and M. Yaguchi. *"Bifidobacteria* and *Bifidogenic* Factors," <u>Journal of Canadian Institute of Food Science and Technology</u>, 21, no. 1 (1990): 29-41. *(Copy available from Canary Connect, see Appendix G.)*

Morse, Roger A., Ph.D. "Honey Fact Sheets." Information sheets from the National Honey Board, 420 21st Avenue, Suite #203, Longmont, CO 80501.

The New Encyclopaedia Britannica, 1990 ed. S.v. "Arrowroot," 1: 589.

The New Encyclopaedia Britannica, 1990 ed. S.v. "Tapioca," 11: 554.

The 1996 National Organic Directory: A Guide to Organic Information and Resources. Davis, CA: CAFF, 1996: 147–158. *(Community Alliance with Family Farmers, PO Box 464, Davis, CA 95617)*

"Nutritional Analysis of Kamut® Brand Grain." Information sheet from the Kamut® Association of North America, 295 Distribution Street, San Marco, CA 92069 (September, 1992).

Oku, T, T. Tokunaga, and N. Hosoya. "Nondigestibility of a New Sweetener, 'Neosugar', in the Rat," Journal of Nutrition, 114 (1984): 1574-1581. Abstract. *(Copy available from Canary Connect, see Appendix G.)*

"Organically Grown Food: Answers to Some Common Questions." Pamphlet from Organic Farms, Inc., 10714 Hanna Street, Beltsville, MD 20705.

"Organically Grown Wild Rice." Pamphlet from Manitok Wild Rice, PO Box 97, Callaway, MN 56521.

Perna, Peter J., Ph.D., Manager. "Fructooligosaccharides (FOS): An All Natural Food which Promotes *Bifidobacteria* and *Lactobacillus*." Broomfield, CO: Center for Applied Nutrition, ZeaGen, Inc., 530 Interlocken Boulevard, 80021. (Available from Canary Connect, see Appendix G.)

Phillips, Sheila. "Natural Foods Primer: Grains." Information sheet from Blooming Prairie Warehouse, 2340 Heinz Road, Iowa City, IA 52240.

_____. "Oils." Information sheet from Blooming Prairie Warehouse, 2340 Heinz Road, Iowa City, IA 52240.

_____. "Sweeteners." Information sheet from Blooming Prairie Warehouse, 2340 Heinz Road, Iowa City, IA 52240.

Pomeranz, Yeshajahu and George S. Robbins. "Amino Acid Composition of Buckwheat," Agricultural and Food Chemistry, 20, no. 2 (March/April 1972): 270. *(Available from The National Buckwheat Institute, PO Box 440, Penn Yan, NY 14527.)*

"Purity Farms Clarified Butter." Pamphlet from Purity Farms, Inc., 14635 Westcreek Road, Sedalia, CO 80135.

Randolph, Theron G., M.D. and Ralph W. Moss, Ph.D. An Alternative Approach to Allergies. New York, NY: Bantam Books, Inc., 1980.

Rinkel, Herbert John, Theron G. Randolph, and Michael Zeller. Food Allergy. Springfield, IL: Thomas, 1951.

Rockwell, Sally, Nutritionist. Coping with *Candida* Cookbook (Revised). Seattle, WA: By the author, 1986. *(Sally J. Rockwell, PO Box 31065, Seattle, WA 98103)*

Rogers, Sherry A., M.D. The E.I. Syndrome. Syracuse, NY: Prestige Publishers, 1986. *(Prestige Publishers, Box 3161, 3502 Brewerton Road, Syracuse, NY 13220)*

Saltzman, Joanne. Amazing Grains. Tiburon, CA: H.J. Kramer, Inc., 1990. *(H.J. Kramer, Inc., PO Box 1082, Tiburon, CA 94920)*

Sano, T. "Effect of Neosugar (Fructooligosaccharides) on Constipation, Intestinal Microflora and Gallbladder Contraction in Diabetics," Proceedings of the 3rd Neosugar Conference, Tokyo (1986). Abstract. *(Copy available from Canary Connect, see Appendix G.)*

Santillo, Humbart. Food Enzymes: The Missing Link to Radiant Health. Prescott, AZ: Hohm Press, 1993.

Semon, Bruce, M.D., Ph.D. "Understanding the Yeast Problem," Allergy Connections, 1, no. 4 (Winter 1992): 8. *(Allergy Connections, PO Box 154, Pewaukee, WI 53072)*

"Sidestepping Food Sensitivities." Informational brochure distributed by Good Earth Restaurants, Corporate Office, 3001 Hennepin Avenue South, Suite 301-A, Minneapolis, MN 55408-2647 [(612) 822-0016].

Skerritt, J.H. "Molecular Comparison of Alcohol-Soluble Wheat and Buckwheat Proteins," Cereal Chemistry, 63, no. 4: 365-369. *(Available from The National Buckwheat Institute, PO Box 440, Penn Yan, NY 14527.)*

Spiegel, J.E., R. Rose, P. Karabell, V.H. Frankos, and D.F. Schmitt. "Safety and Benefits of Fructooligosaccharides as Food Ingredients," Food Technology (January 1994): 85-89. *(Copy available from Canary Connect, see Appendix G.)*

Springer, Jerry. <u>Allergies - Making Kids Crazy</u>. Interview with Doris Rapp, M.D. Air Date: December 17, 1992. 45 min., Multimedia Entertainment, Inc., 1994. Videocassette. *(Available from Video Archives, Inc., 41 Paoli Plaza #3D, Paoli, PA 19301.)*

"Stevia Rebaudiana." Information sheet from Allergy Resources, Inc., PO Box 444, Guffey, CO 80820.

Strehlow, Wighard, M.D. <u>The Wonder Food Spelt</u>. Konstanz, Germany: By the author, 1989. *(Available from Purity Foods, Inc., 2871 W. Jolly Road, Okemos, MI 48864.)*

Takahashi, Y. "Effects of Neosugar (Fructooligosaccharides) in the Chronic Renal-Failure Patient," <u>Proceedings of the 3rd Neosugar Conference</u>, Tokyo (1986). Abstract. *(Copy available from Canary Connect, see App. G.)*

"Thickeners and Binders for Non-Gluten Recipes." Information sheet from FoodCare, Inc., PO Box 40, Seymour, IL 61875. *(FoodCare is no longer in business.)*

Tokunaga, T, T. Oku, and N. Hosoya. "Utilization and Excretion of a New Sweetener, Fructooligosaccharides (Neosugar), in Rats," <u>Journal of Nutrition</u>, 119 (1989): 553-559. Abstract. *(Copy available from Canary Connect, see Appendix G.)*

Truss, C. Orian, M.D. <u>The Missing Diagnosis</u>. Birmingham, AL: By the author, 1982. *(The Missing Diagnosis, PO Box 26508, Birmingham, AL 35226)*

U.S. Department of Agriculture. <u>Food Guide Pyramid: A Guide to Daily Food Choices</u>. Washington, DC: Government Printing Office, 1992. (Provided by the Iowa State University Extension Service.)

Waters, Jim. "Why Organic Agriculture?" Information sheet from Blooming Prairie Warehouse, 2340 Heinz Road, Iowa City, IA 52240.

<u>Webster's New Universal Unabridged Dictionary</u>. Deluxe Second Edition. New York, NY: Simon and Schuster, 1983.

"What Is a Coop Food Buying Club?," <u>An Organizers' Manual for Cooperative Food Buying Clubs</u>. Iowa City, IA: Central States Cooperative: 2. *(Central States Cooperative, 2340 Heinz Road, Iowa City, IA 52240)*

Williams, C.H., S.W. Witherly, and R.K. Buddington. "Influence of Dietary Neosugar on Selected Bacterial Groups of the Human Faecal Flora," <u>Microbial Ecology in Health and Disease</u>, 7 (1994): (accepted for publication). *(Copy available from Canary Connect, see Appendix G.)*

Wood, Rebecca. "The Incredible 'New' Wheat," <u>Men's Fitness</u>, 5 (November 1989).

Yamashita, K., K. Kawai, and M. Itakura. "Effects of Fructo-oligosaccharides on Blood Glucose and Serum Lipids in Diabetic Subjects," <u>Nutrition Research</u>, 4 (1984): 961-966.9. *(Copy available from Canary Connect, see Appendix G.)*

Yunginger, John W., M.D. "Food Ingredient Labeling: How Many Ways Can Wheat Be Spelt?" <u>Allergy Proceedings</u>, 15, no. 4 (July-August 1994): 219-220.

APPENDIX A
FOOD FAMILIES

Foods are grouped into botanical families based on biological origin. Each food family is assigned an identification name and number. List 1 provides an alphabetical listing of individual foods with their assigned number. List 2 gives the foods divided into numerical groupings called food families. These lists are used to construct a Rotary Diversified Diet. List 2 is especially helpful in enabling the reader to avoid eating foods from the same family group in a repetitive way. The lists also include nonedible plants because persons allergic to a weed or plant may need to avoid foods in the same family. For more information on using these lists to construct a Rotary Diversified Diet or revise the diet contained in this cookbook, see Chapter 4—Rotational Diet.

These lists were compiled from various sources, which include the following books. (See bibliography for compete listing.)

Coping with Your Allergies by Golos and Golbitz
An Alternative Approach to Allergies by Randolph and Moss
Rotational Bon Appetite! by Hayes and Maynard
If This Is Tuesday, It Must Be Chicken by Golos and Golbitz

List 1: Food Families (Alphabetical)

A

81	abalone
80	absinthe
41	acacia (gum)
46	acerola
79	acorn squash
41	adzuki beans
1	agar agar
12	agave
98	albacore
41	alfalfa
1	Algae Family
63	allspice
40b	almond
11	*Aloe vera*
54	althea root
30	amaranth
12	Amaryllis Family
94	amberjack
86	American eel
64	American Ginseng
68	American persimmon
117	Amphibians
41	anasazi beans
85	anchovy
85	Anchovy Family
65	angelica
65	anise
38	annatto
136	antelope
40a	apple

73	apple mint
40b	apricot
47	arrowroot, Brazilian (tapioca)
9	arrowroot (*Colocasia*)
17	arrowroot, East Indian (*Curcuma*)
19	Arrowroot Family
13	arrowroot, Fiji (*Tacca*)
4	arrowroot, Florida (*Zamia*)
19	arrowroot (*Maranta* starch)
16	arrowroot (*Musa*)
18	arrowroot, Queensland
80	artichoke flour
80	artichoke, globe
80	artichoke, Jerusalem
9	Arum Family
11	asparagus
2	*Aspergillus*
34	avocado

B

134	bacon
2	baker's yeast
6	bamboo shoots
16	banana
16	Banana Family
46	Barbados cherry
6	barley
73	basil
114	bass (black)
113	Bass Family

113	bass (yellow)
53	basswood
34	bay leaf
41	beans
132	bear
132	Bear Family
66	bearberry
24	Beech Family
137	beef
137	beef by-products
28	beet
74	bell pepper
73	bergamot
23	Birch Family
121	Birds
38	Bixa Family
114	black bass
41	black-eyed peas
21	black pepper
40c	black raspberry
80	black salsify
41	black turtle beans
22	black walnut
40c	blackberry
66	blueberry
93	bluefish
93	Bluefish Family
36	bok choy
80	boneset
98	bonito
79	Boston marrow

71	borage	47 cassava	73 clary
71 Borage Family	34 cassia bark	63 clove
40c boysenberry	47 castor bean	41 clover
137 Bovine Family	47 castor oil	81 cockle
6 bran	112 Catfish Family	55 cocoa
52 brandy	88 catfish (ocean)	55 cocoa butter
47 Brazilian arrowroot	112 catfish species	8 coconut
62 Brazil nut	73 catnip	8 coconut meal
25 breadfruit	36 cauliflower	8 coconut oil
2 brewer's yeast	104 caviar	79 cocozelle
36 broccoli	74 cayenne (red) pepper	87 cod (scrod)
36 Brussels sprouts	65 celeriac	87 Codfish Family
27 buckwheat	65 celery	76 coffee
27 Buckwheat Family	65 celery leaf	55 cola nut
137 buffalo (bison)	65 celery seed	36 collards
6 bulgur	80 celtuce	80 coltsfoot
80 burdock root	81 Cephalopod	36 colza shoots
40d burnet	9 ceriman	71 comfrey
137 butter	80 chamomile	80 Composite Family
31 Buttercup Family	52 champagne	5 Conifer Family
79 buttercup squash	28 chard	65 coriander (cilantro)
101 butterfish	79 chayote	6 corn
22 butternut	137 cheese, goat	124 cornish hen
79 butternut squash	137 cheese, milk	6 corn meal

C

	40b cherry	6 corn oil
	65 chervil	6 corn products
36 cabbage	24 chestnut	78 corn salad
55 cacao	73 chia seed	6 cornstarch
60 Cactus Family	124 chicken	6 corn sugar
6 cane sugar	41 chickpea	6 corn syrup
18 Canna Family	67 chicle	80 costmary
36 canola oil	80 chicory	54 cottonseed oil
79 cantaloupe	80 chicory, witloof	41 coumarin
37 caper	74 chili pepper	36 couve tronchuda
37 Caper Family	36 Chinese cabbage (bok choy)	41 cowpea
74 *Capsicum*	64 Chinese Ginseng	82 crab
42 carambola	56 Chinese gooseberry	40a crabapple
65 caraway seed	14 Chinese potato (yam)	66 cranberry
17 cardamon	79 Chinese preserving melon	114 crappie
80 cardoon	7 Chinese water chestnut	82 crayfish
135 caribou	24 chinquapin	52 cream of tartar
41 carob	11 chives	79 Crenshaw melon
41 carob syrup	55 chocolate	96 croaker
111 carp	111 chub	96 Croaker Family
29 Carpetweed Family	7 chufa	79 crookneck squash
1 carageen	40b cider	82 Crustaceans
65 carrot	65 cilantro (coriander)	79 cucumber
65 Carrot Family	34 cinnamon	65 cumin
65 carrot syrup	2 citric acid	36 curly cress
79 casaba melon	45 citron	39 currant
79 caserta squash	6 citronella	79 cushaw squash
48 cashew	45 Citrus Family (Rue)	87 cusk
48 Cashew Family	81 clam	32 custard-apple

41	kidney bean
56	kiwi berry
36	kohlrabi
41	kudzu
45	kumquat
41	kuzu

L

137	lactose
137	lamb
28	lamb's-quarters
134	lard
34	Laurel Family
73	lavender
41	lecithin
11	leek
41	Legume Family
45	lemon
73	lemon balm
6	lemon grass
72	lemon verbena
41	lentil
80	lettuce
41	licorice
11	Lily Family
41	lima bean
45	lime
53	linden
44	linseed
53	Linden Family
51	litchi
82	lobster
40c	loganberry
40c	longberry
79	loofah
40a	loquat
65	lovage
79	*Luffa*
51	lychee

M

26	macadamia
33	mace
98	mackerel
98	Mackerel Family
76	Madder Family
9	malanga
54	Mallow Family
46	Malpighia Family
6	malt
6	maltose
127	Mammals
48	mango
50	Maple Family

50	maple products
50	maple sugar
50	maple syrup
19	*Maranta* starch
73	marjoram
99	marlin
99	Marlin Family
49	maté
74	melon pear
84	menhaden
12	mescal
137	milk, cow's
137	milk, goat's
6	millet
111	Minnow Family
73	Mint Family
6	molasses
2	mold
81	Mollusks
135	moose
2	morel
70	Morning-Glory Family
25	mulberry
25	Mulberry Family
89	mullet
89	Mullet Family
41	mung bean
45	murcot
52	muscadine
2	mushroom
109	muskellunge
79	muskmelon
81	mussel
36	Mustard Family
36	mustard greens
36	mustard seed
137	mutton
63	Myrtle Family

N

14	ñame
43	nasturtium
43	Nasturtium Family
41	navy bean
40b	nectarine
29	New Zealand spinach
74	Nightshade Family
41	northern beans
97	northern scup
33	nutmeg
33	Nutmeg Family
2	nutritional yeast

O

6	oat
6	oatmeal
88	ocean catfish
102	ocean perch
23	oil of birch
54	okra
137	oleomargarine
69	olive
69	Olive Family
69	olive oil
11	onion
128	opossum
128	Opossum Family
45	orange
20	Orchid Family
73	oregano
15	orris root
42	oxalis
42	Oxalis Family
81	oyster
80	oyster plant

P

8	palm cabbage
8	Palm Family
59	papaya
59	Papaya Family
74	paprika
62	paradise nut
65	parsley
65	parsnip
123	partridge
58	Passion Flower Family
58	passion fruit
6	patent flour
79	pattypan squash
32	pawpaw
41	pea
40b	peach
124	peafowl
41	peanut
41	peanut oil
40a	pear
22	pecan
40a	pectin
75	Pedalium Family
81	Pelecypods
73	pennyroyal
74	pepino
74	pepper, sweet, all colors
21	peppercorn
21	Pepper Family

73 peppermint
115 Perch Family
102 perch (ocean)
113 perch (white)
115 perch (yellow)
79 Persian melon
68 persimmon
124 pheasant
124 Pheasant Family
109 pickerel
122 pigeon (squab)
30 pigweed
109 pike
109 Pike Family
84 pilchard (sardine)
63 *Pimenta*
74 pimiento
10 pineapple
10 Pineapple Family
5 pine nut
41 pinto beans
21 *Piper*
48 pistachio
103 plaice
16 plantain
40b plum
9 poi
48 poison ivy
48 poison oak
48 poison sumac
87 pollack
61 pomegranate
61 Pomegranate Family
94 pompano
6 popcorn
35 Poppy Family
35 poppyseed
97 porgy
134 pork
134 pork gelatin
74 potato
74 Potato Family
82 prawn
79 preserving melon
60 prickly pear
136 Pronghorn Family
26 Protea Family
40b prune
2 puffball
12 pulque
45 pummelo
79 pumpkin
79 pumpkin meal

79 pumpkin seed
114 pumpkinseed (sunfish)
40c purple raspberry
30 purslane
30 Purslane Family
80 pyrethrum

Q

124 quail
18 Queensland arrowroot
26 Queensland nut
40a quince
28 quinoa

R

129 rabbit
36 radish
52 raisin
11 ramp
36 rape
40c raspberry, all colors
119 rattlesnake
6 raw sugar
41 red clover
40c red raspberry
135 reindeer
137 rennin (rennet)
118 Reptiles
27 rhubarb
6 rice
6 rice bran
6 rice flour
137 Rocky Mountain sheep
105 roe
80 romaine
40 Rose Family
102 rosefish
40a rosehips
54 roselle
73 rosemary
45 Rue Family
123 ruffed grouse
36 rutabaga
6 rye

S

80 safflower oil
15 saffron
73 sage
8 sago starch
99 sailfish
106 Salmon Family
106 salmon species
80 salsify

80 santolina
67 Sapodilla Family
62 Sapucaya Family
62 sapucaya nut
84 sardine
11 sarsaparilla
34 sassafras
115 sauger (perch)
137 sausage casings (beef)
134 sausage (pork)
73 savory
39 Saxifrage Family
81 scallop
80 scolymus
102 Scorpionfish Family
80 scorzonera
134 scrapple (pork)
91 sea bass
91 Sea Bass Family
88 Sea Catfish Family
27 sea grape
84 sea herring
96 sea trout
1 seaweed
7 Sedge Family
41 senna
75 sesame
75 sesame oil
105 shad
11 shallot
3 shavegrass
137 sheep
82 shrimp
96 silver perch
90 silverside
90 Silverside Family
98 skipjack
40b sloe
108 smelt
108 Smelt Family
81 snail
119 Snake Family
51 Soapberry Family
11 soap plant
103 sole
6 sorghum
27 sorrel
80 southernwood
41 soybean
41 soy products
79 spaghetti, vegetable
80 Spanish oyster plant
73 spearmint

28	spinach
29	spinach, New Zealand
6	spelt
96	spot
96	spotted sea trout
137	spray dried milk
47	Spurge Family
79	squash
81	squid
130	squirrel
130	Squirrel Family
55	Sterculia Family
80	stevia
79	straightneck squash
40c	strawberry
41	string bean
104	sturgeon
104	Sturgeon Family
110	sucker
110	Sucker Family
137	suet
28	sugar beet
6	sugar cane
6	sugar, raw
73	summer savory
114	sunfish
114	Sunfish Family
80	sunflower meal
80	sunflower oil
80	sunflower seed
80	sunflower seed products
36	swede
65	sweet cicely
6	sweet corn
74	sweet pepper
70	sweet potato
134	Swine Family
100	swordfish
100	Swordfish Family
6	syrup, sorghum

T

13	Tacca Family
75	tahini
41	tamarind
28	tampala
45	tangelo
45	tangerine
80	tansy
47	tapioca
9	taro
80	tarragon
57	tea

57	Tea Family
6	teff
41	tempeh
12	tequila
120	terrapin
73	thyme
92	tilefish
92	Tilefish Family
74	tobacco
41	tofu
74	tomatillo
74	tomato
41	tonka bean
74	tree tomato
6	triticale
106	trout species
2	truffle
98	tuna
79	turban squash
103	turbot
126	turkey
126	turkey eggs
126	Turkey Family
17	turmeric
36	turnip
120	Turtle Family
120	turtle species

U

36	upland cress

V

78	Valerian Family
20	vanilla
137	veal
79	vegetable spaghetti
79	vegetable sponge
135	venison
72	Verbena Family
40a	vinegar

W

115	walleye
22	Walnut Family
36	watercress

79	watermelon
96	weakfish
131	whale
131	Whale Family
6	wheat
6	wheat flour
6	wheat germ
90	whitebait
107	whitefish
107	Whitefish Family
21	white pepper
113	white perch
6	whole wheat
6	wild rice
52	wine
40c	wineberry
52	wine vinegar
23	wintergreen
73	winter savory
80	witloof chicory
76	woodruff
80	wormwood

X

23	xylitol

Y

14	yam
14	Yam Family
14	yampi
80	yarrow
9	yautia
2	yeast, brewer's or nutritional
113	yellow bass
94	yellow jack
115	yellow perch
49	yerba maté
137	yogurt
40c	youngberry
47	yuca
11	yucca

Z

4	*Zamia*
79	zucchini

List 2: Food Families (Numerical)

Plant

1 **Algae**
agar-agar
carrageen (Irish moss)
dulse*
kelp (seaweed)

2 **Fungi**
baker's yeast ("Red Star")
brewer's or nutritional yeast
mold (in certain cheeses)
citric acid (*Aspergillus*)
morel
mushroom
puffball
truffle

3 **Horsetail Family,**
Equisetaceae
shavegrass (horsetail)*

4 **Cycad Family,** *Cycadaceae*
Florida arrowroot (*Zamia*)

5 **Conifer Family,** *Coniferae*
juniper (gin)*
pine nut (piñon, pinyon)

6 **Grass Family,** *Gramineae*
barley
malt
maltose
bamboo shoots
corn (mature)
corn meal
corn oil
cornstarch
corn sugar
corn syrup
hominy
hominy grits
popcorn
Job's tears
Kamut
lemon grass
citronella
millet
oat
oat bran
oatmeal
rice
rice bran
rice flour
rye

sorghum grain
syrup
spelt
sugar cane
cane sugar
molasses
raw sugar
sweet corn
teff
triticale
wheat
bran
bulgur
flour
gluten
graham
patent
whole wheat
wheat germ
wild rice

7 **Sedge Family,** *Cyperaceae*
Chinese water chestnut
chufa (groundnut)

8 **Palm Family,** *Palmaceae*
coconut
coconut meal
coconut oil
date
date sugar
palm cabbage
sago starch (*Metroxylon*)

9 **Arum Family,** *Araceae*
ceriman (*Monstera*)
dasheen (*Colocasia*)
arrowroot
taro (*Colocasia*)
arrowroot
poi
malanga (*Xanthosoma*)
yautia (*Xanthosoma*)

10 **Pineapple Family,**
Bromeliaceae
pineapple

11 **Lily Family,** *Liliaceae*
Aloe vera
asparagus
chives
garlic
leek

onion
ramp
sarsaparilla*
shallot
yucca (soap plant)

12 **Amaryllis Family,**
Amaryllidaceae
agave
mescal, pulque, and
tequila

13 **Tacca Family,** *Taccaceae*
Fiji arrowroot (*Tacca*)

14 **Yam Family,** *Dioscoreaceae*
Chinese potato (yam)
ñame (yampi)

15 **Iris Family,** *Iridaceae*
orris root (scent)
saffron (*Crocus*)

16 **Banana Family,** *Musaceae*
arrowroot (*Musa*)
banana
plantain

17 **Ginger Family,**
Zingiberaceae
cardamon
East Indian arrowroot,
(*Curcuma*)
ginger
tumeric

18 **Canna Family,** *Cannaceae*
Queensland arrowroot

19 **Arrowroot Family,**
Marantaceae
arrowroot (*Maranta* starch)

20 **Orchid Family,** *Orchidaceae*
vanilla

21 **Pepper Family,** *Piperaceae*
peppercorn (*Piper*)
black pepper
white pepper

22 **Walnut Family,**
Juglandaceae
black walnut
butternut
English walnut
heartnut
hickory nut
pecan

*One or more plant parts (leaf, root, seed, etc.) used as a beverage.

23 **Birch Family,** *Betulaceae*
   filbert (hazelnut)
   oil of birch (wintergreen)
      (some wintergreen flavor is
      methyl salicylate)
   xylitol
24 **Beech Family,** *Fagaceae*
   chestnut
   chinquapin
25 **Mulberry Family,** *Moraceae*
   breadfruit
   fig
   hop*
   mulberry
26 **Protea Family,** *Proteaceae*
   macadamia (Queensland nut)
27 **Buckwheat Family,**
   Polygonaceae
   buckwheat
   garden sorrel
   rhubarb
   sea grape
28 **Goosefoot Family,**
   Cheopodiaceae
   beet
   chard
   lamb's-quarters
   quinoa
   spinach
   sugar beet
   tampala
29 **Carpetweed Family,**
   Aizoaceae
   New Zealand spinach
30 **Purslane Family,**
   Portulacaceae
   amaranth
   pigweed (purslane)
31 **Buttercup Family,**
   Ranunculaceae
   golden seal*
32 **Custard-Apple Family,**
   Annona species
   custard-apple
   papaw (pawpaw)
33 **Nutmeg Family,**
   Myristicacae
   nutmeg
      mace

34 **Laurel Family,** *Lauraceae*
   avocado
   bay leaf
   cassia bark
   cinnamon
   sassafras*
      filé (powdered leaves)
35 **Poppy Family,**
   Papaveraceae
   poppyseed
36 **Mustard Family,** *Cruciferae*
   broccoli
   Brussels sprouts
   cabbage
   cauliflower
   Chinese cabbage (bok choy)
   collards
   colza shoots
   couve tronchuda
   curly cress
   horseradish
   kale
   kohlrabi
   mustard greens
   mustard seed
   radish
   rape
   canola oil
   rutabaga (swede)
   turnip and turnip greens
   upland cress
   watercress
37 **Caper Family,**
   Capparidaceae
   caper
38 **Bixa Family,** *Bixaceae*
   annatto (natural yellow dye)
39 **Saxifrage Family,**
   Saxifragaceae
   currant
   gooseberry
40 **Rose Family,** *Rosaceae*
   a. pomes
      apple
         cider
         vinegar
         pectin
      crabapple
      loquat
      pear
      quince
      rosehips*

   b. *stone fruits*
      almond
      apricot
      cherry
      peach (nectarine)
      plum (prune)
      sloe
   c. *berries*
      blackberry
         boysenberry
         dewberry
         loganberry
         longberry
         youngberry
      raspberry (leaf)*
         black raspberry
         red raspberry
         purple raspberry
         wineberry
      strawberry (leaf)*
   d. herb
      burnet (cucumber flavor)
41 **Legume Family,**
   Leguminoseae
   alfalfa (sprouts)*
   beans
      adzuki
      anasazi
      black turtle
      fava
      lima
      mung (sprouts)
      navy
      northern
      pinto
      string (kidney)
   black-eyed pea (cowpea)
   carob*
      carob syrup
   chickpea (garbanzo)
   cloves
   fenugreek*
   garbanzo (chickpea)
   guar gum
   gum acacia
   gum tragacanth
   jicama
   kudzu (kuzu)
   lentil
   licorice*
   pea

*One or more plant parts (leaf, root, seed, etc.) used as a beverage.

peanut
  peanut oil
red clover*
senna*
soybean
  lecithin
  soy flour
  soy grits
  soy milk
  soy oil
  tempeh
  tofu
tamarind
tonka bean
coumarin

42 Oxalis Family, *Oxalidaceae*
carambola
oxalis

43 Nasturtium Family, *Tropaeolaceae*
nasturtium

44 Flax Family, *Linacaea*
flaxseed*
linseed oil

45 Rue (Citrus) Family, *Rutaceae*
citron
grapefruit
kumquat
lemon
lime
murcot
orange
pummelo
tangelo
tangerine

46 Malpighia Family, *Malpighiaceae*
acerola (Barbados cherry)

47 Spurge Family, *Euphorbiaceae*
cassava or yuca (*Manihot*)
  cassava meal
  tapioca (Brazilian arrowroot)
castor bean
  castor oil

48 Cashew Family, *Anacardiaceae*
cashew
mango
pistachio

poison ivy
poison oak
poison sumac

49 Holly Family, *Aquifoliaceae*
maté (yerba maté)

50 Maple Family
maple sugar
maple syrup

51 Soapberry Family, *Sapindaceae*
litchi (lychee)

52 Grape Family, *Vitaceae*
grape
  brandy
  champagne
  cream of tartar
  dried "currant"
  raisin
  wine
  wine vinegar
  muscadine

53 Linden Family, *Tiliaceae*
basswood (linden)*

54 Mallow Family, *Malvaceae*
althea root*
cottonseed oil
hibiscus (roselle)*
okra

55 Sterculia Family, *Sterculiaceae*
chocolate (cacao)*
cocoa*
  cocoa butter
cola nut

56 Dillenia Family, *Dilleniaceae*
Chinese gooseberry (kiwi berry)

57 Tea Family, *Theaceae*
tea*

58 Passion Flower Family, *Passifloraceae*
granadilla (passion fruit)

59 Papaya Family, *Caricaceae*
papaya

60 Cactus Family, *Cactaceae*
maguey (Aguamiel)
prickly pear

61 Pomegranate Family, *Puniceae*
pomegranate
  grenadine

62 Sapucaya Family, *Lecythidaceae*
Brazil nut
sapucaya nut (paradise nut)

63 Myrtle Family, *Myrtaceae*
allspice (*Pimenta*)
clove
eucalyptus*
guava

64 Ginseng Family, *Araliaceae*
American Ginseng*
Chinese Ginseng*

65 Carrot Family, *Umbelliferae*
angelica
anise
caraway
carrot
  carrot syrup
celeriac (celery root)
celery
  seed & leaf*
chervil
coriander (cilantro)
cumin
dill
  dill seed
fennel*
  finocchio
    Florence fennel
gotu kola*
lovage*
parsley*
parsnip
sweet cecily

66 Heath Family, *Ericaceae*
bearberry*
blueberry*
cranberry
huckleberry*

67 Sapodilla Family, *Sapotaceae*
chicle (chewing gum)

68 Ebony Family, *Ebonaceae*
American persimmon
kaki (Japanese persimmon)

69 Olive Family, *Oleaceae*
olive (green or ripe)
olive oil

70 Morning-Glory Family, *Convolvulacea*
sweet potato

*One or more plant parts (leaf, root, seed, etc.) used as a beverage.

71 Borage Family,
Boraginaceae (Herbs)
  borage
  comfrey (leaf & root)*

72 Verbena Family,
Verbenaceae
  lemon verbena*

73 Mint Family, *Labiatae* (Herbs)
  apple mint
  basil
  bergamot
  catnip*
  chia seed*
  clary
  dittany*
  horehound*
  hyssop*
  lavender
  lemon balm*
  marjoram
  oregano
  pennyroyal*
  peppermint*
  rosemary
  sage
  spearmint*
  summer savory
  thyme
  winter savory

74 Nightshade (Potato) Family,
Solanaceae
  eggplant
  ground cherry
  pepino (melon pear)
  pepper (Capsicum)
    bell, sweet (all colors)
    cayenne (red)
    chili
    paprika
    pimiento
  potato
  tobacco
  tomatillo
  tomato
  tree tomato

75 Pedalium Family,
Pedaliaceae
  sesame seed
    sesame oil
    tahini

76 Madder Family, *Rubiaceae*
  coffee*
  woodruff

77 Honeysuckle Family,
Caprifoliaceae
  elderberry
    elderberry flowers

78 Valerian Family,
Valerianaceae
  corn salad (fetticus)

79 Gourd Family, *Cucurbitaceae*
  chayote
  Chinese preserving melon
  cucumber
  gherkin
  loofah (*Luffa*) (vegetable sponge)
  muskmelons
    cantaloupe
    casaba
    crenshaw
    honeydew
    Persian melon
  pumpkin
    pumpkin seed & meal
  squashes
    acorn
    buttercup
    butternut
    Boston marrow
    caserta
    cocozelle
    crookneck & straightneck
    cushaw
    golden nugget
    Hubbard varieties
    pattypan
    turban
    vegetable spaghetti
    zucchini
  watermelon

80 Composite Family,
Compositae
  absinthe
  boneset*
  burdock root*
  cardoon
  chamomile
  chicory*
  coltsfoot
  costmary

dahlia (Dacopa beverage)
dandelion
endive
escarole
globe artichoke
goldenrod*
Jerusalem artichoke
  artichoke flour
lettuce
  celtuce
pyrethrum
romaine
safflower oil
salsify (oyster plant)
santolina (herb)
scolymus (Spanish oyster plant)
scorzonera
southernwood
stevia (sweet herb)
sunflower
  sunflower seed, meal, and oil
tansy (herb)
tarragon (herb)
witloof chicory (French endive)
wormwood (absinthe)
yarrow*

Animal

81 Mollusks
  Gastropods
    abalone
    snail
  Cephalopod
    squid
  Pelecypods
    clam
    cockle
    mussel
    oyster
    scallop

82 Crustaceans
  crab
  crayfish
  lobster
  prawn
  shrimp

83 Fishes (Saltwater)

84 Herring Family
  menhaden
  pilchard (sardine)
  sea herring

*One or more plant parts (leaf, root, seed, etc.) used as a beverage.

85 Anchovy Family
  anchovy
86 Eel Family
  American eel
87 Codfish Family
  cod (scrod)
  cusk
  haddock
  hake
  pollack
88 Sea Catfish Family
  ocean catfish
89 Mullet Family
  mullet
90 Silverside Family
  silverside (whitebait)
91 Sea Bass Family
  grouper
  sea bass
92 Tilefish Family
  tilefish
93 Bluefish Family
  bluefish
94 Jack Family
  amberjack
  pompano
  yellow jack
95 Dolphin Family
  dolphin
96 Croaker Family
  croaker
  drum
  sea trout
  silver perch
  spot
  weakfish (spotted sea trout)
97 Porgy Family
  northern scup (porgy)
98 Mackerel Family
  albacore
  bonito
  mackerel
  skipjack
  tuna
99 Marlin Family
  marlin
  sailfish
100 Swordfish Family
  swordfish

101 Harvestfish Family
  butterfish
  harvestfish
102 Scorpionfish Family
  rosefish (ocean perch)
103 Flounder Family
  dab
  flounder
  halibut
  plaice
  sole
  turbot

104 *Fishes (freshwater)*
104 Sturgeon Family
  sturgeon (caviar)
105 Herring Family
  shad (roe)
106 Salmon Family
  salmon species
  trout species
107 Whitefish Family
  whitefish
108 Smelt Family
  smelt
109 Pike Family
  muskellunge
  pickerel
  pike
110 Sucker Family
  buffalofish
  sucker
111 Minnow Family
  carp
  chub
112 Catfish Family
  catfish species
113 Bass Family
  white perch
  yellow bass
114 Sunfish Family
  black bass species
  sunfish species
    pumpkinseed
  crappie
115 Perch Family
  sauger
  walleye
  yellow perch
116 Croaker Family
  freshwater drum

117 *Amphibians*
117 Frog Family
  frog (frogs' legs)

118 Reptiles
119 Snake Family
  rattlesnake
120 Turtle Family
  terrapin
  turtle species

121 Birds
121 Duck Family
  duck
    eggs
  goose
    eggs
122 Dove Family
  dove
  pigeon (squab)
123 Grouse Family
  ruffed grouse (partridge)
124 Pheasant Family
  chicken
    eggs
  cornish hen
  peafowl
  pheasant
  quail
125 Guinea Fowl Family
  guinea fowl
    eggs
126 Turkey Family
  turkey
    eggs

127 Mammals
128 Opossum Family
  opossum
129 Hare Family
  rabbit
130 Squirrel Family
  squirrel
131 Whale Family
  whale
132 Bear Family
  bear
133 Horse Family
  horse
134 Swine Family
  hog (pork)
  bacon

ham	**137 Bovine Family**	lactose
lard	beef cattle	spray dried milk
pork gelatin	beef	yogurt
sausage	beef by-products	veal
scrapple	gelatin	buffalo (bison)
135 Deer Family	oleomargarine	goat (kid)
caribou	rennin (rennet)	cheese
deer (venison)	sausage casings	ice cream
elk	suet	milk
moose	milk products	sheep (domestic)
reindeer	butter	lamb
136 Pronghorn Family	cheese	mutton
antelope	ice cream	Rocky Mountain sheep

Appendix B
Candida Questionnaire and Score Sheet*

This questionnaire lists factors in your medical history that promote the growth of *Candida Albicans* and that frequently are found in people with yeast-related health problems (Section A), and symptoms commonly found in individuals with yeast-related health problems (Sections B and C).

For each yes answer in Section A, circle the Point Score in that section. Total your score, and record it in the box at the end of the section. Then move on to Sections B and C, and score as directed.

Section A: History

		Point Score
1.	Have you taken tetracyclines or other antibiotics for acne for 1 month (or longer)?	35
2.	Have you at any time in your life taken "broad spectrum" antibiotics or other antibacterial medication for respiratory, urinary, or other infections for 2 months or longer, or in shorter courses 4 or more times in a 1-year period?	35
3.	Have you taken a broad spectrum antibiotic drug—even in a single dose?	6
4.	Have you, at any time in your life, been bothered by persistent prostatitis, vaginitis, or other problems affecting your reproductive organs?	25
5.	Are you bothered by memory or concentration problems—do you sometimes feel spaced out?	20
6.	Do you feel "sick all over" yet, in spite of visits to many different physicians, the causes haven't been found?	20
7.	Have you been pregnant... 2 or more times?	5
	1 time?	3
8.	Have you taken birth control pills... For more than 2 years?	15
	For 6 months to 2 years?	8
9.	Have you taken steroids orally, by injection or inhalation? For more than 2 weeks?	15
	For 2 weeks or less?	6
	(continued)	

*Filling out and scoring this questionnaire should help you and your physician evaluate the possible role *Candida albicans* contributes to your health problems. Yet it will not provide an automatic yes or no answer. A comprehensive history and physical examination are important.

---

* Adapted from <u>The Yeast Connection Handbook</u> by William G. Crook, M.D., and used with his permission. (Jackson, TN: Professional Books, 1996.)

Section A: History (continued)		Point Score
10.	Does exposure to perfumes, insecticides, fabric shop odors and other chemicals provoke..	
	Moderate to severe symptoms?	20
	Mild symptoms?	5
11.	Does tobacco smoke *really* bother you?	10
12.	Are your symptoms worse on damp, muggy days or in moldy places?	20
13.	Have you had athlete's foot, ring worm, "jock itch," or other chronic fungous infections of the skin or nails? Have such infections been... Severe or persistent?	20
	Mild to moderate?	10
14.	Do you crave sugar?	10
	Total Score, Section A	

Section B: Major Symptoms

For each of your symptoms, enter the appropriate number in the Point Score column:

    If a symptom is **occasional or mild**   3 points

    If a symptom is **frequent and/or moderately severe**   6 points

    If a symptom is **severe and/or disabling**   9 points

Add total score and record it in the box at the end of this section.

		Point Score
1.	Fatigue or lethargy	
2.	Feeling of being "drained"	
3.	Depression or manic depression	
4.	Numbness, burning, or tingling	
5.	Headache	
6.	Muscle aches	
7.	Muscle weakness or paralysis	
8.	Pain and/or swelling in joints	
9.	Abdominal pain	
10.	Constipation and/or diarrhea	
11.	Bloating, belching, or intestinal gas	
12.	Troublesome vaginal burning, itching, or discharge	
13.	Prostatitis	
14.	Impotence	
15.	Loss of sexual desire or feeling	
16.	Endometriosis or infertility	
17.	Cramps and/or other menstrual irregularities	
18.	Premenstrual tension	
19.	Attacks of anxiety or crying	
20.	Cold hands or feet, low body temperature	
21.	Hypothyroidism	
22.	Shaking or irritable when hungry	
23.	Cystitis or interstitial cystitis	
	Total Score, Section B	

Section C: Other Symptoms

For each of your symptoms, enter the appropriate number in the Point Score column:

If a symptom is **occasional or mild**	1 points
If a symptom is **frequent and/or moderately severe**	2 points
If a symptom is **severe and/or disabling**	3 points

Add total score and record it in the box at the end of this section.

Section C—Column 1	Point Score
1. Drowsiness, including inappropriate drowsiness	
2. Irritability	
3. Incoordination	
4. Frequent mood swings	
5. Insomnia	
6. Dizziness/loss of balance	
7. Pressure above ears...feeling of head swelling	
8. Sinus problems...tenderness of cheekbones or forehead	
9. Tendency to bruise easily	
10. Eczema, itching eyes	
11. Psoriasis	
12. Chronic hives (urticaria)	
13. Indigestion or heartburn	
14. Sensitivity to milk, wheat, corn, or other common foods	
15. Mucus in stools	
16. Rectal itching	
17. Dry mouth or throat	
18. Mouth rashes, including "white" tongue	
Continued in Column 2	

Section C—Column 2	Point Score
19. Bad breath	
20. Foot, hair, or body odor not relieved by washing	
21. Nasal congestion or post nasal drip	
22. Nasal itching	
23. Sore throat	
24. Laryngitis, loss of voice	
25. Cough or recurrent bronchitis	
26. Pain or tightness in chest	
27. Wheezing or shortness of breath	
28. Urinary frequency or urgency	
29. Burning on urination	
30. Spots in front of eyes or erratic vision	
31. Burning or tearing of eyes	
32. Recurrent infections or fluid in ears	
33. Ear pain or deafness	

Total Score, Section C	
Total Score, Section A	
Total Score, Section B	

GRAND TOTAL SCORE (Add totals from Sections A, B, and C)	

The Grand Total Score will help you and your physician decide if your health problems are yeast connected. Scores in women will run higher as 7 items in the questionnaire apply exclusively to women, while only 2 apply exclusively to men.

Yeast-connected health problems are almost certainly present in women with scores **more than 180**, and in men with scores **more than 140**.

Yeast-connected health problems are probably present in women with scores **more than 120**, and in men with scores **more than 90**.

Yeast-connected health problems are possibly present in women with scores **more than 60**, and in men with scores **more than 40**.

With scores of less than 60 in women and 40 in men, yeasts are less apt to cause health problems.

APPENDIX C
RESOURCES

This resource appendix is for the reader's information only. At publication date, to the best of our knowledge all of the companies or organizations listed in this appendix are reputable sources for the indicated products and/or services. As an individual, it is your responsibility to ask the appropriate questions to ensure that the products or information you order meet your specific needs. No fee was paid for a listing in this book. When you contact them for information or to place an order, please mention where you learned of their service.

Since products and supplies change rapidly, often more rapidly than catalogs can be changed, mail-order companies may carry products not listed in their catalog. If you cannot locate a product in the catalog, ask the company about its availability if they list similar products. For example, when ordering an assortment of legume flours from Allergy Resources I happened to mention that I could not find garbanzo bean flour. They informed me that it was available but not currently listed in their catalog.

The appendix is divided into six sections.

◆　Section 1: Resources for Food and Non-Food Products
◆　Section 2: Resource Guides
◆　Section 3: Resources for Personalized Assistance for Food Allergy and Rotational Diet Planning
◆　Section 4: Resources for Locating a Physician
◆　Section 5: Resources for *Candida* and Food Allergy Diagnosis and Other Testing
◆　Section 6: Resources for a Personal Support System

If you know of additional mail order sources for the listed products or of resources for the other sections, please forward the name, address, phone, and product information and/or service provided to Canary Connect Publications for inclusion in <u>Canary Connect News</u> newsletter (see Appendix G).

Section 1: Resources for Food and Non-Food Products

This section contains two lists. List A: Products is divided into Food Products and Non-food Products listed in alphabetical order along with the names of nationwide mail-order companies. List B: Addresses gives the name, address, and phone number for the companies mentioned in List A.

List A: Products

<u>Food Products</u>

Adzuki beans, *organic*
　Jaffe Brothers, Inc.
　Gold Mine Natural Food
　"New" Mountain Ark Trading
Agar powder
　Fruitful Yield
　Allergy Resources
Almond butter, *organic*
　Jaffe Brothers, Inc.
　Allergy Resources
　Walnut Acres Organic Farms
Almond oil, *organic*
　Flora, Inc.
　Allergy Resources
Almonds, *organic*
　Allergy Resources
　Jaffe Brothers, Inc.

Almonds, *organic* **(continued)**
　Gold Mine Natural Food
　Walnut Acres Organic Farms
Amaranth flat bread
　Nu-World Amaranth
Amaranth flour
　Nu-World Amaranth
　Arrowhead Mills (*organic*)
　Jaffe Brothers, Inc. (*organic*)
　Fruitful Yield (*organic*)
　Allergy Resources (*organic*)
Amaranth garden seed
　Nu-World Amaranth
　Seeds of Change (*organic*)
Amaranth pasta (*organic*)
　Mio Amore Pasta

Amaranth, puffed
　Nu-World Amaranth
　Allergy Resources
　Gold Mine Natural Food
Amaranth, whole seed
　Nu-World Amaranth
　Arrowhead Mills (*organic*)
　Jaffe Brothers, Inc. (*organic*)
　Fruitful Yield (*organic*)
　Gold Mine Natural Food
　　(*organic*)
　"New" Mountain Ark Trading
　　(*organic*)
　Allergy Resources (*organic*)
Apple juice, *organic*
　Mountain Sun
　Walnut Acres Organic Farms

Applesauce, *organic*
Jaffe Brothers, Inc.
Arrowroot starch
Fruitful Yield
Allergy Resources
Walnut Acres Organic Farms

Bagles
Francis Simun Bakery
Pacific Bakery
Baking powder, Featherweight Brand
Ener-G Foods, Inc.
Barley flour, *organic*
Arrowhead Mills
Allergy Resources
Walnut Acres Organic Farms
Barley, pearled, *organic*
Arrowhead Mills
"New" Mountain Ark Trading
Beans (*see individual listings*)
Adzuki, Black turtle, Garbanzo,
Kidney, Lentils, Navy, Peas
(green split), Pinto
Beef, *natural/organic*
Walnut Acres Organic Farms
Bits of Barley cereal
Arrowhead Mills
Black turtle beans, *organic*
Arrowhead Mills
"New" Mountain Ark Trading
Gold Mine Natural Food
Jaffe Brothers, Inc.
Allergy Resources
Brazil nuts
Jaffe Brothers, Inc.
Walnut Acres Organic Farms
Breads (*see individual listings*)
Amaranth, flat bread; Bagles;
Buns; Flat Breads; Kamut,
sourdough; Millet, yeast-free;
Rice, yeast-free; Rye, sour-
dough; Spelt, sourdough
Brown rice products (*see Rice,
brown*)
Buckwheat cereal, *Pocono brand*
Birkett Mills
Buckwheat flour, light & dark
Birkett Mills
Arrowhead Mills (*dark only*)
Buckwheat groats, *organic*
Birkett Mills
"New" Mountain Ark Trading
Gold Mine Natural Food
(continued in next column)

Buckwheat groats, *org. (cont.)*
Jaffe Brothers, Inc.
Allergy Resources
Buckwheat groats, roasted, *org.*
Birkett Mills (*available in 4
granulations*)
Arrowhead Mills
Allergy Resources
Gold Mine Natural Food
"New" Mountain Ark Trading
Buckwheat soba noodles, 100%,
organic
"New" Mountain Ark Trading
Allergy Resources
Gold Mine Natural Food
Buffalo
D'Angelo Brother Products
Family Pride Meats
Czimer Game & Seafood
Game Sales International, Inc.
Buns, "hamburger"
Summercorn Foods
Butter (*see individual listings*)
Almond, Cashew,
Clarified (Ghee), Sunflower

Canola oil, *organic*
Flora, Inc.
Walnut Acres Organic Farms
Caraway seed
Frontier Cooperative Herbs
Carob chips, unsweetened
Fruitful Yield
Carob powder
Allergy Resources
Jaffe Brothers, Inc.
Cashew butter
Jaffe Brothers, Inc.
Cashews, raw
Fruitful Yield
Jaffe Brothers, Inc.
Walnut Acres Organic Farms
Celiac products
Food for Thought
Foods Naturally
Chestnut flour, *organic*
Gold Mine Natural Food
Chestnuts, dried *organic*
Gold Mine Natural Food
"New" Mountain Ark Trading

Chicken, *natural/organic*
D'Angelo Brother Products
Jedlicka Farm (eastern Iowa)
Walnut Acres Organic Farms
Chickpea (*see Garbanzo*)
Citrus pectin
Fruitful Yield
Allergy Resources
Clarified butter (Ghee)
Allergy Resources
Walnut Acres Organic Farms
Cranberry juice, unsweetened
Walnut Acres Organic Farms

Dacopa (beverage from dahlia tubers)
An Ounce of Prevention
Allergy Resources
DevanSweet™
Devansoy Farms, Inc.

Egg replacer, Ener-G brand
Allergy Resources
Ener-G Foods, Inc.
Exotic meats (*see Wild game*)
Extracts & flavorings,
alcohol-free
Frontier Cooperative Herbs

Filbert oil (hazelnut), *organic*
Allergy Resources
Filberts (hazelnuts)
Jaffe Brothers, Inc. (*organic*)
Walnut Acres Organic Farms
Flavorings (*see Extracts*)
Flatbreads
Francis Simun Bakery
Nu-World Amaranth
Flaxseed, *organic*
Arrowhead Mills
Allergy Resources
Fruitful Yield
Gold Mine Natural Food
Jaffe Brothers, Inc.
Walnut Acres Organic Farms
Flaxseed meal, *organic*
Allergy Resources
Fruitful Yield
Flaxseed oil, *organic*
Flora, Inc.
Arrowhead Mills
Gold Mine Natural Food
Jaffe Brothers, Inc.
Allergy Resources

Flours *(see Legume Flours and individual listings for grains/nongrains)*

Flours, freshly ground
Special Foods
Gold Mine Natural Food

Fish/shellfish *(see Salmon, Shrimp, Tuna)*

FOS (Fructo-oligo saccharides)
Canary Connect

FruitSource Sweetener (liquid & granular)
Gold Mine Natural Food

Fruit Sweet, Wax Orchards brand
Wax Orchards

Garbanzo bean flour
Allergy Resources
Bob's Red Mill Natural Foods

Garbanzo beans (chickpea), *org.*
Arrowhead Mills
"New" Mountain Ark Trading
Gold Mine Natural Food
Walnut Acres Organic Farms
Allergy Resources
Jaffe Brothers, Inc.

Garlic *(some organic)*
Walnut Acres Organic Farms
Watkins
Frontier Cooperative Herbs

Ghee *(see Clarified butter)*

Green split peas *(see Peas, green split)*

Guar gum
Fruitful Yield
Allergy Resources

Hazelnuts *(see Filberts)*

Herbs & spices
Atlantic Spice Company *(org.)*
San Francisco Herb Co. *(org.)*
Trout Lake Farm *(organic)*
Walnut Acres Organic Farms
Frontier Cooperative Herbs
Watkins

Honey
Walnut Acres Organic Farms

Jam/jelly, all fruit spreads
Walnut Acres Organic Farms

Jerusalem artichoke flour
Fruitful Yield
Allergy Resources

Kamut bread, sourdough, *organic*
Nokomis
Allergy Resources
Summercorn Foods
Pacific Bakery
French Meadow Bakery

Kamut buns, sourdough, *organic*
Summercorn Foods

Kamut flakes, quick cooking, *org.*
Grain Place Foods, Inc.
(Golden Kamut)

Kamut flour, *organic*
Arrowhead Mills
Jaffe Brothers, Inc.
Allergy Resources

Kamut grain, *organic*
"New" Mountain Ark Trading
Gold Mine Natural Food
Jaffe Brothers, Inc.
Allergy Resources

Kamut pasta, *organic*
Gold Mine Natural Food
Jaffe Brothers, Inc.
Allergy Resources

Kamut, puffed, *organic*
Arrowhead Mills

Kasha *(see Buckwheat, roasted)*

Kidney beans, *organic*
Arrowhead Mills
Jaffe Brothers, Inc.
Gold Mine Natural Food
"New" Mountain Ark Trading
Walnut Acres Organic Farms
Allergy Resources

Kombu
Gold Mine Natural Food
"New" Mountain Ark Trading

Kudzu (Kuzu)
Gold Mine Natural Food *(org.)*
"New" Mountain Ark Trading
Allergy Resources

Lamb, *organic*
Game Sales International, Inc.

Lemonade, Mountain Sun brand, *organic*
Mountain Sun

Legume flours *several varieties*
Allergy Resources
Bob's Red Mill Natural Foods

Lentil Flour
Allergy Resources
Bob's Red Mill Natural Foods

Lentils, green *organic*
Arrowhead Mills
"New" Mountain Ark Trading
Gold Mine Natural Food
Jaffe Brothers, Inc.
Walnut Acres Organic Farms
Allergy Resources

Lentils, red
Arrowhead Mills
Jaffe Brothers, Inc. *(organic)*
"New" Mountain Ark Trading
Walnut Acres Organic Farms

Macadamia nut oil, *organic*
Allergy Resources

Macadamia nuts
Jaffe Brothers, Inc. *(organic)*
Walnut Acres Organic Farms

Maple granules, *organic*
Walnut Acres Organic Farms
Jaffe Brothers, Inc.
Allergy Resources

Maple syrup, 100% pure, *organic*
"New" Mountain Ark Trading
Walnut Acres Organic Farms

Meats *(see individual listings)*
Beef, Buffalo, Chicken, Lamb, Pheasant, Rabbit, Turkey, Venison, Wild game and exotic meats

Millet bread, sourdough, *organic*
Allergy Resources

Millet, hulled, *organic*
Arrowhead Mills
Gold Mine Natural Food
"New" Mountain Ark Trading
Jaffe Brothers, Inc.
Walnut Acres Organic Farms
Allergy Resources

Millet, puffed
Arrowhead Mills

Navy beans, *organic*
Allergy Resources
Gold Mine Natural Food
Jaffe Brothers, Inc.
"New" Mountain Ark Trading

Nuts *(see individual listings)*
Almonds, Brazil nuts, Cashews, Filberts, Macadamia nuts, Pecans, Walnuts

Oat bran, *organic*
  Arrowhead Mills
  Allergy Resources
  Jaffe Brothers, Inc.
Oat flour, *organic*
  Arrowhead Mills
  Walnut Acres Organic Farms
  Allergy Resources
Oat milk
  Walnut Acres Organic Farms
Oats, old fashioned rolled, *org.*
  Arrowhead Mills
  Allergy Resources
  Gold Mine Natural Food
  Jaffe Brothers, Inc.
Oil *(see individual listings)*
  Almond, Canola, Filbert,
  Macadamia, Olive, Pumpkin,
  Safflower, Sesame, Sunflower,
  Walnut
Olive oil, *organic*
  Flora, Inc.
  Gold Mine Natural Food

Pastry poppers, wheat-free
  Walnut Acres Organic Farms
Pau D'Arco tea (Argentinian La
  Pacho/Taheebo Bark)
  Atlantic Spice Co.
  San Francisco Herb Co.
  An Ounce of Prevention
    (bags only)
  Allergy Resources
Peas, green split, *organic*
  Arrowhead Mills
  Gold Mine Natural Food
  "New" Mountain Ark Trading
  Jaffe Brothers, Inc.
Pecans, *organic*
  Jaffe Brothers, Inc.
  Walnut Acres Organic Farms
Pheasant
  Czimer Game & Seafood
  Games Sales International, Inc.
Pinto beans, *organic*
  Arrowhead Mills
  "New" Mountain Ark Trading
  Gold Mine Natural Food
  Walnut Acres Organic Farms
  Allergy Resources
  Jaffe Brothers, Inc.
Pizza crust, amaranth
  Nu-World Amaranth

Potato flour
  Fruitful Yield
Potato starch flour
  Ener-G Foods, Inc
Poultry *(see Chicken, Pheasant, and
  Turkey))*
Produce, organic *(mail-order)*
  Diamond Organics
  Walnut Acres Organic Farms
  Your area food-buying
    cooperative warehouse (See
    Appendix E)
Pumpkin seed oil
  Flora, Inc.
  Allergy resources
Pumpkin seeds
  Fruitful Yield
  Gold Mine Natural Food
  Jaffe Brothers, Inc.
  Walnut Acres Organic Farms

Quinoa flakes
  The Quinoa Corporation
  Gold Mine Natural Food
Quinoa flour, *organic*
  Quinoa Corporation
  Allergy Resources
Quinoa pasta *(also contains corn)*
  Quinoa Corporation
  Allergy Resources
Quinoa, whole seed, *organic*
  Quinoa Corporation
  Arrowhead Mills
  Fruitful Yield
  "New" Mountain Ark Trading
  Walnut Acres Organic Farms
  Allergy Resources
  Gold Mine Natural Food
  Jaffe Brothers, Inc.

Rabbit
  D'Angelo Brother Products
  Game Sales International, Inc.
Rice & Shine Cereal
  Arrowhead Mills
Rice bread, yeast-free
  Allergy Resources
  Ener-G Foods, Inc.
Rice, brown basmati, *organic*
  Arrowhead Mills
  "New" Mountain Ark Trading
  Gold Mine Natural Food
  Jaffe Brothers, Inc.
  Walnut Acres Organic Farms

Rice cakes, *organic*
  "New" Mountain Ark Trading
Rice cereal, brown, *organic*
  Walnut Acres Organic Farms
**Rice cereal—Purely Organic
  Hot Rice™ Cereal**
  Lundberg Family Farms
Rice flour, brown, *organic*
  Arrowhead Mills
  Fruitful Yield
  Jaffe Brothers, Inc.
  Allergy Resources
Rice, long-grain, brown, *organic*
  Arrowhead Mills
  "New" Mountain Ark Trading
  Gold Mine Natural Food
  Walnut Acres Organic Farms
  Jaffe Brothers, Inc.
Rice, medium-grain, brown, *org.*
  "New" Mountain Ark Trading
  Gold Mine Natural Food
Rice, short-grain, brown, *organic*
  "New" Mountain Ark Trading
  Allergy Resources
  Gold Mine Natural Food
  Walnut Acres Organic Farms
  Jaffe Brothers, Inc.
Rice pasta
  Jaffe Brothers, Inc. (*brown, org.*)
  Walnut Acres Organic Farms
    (*brown*)
  Allergy Resources
Rice, puffed
  Arrowhead Mills
Rice syrup, brown, *organic*
  Lundberg Family Farms
  "New" Mountain Ark Trading
  Walnut Acres Organic Farms
Rice syrup, flavored
  "New" Mountain Ark Trading
  Walnut Acres Organic Farms
Rice, white basmati, *organic*
  Gold Mine Natural Food
  "New" Mountain Ark Trading
  Walnut Acres Organic Farms
Rock salt *(see Salt: Orsa real salt)*
Rye bread, sourdough, yeast-free
  French Meadow Bakery
Rye flour
  Jaffe Brothers, Inc. (*organic*)
  Arrowhead Mills
  Walnut Acres Organic Farms

Rye pasta
    Mio Amore Pasta (*organic*)
    Allergy Resources

Safflower oil, *organic*
    Flora, Inc.
Salmon (*packed in glass jars*)
    Chuck's Seafood Products (*sold by 12/case*
    Canary Connect (*Chuck's brand, sold by individual jar*
Salt
    Natural mineral salt (*unrefined*)
        Jaffe Brothers, Inc.
        "New" Mountain Ark Trading
        Walnut Acres Organic Farms
    Orsa real salt
        Allergy Resources
    Sea salt (*refined*)
        Gold Mine Natural Food
        Jaffe Brothers, Inc.
        Walnut Acres Organic Farms
Salsa Seasoning Blend, Watkins
    Watkins (product number 1401)
Seeds (*see individual listings*)
    Caraway, Flax, Pumpkin, Sesame, Sunflower
Sesame oil, *organic*
    Flora, Inc.
    Gold Mine Natural Food
Sesame seeds, *organic*
    Arrowhead Mills
    Fruitful Yield
    Gold Mine Natural Food
    Allergy Resources (*brown*)
    "New" Mountain Ark Trading
    Jaffe Brothers, Inc.
    Walnut Acres Organic Farms
Shrimp
    Schwan's Sales Enterprises (*Seafarer's Choice medium peeled and deveined shrimp.*)
Soybeans (*snack*)
    Fruitful Yield
Soy Quick, Ener-G brand Pure
    Ener-G Foods, Inc.
Soy, flour (*also other soy products*)
    Arrowhead Mills
    Jaffe Brothers, Inc.
Spelt bread, sourdough, *organic*
    Nokomis
    Summercorn Foods
    Allergy Resources
    French Meadow Bakery

Spelt buns, sourdough, *organic*
    Summercorn Foods
Spelt flakes, quick cooking, *org.*
    Grain Place Foods, Inc. (*Nature's Spelt*)
Spelt flour, *organic*
    Arrowhead Mills
    Walnut Acres Organic Farms
    Allergy Resources
Spelt grain, *organic*
    "New" Mountain Ark Trading
    Gold Mine Natural Food
    Allergy Resources
    Jaffe Brothers, Inc.
Spelt pasta, *organic*
    Allergy Resources
    Jaffe Brothers, Inc.
    "New" Mountain Ark Trading
    Walnut Acres Organic Farms
Spices (*see Herbs*)
Starches (*see individual listings*)
    Arrowroot, Kudzu (Kuzu), Potato, Tapioca
Stevia, white powder concentrate
    Fruitful Yield
    Body Ecology Diet
Sunflower oil, *organic*
    Flora, Inc.
Sunflower seeds, raw
    Arrowhead Mills
    Fruitful Yield (*organic*)
    Gold Mine Natural Food (*org.*)
    Jaffe Brothers, Inc. (*organic*)
    "New" Mountain Ark Trading (*organic*)
    Walnut Acres Organic Farms (*organic*)

Tahini, *organic*
    Walnut Acres Organic Farms
    Allergy Resources
    Jaffe Brothers, Inc.
Tapioca starch flour
    Fruitful Yield
    Allergy Resources
Teff grain, brown and ivory
    The Teff Company (*bulk quantities*)
    Allergy Resources (*brown only*
    Gold Mine Natural Food
    "New" Mountain Ark Trading

Teff flour, brown and ivory
    The Teff Company (*bulk quantities*)
    Allergy Resources (*brown only*)
Tomato products, Muir Glen, *org.*
    Jaffe brothers, Inc.
    Good Eats
    Walnut Acres Organic Farms
Tuna (*packed in glass jars*)
    Chuck's Seafood Products (*sold by 12/case*
    Canary Connect (*Chuck's brand, sold by individual jar*)
Turkey
    D'Angelo Brother Products

Venison
    Allergy Resources
    D'Angelo Brother Products
    Czimer Game & Seafood
    Game Sales International, Inc.
Vitamin C crystals, unbuffered, corn-free (use with baking soda for leavening & to replace vinegar in salad dressings)
    Freeda Vitamins (product #0150)
    Bronson Pharmaceuticals (product #49)
    An Ounce of Prevention (Vital Life Brand)

Walnut oil
    Flora, Inc.
    Allergy Resources
Walnuts, *organic*
    Jaffe Brothers, Inc.
    Allergy Resources
    Gold Mine Natural Food
White bean flour
    Allergy Resources
    Bob's Red Mill Natural Foods
Wild game and exotic meat
    D'Angelo Brother Products
    Czimer Game & Seafood
    Family Pride Meats
    Game Sales International, Inc.
Wild rice, *organic*
    Gold Mine Natural Food
    Walnut Acres Organic Farms
    Jaffe Brothers, Inc.
    "New" Mountain Ark Trading
Wild-rice pasta, *organic*
    Mio Amore Pasta
    Allergy Resources

Non-food Products

Acidophilus supplements,
Lactobacillus acidophiilus
NCFM Superstrain (see pg. 14)
Metagenics
Acu-Trol (see page 16)
Acu-Trol, Inc.
Alka-Aid (see page 20)
Wellness Health & Pharmacu.

Books
Allergy Alternative
Allergy Resources
Amer. Environ. Health Found.
The Cotton Place
E.L. Foust Co., Inc.
Gold Mine Natural Food
The Living Source
"New" Mountain Ark Trading

Cellophane bags
Pak-Sel
Janice Corporation
The Living Source
Seventh Generation

Cookware/bakeware, stain. steel
Saladmaster
Estia Corporation
(continued in next column)

Cookware/bakeware (continued)
Walnut Acres Organic Farms
Gold Mine Natural Food
Miracle Exclusives, Inc.
"New" Mountain Ark Trading
Vita-Mix

Filtered water systems
R. H. of Texas
An Ounce of Prevention
N.E.E.D.S.
Nigra Enterprises
FOS (Fructo-oligo saccharides)
Canary Connect

Garden plants, *organic*
The Natural Gardening Co.
Garden seeds, *organic*
Nu-World Amaranth (amaranth)
Seeds of Change, organic
**Granny's Old Fashioned
Products** *(household and
personal care products)*
Canary Connect

Juicer
Pak-Sel *(Champion brand)*
Vita-Mix

Knives (cutlery)
Cutco Cutlery Corporation

Nutritional supplements
Allergy Alternative
An Ounce of Prevention
Canary Connect (FOS)
Freeda Vitamins
Klaire Laboratories, Inc.
N.E.E.D.S.
The Living Source

Oil of Oregano
An Ounce of Prevention
Oxygen supplies for chemically
sensitive persons *(ceramic
masks/tygon tubing)*
Amer. Environ. Health Found.

ParaMicrocidin
Allergy Research/Nutricology

UltraClear® products
HealthComm International, Inc.

**Vitamin C powder, buffered,
corn-free, citrus-free**
Allergy Research/Nutricology
Twin Labs

List B: Addresses

Acu-Trol, Inc.
2 Willow Road
St. Paul, MN 55127
(800) 594-4675
PHONE/FAX: (612) 483-5679
(Catalog available.)

Allergy Alternative
526 Shagbark Street
Windsor, CA 95492
(707) 838-1514
Orders: (800) 838-1514
(Catalog available.)

Allergy Research/Nutricology
PO Box 489
400 Preda Street
San Leandro, CA 94577-0489
(800) 545-9960
Order: (800) 782-4274
(Catalog available.)

Allergy Resources
PO Box 444
Guffey, CO 80820
Order line: (800) 873-3529
Customer Service: (719) 689-2969
FAX: (719) 689-2303
(Catalog available.)

**American Environmental Health
Foundation**
8345 Walnut Hill Lane   Ste. 225
Dallas, TX 75231
(800) 428-2343
(214) 361-9515

Arrowhead Mills
110 S. Lawton
PO Box 2059
Hereford, TX 79045
(800) 749-0730
FAX: (806) 364-8242
*(Product list available. Ask your local
health-food store to stock their
products.)*

Atlantic Spice Company
PO Box 205
North Truro, MA 02652
(800) 316-7965
FAX: (508) 487-2550
(Catalog available.)

An Ounce of Prevention
8200 E. Phillips Place
Englewood, CO 80112
(303) 770-8808
Orders: (800) 693-8808
*(Products for the chemically sensitive,
catalog available, personal attention.)*

Birkett Mills
PO Box 440A
Penn Yan, NY 14527
(315) 536-3311
FAX: (315) 536-6740
(Product list available.)

Bob's Red Mill Natural Foods, Inc.
5209 SE International Way
Milwaukie, OR 97222
(503) 654-3215
(Catalog available.)

Body Ecology Diet
1266 W. Paces Ferry Road
Suite 505-B
Atlanta, GA 30327
(404) 266-1366
FAX: (404) 266-2156

Bronson Pharmaceuticals
1945 Craig Road
St. Louis, MO 63146
(800) 235-3200
FAX: (800) 722-3821

Canary Connect
PO Box 5317
Coralville, IA 52241–0317
(319) 351-2317
FAX: (319) 351-2317 (auto mode)
(See Appendix G for more details.)

Chuck's Seafood Products
PO Box 5488
Charleston, OR 97420–0613
(541) 888-4600
FAX: (541) 888-2121
(Product list available.)

The Cotton Place
PO Box 7715
Waco, TX 76714-7715
Local: (817) 751-7730
Outside Dallas area: (800) 451-8866
FAX: (817) 751-7821
(Catalog available.)

Cutco Cutlery Corporation
1116 East State Street
Olean, NY 14760
Customer Service: (800) 828-0448
FAX: (716) 373-6145

Czimer Game & Seafood
13136 W. 159th Street
Lockport, IL 60441
(708) 301-0500
(Several exotic meats available. Grass-fed animals, no antibiotics or steriods. Product list available.)

D'Angelo Brother Products
909 South 9th Street
Philadelphia, PA 19147
(215) 923-5637
(Widest selection—50 or more—of organic farm fed exotic animals. No antibiotics or steriods, not hunted. Free-range. Quality care. Product list available.)

Devansoy Farm, Inc.
PO Box 885
Carroll, IA 51401
(800) 747-8605

Diamond Organics
PO Box 2159   *(Catalog available.)*
Freedom, CA 95019
(800) 922-2396
(888) ORGANIC (674-2642)

E.L. Foust Company, Inc.
PO Box 105   *(Catalog available.)*
Elmhurst, IL 60126
Illinois: (630) 834-4952
Outside Illinois: 1-800-225-9549

Ener-G Foods, Inc.
PO Box 84487
Seattle, WA 98124–5787
(800) 331-5222
FAX: (206) 764-3398
(Contact your local health-food store or above address for Ener-G brand bread and baking products.)

Estia Corporation
350 Gotham Parkway
Carlstadt, NJ 07072
(201) 939-4925
(Catalog available.)

Family Pride Meats
19 Main Street
PO Box 6
Ipswich, SD 57451
(605) 426-6343 or
FAX: (605) 426-6288
(Buffalo with no antibiotics or steriods. Also ask about availability of other exotic meats. Product list available.)

Flora, Inc.
Box 73
East Badger Road
Lynden, WA 98264
1-800-446-2110
FAX: (360) 354-5355
(Product list available.)

Food for Thought
Riverview Square
470 First Avenue
Coralville, IA 52241
(319) 341-3354   *(Celiac products.)*
FAX: (319) 341-3355
Online Address:
http://www.avalon.net/~wmiller

Foods Naturally
603 B Avenue
Kalona, IA 52247
(319) 656-3437   *(Celiac products.)*
Online Address: http://www.net
ins.net/balancedlife/foodsnat.htm

Francis Simun Bakery
3106 Commerce Street
Dallas, TX 75226
(214) 741-4242
(Yeast-free flat breads and bagels in a wide variety of flours.)

Freeda Vitamins
36 E. 41st Street
New York, NY 10017
In NY State: (212) 685-4980
Out of NY State: (800) 777-3737
(Catalog available.)

French Meadow Bakery
2610 Lyndale Avenue S.
Minneapolis, MN 55408
(612) 870-4740
FAX: (612) 870-0907
(Mail order or ask your local health-food store to carry their special bread products.)

Frontier Cooperative Herbs
3021 78th Street
PO Box 299   *(Catalog available.)*
Norway, IA 52318
(800) 786-1388
FAX: (319) 227-7966

Fruitful Yield
2111 Bloomingdale Road
Glendale Heights, IL 60139
(800) 469-5552   *(Catalog available.)*
FAX: (708) 894-0206

Game Sales International, Inc.
PO Box 7719
2456 E. 13th Street
Loveland, CO 80537-0719
Local: (970) 667-4090
(800) 729-2090
FAX: (970) 669-9041
(Exotic animals. Product list available.)

Gold Mine Natural Food Co.
3419 Hancock Street
San Diego, CA 92110–4307
Order line: (800) 475-3663
Customer Service: (619) 296-8536
FAX: (619) 296-9756
(Catalog available.)

Good Eats
5 Louise Drive
Ivyland, PA 18974
(800) 490-0044
FAX: (215) 443-7087

Grain Place Foods, Inc.
1904 N. Highway 14
Marquette, NE 68854
(402) 854-3195
FAX: (402) 854-2566
(Product list available.)

HealthComm International, Inc.
5800 Soundview Dr.   Bldg. B
PO Box 1729
Gig Harbor, WA 98335
(800) 843-9660
(Information on UltraClear® products & health-care professionals using them.)

Jaffe Brothers, Inc.
PO Box 636   *(Catalog available.)*
Valley Center, CA 92082–0636
(619) 749-1133
FAX: (619) 749-1282

Janice Corporation
198 US Highway 46
Budd Lake, NJ 07828–3001
(800) 526-4237   *(Catalog available.)*
FAX: (201) 691-5459

Jedlicka Farm
2019 Vincent Avenue NE
Solon, IA 52333
(319) 644-2686
(Natural/organic chicken, eastern Iowa.)

Klaire Laboratories, Inc.
1573 West Seminole
San Marcos, CA 92069
(800) 533-7255 & (619) 744-9680
(Catalog available.)

The Living Source
PO Box 20155
Waco, TX 76702
(817) 776-4878
Order: (800) 662-8787
FAX: (817) 776-9329
(Catalog available.)

Lundberg Family Farms
PO Box 369
Richvale, CA 95974
(916) 882-4551
FAX: (916) 882-4500
(Product list available.)

Metagenics
921 Calle Negocio
San Clemente, CA 92673-6259
(714) 366-0818
(Lactobacillus acidophiilus NCFM Super-strain [pg. 14] sold under Metagenics label is only available through health profession-als, i.e. chiropractors, physical therapists, MDs. Health-food stores may have same product under Ethical Nutrients label.)

Mio Amore Pasta
PO Box 86   *(Product list available.)*
Edgar, NE 68935
(402) 224-4010

Miracle Exclusives, Inc.
62 Seaview Blvd.
Port Washington, NY 11050
(800) 645-6360 & (516) 484-2121
FAX: (516) 484-2199
(Catalog available.)

Mountain Sun
18390 Hwy 145
Delores, CO 81323
(970) 882-2283
FAX: (970) 882-2270
(Ask for your geographic distributor.)

The Natural Gardening Company
217 San Anselmo Avenue
San Anselmo, CA 94960
(707) 766-9303
FAX: (707) 766-9747

N.E.E.D.S.
527 Charles Avenue 12-A
Syracuse, NY 13209
1-800-634-1380
FAX: (800) 295-NEED (6333)
(Catalog available.)

"New" Mountain Ark Trading Co.
799 Old Leicester Hwy.
Ashville, NC 28806
(800) 643-8909   *(Catalog available.)*
(704) 252-9479

Nigra Enterprises
5699 Kanan Road
Agoura, CA 91301-3328
(818) 889-6877

Nokomis
W2 495 County Road E.S.
East Troy, WI 53120
(800) 367-0358
FAX: (414) 642-5517
(Request information packet.)

Nu-World Amaranth, Inc.
Attention: Larry Walters
PO Box 2202
Naperville, Illinois 60567
(708) 369-6819
FAX: (708) 369-6851
(Product list available.)

Pacific Bakery
PO Box 950
Oceanside, CA 92049
(619) 757-6020
(Yeast-free Kamut bread and bagels. Mail order, but due to shipping costs you may wish to encourage your local health-food store to carry this brand.)

Pak Sel
7205 S.E. Johnson Creek Blvd.
Portland, Oregon 97206
1-800-635-BAGS (2247)
(503) 771-9404
FAX: (503) 771-9413
(Product list available.)

Quinoa Corporation
PO 1039
Torrance, California 90505
(310) 530-8666
FAX: (310) 530-8764

R. H. of Texas
Box 780392
Dallas, TX 75378
(214) 351-6681
(Specializes in designing water purification systems for the chemically sensitive.)

Saladmaster International Headquarters
912 113th Street
Arlington, TX 76011
(817) 633-3555
FAX: (817) 633-5544
(Catalog available.)

San Francisco Herb Company
250 14th Street   *(Catalog available.)*
San Francisco, CA 94103
(800) 227-4530
FAX: (415) 861-4440

Schwan's Sales Enterprises
Corporate Office *(home delivery co.)*
115 W. College Drive
Marshall, MN 56258
(800) 533-5290
Quality Assurance: (507) 537-8338
Customer Service: (800) 544-8708
(Quality assurance extension #8144.)

Seeds of Change
PO Box 15700
Santa Fe, NM 87506–5700
(505) 438-8080
Customer Service: (888) 762-7333
Catalog: (800) 957-3337
FAX: (888) 329-4762
(Catalog available.)

Seventh Generation
#1 Mill Street
PO Box A26
Burlington, VT 05401
(800) 456-1177
FAX: (800) 456-1139
(Catalog available.)

Special Foods
9207 Shotgun Court
Springfield, VA 22153
(703) 644-0991
FAX: (703) 644-1006
*(Very specialized flours, baking
powders, baked products, pastas, and
lip balms. Product list available.)*

Summercorn Foods
1410 Cato Springs Road
Fayetteville, AR 72701
(501) 521-9338
FAX: (501) 443-5771
*(Yeast-free Kamut and spelt breads and
"hamburger" buns. Product list available.)*

The Teff Company
P. O. Box A
Caldwell, Idaho 83606
(208) 454-3330
*(For bulk orders. Product list
available.)*

Trout Lake Farm
42 Warner Road
Trout Lake, WA 98650
(800) 395-6093
FAX: (509) 395-2645

Twin Laboratories, Inc.
2120 Smithtown Avenue
Ronkonkoma, NY 11779
In NY State: (516) 467-3140
Outside NY State: (800) 645-5626
*(Products available through health-
food stores and food-buying
cooperatives. Catalog of product
information available.)*

Vita-Mix
8615 Usher Road
Cleveland, OH 44138
(800) 848-2649
FAX: (216) 235-3726
(Catalog available.)

Walnut Acres Organic Farms
Penns Creek, PA 17862
(800) 433-3998
FAX: (717) 837-1146
(Catalog available.)

Watkins, Inc.
P. O. 5570
Winona, MN 55987-0570
Customer Service: (800) 243-9423
Credit Card Order: (800) 247-5907
FAX: (507) 452-6723
ID# 00201
(Catalog available.)

Wax Orchards
22744 Wax orchard Road SW
Vashon, WA 98070
(800) 634-6132
FAX: (206) 463-9731

**Wellness Health &
Pharmaceuticals**
2800 S. 18th Street
Birmingham, AL 35209
(800) 227-2627

Section 2: Resource Guides

Resource guides/books providing additional information on locating organic food, clothing, bedding, cleaning products, and more for the chemically sensitive and environmentally aware.

Highways to Health
The S.T.A.T.E. Foundation
(Sensitive to a Toxic Environment)
PO Box 834
Orchard Park, NY 14127
(716) 675-1164
Donations very helpful.

Nontoxic, Natural, and Earthwise: How to Protect Yourself and Your Family from Harmful Products and Live in Harmony with the Earth. Book by Debra Lynn Dadd in collaboration with Steve Lett and Judy Collins. Los Angeles, CA: Jeremy P. Tarcher, Inc., 1990. Contains an excellent resource section.

Section 3: Resources for Personalized Assistance for Food Allergy and Rotational Diet Planning

Resources which offer personalized assistance in rotational diet planning and specialized recipes.

Rotational Diet Planning

Allergy Adapt, Inc.
Nicolette Dumke
1877 Polk Avenue
Louisville, CO 80027
(303) 666-8253

Better Health U.S.A.
1620 W. Oakland Park Blvd.
Ft. Lauderdale, FL 33311
(800) 684-2231 & (954) 486-4500
FAX: (954) 739-2780
(Food allergy and Candida testing. Results used to provide a personalized rotational diet.)

Specialized Recipes

Canary Connect
A Division of SOBOLE, Inc.
P. O. Box 5317
Coralville, IA 52241-0317
Phone/FAX: (319) 351-2317
(Send copy of your personalized rotational diet and the type of recipe(s)—by Day—that you need: i.e., soups for Day 1, desserts for Day 4, etc. Submit fee of $10.00 for initial consultation and analysis. Response will include ideas and options along with cost estimate for further services.)

Section 4: Resources for Locating a Physician

The following sources may be contacted for information on physicians who treat CRC in your geographical area. These organizations may require a small monetary fee for their list.

American Academy of Environmental Medicine
4510 W. 89th Street   Suite 110
Prairie Village, KS 66207-2282
(913) 642-6062
Enclose a $3 donation, a self-addressed stamped #10 envelope, and state the geographic area in which you are interested.

American Association of Naturopathic Physicians
2366 Eastlake Avenue East
Suite 322
Seattle, WA 98102
Phone: (206) 323-7610
($5 fee for referral information.)

American College for Advancement in Medicine
23121 Verdugo Drive #204
PO Box 3427
Laguna Hills, CA 92654
(714) 583-7666
(Send self-addressed, stamped envelope—2 stamps.)

American Holistic Medical Association
4101 Lake Boone Trail   Ste. 201
Raleigh, NC 27607
(Send donation of $8.75 for names of AHMA physicians in your area and three association brochures.)

Chemical Injury Information Network (CIIN)
PO Box 301
White Sulphur Springs, MT 59645
Phone/FAX: (406) 547-2255

Immuno Laboratories
1620 W. Oakland Park Blvd.
Ft. Lauderdale, FL 33311
(800) 231-9197
(954) 486-4500
FAX: (954) 739-6563
(Information and referrals for physicians treating Candida Related Complex and/or food allergies.)

World Research Foundation
20501 Ventura Blvd. S. #1
Woodland Hills, CA 91364
(818) 907-5483
FAX: (818) 227-6484
($2 fee for initial introduction packet. Includes listing for other services/fees.)

Price-Pottenger Nutrition Foundation (PPNF)
PO Box 2614
LaMesa, CA 91943–2614
(619) 574-7763
FAX: (619) 574-1314
Enclose a $6 donation, a self-addressed stamped #10 envelope, and state the geographic area in which you are interested.

Following are information and referral resources for physicians offering EPD (Enzyme Potentialted Desensitization) treatments (see page 20). When contacting them, be sure to provide information on the state or geographical area you are interested in.

Marjorie Hurt Jones, RN
MAST Enterprises, Inc.
2614 N. Fourth Street #616
Coeur d'Alene, ID 83814
(208) 772-8213

Santa Fe Center of Allergy & Environmental Medicine
141 Paseo de Peralta   Suite A
Santa Fe, NM 87501
(505) 983-8890
FAX: (505) 820-7315

Section 5: Resources for *Candida* and Food Allergy Diagnosis and Other Testing

Some health-care professionals have found certain blood and stool diagnostic analysis tests helpful in diagnosing CRC as well as food sensitivities (see page 3, Diagnosis of CRC) and/or parasites. Some laboratories which perform these tests are listed below. You may be able to work directly with some of the labs listed regarding your diagnostic needs while others prefer working with health-care professionals regarding test results. Your physician and/or other health-care professional may be able to work with you in determining appropriate tests and submitting required samples for evaluation.

Immuno Laboratories
1620 W. Oakland Park Blvd.
Suite 300
Ft. Lauderdale, FL 33311
(800) 231-9197
(954) 486-4500
FAX: (954) 739-6563
(Food allergy and Candida testing.
Results used to provide a personalized
rotational diet.)

Great Smokies Diagnostic Laboratory
18A Regent Park Blvd.
Asheville, NC 28806
(704) 253-0621

Institute of Parasitic Diseases
O.M. Amin, Ph.D.
3530 E. Indian School Road
Phoenix, AZ 85018
(602) 955-4211
FAX: (602) 955-4102
To Purchase Test Kit Contact:
Urokeep, Inc.
(602) 545-9236

Section 6: Resources for a Personal Support System

As discussed on page 25, developing a personal support system is an important, beneficial element of the healing process. The following organizations can provide information on support groups in your area, how to form a support group, writing circles, and/or other resources as listed.

Candida & Dysbiosis Information Foundation
PO Drawer JF
College Station, TX 77841-5146
Hot Line: (409) 694-8687
(Nonprofit educational foundation run on a volunteer
basis. Hot Line has limited hours. A substantial
information packet and an irregularly published newsletter
are available for a minimum initial $25.00 donation. Good
support and information source.)

Chemical Injury Information Network (CIIN)
PO Box 301
White Sulphur Springs, MT 59645
Phone/FAX: (406) 547-2255
(Help in finding a local support group. Publish a monthly
newsletter, Our Toxic Times, on a donation basis.)

Human Ecology Action League (HEAL)
PO Box 29629
Atlanta, GA 30359–1126
(404) 248-1898
FAX: (404) 248-1898
(An excellent resource for local HEAL support groups.
Publish a quarterly newsletter, Human Ecologist.
Donations very helpful.)

Sondra Lewis
c/o Canary Connect Publications
A Division of SOBOLE, Inc.
PO Box 5317
Coralville, IA 52241-0317
[Writing circles divided into groups: 1) Multiple Chemical
Sensitivities (MCS) and other health challenges OR
2) Candida Related Complex (CRC). For information,
send a #10 self-addressed, stamped envelope.]

APPENDIX D
RECOMMENDED READING

Books

Balch, James F., M.D. and Phyllis A. Balch, C.N.C. <u>Prescription for Nutritional Healing</u>. Garden City Park, NY: Avery Publishing Group, Inc., 1990.

Balch, Phyllis A., C.N.C. and James F. Balch, M.D. <u>Prescription for Dietary Wellness</u>. Greenfield, IN: PAB Books, Inc., 1992.

<u>*Candida Albicans* - Booklet of Reprints</u>. San Diego, CA: Price-Pottenger Nutrition Foundation. *(Price-Pottenger Nutrition Foundation, P.O. Box 2614, LaMesa, CA 91943-2614)*

Crook, William G., M.D. <u>Chronic Fatigue Syndrome and the Yeast Connection</u>. Jackson, TN: Professional Books, Inc., 1992. *(Professional Books, Inc., Box 3246, Jackson, TN 38303)*

_____. <u>Detecting Your Hidden Allergies</u>. Jackson, TN: Professional Books, Inc., 1988. *(See above.)*

_____. <u>The Yeast Connection and the Woman</u>. Jackson, TN: Professional Books, Inc., 1995. *(Professional Books, Inc., Box 3246, Jackson, TN 38303)*

_____. <u>The Yeast Connection Handbook</u>. Jackson, TN: Professional Books, Inc., 1996. *(See above.)*

_____ and Marjorie Hurt Jones, R.N. <u>The Yeast Connection Cookbook</u>. Jackson, TN: Professional Books, 1989. *[Available from Professional Books, Inc. (see above) or Mast Enterprises, Inc., 2615 N. Fourth Street #616, Coeur d'Alene, ID 83814.]*

Dadd, Debra Lynn. <u>Nontoxic, Natural, and Earthwise</u>. Los Angeles, CA: Jeremy P. Tarcher, Inc., 1990.

"Fresh Flax Oil." Pamphlet from Allergy Resources, Inc., P.O. Box 888, 264 Brookridge, Palmer Lake, CO 80133.

Golos, Natalie and Frances Golos Golbitz. <u>Coping with Your Allergies</u>. New York, NY: A Fireside Book, Published by Simon and Schuster, Inc., 1986.

Golos, Natalie and William J. Rea, M.D. <u>Success in the Clean Bedroom</u>. Rochester, NY: Pinnacle Publishers, 1992.

Levin, Alan Scott, M.D. and Merla Zellerbach. <u>The Type 1/Type 2 Allergy Relief Program</u>. Los Angeles, CA: Jeremy P. Tarcher, Inc., 1983.

Mandell, Marshall, Ph.D. and Lynne Waller Scanlon. <u>5-Day Allergy Relief System</u>. New York, NY: Pocket Books, a Division of Simon and Schuster, Inc., 1979.

Randolph, Theron G., M.D. and Ralph W. Moss, Ph.D. <u>An Alternative Approach to Allergies</u>. New York, NY: Bantam Books, Inc., 1980.

Riotte, Louise. <u>Carrots Love Tomatoes: Secrets of Companion Planting for Successful Gardening</u>. Pownal, VT: Garden Way Publishing, a division of Storey Communications, Inc., 1975.

Rogers, Sherry A., M.D. <u>The E.I. Syndrome</u>. Syracuse, NY: Prestige Publishers, 1986. *(Prestige Publishers, Box 3161, 3502 Brewerton Road, Syracuse, NY 13220)*

Springer, Jerry. <u>Allergies - Making Kids Crazy</u>. Interview with Doris Rapp, M.D. Air Date: December 17, 1992. 45 min., Multimedia Entertainment, Inc., 1994. Videocassette. *(Available from Video Archives, Inc., 41 Paoli Plaza #3D, Paoli, PA 19301.)*

Thomas, Sherry and Jeanne Tetrault. <u>Country Woman: A Handbook for the New Farmer</u>. San Angelo, TX: Anchor Press, 1976. This book is currently out of print, but you should be able to find it in your local library.

Truss, C. Orian, M.D. <u>The Missing Diagnosis</u>. Birmingham, AL: By the author, 2614 Highland Avenue, 1982. *(The Missing Diagnosis, P.O. Box 26508, Birmingham, AL 35226)*

Cookbooks

Crook, William G., M.D. and Marjorie Hurt Jones, R.N. The Yeast Connection Cookbook. Jackson, TN: Professional Books, 1989. *Especially for vegetable cookery and salad dressings, as well as helpful ideas.* (Available from Professional Books, Inc., Box 3246, Jackson, TN 38303 or Mast Enterprises, Inc., 2615 N. Fourth Street #616, Coeur d'Alene, ID 83814.)

Dumke, Nicolette M. Allergy Cooking with Ease. Lancaster, PA: Starburst Publishers, 1992. *Especially for alternative meats and gluten-free bread and pastas.* (Available from Allergy Adapt, Inc., 1877 Polk Avenue, Louisville, CO 80027, (303) 666-8253.)

_____. Easy Bread Making for Special Diets. Louisville, CO: Allergy Adapt, Inc., 1995. *Especially for wheat-free bread prepared in bread machines (includes yeast and yeast-free recipes).* (See above.)

_____. The EPD Patient's Cooking and Lifestyle Guide. Louisville, CO: Allergy Adapt, Inc., 1994. *A must for persons using EPD treatment..* (EPD is Enzyme Potentiated Desensitization allergy treatment.) (See above.)

_____. A Preview of The Allergy Diet Guide and Cookbook. Louisville, CO: Allergy Adapt, Inc. *The Allergy Diet Guide and Cookbook is scheduled for publication in 1997.* (See above to order the Preview.)

Gates, Donna with Linda Schatz. The Body Ecology Diet: Recovering Your Health and Rebuilding Your Immunity. Atlanta, GA: B.E.D. Publications, 1993. *Especially for meat-free recipes.* (B.E.D. Publications, 1266 West Paces Ferry Road, Suite 505, Atlanta, GA 30327)

Gioannini, Marilyn. The Complete Food Allergy Cookbook. Rocklin, CA: Prima Publishing, 1996. (Prima Publishing, PO Box 1260BK, Rocklin, CA 95677)

Golos, Natalie and Frances Golos Golbitz. If This Is Tuesday, It Must Be Chicken. New Canaan, CT: Keats Publishing, Inc., 1983. *Especially for information on rotation.* (Keats Publishing, Inc., 27 Pine Street [Box 876], New Canaan, CT 06840)

Grimmett, Charlene. Beat the Yeast Cookbook. Aurora, IL: By the author, 1985. *Especially for low carbohydrate recipes.* (Charlene Grimmett, P.O. Box 1971, Aurora, IL 60507)

Hayes, Stephanie, R.D. and Barbara Maynard, R.D. Rotational Bon Appetite! Dallas, TX: WJR and Associates, P.A. dba Environmental Health Center-Dallas, 1986. *Especially for information on rotation.* (Environmental Health Center–Dallas, 8345 Walnut Hill Lane, Suite 205, Dallas, TX 75231)

Jones, Marjorie Hurt, R.N. Super Foods. Coeur d'Alene, ID: Mast Enterprises, Inc., 1990. *Especially for specialty grains (Super Foods) recipes.* (Mast Enterprises, Inc., 2615 N. Fourth Street #616, Coeur d'Alene, ID 83814)

Rockwell, Sally, Nutritionist. Coping with Candida Cookbook (Revised). Seattle, WA: By the author, 1986. *Especially as a carbohydrate level resource.* (Sally J. Rockwell, P.O. Box 31065, Seattle, WA 98103)

Saltzman, Joanne. Amazing Grains. Tiburon, CA: H.J. Kramer, Inc., 1990. Especially for meat-free recipes. (H.J. Kramer, Inc., P.O. Box 1082, Tiburon, CA 94920)

Vierra, Danny and Charise Vierra. Vegetarian Cooking School Cookbook. Brushton, NY: TEACH Services, Inc., 1996. Especially for vegetarian recipes. (Modern Manna Ministries, 517 S. Central Ave., Lodi, CA 95240, (209) 334-3868)

Newsletters

The following newsletters are excellent resources and a subscription would be a valuable addition to your personal informational library.

Canary Connect News. Editors: Sondra K. Lewis and Lonnett Dietrich Blakley. Canary Connect Publications, P.O. Box 5317, Coralville, IA 52241-0317. Phone: (319) 351-2371. 4 issues/year—first issue, January-March 1995. Back issues available. See ordering information on pages 270 and 271.

MFA Collection. Editor: Marjorie Hurt Jones, R.N. MAST Enterprises, Inc., 2615 N. Fourth Street #616, Coeur d'Alene, ID 83814. Phone: (208) 772-8213. The MFA Collection contains all the issues of Mastering Food Allergies Newsletter. This newsletter was published from December 1985–January 1986 through May–June 1996. Individual issues are available from MAST Enterprises. Highly recommended.

APPENDIX E
COOPERATIVE FOOD WAREHOUSES
IN THE UNITED STATES

If you know of U.S. cooperative food warehouses not included in this list, please send the name, address, phone number, and geographical area serviced for each so we may share this information through Canary Connect News newsletter (see page 269). Formerly we had listed some cooperative buying clubs in southern California since we were unable to locate cooperative food warehouse resources in this area. Many thanks to V.R. of Kansas for forwarding California information included in this updated listing!

Northeastern States

Hudson Valley Federation of
  Food Cooperatives
6 Noxon Road
Poughkeepsie, NY 12603

(914) 473-5400
FAX: (914) 473-5458

New York, New Jersey, Eastern Pennsylvania,
Western Connecticut

Northeast Cooperatives
P.O. Box 8188
Brattleboro, VT 05304

(802) 257-5856
FAX: (802) 257-7039

Massachusettes, Maine, Rhode Island,
New Hampshire, Vermont, Connecticut,
Eastern New York

Southern States

Ozark Cooperative Warehouse
P.O.Box 1528
Fayetteville, AR 72702

(501) 521-2667
FAX: (501) 521-9100

Alabama, Arkansas, Georgia, Louisiana, Texas,
Oklahoma, Mississippi, Western Texas,
Part of Florida, Southern Missouri

Midwestern States

Blooming Prairie Warehouse
2340 Heinz Road
Iowa City, IA 52240

(800) 323-2131
(319) 337-6448
FAX: (319) 337-4592

Iowa, Nebraska, Illinois, Indiana, Northern Kansas
and Missouri, Southwestern Wyoming, Michigan,
Southern South Dakota and Wisconsin

Blooming Prairie Natural Foods
510 Kasota Avenue SE
Minneapolis, MN 55414

(800) 322-8324 in MN
(800) 328-8241
  outside MN
FAX: (612) 378-9780

Southern Minnesota, Western Wisconsin, South
Dakota, North Dakota, Parts of Iowa

Federation of Ohio River
  Cooperatives
320 Outerbelt Street
Columbus, OH 43213-1597

(614) 861-2446
FAX: (614) 861-7638

District of Columbia, Kentucky, Maryland,
Michigan, Northern North Carolina, Ohio,
Southeast Indiana, Tennessee, Virginia,
West Virginia, Western Pennsylvania

North Farm
204 Regas Road
Madison, WI 53714

(608) 241-2667
FAX: (608) 241-0688

Illinois, Indiana, Michigan, North Dakota,
Wisconsin; Parts of Minnesota, Montana, Ohio,
South Dakota, and Wyoming; Small Areas of Iowa
and Missouri

Southwestern States

Tucson Cooperative Warehouse
350 S. Toole Avenue
Tucson, AZ 85701

(800) 351-2667
  Outside AZ
(602) 884-9951
FAX: (602) 792-3258

Arizona, New Mexico, Las Vegas area, Southern
California and Colorado, Middle Texas,
Some of Utah

Continued ...

Southwestern States (continued)

Mountain People's Warehouse 12745 Earhart Avenue Auburn, CA 95602	(800) 679-6733 (916) 889-9531 FAX: (916) 889-9544 (FAX for Order Dept.)	California, Nevada, Idaho, Oregon, Montana, Wyoming, Arizona, Colorado, Utah, Washington, Parts of Texas

Northwestern States

Mountain People's Northwest 4005 6th Avenue S. Seattle, WA 98108	(800) 336-8872 FAX: (800) 210-0104	Washington, Oregon, Northern Idaho, Alaska, Hawaii

APPENDIX F
ORGANIZATIONS PROVIDING INFORMATION ON ORGANIC FOOD PRODUCTION AND AVAILABILITY

At publication date the following organizations have been contacted and have indicated their willingness to act as an informational resource regarding organic food production and availability in their geographical area. You should be aware, however, that the contact person for some of these organizations may change in the future. If a change does occur, the person listed should be able to direct you to the currect contact person. When you contact these resources, please mention where you found them.

Northeastern States

Maine Organic Farmers and
Gardeners Association
PO Box 2176
Augusta, ME 04338-2176
(207) 622-3118

New Hampshire Department of
Agriculture, Markets, & Food
Bureau of Markets
PO Box 2042
Concord, NH 03302-2042
(603) 271-3685 & 271-2753
FAX: (603) 271-1109
Ask for the Certified Organic Farm List.

Northeast Organic Farming Assoc.
—Connecticut (NOFA)
69 Meetinghouse Hill Road
Durham, CT 06422
(860) 349-1417
OR P.O. Box 386
Northford, CT 06471
(860) 484-2445 (message only)
*Ask about Annual Directory of Organic
Growers.*

Northeast Organic Farming Assoc.
—Massachusetts (NOFA)
411 Sheldon Road
Barre, MA 01005-9252
(508) 355-2853

Northeast Organic Farming Assoc.
—New Jersey (NOFA)
33 Titus Mill Road
Pennington, NJ 08534
(609) 737-6848
FAX: (609) 737-2366
*Ask for Fine Foods Organically Grown
in New Jersey & Pennsylvania.*

Northeast Organic Farming Assoc.
—New York (NOFA)
472 Monkey Run Road
Port Crane, NY 13833
(607) 648-5557

Northeast Organic Farming Assoc.
—Rhode Island (NOFA)
2325 Boston Neck Road
Saunderstown, RI 02874
(401) 295-1030

Northeast Organic Farming Assoc.
—Vermont (NOFA)
P.O. Box 697
Richmond, VT 05477
(802) 434-4122

Virginia Association for Biological
Farming
PO Box 10721
Blacksburg, VA 24062-0721
(540) 381-5082

Southeastern States

Carolina Farm Stewardship Assoc.
115 West Main Street
Carrboro, NC 27510
(919) 968-1030
FAX: (919) 933-4465

Florida Certified Organic Growers
and Consumers, Inc. (FOG)
PO Box 12311
Gainesville, FL 32604
Phone/FAX: (352) 337-6345

Kentucky Dept. of Agriculture
100 Fairoaks Lane Suite 252
Frankfurt, KY 40601
(502) 564-6571
FAX: (502) 564-7852
Ask for list of organic growers.

Louisiana Dept. of Agriculture &
Forestry/Office of Agricultural
& Environmental Services
Attn: Kyle Moppert
PO Box 3596
Baton Rouge, LA 70821-3596
(504) 925-3789
FAX: (504) 925-3760

Louisiana Organic Growers Assoc.
PO Box 1296
Denham Springs, LA 70727-1296
(504) 664-5368
FAX: (504) 664-7734

Ozark Organic Growers Assoc.
HC73 Box 42
Jerusalem, AR 72080
(501) 745-5465
FAX: (501) 745-2589

Midwestern States

Farm Verified Organic, Inc.
RR 1 Box 40A
Medina, ND 58467
(701) 486-3478
FAX: (701) 486-3580

Minnesota Grown Program
Minnesota Dept. of Agriculture
90 W. Plato Boulevard
St. Paul, MN 55107
(800) 657-3878
(612) 297-2301 & 297-8695
*Request a copy of Minnesota Grown
Farmer to Consumer Directory.*

Missouri Organic Association
2832 Olde Chelsea
St. Charles, MO 63301
(314) 657-4156

Nebraska Sustainable Agriculture
Society
PO Box 736
Hartington, NE 68739
(402) 254-2289
FAX: (402) 254-6891

Northern Plains Sustainable
 Agriculture Society
HC5 Box 104
Langdon, ND 58249
(701) 256-2424

Oklahoma Dept. of Agriculture
Market Development Dept.
2800 North Lincoln Boulevard
Oklahoma City, OK 73105-4298
(405) 521-3864
FAX: (405) 521-4912
*Ask for Oklahoma Fruit & Vegetable
Buyers Guide.*

Organic Crop Improvement
 Association—Chapter 1 of Iowa
6534 220th Street
Arthur, IA 51431
(712) 367-2442
FAX: (712) 367-2342

Organic Crop Improvement
 Association—Wisconsin
N7834 County Road B
Spring Valley, WI 54767
Mail to: PO Box 52
         Viroqua, WI 54665
(608) 734-3273
FAX: (608) 734-3306

Prairie Talk
PO Box 733
Solon, IA 52333
(319) 644-3052
(319) 644-3291

Texas Department of Agriculture
Texas Certified Organic Program
PO Box 12847
Austin, TX 78711
(512) 475-1641
FAX: (512) 463-7643
*(Request a Certification List of certified
organic growers.)*

Northwestern States

Alternative Energy Resources
 Organization
25 South Ewing Street   Ste. 214
Helena, MT 59601
(406) 443-7272
FAX: (406) 442-9120

Idaho Department of Agriculture
Attn: Jim Boatman
PO Box 790
Boise, IDA 83701-0790
(208) 332-8660
FAX: (208) 334-2170
*Ask for Organic Directory and Growers
Brochure.*

Idaho Organic Producers Assoc.
2260 E., 4300 N.
Filer, ID 83328
(208) 326-4101
FAX: (208) 326-8684

Oregon Tilth Certified Organic
11535 SW Durham Road
Suite C1
Tigard, OR 97224-3474
(503) 620-2829
FAX: (503) 624-1386

Washington State Department of
Agriculture
Organic Food Program
PO Box 42560
Olympia, WA 98504
(360) 902-1877
FAX: (360) 902-2087
*Ask for Organic Growers, Processors,
& Handlers List.*

Southwestern States

California Certified Organic
 Farmers
1115 Mission Street
Santa Cruz, CA 95060
(408) 423-2263
FAX: (408) 423-4528

Colorado Organic Producers
 Association
8890 Lane 4 North
Moscow, CO 81146
Phone/FAX: (719) 378-2436

   If you know of other organizations providing information on organic food production and availability for states not listed in this appendix, please send Canary Connect Publications the name, address, and phone number for each so the information may be included in <u>Canary Connect News</u> newsletter (see Appendix G).

APPENDIX G
CANARY CONNECT

Canary ConnecT™

Thank you for purchasing <u>Allergy & Candida Cooking Made Easy</u>. We hope you enjoy reading and using it and that the information and recipes it contains will aid you in your journey towards better health.

We would love to hear from you regarding how this book has affected your life. We also look forward to our future projects and to the continuing effort to provide you with the best, most complete information possible to enhance your health and lifestyle. <u>Canary Connect News</u> newsletter is an excellent resource for continuing the learning process. See below and pages 270 and 271 for more information on the newsletter and subscription procedures.

Please accept our best wishes as you use this book. You will be in our prayers as you continue the adventure of life and learning.

Sondra   *Lonnett*

* * * * * * *

Ongoing and Upcoming Projects for Canary Connect

- <u>Canary Connect News</u> newsletter, published quarterly, see below and pages 270 and 271.
- Cooking Video Series, first of the series expected to be released in Spring 1997.
- Booklet—<u>Traveling with Food Allergies</u> is currently a series article published in issues #3–6 of <u>Canary Connect News</u>, newsletter. Projected publication date is not currently set for booklet. Booklet will include "good" choice places to eat—delis, restaurants, health-food stores, bed and breakfasts in United States.
- Seminars and workshops on Managing Food Allergies, *Candida* Related Complex, and Rotational Diet can be scheduled. Some of these seminars and workshops are available on videotape.

Canary Connect News—Past, Current, and Projected Articles and Columns

Our goal for the newsletter is to fit your needs. Send us your opinions regarding this list so we can know of your interests. You may also send us your list of suggested additions. A highlights list for back issues of <u>Canary Connect News</u> (CCN) available as of the publication of this book can be found on page 270. An up-to-date highlights list is available upon request.

- Information on current research, alternative treatments, and/or supplements investigated by us and/or shared by CCN readers on: *Candida* Related Complex (CRC), Chronic Fatigue and Immune Dysfunction Syndrome (CFIDS), Fibromyalgia (FM), food allergies, and Multiple Chemical Sensitivities/Environmental Illness (MCS/EI).
- A "Question & Answer" column where CCN readers can submit questions as well as responses to the requests and questions of other readers—truly a "making a connection with others" forum
- Helpful hints from us and/or CCN readers regarding food preparation, food allergies, chemical sensitivities, etc.
- Meal Planning Ideas—especially Quick & Easy Meals and Meals Away from Home
- Resources for hard-to-find food and health-care products and services
- A special series of articles on several types of health-care providers focusing on their importance in a health-care regimen, how they help, and guidelines for choosing a provider beneficial in an individual's unique situation
- Special tips/techniques/recipes for reclaiming holidays such as picnics/potlucks, birthdays, Thanksgiving, Christmas, New Years, etc.
- Veggie Corner columns on less-familiar vegetables (ex. bok choy, chard, collards, kale, okra, artichoke, etc.)
- Current information and research on FOS (Fructo-oligo-saccharides)
- Recipes, recipes, and more recipes that: follow the *Candida* control and rotational diet set forth in this book, follow the *Candida* control diet, and/or are from you, the readers of <u>Canary Connect News</u>.
- Organic gardening—including growing amaranth greens cooking herbs
- Coping strategies for persons dealing with health challenges, including Traveling Tips
- Sprouting whole grains, beans, etc.

What Does Canary Connect Mean?

The name Canary Connect was chosen to illustrate the focus of my endeavors and as a symbol of my goal and purpose. Canaries were used in coal mine tunnels to warn miners of dangerous coal gases. Since canaries are more sensitive to coal gases than humans, they would stop singing (or even die) when the dangerous gases were present in the mine shafts. Coal miners would then know to leave immediately.

Those of us affected by Multiple Chemical Sensitivities/Environmental Illness (MCS/EI) have come to regard ourselves as warning "canaries" for today's world. Since we are more sensitive to chemicals and other dangerous substances present in today's world, we "human canaries" are singing out the message of danger to any and all who will hear and respond. We "sing" not only to reach those around us, but to connect with other "canaries."

In addition, persons dealing with *Candida* Related Complex, food allergies, and/or other health challenges can also consider themselves to be "canaries." They can "sing" out regarding the multi-facetted causes of these challenges, the importance of incorporating a healthy, chemical-free diet, and the lifestyle choices that will help prevent the development of life-changing health challenges.

By forming an interconnecting network amount ourselves, we can provide support and encouragement for each other. We can realize that we are not alone as we face our health challenges. We can share our individual solutions for situations such as the frustration faced when dealing with persons who do not take our symptoms seriously. Also, we can share the information, techniques, and knowledge we acquire as we learn to deal with the health challenges in our daily lives.

By extending this connection to include the non-"canaries" around us, we can also help them understand who we are, the challenges we face, and the dedication we have to improving the world in which we and they live.

To accomplish the goal of forming this network and helping others, we need your input—your recipes, helpful hints, questions, experiences, challenges, solutions, etc. You are cordially invited to be an active participant in the ongoing adventure that is Canary Connect News.

Guidelines for Submitting a Question for Newsletter or Personal Response

—To submit a question, recipe, request, helpful hint, etc. to Canary Connect News (CCN) newsletter, please keep submission(s) concise but detailed enough for us to understand. Include your name, address, and phone number and indicate if you would prefer that your name not be used. Usually we credit submissions using the format: Mary S., IA. No fee involved. Submissions will be included in CCN as space is available. For mailing address, see item #8 below.

—To submit a question for a personal response, please use the following guidelines.
1. Submit only one question per page or half page of paper so that we may respond to each question separately. This may help us respond more quickly to the less-time-consuming questions. Questions requiring research may require a longer time to answer.
2. Keep questions concise but detailed enough for us to understand and give an accurate response.
3. Include your name, address, and phone number on each page you send.
5. Realize that some questions may be beyond our knowledge, but we will try to at least direct you to another source. Also, we may include your question in Canary Connect News and request responses from others.
6. Questions submitted for personal response do involve a fee. When submitting your question(s), include a payment of $10.00 US—check, money order, or MasterCard/Visa (see form on page 273). If the total cost for processing your submission will be over $10.00, we will inform you of the estimated total for your approval and payment prior to undertaking the processing and/or research. (The fee is $10.00 per submission—not $10 per question.)
7. If you prefer to call us with your questions, we are happy to use this format. If we are not available to consult with you at the time of your initial call, a date and time will be set up when we are able to do so. Do realize that there is an hourly phone consultation fee (charged by portions of an hour). Inquire about the fee rates when you call. Please have your credit card (MasterCard or VISA—see form on page 273) handy when you call so the information can be entered before the consultation begins.
8. Questions should be submitted to the following address/phone: Canary Connect Publications, A Division of SOBOLE, Inc., PO Box 5317, Coralville, IA 52241-0317, (319) 351-2317.

Canary Connect News Back Issue Highlights

The following highlights are for issues of Canary Connect News in print or pending at the publication date of this book. To request an updated Current Back Issue Highlights List for Canary Connect News Newsletter, see the order form on page 273.

Highlights in Issue #1!
(January-March 1995)
Welcome to Canary Connect News!
What Does Canary Connect Mean?
Issue #1 contains information on the sweetener and probiotic enhancer FOS (fructo-oligo-saccharides) and results from an FOS customer survey. A **FREE** copy is available upon request (see order form on page 273).

Highlights in Issue #2!
(April-June 1995)
Learn about "Greens" Cookery and explore using chard, spinach, collards, and kale to spruce up your diet (includes 7 recipes). Kid's Corner has a great recipe for Spiced Baked Potatoes. Reclaim Picnics/Potlucks with recipes for 7 Layer Salad, Rhubarb or Strawberry-Rhubarb Crisp, Fresh Strawberry Pie with Kamut Pie Crust, and other take-along ideas. "Q&A" Exchange includes ideas for a hot drink when coffee or regular tea is not an option.

Highlights in Issue #3!
(July-September 1995)
In the first of a four-part article on Traveling Tips, Preplanning for Success is discussed. Reclaim Birthdays using these cake recipes—'Cherub' (Angel) Food, Quinoa or Rice Carob. Oatmeal Cookies in Kid's Corner and Pear Crisp in Recipe Corner provide two great dessert ideas. Veggie Corner features bok choy complete with several recipe ideas. Learn about a Canary Entrepreneur who hasn't let Multiple Chemical Sensitivities stop her dreams and goals. "Q&A" Exchange includes information on rotating immune strengthening herbs.

Highlights in Issue #4!
(October-December 1995)
Several recipe variations for Pumpkin Pie are included in ideas for Reclaiming Thanksgiving, Christmas, and New Years. Veggie Corner takes pumpkin even further with recipes for   a delicious Tomato-Free Spaghetti/ Pizza Sauce and Buckwheat Pizza Crust.   Reader-submitted recipes include Sweetener-Free Butternut Squash Pie, Spinach/Water Chestnut Salad, Sprout Salad, and Pancake "Maple Syrup." Traveling Tips: Part 2 focuses on dealing with chemical exposures, bathroom stops, and vehicle refueling.

Highlights in Issue #5!
(January-March 1996)
Working Toward Emotional and Spiritual Healing is the subject of an inspirational two-part interview with Susanne Michler, Counselor, entitled Chasing the "Blues" Away! Traveling Tips: Part 3 explores options and procedures for hotels/motels and "getting there with wearable clothes." Lentil Casserole (with lamb, pork, and vegetarian variations) is delicious, easy, and filling! "Q&A" Exchange addresses various digestion issues and weight maintenance.

Highlights in Issue #6!
(April-June 1996)
Traveling Tips: Part 4 details food and meal planning ideas. In part 2 we conclude the Susanne Michler interview—Chasing the "Blues" Away! "Dear Friends" discusses broadening your support system through writing circles. Quick and easy recipes include salad dressing, griddle bread with several gluten-free variations, and Lentil or Ground Meat Sloppy Joes. "Q&A" Exchange covers short- and long-term techniques to use when dealing with food or chemical exposures.

Highlights in Issue #7!
(July-September 1996)
An interview with James Luth describes how Shiatsu massage therapy can aid in detoxification and relaxation in The "Finger Touch" of Improved Health. "Q&A" Exchange includes great sources for yeast-free breads, a solution to help remove a mold problem in a vehicle air conditioning system, and several reader input requests. Kid's Corner gives a dairy- and sugar-free ice cream recipe with several variations. Easy meat or lentil taco recipes with be a hit with your whole family. An inspiring personal story appears in Canary Entrepreneurs.

Coming Up in Issue #8!
(October-December 1996)
Vegetarian Delights will include delicious recipes for Amazing Cheese-free "Mac and Cheese," Quick and Easy Bean and Lentil Patties. The Reclaiming Holidays column will include a recipe for dairy-free whipped topping.   As always, the reader-favorite "Q&A" Exchange.

RETURN THIS PAGE OR A PHOTOCOPY OF IT TO ORDER

Allergy & *Candida* Cooking Made Easy

by Sondra K. Lewis
with Lonnett Dietrich Blakley

Canary Connect News

A quarterly newsletter edited by
Sondra K. Lewis and
Lonnett Dietrich Blakley

Did you enjoy the recipes, meal planning ideas, helpful hints, general information, and ideas in this book? Do you desire on-going support regarding *Candida* Related Complex (CRC), food allergies, rotational diet, Multiple Chemical Sensitivities (MCS), and/or other health challenges?

Then Canary Connect News quarterly newsletter is your answer. **Make the connection! Subscribe today!** For more information, see pages 268 and 270. A one-year subscription (4 issues) is $15.00. Back issues are available, see page 270 for issue highlights. An updated list will be forwarded upon your request.

Quantity	Description		Unit Price	Total Price
	Allergy & *Candida* Cooking Made Easy		$29.95	
	Iowa Residents add 5% Sales Tax to Book Cost		$1.50 / copy	
	Canary Connect News—1 year subscription	US & Canada Other countries	$15/year $20/year	
	Canary Connect News Back Issues (see listing, page 270) Please send back issues #: _____, _____, _____, _____, _____		$5/each 4 for $15	
Book Shipping Options: (Book price includes US Bookrate shipping.)		For US Priority Rate, add $1.50 per book For Canada (Air), add $4.50 per book		
Check or money order payable to Canary Connect (US Funds Only) OR Complete Credit Card Information Below			**TOTAL ENCLOSED**	

Ship book(s) and/or newsletter to:

Name	**Phone ( )** (Required for credit card orders)
Address	
City/State/Zip	

Mail completed form and payment to:
Canary Connect Publications
A Division of SOBOLE, Inc.
PO Box 5317   Coralville, IA 52241-0317
Phone/FAX: (319) 351-2317 (AUTO MODE)

Thank You for Your Order!

FYI: Due to bookkeeping procedures/requirements, we are unable to process and will return orders received with insufficient payment, lack of cardholder's signature (when required), and/or incomplete/inadequate order information. Prepare your order carefully. Thank you.
Canary Connect does not give out or sell customer information.

Please autograph and dedicate cookbook(s) to:

_____

PLEASE NOTE: Dedicated books are not refundable.

CREDIT CARD INFORMATION—
Circle One: MasterCard   VISA
Card # _____ _____ _____ _____
Expires: _____
Cardholder's Signature (required):

_____

Cardholder's Name/Address (if different from above):
_____
_____

Use this page or a photocopy of it to order general information from CANARY CONNECT.

Or you may use a separate sheet of paper, order by code in left column, enclose appropriate fee listed in right column, and provide requested mailing address information. See reverse side of form for FOS articles/abstracts.

SEND REQUESTED INFORMATION AND/OR PRODUCTS TO:

Name	Phone ( ) (Required for credit card orders)
Address	
City/State/Zip	

CIRCLE CODE IN LEFT COLUMN TO REQUEST INFORMATION AND/OR PRODUCTS. PREPARE YOUR ORDER CAREFULLY—SEE FYI BELOW.

CODE	DESCRIPTION	PRICE*
INFO	**Basic Information Packet on Products and Services Available from Canary Connect** Following items are available at publication date. —Basic FOS information including Sondra's success story with *Candida* and food allergies, complimentary copy of CCN#1, order form, and research article (Perna, Peter J., Ph.D., Manager. "Fructooligosaccharides (FOS): An All Natural Food which Promotes *Bifidobacteria* and *Lactobacillus*." Broomfield, CO: Center for Applied Nutrition, ZeaGen, Inc. 530 Interlocken Boulevard, 80021) —Chuck's Seafood—Tuna and Salmon (packed in glass jars) —Food Enzyme Supplements —Granny's Old Fashioned Household and Personal Care Products. Specially formulated for the chemically sensitive. Economical, effective, environmentally friendly. Fragrance, phosphate, formaldehyde, and dye free. All Granny's products are in liquid form. (See below for low-cost trial sizes available for purchase.)	NO CHARGE
BIH	Current Back Issue Highlights List for Canary Connect News Newsletter	NO CHARGE
WC	Writing Circle Information packet—information on participation and guidelines (See page 261.)	NO CHARGE
VC	Information on Video Cooking Series or other publications by Canary Connect Publications as it becomes available	NO CHARGE
PR	Personalized assistance regarding specialized recipes and meal planning to fit a personalized rotation (Initial submission fee of $10 required. See page 269 for more details and instructions.)	$10.00
TGR	Granny's 2 ounce Trial Size—$1.50 each or all 7 for $7 TOTAL # ORDERED: _____ (Price includes shipping. Iowa residents add 5% sales tax.) <u>Circle choice(s):</u> Laundry Liquid Dish/All Purpose Cleaner Hand/Body Liquid Soap Protein Shampoo Tearless Shampoo Creme Rinse Hand/Body Moisturizing Lotion	
	Subtotal to Be Carried Over to Reverse Side of This Page $	

*Prices subject to change without notice.

Mail completed form and payment to:

Canary Connect Publications
A Division of SOBOLE, Inc.
PO Box 5317   Coralville, IA 52241-0317
Phone/FAX: (319) 351-2317 (AUTO MODE)

CREDIT CARD INFORMATION—
Circle One: MasterCard   VISA
Card # _____ _____ _____ _____
Expires: _____
Cardholder's Signature (required):
_____
Cardholder's Name/Address (if different from above):
_____
_____

FYI: Due to bookkeeping procedures/requirements, we are unable to process and will return orders received with insufficient payment, lack of cardholder's signature (when required), and/or incomplete/inadequate order information. Prepare your order carefully. Thank you.
Canary Connect does not give out/sell customer information.

Thank You for Your Request!

Order Form for General Information from Canary Connect (continued)

Bᴇ sᴜʀᴇ ᴛᴏ ᴄᴏᴍᴘʟᴇᴛᴇ ᴍᴀɪʟɪɴɢ ɪɴғᴏʀᴍᴀᴛɪᴏɴ ᴏɴ ʀᴇᴠᴇʀsᴇ sɪᴅᴇ ᴏғ ᴛʜɪs ғᴏʀᴍ.

#	Iɴғᴏʀᴍᴀᴛɪᴏɴ Dᴇsᴄʀɪᴘᴛɪᴏɴ	Pʀɪᴄᴇ*
R3	The items found in codes R3 and R13 are scientific articles on FOS, its uses, and available research on its effects. May be more appropriate for persons in health-care professions. **The following three (3) scientific articles and abstracts on FOS:** Modler, H.W., R.C. McKellar, and M. Yaguchi. "_Bifidobacteria_ and _Bifidogenic_ Factors," Journal of Canadian Institute of Food Science and Technology, 21, no. 1 (1990): 29-41. Hosoya, N., D. Dhorranintra, and H. Hidaka. "Utilization of [U-14C] Fructooligosaccharides in Man as Energy Resources," Journal of Clinical Biochemical Nutrition, 5 (1988): 67-74. Abstract. Hidaka, H., T. Eida, T. Takizawa, T. Tokunaga, and Y. Tahiro. "Effects of Fructooligosaccharides on Intestinal Flora and Human Health," _Bifidobacteria_ Microflora, 5, no. 1 (1986): 37-50. Abstract.	Sʜɪᴘᴘɪɴɢ ᴀɴᴅ Hᴀɴᴅʟɪɴɢ Cʜᴀʀɢᴇ ᴏғ $3.00
R13	**The three (3) articles and abstracts listed above plus the following thirteen (13) scientific articles and abstracts on FOS:** Fukuyasu, T., T. Oshida, and K. Ashida. "Effect of Oligosaccharides on Growth of Piglets and on Bacterial Flora, Putrefactive Substances and Volatile Fatty Acids in Their Feces," Bulletin of Animal Hygiene, 26 (1987): 15-22. Abstract Hidaka, H., Y. Tashiro, and T. Eida. "Proliferation of Bifidobacteria by Oligosaccharides and Their Useful Effect on Human Health," Bifidobacteria Microflora, 10, no. 1 (1991): 65-79. McKellar, R.C. and H.W. Modler. "Metabolism of Fructooligosaccharides by _Bifidobacterium sp._," Applied Microbiology Biotechnology, 31 (1989): 537-541. Abstract. Mitsuoka, T. "_Bifidobacteria_ and Their Role in Human Health," Journal of Industrial Microbiology, 6 (1990): 263-268. Mitsuoka, T. "Effects of Long-term Intake of Neosugar (Fructooligosaccharides) on Intestinal Flora and Serum Lipids," Proceedings of the 3rd Neosugar Conference, Tokyo (1986). Abstract. Mitsuoka, T.; H. Hidaka, and T. Eida. "Effect of Fructooligosaccharides on Intestinal Microflora," Die Nahrung, 31, no. 5-6 (1987): 427-436. Oku, T, T. Tokunaga, and N. Hosoya. "Nondigestibility of a New Sweetener, 'Neosugar', in the Rat," Journal of Nutrition, 114 (1984): 1574-1581. Abstract. Sano, T. "Effect of Neosugar (Fructooligosaccharides) on Constipation, Intestinal Microflora and Gallbladder Contraction in Diabetics," Proceedings of the 3rd Neosugar Conference, Tokyo (1986). Abstract. Spiegel, J.E., R. Rose, P. Karabell, V.H. Frankos, and D.F. Schmitt. "Safety and Benefits of Fructooligosaccharides as Food Ingredients," Food Technology (January 1994): 85-89. Takahashi, Y. "Effects of Neosugar (Fructooligosaccharides) in the Chronic Renal-Failure Patient," Proceedings of the 3rd Neosugar Conference, Tokyo (1986). Abstract. Tokunaga, T, T. Oku, and N. Hosoya. "Utilization and Excretion of a New Sweetener, Fructooligosaccharides (Neosugar), in Rats," Journal of Nutrition, 119 (1989): 553-559. Abstract Williams, C.H., S.W. Witherly, and R.K. Buddington. "Influence of Dietary Neosugar on Selected Bacterial Groups of the Human Faecal Flora," Microbial Ecology in Health and Disease, 7 (1994): (accepted for publication). Yamashita, K., K. Kawai, and M. Itakura. "Effects of Fructo-oligosaccharides on Blood Glucose and Serum Lipids in Diabetic Subjects," Nutrition Research, 4 (1984): 961-966.9.	Sʜɪᴘᴘɪɴɢ ᴀɴᴅ Hᴀɴᴅʟɪɴɢ Cʜᴀʀɢᴇ ᴏғ $9.00
	Subtotal from This Side $	
	Iowa Residents Add 5% Sales Tax $	
	Subtotal from Other Side $	
Check or money order payable to Canary Connect (US Funds Only) OR Complete Credit Card Information on Other Side of Form	**TOTAL ENCLOSED**	

*Prices subject to change without notice.

FYI: Due to bookkeeping procedures/requirements, we are unable to process and will return orders received with insufficient payment, lack of cardholder's signature (when required), and/or incomplete/inadequate order information. Prepare your order carefully. Thank you. Canary Connect does not give out or sell customer information.

Evaluation Form for Allergy & *Candida* Cooking Made Easy

Your comments regarding this book are greatly appreciated. Please take a few minutes to complete this evaluation form (or a photocopy of it) and forward it to us. Include information on any errors (such as typos, grammar, or spelling) that you see in the cookbook (no matter how small or insignificant). We will use your comments to correct/improve the book for future printings and/or editions, and in future works by the authors in the form of book, video, or newsletter. We would request that you sign your evaluation only so that we may contact you if we have a question regarding your comments.

This book was developed to be clear and concise, while detailed especially for the inexperienced cook. All efforts have been made to make it informative, readable, and understandable by people at all levels of experience or expertise in the areas of subject matter and cooking skills.

If you want a personal answer to a question (rather than a response printed in <u>Canary Connect News</u> newsletter), see page 269 for guidelines and fees regarding this procedure. Please allow several weeks for response.

For each category listed below, please evaluate clarity (CLEAR), information (INFO), and usability (USE) with a ranking of 1 to 10 (1 = lowest / 10 = highest).

Book Section	CLEAR	INFO	USE
Table of Contents			
How to Use This Book			
1. *Candida* Related Complex			
2. Treatments for *Candida* Related Complex (CRC)			
3. Food Allergies			
4. Rotational Diet			
5. Specialty Foods			
6. Organics–The Only Way to Go!			
7. Quintessential Odds and Ends			
8. Meal Planning			
9. Recipe Table of Contents			
10. Recipes: Cereals and Basic Grains/Nongrains			
Breads, Muffins, Pancakes			
Main Dishes			
Salads and Dressings			
Vegetables			
Desserts			
Beverages and Misc.			
Bibliography			

Book Section	CLEAR	INFO	USE
Appendix A: Food Families			
Appendix B: *Candida* Questionnaire and Score Sheet			
Appendix C: Resources			
Appendix D: Recommended Reading			
Appendix E: Cooperative Food Warehouses in the US			
Appendix F: Organizations Providing Info. on Organic Food Production & Availability			
Appendix G: Canary Connect			
Subject Index			
Recipe Index			
Commonly Asked Questions and Answers			
Nutritional Analysis			
Graphics/Tables/Charts			
Special Sayings			
Book Cover			
Spiral Binding			

Please Circle Your Response:

Did you appreciate that the book was printed with soy bean ink?   Yes   No   No Opinion

How much of the book have you read and begun to apply?   all   most   about half   very little   none

How many of the recipes have you prepared?   up to 10   11–30   31–50   over 50

Would you recommend this book to friends, family, health-care professionals, etc.?   Yes   No   Maybe

Would you recommend that your local health-food store carry this book?   Yes   No   Maybe

Continued on Next Page

Evaluation Form for Allergy & *Candida* Cooking Made Easy (continued)

Other Comments:

_____
_____
_____
_____
_____
_____
_____
_____
_____
_____
_____
_____
_____
_____
_____
_____
_____
_____
_____
_____
_____
_____
_____

Evaluation
Date: _____

Name: _____

Address: _____

City/State/Zip: _____

Phone: _____

Please send evaluation form to:

Canary Connect Publications
A Division of SOBOLE, Inc.
PO Box 5317
Coralville, IA 52241-0317
Phone/FAX: (319) 351-2317
(FAX IN AUTO MODE)

Thank you for taking the time to inform us of your opinions!
They are important to us.

SUBJECT INDEX

The heart has eyes which the brain knows nothing of.
          Charles H. Parkhurst

Time is like money; the less we have of it to spare the further we make it go.
          Josh Billings

RECIPE INDEX

> *Character is the result of two things—mental attitude and the way we spend our time.*
> Elbert Hubbard

> *To carry care to bed is to sleep with a pack on your back.*
> Thomas C. Haliburton

> *I'm not afraid of storms, for I'm learning how to sail my ship.*
> Louisa May Alcott

> *Never give in—*
> *in nothing great or small,*
> *large or petty—*
> *never give in.*
> —*Winston Churchill*

> *Hold fast to dreams; for if dreams die, life*
> *is a broken-winged bird that cannot fly.*
> —*Lanston Hughes*

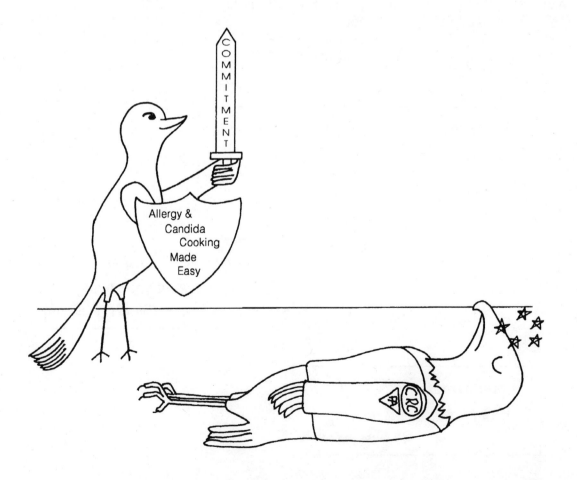

Thank you for purchasing <u>Allergy & *Candida* Cooking Made Easy</u>!

As an <u>Allergy & *Candida* Cooking Made Easy</u> (ACCME) purchaser, you have the opportunity to add the quarterly newsletter <u>Canary Connect News</u> to your personal resources at a **substantial savings** by taking advantage of this special offer. Simply tear out this page (photocopies not accepted), complete the information below, and send it with your payment or credit card information to Canary Connect (see address below).

Make the "CONNECTION"

Up-to-date Information
"Question & Answer" Exchange
Reclaiming Holidays/Celebrations
Coping Strategies — Cooking Tips
RECIPES–RECIPES–RECIPES

Look at How Much You Save!		
Item	Regularly	Special Offer
2 Year Subscription (8 issues—#2 through #9)	$30.00	**$15.00**
Individual Back Issues	$5.00 each or 4 for $15.00	**$3.00 Each**

These are just a sample of the enjoyable, informative, helpful articles included in *Canary Connect News* (CCN), a quarterly newsletter edited by Sondra K. Lewis and Lonnett Dietrich Blakley, the authors of the cookbook and resource guides, <u>Allergy & *Candida* Cooking—Rotational Style</u> and <u>Allergy & *Candida* Cooking Made Easy</u>. Each reader-friendly issue comes chock full of information to aid you in your personal journey whether you are exploring using alternative foods; adding more diversity to your diet; and/or dealing with health challenges such as *Candida* Related Complex, food allergies, and other health challenges as listed on page 268 of ACCME. CCN recipes are based on the *Candida*-control diet and are designed to provide diversity, good nutrition, and most of all delicious taste. For a listing of articles and information projected for upcoming issues, see page 268 in ACCME.

Connecting with others to provide up-to-date information, on-going support, and encouragement is CCN's major goal. In fact, the "Question & Answer" Exchange in each issue is a reader-favorite. Come join us as we help ourselves and others through communication and caring. Take advantage of this special offer to bring all of this information into your home. Highlights of back issues are listed on the back of this page to illustrate the wealth of information available and aid you in making your back issue order choices.

Mail completed form and payment to:

Canary Connect Publications
A Division of SOBOLE, Inc.
PO Box 5317   Coralville, IA   52241-0317
Phone: (319) 351-2317
PLEASE NOTE: Form may not be photocopied.

FYI: Due to bookkeeping procedures/requirements, we are unable to process and will return orders received with insufficient payment, lack of cardholder's signature (when required), and/or incomplete/inadequate order information. Prepare your order carefully. Thank you.
Canary Connect does not give out or sell customer information.

Canary Connect News—ACCME Purchase Special Offer

NAME _____

ADDR _____

_____

PHONE _____
PHONE NUMBER REQUIRED FOR CREDIT CARD ORDERS

<u>CHECK ALL THAT APPLY</u>:
___ Please send issues #2–9 of <u>Canary Connect News</u> at the special price of $15.00).
___ Please send back issues of <u>Canary Connect News</u> as indicated below **$3.00 each**.

Issues: #____ #____ #____ #____ #____

TOTAL AMOUNT DUE: $_____

I have enclosed check or money order in **US Funds** for payment of the total amount due. **OR** Bill my credit card account as indicated above.

CREDIT CARD INFORMATION—
Circle One: MasterCard   VISA
Card # _____ _____ _____ _____
Expires: _____
Cardholder's Signature (required):

_____

Cardholder's Name/Address (if different from above):

_____

_____

Special offer available to ACCME purchasers only. This form may not be photocopied.

*Thank You for
Your Order!*

Canary Connect News Back Issue Highlights

The following highlights are for issues of Canary Connect News in print or pending at the publication date of Allergy & *Candida* Cooking Made Easy. To request an updated Current Back Issue Highlights List for Canary Connect News Newsletter, see the order form on page 273.

Highlights in Issue #1!
(January-March 1995)
Welcome to Canary Connect News!
What Does Canary Connect Mean?
Issue #1 contains information on the sweetener and probiotic enhancer FOS (fructo-oligo-saccharides) and results from an FOS customer survey. A copy will be sent to you **FREE**.

Highlights in Issue #2!
(April-June 1995)
Learn about "Greens" Cookery and explore using chard, spinach, collards, and kale to spruce up your diet (includes 7 recipes). Kid's Corner has a great recipe for Spiced Baked Potatoes. Reclaim Picnics/Potlucks with recipes for 7 Layer Salad, Rhubarb or Strawberry-Rhubarb Crisp, Fresh Strawberry Pie with Kamut Pie Crust, and other take-along ideas. "Q&A" Exchange includes ideas for a hot drink when coffee or regular tea is not an option.

Highlights in Issue #3!
(July-September 1995)
In the first of a four-part article on Traveling Tips, Preplanning for Success is discussed. Reclaim Birthdays using these cake recipes—'Cherub' (Angel) Food, Quinoa or Rice Carob. Oatmeal Cookies in Kid's Corner and Pear Crisp in Recipe Corner provide two great dessert ideas. Veggie Corner features bok choy complete with several recipe ideas. Learn about a Canary Entrepreneur who hasn't let Multiple Chemical Sensitivities stop her dreams and goals. "Q&A" Exchange includes information on rotating immune strengthening herbs.

Highlights in Issue #4!
(October-December 1995)
Several recipe variations for Pumpkin Pie are included in ideas for Reclaiming Thanksgiving, Christmas, and New Years. Veggie Corner takes pumpkin even further with recipes for a delicious Tomato-Free Spaghetti/ Pizza Sauce and Buckwheat Pizza Crust. Reader-submitted recipes include Sweetener-Free Butternut Squash Pie, Spinach/Water Chestnut Salad, Sprout Salad, and Pancake "Maple Syrup." Traveling Tips: Part 2 focuses on dealing with chemical exposures, bathroom stops, and vehicle refueling.

Highlights in Issue #5!
(January-March 1996)
Working Toward Emotional and Spiritual Healing is the subject of an inspirational two-part interview with Susanne Michler, Counselor, entitled Chasing the "Blues" Away! Traveling Tips: Part 3 explores options and procedures for hotels/motels and "getting there with wearable clothes." Lentil Casserole (with lamb, pork, and vegetarian variations) is delicious, easy, and filling! "Q&A" Exchange addresses various digestion issues and weight maintenance.

Highlights in Issue #6!
(April-June 1996)
Traveling Tips: Part 4 details food and meal planning ideas. In part 2 we conclude the Susanne Michler interview—Chasing the "Blues" Away! "Dear Friends" discusses broadening your support system through writing circles. Quick and easy recipes include salad dressing, griddle bread with several gluten-free variations, and Lentil or Ground Meat Sloppy Joes. "Q&A" Exchange covers short- and long-term techniques to use when dealing with food or chemical exposures.

Highlights in Issue #7!
(July-September 1996)
An interview with James Luth describes how Shiatsu massage therapy can aid in detoxification and relaxation in The "Finger Touch" of Improved Health. "Q&A" Exchange includes great sources for yeast-free breads, a solution to help remove a mold problem in a vehicle air conditioning system, and several reader input requests. Kid's Corner gives a dairy- and sugar-free ice cream recipe with several variations. Easy meat or lentil taco recipes with be a hit with your whole family. An inspiring personal story appears in Canary Entrepreneurs.

Coming Up in Issue #8!
(October-December 1996)
Vegetarian Delights will include delicious recipes for Amazing Cheese-free "Mac and Cheese," Quick and Easy Bean and Lentil Patties. The Reclaiming Holidays column will include a recipe for dairy-free whipped topping. As always, the reader-favorite "Q&A" Exchange.